EVANGELICALS AND POLITICS
IN AFRICA, ASIA AND LATIN AMERICA

The global expansion of evangelical Christianity is one of the most important religious developments in recent decades, but its political dimension is little studied by the comparative literature on religion and world politics. Paul Freston's book is a pioneering comparative study of the political aspects of the new mass evangelical Protestantism of sub-Saharan Africa, Latin America and parts of Asia. The book examines twenty-seven countries from the three major continents of the Third World, burrowing deep into the specificities of each country's religious and political fields, but keeping in view the need for cross-continental comparisons. The conclusion looks at the implications of evangelical politics for democracy, nationalism and globalisation.

This unique account of the politics of global evangelicalism will be of interest across disciplines and in many different parts of the world.

PAUL FRESTON is Lecturer in Sociology at the Federal University of São Carlos, Brazil. He has published six books in Portuguese and many articles in Portuguese, Spanish and English on the sociology of Protestantism in Brazil and Latin America. He is the author of *Pentecostalismo* (Belém, Unipop, 1996) and co-author of *Nem Anjos Nem Demônios: Interpretações Sociológicas do Pentecostalismo* (Petrópolis, Vozes, 1994).

EVANGELICALS AND POLITICS IN AFRICA, ASIA AND LATIN AMERICA

PAUL FRESTON

CAMBRIDGE
UNIVERSITY PRESS

PUBLISHED BY THE PRESS SYNDICATE OF THE UNIVERSITY OF CAMBRIDGE
The Pitt Building, Trumpington Street, Cambridge, United Kingdom

CAMBRIDGE UNIVERSITY PRESS
The Edinburgh Building, Cambridge CB2 2RU, UK
40 West 20th Street, New York NY 10011–4211, USA
477 Williamstown Road, Port Melbourne, VIC 3207, Australia
Ruiz de Alarcón 13, 28014, Madrid, Spain
Dock House, The Waterfront, Cape Town 8001, South Africa

http://www.cambridge.org

First published 2001
Reprinted 2003

Printed in the United Kingdom at the University Press, Cambridge

Typeface Baskerville 11/12.5pt   *System* Poltype® [V N]

A catalogue record for this book is available from the British Library

Library of Congress cataloguing in publication data
Freston, Paul.
Evangelicals and politics in Africa, Asia and Latin America / Paul Freston.
p.   cm.
Includes bibliographical references.
ISBN 0 521 80041 2 (hardback)
1. Evangelicalism – Political aspects – Africa, Sub-Sahara.   2. Christianity and
politics – Africa, Sub-Sahara.   3. Evangelicalism – Political aspects – Asia.   4. Christianity
and politics – Asia.   5. Evangelicalism – Political aspects – Latin America.   6. Christianity
and politics – Latin America.   I. Title

BR1642.A357 F74 2001
322'.1'0882044–dc21   00-063098 CIP

ISBN 0 521 80041 2 hardback

For
my wife Yolanda
my children Rodrigo, Giovanna and Raphael
my father Frank
my mother-in-law Aliete

Contents

Foreword

There have been several surveys of the global role of the Roman Catholic Church including its very varied contributions to politics. In respect of Catholicism nobody could possibly suppose that its contribution in Spain in the 1930s is on a par with its contribution in Korea in the 1990s. Time and place are crucial, and the fact that Catholicism itself is centralised and hierarchical and based on mediation cannot be read as implying an analogous approach in politics.

The same considerations apply to evangelicalism, and to its most potent variant in the developing world, pentecostalism. Time and context are crucial, and the fact that pentecostalism in particular encourages the poor to raise their voice does not mean this can be translated into the promotion of populist democracy. Unfortunately we have lacked a comprehensive survey of the global role of evangelical and pentecostal movements, partly no doubt because of their internal variation and fissiparousness. They belong to a pluralistic world and to bring their many political contributions together is not only intellectually demanding but requires burrowing in obscure places and acquaintance with extremely varied contexts. It seems to me that Paul Freston's book triumphantly meets the intellectual demands and shows a detailed understanding of the diversity. What he offers is *the* guide to evangelical politics worldwide.

My own concerns with pentecostalism in Latin America (and more recently globally) have focused on the changes it initiates and manifests as a form of cultural revolution. I believe such an approach finds its complement in studies focused more on the level of politics, and over the past decade I have taken the work of Paul Freston as the most reliable, conscientious and balanced guide in that area, in Brazil, in Latin America generally, and now, with the present work, on a global scale. Anyone reading his conclusion will see that he is not prey to false generalisation, to facile hopes or fears, let alone to conspiracy theories, but someone who roots his work in the classical and current literature on political culture, democracy and civil society. For every consideration which might yield one reading he cites other counter-vailing consider-ations, and is always alert to unintended consequences.

There is, of course, a vast literature on such issues as the evangelical contribution to politics in the Anglo-American ambience and one of the problems has been a tendency to read off from that (and the undoubted fact of American cultural radiation) what is happening elsewhere. After Paul Freston's book there will be no more excuse for that particular version of Western 'ethnocentrism'.

DAVID MARTIN

Acknowledgements

I began studying Third World evangelical politics when hunting for a topic for my doctoral thesis in sociology at the University of Campinas. The result, under the supervision of Dr Sergio Miceli and with funding from FAPESP (Fundação de Amparo à Pesquisa do Estado de São Paulo) and ANPOCS (Associação Nacional de Pós-Graduação e Pesquisa em Ciências Sociais), was a study of Protestantism and politics in Brazil. But I was aware that Protestants in other parts of Latin America were doing similar things, and while teaching at the Universidade Federal de São Carlos, with a Bolsa Recém-Doutor from the CNPq (Conselho Nacional de Desenvolvimento Científico e Tecnológico), I extended my research to other countries. The following two years were spent in Oxford, teaching Third World students doing doctoral studies at the Open University and the University of Wales in association with the Oxford Centre for Mission Studies (OCMS). I also spent six months as a Senior Associate Member of St Antony's College, through the good offices of Professor Terence Ranger. All this was instrumental in broadening my perspective and giving me the courage to conceive of a comparative work spanning three continents.

I returned to Brazil with cases full of material. The chance to process it came in 1998, when the Pew Charitable Trusts, via Infemit/OCMS, funded the writing of a report showing the viability of a larger project on evangelicalism and politics in the developing world. I am grateful to Pew for this 'excuse', as the report later took wings and grew into this book. Perceiving the importance of evangelical politics globally, Pew has subsequently started funding a major project on 'Evangelical Christianity and Political Democracy in the Developing World', under the general direction of Dr Vinay Samuel and with myself as Regional Director for Latin America. The project will produce eighteen case studies of evangelical politics.

At the risk of injustice to the many people who have assisted me in various countries, I would like to thank especially: Vinay Samuel for unfailing encouragement and support; Eric Brown (in memoriam), Tim Shah, Simon Lumby, Ricardo Muniz, David Maxwell, Teresa Cruz e Silva and Moss Ntlha for their generosity in sending relevant material; and David Martin who forwarded the manuscript to the eventual publishers and graciously agreed to write the foreword.

The Brazil chapter is partly based on articles published originally in *Social Compass* and the *Journal of Contemporary Religion*.

My family, as usual, has paid a high price for all this, and the result is dedicated to them. They deserve much more . . .

Campinas,
Barzil.

Abbreviations

AG	Assemblies of God
AICs	African Independent Churches
ANC	African National Congress
CAN	Christian Association of Nigeria
CMS	Church Missionary Society
Conep	Concilio Nacional Evangélico del Perú
CPK	Church of the Province of Kenya (Anglican)
DRC	Dutch Reformed Church
IEP	Iglesia Evangélica Pentecostal
IMP	Iglesia Metodista Pentecostal
KNU	Karen National Union
MEP	Movimento Evangélico Progressista
MUC	Movimiento Unión Cristiana
NSCN	National Socialist Council of Nagaland
PNC	Partido Nacional Cristiano
TSPM	Three Self Patriotic Movement
UC	Universal Church of the Kingdom of God
WCC	World Council of Churches
ZAOGA	Zimbabwe Assemblies of God Africa
ZCC	Zion Christian Church

Introduction

This book attempts an initial mapping of evangelical involvement in the politics of the Third World. It represents a pioneer cross-cultural comparative study of the political dimensions of the new mass Protestantism of sub-Saharan Africa, Latin America and parts of Asia.

These political dimensions certainly need mapping, since the terrain is unpredictable. Amongst Third World evangelical presidents, for example, there has been the head of a military junta who delivered televised sermons every Sunday until being overthrown by other generals; a trade-union leader who, in Lech Walesa style, led the opposition to a one-party system and was elected president, only to create a virtual replica of the deposed regime; a former Marxist dictator who converted to democracy and pentecostalism and returned to power via the ballot box; a businessman-cum-prophet who won a democratic election and two years later had to flee the country after suspending the constitution and trying to govern autocratically; and even a 'president in clandestinity', titular head of resistance to an incipient autocracy. At another level, we come across missionary societies specialised at recruiting former soldiers to continue the struggle against communism, as well as socialist guerrillas with an evangelistic music group; not to mention the vice-president of a pentecostal denomination who is also director-general in the office of the presidency of his country, but who under the former regime was arrested as a subversive and tortured by a deacon of his own church.

This introduction explains the dimensions of the work, and surveys some of the relevant literature at a global level. After that, the case of Brazil is presented in detail, as an introduction to the methodological and interpretative concerns which further studies of Third World evangelical politics might have, and as a wall off which to bounce comparative observations regarding other countries. Although there are good reasons for starting with Brazil, the intention is not to treat it as a

I

paradigm but as a convenient base for building a comparative edifice. Each continent is then treated in turn, beginning with continent-wide generalisations before looking at specific countries. The conclusion draws out the major themes examined and talks of the overall state of studies of evangelicalism and politics in the Third World, in terms of substantive knowledge and thematic reflection.

The focus is evangelicals and politics in Africa, Asia and Latin America. Some brief clarifications are necessary. The definition of 'evangelical' is hotly debated in historical and sociological literature. A recent South African debate (Hale 1993; Walker 1994) called the useful-ness of the category into question. The large US literature has produced various definitions and an international focus makes delimitation even harder, since US definitions are by no means universally applicable for a phenomenon generally regarded as originating in eighteenth-century Europe and whose centre of gravity is now in Africa and Latin America. Bebbington's (1989) quadrilateral, used to study British evangelicalism from the 1730s to the 1980s, has found considerable acceptance as a working definition. It consists of four constant characteristics: conver-sionism (emphasis on the need for change of life), activism (emphasis on evangelistic and missionary efforts), biblicism (a special importance attributed to the Bible, though not necessarily the fundamentalist shib-boleth of 'inerrancy') and crucicentrism (emphasis on the centrality of Christ's sacrifice on the cross).

In this book I cast my net broadly, within reasonable substantive criteria (i.e. I have not used self-labelling as a *sine qua non*, or even common labelling by Westerners or locals). This procedure seems especially justified for the Third World, where factors related to colo-nialism and imperialism have often produced movements isolated from mainstream western evangelicalism but which seem basically to meet the substantive criteria. I reject the implicit use of 'evangelical' as a denominational category distinct from 'mainline', as in some of Paul Gifford's works on Africa, which tend to imprison 'evangelicalism' not only denominationally but even politically (it would certainly be ruinous to have a political criterion in our definition of evangelical!). To illus-trate the point: just as 50 per cent of Anglican clergy and 35 per cent of the laity in Britain are evangelical (Sinclair 1993), so also Third World Anglicanism, the most 'mainline' manifestation of Protestantism, has its evangelical wing. Prominent figures, especially in political involve-ment, are the bishop of Recife, Robinson Cavalcanti, a product of the Brazilian evangelical students' movement and of the Latin American

Theological Fraternity, and leader of the evangelical left in Brazil; and the archbishop of Kenya, David Gitari, head of the principal church in the country and renowned for his criticisms of the Moi regime. One could say the same regarding the Presbyterian churches of Ghana or Korea, the Eglise Evangélique du Cameroun or the Church of South India.

While institutional factors should be taken into account in understanding evangelical political attitudes, it is not wise to define evangelicalism in institutional terms. There has always been a strong anti-institutional tendency in evangelicalism, and this should remind us to avoid an excessively institutional approach to political analysis which sees, for example, the pronouncements of a church hierarchy as if they really corresponded to grass-roots members' attitudes and actions.

At the other end of the denominational spectrum, we must take into account the churches which go under labels such as African Independent Churches or spirit churches. As Maxwell (1997b) says, the whole category of independency is questionable, and the continuity with Western evangelicalism greater than often imagined. Most of them come into a broad evangelical category, and thus their political positions must be examined.

Definitional questions aside, the international comparative study of evangelicalism is still in its infancy. The *Evangelicalism and Globalisation* project, with which the author is involved, highlights its significance as a worldwide phenomenon (Hutchinson and Kalu 1998). After Catholicism, evangelicalism is the largest segment of world Christianity, truly global in its reach. The statistician David Barrett places seven hundred and fifty million out of two billion Christians in the evangelical category. Barrett's 1998 categories of 'Protestant', 'Anglican' and 'indigenous non-white' add up to 11.5 per cent of the world's population (Barrett and Johnson 1998). Some 60 per cent of all Christians are in the Third World. But allowing for high rates of non-practice in the developed West, it is evident that a far higher proportion of active Christians live in the Third World. Christianity may already be the leading religion outside the West; only Islam could possibly rival it for that palm. As for evangelical Christianity, its numerical heartland is already in the Third World, and its numerical dynamism even more so. One of the most salient aspects of this has been a trend to political involvement in many countries. Evangelical politics is no longer limited to (or even predominantly located in) its traditional Anglo-Saxon or North Atlantic heartlands.

Such statistics are, of course, fraught with problems, but they give some idea of the dimensions of the phenomenon, which is one of the most important religious developments globally of our time. This is as yet scarcely reflected in scholarship. In the volume which inaugurated the Evangelicalism and Globalisation project, I pointed out (Freston 1998a) that discussions about religion under globalisation have usually failed to take into account what has actually happened to Christianity, especially in its evangelical form, in recent decades: recession in Europe and stagnation in the United States (masked in the latter case by high-visibility political and media activity) have been countered by the expansion of evangelicalism (at the expense largely of nominal Catholicism) in Latin America and the impressive growth of many forms of Christianity in sub-Saharan Africa, the Far East and the Pacific. Yet the only significant non-First World religious phenomena that have impinged on Western academic consciousness are Islamic fundamentalism and Liberation Theology. Beyer's book on religion and globalisation (1994) has five case-studies: the New Christian Right in the United States, Liberation Theology in Latin America, Iran, Zionism and religious environmentalism. The constitution of a global, largely pentecostal, evangelicalism is often ignored because it has occurred mostly independently of Western initiatives. The same could be said for leading scholars of globalisation like Robertson (1992) and Waters (1995), even though both discuss religion. Even specialists on evangelicalism too often imagine parochially that what happens in the Anglo-Saxon world is still determinant globally. Global evangelicalism definitely answers in the positive the concern Harvey Cox (1988) had regarding Catholicism in the wake of the Boff–Ratzinger dispute: 'whether a culturally polycentric Christianity is really possible'. Cox's later *Fire From Heaven* (1996), as well as Poewe's edited volume on *Charismatic Christianity as a Global Culture* (1994), are significant attempts to do justice to the global spread of pentecostal/charismatic Christianity. Also useful are two collections on the global spread of Christianity: the volumes edited by Hefner (*Conversion to Christianity*, 1993) and van der Weer (*Conversion to Modernities*, 1994), some articles of which have direct relevance to our subject.

Of recent works on religion and politics worldwide, Casanova's *Public Religions in the Modern World* (1994) is very useful theoretically, but once again its case-studies are less relevant to our concerns: four of the five treat Catholicism, and the fifth is on evangelicals in the United States. Moyser's 1991 edited volume *Politics and Religion in the Modern World* has a useful introduction and a chapter on Southern Africa by Adrian Hastings. Witte's *Christianity and Democracy in Global Context* (1993) also has a chapter on Africa, by Richard Joseph. De Gruchy's *Christianity and Democracy* (1995), written by a leading South African scholar, has relevant chapters on that country and on sub-Saharan Africa. Finally, the volume edited by Westerlund (1996), *Questioning the Secular State*, includes chapters on evangelicals in Guatemala (Garrard-Burnett) and the Philippines (Rose). But, on the whole, Third World evangelicalism, especially Latin American and Asian, is still poorly served (or totally neglected) in volumes relating religion (or even just Christianity) to politics worldwide. This is the case whether the rubric is 'religion', 'Christianity' or 'fundamentalism': the five edited volumes of the *Fundamentalism Project* (Marty and Appleby 1991, 1993a, 1993b, 1994, 1995) contain only one article (Stoll 1994) directly relevant to our concerns, and the comparative analysis at the end of the *Project* admits that Third World pentecostals sit uneasily in their schema.

We thus have a situation in which the comparative literature on themes which are (for good reasons) academically fashionable ('religion and politics', 'fundamentalism', 'globalisation') does not come to grips with evangelicals in Third World politics. There are, however, a growing number of in-depth country-level studies which treat wholly or principally evangelical Protestantism: Hunter and Chan (1993) on China; Kang (1997) on Korea; Webster (1992) on the Dalit Christians of India (the majority of Indian Christians); Scott (1991) on Mexico; Grenfell (1995) on Guatemala; Lagos (1988) on Chile; Zub (1993) on Nicaragua; Freston (1993a, 1993b, 1994b, 1996) on Brazil; and Gifford (1993) on Liberia. Two collections on Africa contain useful material on evangelicals (as well as material on Catholics and Muslims which situates the evangelical role): the volumes edited by Gifford (1995) on *The Christian Churches and the Democratization of Africa*, and by Hansen and Twaddle (1995) on *Religion and Politics in East Africa*. On Latin America, there are three edited volumes: Padilla (1991) is of uneven value, but some chapters have useful information on several countries; Gutiérrez (1996) treats only Spanish-speaking countries – it is stronger on the historical side but adds little to our knowledge of the recent feverish political activity in many countries; Cleary and Stewart-Gambino (1997) talk specifically of pentecostals – Dodson's chapter has useful theoretical reflections and Wilson's adds to reflection on the Guatemalan case. A few authors have attempted comparisons within a continent. On Africa, there is a long review article by Ranger (1986), a book by Haynes

(1996) and another by Gifford (1998). All have broader interests than evangelicals, and Ranger's fine article is now somewhat dated. Gifford certainly gives evangelical Christianity its due weight in his case-studies (Ghana, Uganda, Zambia and Cameroon). On Latin America, three books have tried to treat Protestantism at the continental level: Stoll, Martin and Bastian (all published in 1990). They are not specifically on politics, and all except Martin are heavily biased towards the northern end of the region. The only works attempting cross-continental comparisons are Haynes (1993), Martin (1996) and Freston (1998b). Each has limitations for our purposes: Haynes is heavy on Islam and light on evangelicalism; Martin is heavy on actual political activity of Christians of all persuasions in Eastern Europe, but light on actual pentecostal politics (as opposed to potentialities) in Latin America; and Freston's article is a first attempt to address some of the specific questions we are concerned with here, but without taking Asia into account. The immense variety of political realities in which the new mass Protestantism of the Third World is situated and increasingly active is, as yet, a largely untapped vein of rich comparative potential.

There is clearly a need for comparative analysis of evangelical political militancy in Latin America, Africa and Asia, but such analysis has scarcely begun. This is partly for linguistic reasons; much of the best literature (and all the source material) on Latin America is in Spanish or Portuguese, often inaccessible to experts on Africa and Asia. Some Asian countries such as Korea present their own linguistic limitations. There is little quality study of Korean evangelicalism in Western languages; whether the material in Korean is better is hard to say – it is, presumably, richer in detail.

This book will represent a step towards filling this gap. It will examine evangelical involvement in the politics of twenty-seven countries in Africa, Asia and Latin America. The ideal choice of countries would be based on a balance of three criteria: objective political importance, size of the evangelical community, and actual evangelical impact on politics. In practice, the choice has also been constrained by availability of materials. Of the countries effectively undersold here, the most important from the evangelical standpoint is probably Indonesia.

The main focus will be contemporary rather than historical; history will be employed as a background for understanding the current situation. The focus will take both the religious and the political poles seriously, situating evangelicalism within the national religious field in which it functions, and within the national political reality in which it tries to locate itself. Between church doctrine and political practice, many factors come into play, from inside and outside the religious field. In addition, there are global dimensions to the context of evangelical politics. One is the spread of differentiation in the modern world, which links up in unique ways with different national traditions regarding religion and politics. Another is the end of the Cold War and the 'third wave' of democratisation which, while beginning earlier in Latin America, is influential in Africa and Asia mainly after 1989. Yet another is the onward march of global capitalism under neoliberal auspices.

Politics has many levels and dimensions, and no cross-continental comparative study could do justice to local government, communal politics and social movements, as well as national governments, parliaments, political parties and electoral behaviour. Our survey will privilege various levels, according to the demands of varied political and religious realities, but also due to the availability or otherwise of information. Sources are mixed, including direct observation, documentary research (church publications, material produced by evangelical politicians, the secular media), interviews with politicians and evangelical leaders in many countries, as well as participation in congresses and bibliographical research.

The unevenness of information from country to country is sometimes due to research limitations, but often reflects real gaps in empirical knowledge. Other gaps have to do with comparative understanding or thematic issues. These give rise to many suggestions for future research, scattered throughout the book.

PART ONE

Brazil

CHAPTER I

Brazil

Brazil is the case the author has personally researched most, and is therefore a convenient benchmark for developing comparative observations as we look at the three continents. However, there are other good reasons for starting with Brazil. It has the largest evangelical community, in absolute terms, in the Third World (with the possible exception of China) and the second largest in the world, behind the United States. Inasmuch as Third World evangelicalisms have common denominators, Brazil can be seen as a possible trendsetter, a test case where phenomena peculiar to the new mass Protestantism of the 'South' of the globe may first appear. This chapter is partly based on my existing studies in Portuguese and English (Freston 1993a, 1993b, 1994b, 1996). The idea is that the analysis should exemplify the sort of information we need on other countries, the questions to ask and the interpretations that might (or might not) be relevant.

Protestants are about 15 per cent of the Brazilian population, some twenty-three million people. (*Protestantes* and *evangélicos* are used interchangeably, and the vast majority would be evangelical in the Anglophone sense.) The social characteristics of this overwhelmingly practising community are illustrated in a survey of Greater Rio de Janeiro (Fernandes 1992): the rapid growth (a new church per day) is largely among the poor (the needier the district, the more churches per capita) and is popular (independent of the initiative of social elites). Of the fifty-two largest denominations in Rio, thirty-seven are of Brazilian origin and all the rest have been long under national control. Denominational creation is definitively nationalised; newly arrived foreign churches no longer create an impact. Protestantism is *national, popular* and *rapidly expanding*.

Thus, characteristics of the Protestant community (size, growth, institutional autonomy and national control) have combined with facets of the culture, media and political systems to make Brazil a key study of the emerging popular Protestantism of the Third World. One example is Brazil's second place (behind the United States) in production of evangelical television programmes. And, since 1986, it has been (together with Guatemala) the major example of a significant Protestant political presence in a traditionally Catholic country. But the Brazilian phenomenon not only has a firmer sociological base (being less influenced by one key figure such as Ríos Montt in Guatemala), but also has elements which make it historically unique.

Protestantism began with German Lutheran immigrants in 1823, reached the Portuguese-speaking population with the missionary efforts of historical churches after 1855 and expanded among the lower classes through pentecostal groups from 1910. The historical (non-pentecostal) churches attract, on average, a membership higher in the social scale than the pentecostals. Sociologically, they are *denominations* (throughout this book, I shall use *denomination, sect* and *church* in italics whenever they have their technical sociology-of-religion meaning), with greater individual freedom and less intense community life. Today, pentecostals constitute two-thirds of all Protestants, but for long the historicals were numerically dominant and much more socially influential, Brazil being the only Latin American country in which historical Protestantism had reasonable success. Until recently, Protestant presence in politics (albeit discreet) was due almost exclusively to the historicals. The 1986 election was the turning-point, quantitatively (number of deputies) and qualitatively (new churches involved, new trajectories, new political styles). The novelty were the pentecostals, who exchanged their apolitical slogan 'believers do not mess with politics' for the corporatist 'brother votes for brother', electing a numerous and vocal caucus.

The sheer size of Protestantism is relevant to this corporatist politics, but does not explain it. There is no automatic relationship between numbers and political presence. A small church can have great influence through socially prominent members elected on a non-religious vote, while a large church may reject both individual and corporate participation. In addition, Protestantism is extremely segmented. This is functional for expansion (stimulus to flexibility, competition and localised supply) but not to concerted political action. A factor in its very success impedes the conversion of this strength into a political bloc.

Segmentation, however, is not infinite. Despite the existence of hundreds of pentecostal denominations, a few larger ones dominate the field. We shall look briefly at these and their diverse political postures.

Brazilian pentecostalism has had three waves of institutional creation (Freston 1995). The first occurred in the 1910s, with the arrival of the Christian Congregation (1910) and the Assemblies of God (AG) (1911). The Christian Congregation remained more limited in scope, but the AG expanded to become the nationwide Protestant church *par excellence*. The second wave occurred in the 1950s and early 1960s; the pentecostal field fragmented, relationship to society became more dynamic and three large groups (among dozens of smaller ones) were formed: the Church of the Four-Square Gospel (1951), Brazil for Christ (1955) and God is Love (1962). All began in São Paulo. The third wave started in the late 1970s and gained strength in the 1980s. Its main representatives are the Universal Church of the Kingdom of God (1977) and the International Church of the Grace of God (1980). Once again, these groups, which start in Rio, update pentecostalism's relationship to society, extending its range of theological, liturgical, ethical and aesthetical possibilities.

The Assemblies of God, founded by Swedes in 1911, represent a third of all Protestants. Their change in political posture was crucial in giving a national dimension to the new Protestant politics.

The origin of the missionaries, the beginnings in the North and the handover to national control in 1930 when the church had scarcely penetrated the South-Eastern cities gave the AG a Swedish/North-Eastern ethos which reflected the cultural marginalisation of early Swedish Pentecostalism and the patriarchal pre-industrial society of the Brazilian North-East before the 1960s. Many leaders are still elderly North-Easterners of rural origin. The government is oligarchical, grouped in lineages around *caudilho*-type *pastores-presidentes* who are virtual bishops. The General Convention, comprised of some fifty state conventions and affiliated ministries, is a relatively weak centre.

The main route to the pastorate is a lengthy apprenticeship to a *caudilho*. The generally slow ladder of promotion is a strong means of social control in the hands of the *pastores-presidentes*. The latter often rule for thirty years, creating a patriarchal style of administration. This model, in which no specialised education separates clergy and laity, is contested by some younger pastors who are products of an alternative route involving seminary education. The AG model also faces other crises, especially the schism between Madureira Convention and the General Convention in 1989. Madureira is an especially successful oligarchical lineage whose growth threatened the survival of the others, leading to its exclusion from the General Convention. There have also been small schisms of upwardly mobile groups who wish to modify the behavioural taboos. The AG is riven by tensions between the desire for respectability and the 'populist' religious tradition which values the socially 'humble' person as more receptive to the gospel. The outcome will have implications for the current corporatist politics.

The other large church of the first wave, the Christian Congregation (CC), founded among Italian immigrants in São Paulo in 1910 by an Italian layman living in Chicago (the only foreigner ever to work with the church), is the chief remaining case of pentecostal opposition to electoral politics. Members are effectively banned from politics. There are several pillars to this aversion to politics, making it unlikely to change in the near future. The CC rejects all mass proselytism through radio, television, open-air preaching or literature. This affects its relationship to modernity. Its doctrine of predestination frees it from pressure to adapt to modern methods of communication, whereas the practical Arminianism (the predominance of free will in salvation) of all other Brazilian churches obliges them to modernise as propaganda agencies in the name of efficacy. The rejection of mass media also protects the CC from one source of pressure to enter politics. Strong *sectarian* elements (extreme 'rejection of the world' which protects from status anxiety) and the absence of paid clergy also contribute to apolitical attitudes by reducing operating costs and avoiding careerist tendencies of professional pastors.

Pioneer of the second pentecostal wave, the Four-Square Church was the last foreign church to succeed in Brazil. Indeed, of the large pentecostal groups, it is the only one of American origin. It has multifocal leadership. Gaining total independence from the Americans in the 1980s, it also freed itself from their apolitical stance. Besides choosing official candidates in internal elections after the fashion of the AG, many leaders (especially former pioneer faith-healers) are themselves politicians.

The first large Pentecostal church founded by a Brazilian, Brazil for Christ was also the first to elect politicians from its own ranks on a corporate vote. The charismatic founder, Manoel de Mello, a poor migrant from the North-East, built a new relationship with society and with São Paulo's populist political culture of the period. His pioneering role reflected not only his Brazilian citizenship but also his personalist leadership in a church without an apolitical tradition and the church's concentration in the most developed urban centre of the country with the freest electorate. The example of the federal deputy elected in 1962 and 1966 would only be imitated by other pentecostals over twenty years later. But it did not last, due partly to the disincentive of the legislature's restricted powers during the 1964–85 military regime, but also to the internal evolution of the church in which Mello's personalism gave way to a faceless structure which did not facilitate such initiatives.

Although famous in the 1960s for criticisms of the military regime and affiliation to the World Council of Churches (WCC), Mello's political progressivism was mainly for external consumption and had little impact on the church. By the late 1970s he had electoral links with the party which supported the military government. Even so, Brazil for Christ's critical stance during the most repressive period of the regime was, amongst Protestants, second only to the Lutherans. Sociologically, this is not surprising, since the latter was the only large *immigrant church*, whose multiclass nature gave it both a perception of the situation and the possibility of protest. This combination approximates the Lutheran Church to the Catholic sociological context. A *church* (in the sociology of religion sense) is more protected in the adoption of politically risky postures. Other Protestant groups either lacked a popular base capable of provoking a pastoral crisis in part of the clergy, or were composed of the poor who were unable to protest without exposing themselves to the full weight of repression. The partial exception confirms the rule: Brazil for Christ was the only pentecostal church to make remarks at all critical of the regime, and the only one to join ecumenical organisations. This affiliation made criticising the regime somewhat less risky.

The third church of the second wave, God is Love, is highly *sectarian* (non-cooperation with other churches and an extreme moralism) and attracts a very poor clientele. It invests heavily in radio but rejects television. Leadership is very personalistic. The founder, Davi Miranda, has avoided politics and built a diversified economic empire.

The largest church of the third wave, the Universal Church of the Kingdom of God, was founded by Edir Macedo, of lower-middle-class origin. With rapid growth in large cities, its cultural ethos is in strong contrast to the AG. The bold vision of penetration of cultural spaces makes political support necessary. Besides electing its own candidates with impressive electoral discipline, the church recruits other political allies through its media empire.

Our survey has shown one church of Swedish origin, one American and four Brazilian. Brazilian pentecostalism is considerably more independent of foreign institutional links (and of foreign personnel) than the historical churches.

Mention should also be made of middle-class charismatic Protestantism. From the 1960s pentecostalising schisms occurred in historical
churches. More important, however, are the newer independent
charismatic denominations, now the main focus of conversion in the
middle and upper classes. However, they are less important than in
Central America, where they form the bulk of middle- and upper-class
Protestantism and produce presidents (Ríos Montt and Serrano).

Many charismatic communities have a political vision based on
'spiritual warfare'. The recipe is ritualism (exorcism of demons which
govern a certain area of life, such as the 'demon of corruption', or of
hereditary curses on the country caused by social sins like slavery or
spiritist religions) and the placing of Christians in power. The multiplication of demons can be a useful metaphor for ideological battles. As
one charismatic, the son of a politician, told me, 'people from the
Workers Party [the main left-wing party] always look oppressed'; the
oppression being demonic and not social.

What is the potential of this abandonment of pietistic individualism in
favour of ritualistic solidarity? As Stoll (1994) says, social exorcism could
be the language of a top-down reform project, or a magical rationalisa-
tion for not treating structural problems. I believe it could also reflect the
desire for a place in 'civil religion'.

Sociologically speaking, exorcising collectivities would require an
environment like an aboriginal corroboree, capable of producing collective effervescence throughout the social group. Without this, the political vision of the charismatic communities remains vague. The gap is
sometimes filled by an American political theology called reconstructionism. This mixture of extreme neoliberalism and Old Testament
theocratic laws offers a ready-made alternative for dissatisfied conservatives. In Central America, defenders of a moderate reconstructionism
are in the vanguard of Protestant politics. In Brazil, reconstructionism
does not have the same importance. Its main strength is in the charismatic communities, but it is unlikely to conquer the current political
vanguard of pentecostal leaders of modest social origin, unaccustomed
to reflecting on national problems. Reconstructionism's themes (elabor-
ated in a context of fuller citizenship), non-dualism, post-millennial
optimism and emphasis on analysis and debate are distant from them.
In short, middle-class charismatic religion is not as central for the
Protestant field, and even less so for its politics, as in Central America.

We have mentioned the large Protestant media in Brazil. Most
televangelism is pentecostal. Media evangelism may be somewhat

more efficacious evangelistically than in the United States, but its main importance is still internal. If in the States it reinforces evangelical values in a secular society, in Brazil it fortifies the self-image of an expanding minority. In addition, it is a way into politics, and politics is also a route to media ownership. The media are easily associated with political activity, through the visibility they give to their presenters, through the power of owners in relation to Protestant leaders who for various reasons (proselytism, status or business) desire access to them, and through concession-holders' need for political support. (Radio and television in Brazil are governed by a mixture of economic and political forces. Concessions of channels are a prerogative of the executive, with congressional approval. Although there are technical and financial criteria, ownership depends, in the last analysis, on political factors.)

Nearly half of the Protestant congressmen since 1986 have had links with the media, whether as presenters of programmes or owners of stations. Some have gone from the media into politics, and others from politics into the media. The Chamber of Deputies' commission on communications always has several Protestants, most of whom have opposed proposals to democratise control of the media.

The Protestant media are neither uniformly political nor politically uniform. Most Protestant media personalities have no electoral activity. But the sizeable minority who do have demonstrate the media's force as intermediary between a conversionist community and public life. The media express the style of *conversionist sects* and are an important business in the growing Protestant market. It is true that there is a close link between media and politics in Brazil as a whole; evangelicals just accentuate the tendency.

The politics of the Universal Church of the Kingdom of God (UC) is closely connected with the media. The church purchased TV Record, the fifth largest network, in 1989; and the need for political support was the main motive for the construction of a solid parliamentary base in 1990. Although the UC's second-in-command had been elected in 1986, he was forced out of the church by Edir Macedo when the latter perceived a danger to his own leadership. The three federal deputies elected in 1990 were not spiritual leaders and could not threaten Macedo's pre-eminence. Electoral discipline is the greatest of any church. In Rio, the Universal vote was divided by computer to guarantee the election of two deputies. One hardly visited the state during the campaign, such was the efficiency of the pastors as vote-gatherers. The UC was already controversial for its money-raising methods and mass exorcisms, and this strengthened members' electoral solidarity. Its deputies frankly admitted defence of the church's interests (especially TV Record) as the reason for their presence in congress. The Universal's political clout (votes, money, media) was demonstrated in the protests against Macedo's preventive imprisonment in 1992. He was released after twelve days.

In executive elections until the mid 1990s, the church favoured conservative candidates and demonised the left. It feared what a left-wing government would mean for its communications empire and for its preaching, based on a recipe for financial success through self-employment. Although many analysts saw its extreme anti-leftism as inevitable, it was in fact too early to weigh the pragmatic and ideological factors.

The church had a long fight to retain control of TV Record. The latter was not acquired by government concession but by purchase of an existing channel: a route which postpones the political work to a second moment, that of government approval of the transfer. Having the money but not yet the political clout, Macedo bought Record in 1989, and did his best to protect himself by supporting Fernando Collor in the presidential election. When in power, Collor broke with Macedo and tried to acquire his own communications network. Macedo might well have lost Record to front men for Collor if the latter had not needed parliamentary help against impeachment in 1992. In the dying moments of Collor's administration, Macedo's possession of TV Record was guaranteed.

Having surveyed the Protestant field and media, we shall now look briefly at the history of Protestant politics in Brazil. Although legal impediments to Protestant political activity were abolished by the electoral law of 1881 and separation of church and state in 1890, social factors (limited suffrage, rigged elections, unfree rural electorate) prevented effective participation. The 1930 Revolution brought new possibilities (secret ballot) and a new incentive (Catholic attempts to implant a neo-Christendom). The first Protestant congressman, a Methodist minister, was elected to the 1933–4 Constituent Assembly. When democracy was restored after Vargas' authoritarian period, the same Methodist was elected to the 1946 Constituent Assembly. After 1950, as structural transformations freed larger portions of the electorate, Protestant representation in congress rose, stabilising at about thirteen. These were historical Protestants. Some had a Protestant electorate, others did

Table 1. *Number of Protestant congressmen (federal deputies and senators) in each legislature, Brazil 1946–2000 (February–February)*

Legislature	Congressmen elected	Total (including substitutes who took office)	Legislature	Congressmen elected	Total (including substitutes who took office)
1946–51	1	1	1975–79	13	14
1951–55	5	7	1979–83	12	13
1955–59	6	8	1983–87	12	17
1959–63	7	11	1987–91	32	36
1963–67	10	13	1991–95	23	35
1967–71	12	13	1995–99	32	38
1971–75	9	11	1999–2003	49	54[a]

[a] Until Feb. 2000.

Table 2. *Protestant congressmen (including substitutes who took office) and terms of office, Brazil 1933–2000 (February–February)*

	Congressmen			Terms of office		
	Total	Historicals	Pentecostals	Total	Historicals	Pentecostals
1933–87	50	47 (94%)	3 (6%)	109	104 (95%)	5 (5%)
1987–2000[a]	104	41 (39%)	63 (61%)	163	64 (39%)	99 (61%)
1933–2000[a]	143[b]	79 (55%)	64 (45%)	272	167 (62%)	104 (38%)

[a] Until Feb. 2000.
[b] Eleven congressmen held seats before and after 1987.

not; some had support from their denominational leaders, others did not; but none had official endorsement from any church.

Although Protestant relationship with the military regime (1964–85) is generally regarded as close, there was no increase in parliamentary representation, and their congressmen were actually more weighted to the opposition than congress as a whole. In short, between 1950 and 1986 a stable presence was established in congress, characterised by party dispersion with no strong ideological concentration, ranging from the non-Marxist left to defence of the military regime. It was concentrated in the more developed South-East and came almost exclusively from the historical churches.

The 1986 election of a Congress-cum-Constituent Assembly following the military's withdrawal from power unexpectedly changed the public face of Protestantism.

Since 1986 there has been a numerical increase and a change in ecclesiastical composition. Pentecostals, previously insignificant, now predominate. This pentecostal irruption is coordinated; the great majority are official candidates of the AG, Universal or Four-Square. Only pentecostals work with this model, the *sectarian* sociological type being basic.

Not all pentecostal churches entered politics. Of the six main churches, only three did so. The Christian Congregation and God is Love have remained apolitical; and Brazil for Christ has not overcome aversion to Mello's old political adventures. The AG was initially pre-eminent. In 1985, its General Convention decided to elect one member from each state to congress. Eighteen states chose candidates in internal polls (occasionally a pentecostal from another denomination); fourteen were elected and another later took office as a substitute.

All this has led to other changes in Protestant politics: in geographical dispersion, social profile, party links and political trajectories.

The AG is the most nationwide church, and its entry into politics caused considerable increase in Protestant representation from the less developed regions. Social origin is lower than that of non-pentecostal congressmen. It is composed of people who, in physical type and style of discourse, typify the clientele of their churches. They identify more with the cultural style of popular Protestantism than with dominant political culture. On the other hand, they are not average church members. Rather, they exemplify the desired results of conversion, either in religious leadership or financial success. They are not people who stand out in the secular world of the poor (such as union leaders), but poor people who have 'succeeded' and are elected on their religious and/or financial prestige.

The previous tendency for Protestant congressmen to be slightly left of the average is reversed. The new Protestant political class practises a party nomadism even greater than the national average. Many switch to smaller parties considered havens for time-servers and those marginalised by large parties. Anti-party sentiment is common in Brazil, but pentecostal *sectarianism* accentuates it. *Sects* usually reject autonomous participation by members in spheres which escape their control. Membership in parties is obligatory, but woe betide the pentecostal politician who makes his party a competing source of authority.

Pentecostal official candidates are typically the following: men prominent in the church as itinerant evangelists, singers or media presenters; sons and sons-in-law of *pastores-presidentes*; and pentecostal businessmen who make agreements with their ecclesiastical leaders.

Why did some pentecostal leaders want to break with the traditional 'believers don't mess with politics' and present their own candidates? And, since the pentecostal vote is not automatic, why were they relatively successful in mobilising their electorate? The new posture was not the result of theological changes; belief in the imminent end of the world, previously a justification for shunning politics, continues.

The causes of pentecostal politicisation have to do with the evolution of the religious field and the defence of *sectarian* frontiers. The first factor is the 'clergy' itself. The main beneficiaries of corporate politics have been the church leaders. Using the analogy of the pastorate as an escalator onto which one generation steps to ascend socially and which the next generation leaves for more attractive alternatives (Martin 1990: 64), corporate politics extends this upward social mobility of pastoral families. Unlike the historical churches, with their tradition, middle-class clientele and bureaucratic standards, the pentecostal field is young, fast-expanding, popular and *sectarian*. Pastors often suffer a double status contradiction: as holders of *de facto* power not legitimated by *sectarian* ideology (which tends to be egalitarian and anti-clerical); and as leaders in the church but marginalised by society (Wilson 1959). These contradictions are not new, but they become more acute as pentecostalism grows. Moreover, it becomes possible to attenuate them. Going into politics, or sending in a relative or protégé, can reduce tensions and help to professionalise one's religious field. Public connection helps internal structuring, strengthening individuals and organisations. Politics also helps access to the media, another way of structuring the pentecostal field. Politics and the media reinforce each other in structuring the Protestant world.

Like all *sects* not geographically isolated, pentecostals oscillate between their own status system and that of society. Although 'despising the world', they often accept 'worldly' opinions about themselves when favourable (ibid.: 503). Many leaders value highly the freedom of the city and other symbolic honours. But politics also brings material resources which help to structure this vast popular religious field whose rapid expansion is always producing new leaders anxious to strengthen their positions.

Pentecostal politicisation also reflects other factors in the religious field. A crucial part in mobilisation is telling 'a reasonably coherent story about why what is wrong is wrong and what can be done about it' (Bruce 1988: 76–7). What story did the AG leaders tell in 1986?

One element is the mystique of the Constituent Assembly (CA) as a moment for rewriting Brazil from scratch, or at least making sure others did not do so. The CA mobilised many 'minorities', as pentecostals knew. But they did not see themselves as one more group seeking a place in the sun. Awareness of numerical growth favoured a new reading of the Scriptures. The Bible which had justified apolitical stances now spoke of a manifest political destiny of the *evangélicos*. 'Let us prize the biblical phrase "the Lord will make you the head and not the tail"' (*Mensageiro da Paz*, March 1985: 2). Brazilian evangelicals are heirs of the Old Testament theocratic promises.

In explaining their involvement, AG leaders talked of a 'threat' to religious freedom. 'The Catholic Bishops' Conference had a scheme to establish Catholicism as the official religion', the president of the AG told me. The future constitution would prohibit open-air preaching, said the *Mensageiro da Paz* (July 1985: 12). The idea of a return to an official religion, a hundred years after separation and without any previous public campaign, seems strange. Were the AG leaders totally out of touch with reality? Or was it cynical manipulation of the faithful for unworthy objectives? Or should we understand 'religious freedom' as a code word for something broader and more anchored in reality?

In fact, it meant more than the mere right to exist in an officially lay state. The AG said they were victims of discrimination. Not the individual abuses of the past, but unequal treatment as a community: *evangélicos* are not consulted on important government decisions as the Catholics are; they have few chaplaincies in the armed forces; Catholic images are still placed in government buildings; public resources go disproportionately to Catholics (Sylvestre 1986: 44). These are the claims of a minority which almost equals the dominant religion in practising members and desires to abolish all signs of its inferiority. Combat on this front is a sociologically correct intuition, in the sense that these things are important for the Catholic project and pentecostals should oppose them *if they wish to compete with the Catholic Church on the same terms*. Expanding popular Protestantism tends to acquire the characteristics of the former dominant religion.

The book *Brother Votes for Brother* (Sylvestre 1986), influential in propagating the new politics of the AG hierarchy, emphasises the motif of religious competition and of acquiring public financing. 'The taxes a believer pays go to finance idolatry [Catholicism] and witchcraft [Umbanda] ... Each parliamentarian receives a part of the federal budget ... See what a fabulous sum could be helping our organizations in the social and educational sector' (ibid.: 62ff.).

Thus, under the slogan of 'threat to religious freedom', pentecostal leaders joined battle with Catholicism for space in civil religion, demanding equal status in public life. The *sect* begins to see itself as the *church* of tomorrow, and seeks public funds as a right justified by its numerical size.

AG leaders also talked of a 'threat to the family'. There were, supposedly, moves to include in the constitution legalisation of abortion on demand, drugs and homosexual marriage. Entry into politics was an act of *cultural defence*: a reaction to changes in the social milieu threatening to undermine the group's capacity to maintain its culture (Bruce 1988: 7, 16).

In many countries, television has been fundamental in spreading metropolitan lifestyles and provoking reactions from those who discern a threat to the family (Martin 1978: 97). In Brazil, the modern communications system was established during the military regime and the television habit extended to all classes. This growth was accompanied by censorship. When censorship was relaxed with redemocratisation, the impact on mores was considerable, making it harder to maintain *sectarian* subculture.

In short, pentecostal politicisation seeks to strengthen internal leaderships, protect the frontiers of *sectarian* reproduction, tap resources for religious expansion and dispute spaces in civil religion. But for these concerns to lead to electoral action, going against church tradition, something else was needed: 'an increasing sense of optimism about the possibility of effective action' (Bruce 1988: 23). Aspects of the political system and immediate context facilitated the pentecostal debut as political actors.

In Protestant countries, one factor in political engagement by theological conservatives is the absence of a two-party system based on class divisions (Wallis and Bruce 1985: 161). Brazil is relatively open to the participation of religious groups, being closer to the American than to the (highly unfavourable) British system. It has a federalist structure, relatively open mass media, weak parties and a proportional electoral system with state-wide voting districts, increasing the electoral chances of a dispersed minority.

With redemocratisation unrestricted multi-party competition returned. Parties sought to diversify their clienteles. But pentecostal politics is not fundamentally a response to outside incentives. There is no evidence that the AG decision to present its own candidates was encouraged by secular politicians. Bruce, writing of the United States, explains the limits on any desire conservative elites might have to politicise religion. 'In so far as non-religious conservatives are prepared to use religion as a means of diverting political choices from economic issues, most will seek to define religion in the most inclusive ... terms ... [to avoid] the disadvantages of social instability and sectarian conflict' (Bruce 1988: 52, 56).

Another possible outside incentive would be from the American religious right. But the numerical success and political ambitions of Brazilian pentecostals are explicable without recourse to a conspiracy theory for which there is no evidence. On the contrary: the AG has few links with the United States, the Universal Church is totally Brazilian and the American president of the Four-Square was against political involvement.

The transformation of the rural electorate since the 1960s helped the AG. It has a strong rural presence, and capitalisation of the countryside freed electors to vote for candidates chosen by the church and not by local bosses.

The economic context was the 'lost decade' of the 1980s which bloated the informal economy and weakened organisations based on the workplace. Economic crisis, urban growth and expectations created by redemocratisation also weakened urban patronage politics. The old rural dependency was built on 'moral bases of kinship', whereas modern urban clientelism is a mercantile relationship lacking in mutual confidence (Zaluar 1985: 234–7). A space thus appears for fusing patronage politician and rural boss in the figure of the 'brother' deputy. *Sectarian* networks have advantages over fragile parties and weakened patronage.

For pentecostals, the 'lost decade' meant the traditional fruits of conversion (honesty, frugality and hard work) became less effective for social mobility, making the collective demands of the poor more attractive. With redemocratisation, repressed currents were allowed free expression, putting at risk the capacity of *sectarian* socialisation to protect from undesirable politicisation. Corporate politics could function, therefore, as a 'pre-emptive' politicisation. But it depended on the 'totalitarianism' of the *sect*, the capacity to interfere in large areas of members' lives, including the right to indicate how to vote, something the historical denominations completely lack.

Thirty-two Protestants were elected to the Constituent Assembly in 1986 and two more took office as substitutes. Eighteen were pentecostals. The number of Protestants was soon appreciated, and a complex dynamic began, involving internal factions and outside forces. President Sarney made early overtures, since the government majority in the Assembly had to be constantly renegotiated. The large parties were internally divided, opening the way for non-party groupings.

Experienced conservative historical deputies took the lead in attempts to form a Protestant bloc. The recipe for united action was to be defence of Protestant institutional interests, a pro-government stance, emphasis on moral questions (abortion, homosexuality, pornography) and indifference on social questions such as land reform. It was immediately opposed by a minority of six (including only one pentecostal) in the name of a different concept of faith and politics.

Leadership in attempts to form a caucus soon passed to pentecostals. They were the majority; many had no position on various questions; and re-election, without the mystique of the CA, would be uncertain. The government was offering rewards for support. This new pentecostal leadership was more 'aggressive' in its self-identification as evangelical, less ideologically committed to the right and bolder in seizing opportunities.

The formula used exploited the lack of a pan-Protestant organism. An Evangelical Confederation which had folded but never been dissolved was resurrected. Most of the new directors were congressmen, and the reinauguration took place, symptomatically, in the presence of important government figures. The Confederation was given property in Brasília and donations from government social programmes, especially before important votes in the CA. The destination of the money is uncertain; appeals of Protestant leaders for public audit of its books were not heeded. Eighteen regional offices were opened, almost all in the states with pentecostal congressmen.

Much of the evangelical community challenged the Confederation's legitimacy and motives. Despite fierce criticism, it survived for three years, due to AG support. Most politicians involved had been official AG candidates. As long as it was receiving federal money, criticisms were overlooked. But what ethical questioning could not do was achieved by the drying up of government money once the CA was over. The Confederation closed in 1990.

The fact that a pan-Protestant organism could arise from the articulations of congressmen shows how vulnerable Brazil's growing and divided Protestantism is to political power. The contrast with Catholicism is stark. But the Confederation's fate also permits a contrast with Umbanda. The role of politicians in organising Umbanda federations is well known. But, in the last resort, the Protestant world does not allow so much liberty to its politicians. It is not so difficult for a politician to work with a federation of *terreiros* organised on clientelistic lines; it is more difficult to work with Protestant denominations organised on communitarian and doctrinal-ethical lines. The Confederation explored the limits of organisational autonomy of the Protestant political class; only in exceptionally favourable circumstances was it able to survive for three years.

The relationship of the Protestant caucus to the conservative *Centrão* group (formed to oppose elements in the first draft of the constitution) reveals other characteristics. Although twenty-five of thirty-two Protestants voted with the *Centrão* initially, most were not ideologically faithful. A group of eighteen linked to the Confederation broke publicly from it. It was this group which became notorious for vote-selling on important issues. In August 1988 the *Jornal do Brasil* denounced these practices. 'Many *evangélicos* are making a profitable trade out of preparing the new constitution, by negotiating their votes in exchange for advantages for their churches, and often for themselves... The list of rewards includes a television channel, at least half a dozen radio stations, important posts in government, benefits of many types and, above all, a lot of money' (7 Aug. 1988). This provoked debate in the Protestant world over the ethics and ideology of the caucus. It became the equivalent of the televangelists' scandal in the United States. Symptomatically, the American scandal occurred in the private sphere; in Brazil, with its weaker private sector, it followed the tradition of channelling public funds. The group most identified with such practices had a nucleus of official AG deputies, with a fringe of other Pentecostals and a few historicals.

The family was a theme of great interest, having been a major justification for electing representatives. There were three proposals for severe legislative restriction on abortion: Protestants, notably pentecostals, were significantly more favourable than the average member of the CA. There is a strong correlation between left-wing evangelical dissidents and opposition to legislative control on abortion. Both evangelical sides echoed classical Christian positions on the legislation of morality.

The homosexuality debate centred on the term 'sexual orientation' in the list of characteristics for which no one should be discriminated against. The Protestant vote again differed from the average, being much less favourable.

The majority Protestant positions on abortion and homosexuality coincided with official Catholic positions. On divorce, however, there is a historic difference. Catholic power barred divorce in Brazil until 1977; Protestants had traditionally defended its introduction. In the CA, an anti-divorce bill was supported by only 13 per cent of congressmen, but 59 per cent of pentecostals. The AG was the vanguard of this new legislative anti-divorcism in Protestantism.

The end of dictatorship was not favourable for retaining artistic censorship. A bill sponsored by two AG deputies was supported by only 22 per cent of congressmen, although 93 per cent of pentecostals were in favour.

There was no danger to religious freedom as such, but pentecostal deputies invested considerably in symbolic measures. Successes were made much of, especially the open Bible in the CA sessions and the name of God in the constitution. The *Mensageiro da Paz* described the latter as 'a bitter defeat for the atheists' (Nov. 1987: 7). When pentecostal leaders embrace politics, they often attach great significance to the penetration of the public sphere (the quintessential 'world' with all its negative doctrinal connotations) by ostentatious religious symbolism and conspicuous ritual performances.

The media were another focus of interest. A polemical point was the question of concessions; nearly all the Protestants on the committee united to prevent changes in the system which has permitted the acquisition of Protestant radio and television empires.

Two votes which influenced the public image of the caucus were land reform and the duration of President Sarney's term of office. A bill to permit effective land redistribution fell thirteen votes short; twenty-two Protestants voted against, most in a last-minute switch. This was widely attributed to donations from the landowners' organisation. In the case of Sarney's term (which would decide whether the first direct elections for president would be in 1988 or 1989), the coin used was different. An insignificant AG deputy, evidently used by the government, was the author of the bill granting an extra year to Sarney. Despite widespread popular protest, the bill was passed by 59 per cent of congress, 76 per cent of Protestants voting favourably. The government was prodigal in its rewards, including four radio stations and one television channel to Protestant deputies.

In the above two votes, there was no great difference between historicals and pentecostals. But in the 'questions of interest to the workers' used by the Trades Unions' Parliamentary Advisory Department (DIAP) to classify the members of the CA, the picture changes. The classification from zero to ten corresponds broadly to the right–left spectrum. The Protestant average was 4.61, below the general average of 4.94. However, historicals averaged 4.09 and pentecostals 5.06. Despite their conservative public image, one cannot label pentecostal politicians *tout court* as a new Christian right (as does Pierucci 1989).

On Kinzo's (1988: 23) classification on five scales (governism, conservatism, democratism, nationalism and opposition to the financial system), pentecostals, as compared to the overall average, were highly 'governist' but slightly less conservative, less 'democratist' but more nationalist, and considerably less opposed to the financial system. Historicals were consistent on all scales, in a centre-right position. But pentecostals' oscillations justify calling them not an ideological right but an opportunist centre.

Official pentecostal politics thus rejected any position even remotely connected with Marxism, but did not adopt neoliberalism. In rejecting anti-capitalism, religious doctrine and social factors intertwined. The AG journal showed the centrality of dispensationalist eschatology in its leaders' world-view. The supposed line-up of forces for the imminent end of the world led to a geopolitical dualism which rejected any non-capitalist ideal. With the collapse of the Soviet bloc, this dualism has weakened. In any case, doctrinal systems are not straitjackets; they are supermarkets from which some products are purchased, others thrown away and others left on the shelf. The apolitical stance which seemed so central to pentecostalism proved to be temporary; geopolitical dualism might also.

There are other reasons for opposing anti-capitalism. Many converts better themselves, or at least broaden their expectations. The ideology of betterment through conversion does not favour restrictions on this possibility in the name of egalitarianism. Pastors are the most threatened, being often the main beneficiaries of conversion. They fear the left will interfere with the competitive religious system in which they prosper. They are also influenced by corporatism: excepting anti-communism, economic postures are based less on principle than on maximisation of gains. In a rapidly growing church, there are factors encouraging pastors to be politically more conservative than their members, and more conservative than the clergy of a numerically stable historical church.

Protestants were the only religious 'caucus' in the CA. Only at the state level are there politicians whose political rationale is the defence of Umbanda. Umbanda does not break a large mass away from Catholicism with a separate identity. It lacks the doctrine and organisation which make possible the new pentecostal politics. The Catholic Church has other channels. Its militants in congress are discreet, as expected of a *territorial church* which, in theory, does not compete with anyone. But it does, of course, defend corporate interests: through politicians sensitive to its influence, through appeals to popular religious sentiment, and through non-religious corporations in which it has weight (such as the association of private schools). This makes its political action less evident. Besides not being in good taste for a *territorial church*, there is no need for it to behave publicly like the pentecostals.

The AG considered the caucus relatively successful. The name of God was in the constitution, religious freedom augmented and religious teaching maintained in public schools. Homosexual 'orientation' and the death penalty were barred. However, pentecostals were defeated on abortion (although existing limitations remain in force), censorship and divorce. But reactions in the Protestant community were divided. AG leaders attributed all criticism to 'false Protestants', but in fact discontent was widespread. A leading (theologically conservative) Protestant journal described the caucus as a 'vile treason of the people... The warped moral stature and the egoistic and conservative interest merit shame and our repulsion' (*Kerygma*, 11, 1988: 23).

In the presidential election of 1989, Brazil's first since 1960, Protestant involvement began with Iris Rezende's attempt to capture the nomination of the largest party, the Partido do Movimento Democrático Brasileiro (PMDB). Rezende is from a small non-pentecostal denomination in Goiás and became the first Protestant to be elected governor of a state. He had never depended on the Protestant vote and had not always been seen as 'one of us' by all Protestants. This changed after 1986 when he became Minister of Agriculture. Record grain harvests were commemorated in thanksgiving services attended by the president and Protestant leaders. This forged a new relationship, with Iris presenting himself as political leader of a nationwide community, and Protestants portraying the harvests as the result of prayer and Protestant administrative efficiency. A mystique developed that Rezende's mere presence in the presidency would bring divine blessing on the country.

Rezende attracted broad Protestant support. Pastors and businessmen (notably the evangelical businessmen's movement Adhonep), launched the Pro-Iris Evangelical Movement. Although the AG journal made no mention of the candidature, the leaders say they would have given enthusiastic support. The Madureira Convention of the AG, strong in Rezende's region, gave support buttressed by prophesies.

After Rezende's failure to get his party's nomination, most church leaders who had supported him did not adopt another candidate in the first round. Even the coordinator of the Evangelical Pro-Collor campaign waited for the PMDB's decision before committing himself to Collor. The candidature of a politically centrist Protestant like Iris, with his optimistic message, moralising fame and administrative efficiency, would have mobilised most Protestant votes and electoral militancy. In the end, the story was very different.

Since the evangelical world is sociologically diverse, when looking at executive elections we need to ask not only what the hierarchies say, but what these pronouncements represent in each denominational structure, what the degree of obedience to their recommendations is and what influence autonomous Protestant campaign movements have.

Historical churches cultivate the ideology of the autonomous citizen. Their bureaucratic structures and middle-class memberships do not encourage electoral definitions by the leadership. Like the Catholic hierarchy, they stick to 'principles'. Despite variations in ideological sympathy, the range of official actions is limited. Churches affiliated to the ecumenical Council of Christian Churches emit pronouncements in the Catholic style, tending more or less explicitly to the centre-left. The effect on members' voting is dubious. The larger historical churches (Baptist and Presbyterian), non-ecumenical, are more democratic internally. This, plus pietistic theology, discourages official pronouncements. The leaders communicate their (usually conservative) preferences indirectly in articles in the official journals.

The main pentecostal hierarchies had another range of positions. However, the political effect is not always the same. Bishop Macedo of the Universal Church has much more power over pastors and influence over members than does the president of the AG.

The Christian Congregation and God is Love kept an apolitical posture which largely corresponds to their practice. The AG and the Four-Square did not adopt a candidate in the first round, but discouraged voting for those associated with 'atheistic Marxism'. In the run-off between conservative Fernando Collor and Workers Party leader Lula, they came out officially for Collor. Brazil for Christ and the Universal Church supported Collor from the first round, the latter campaigning openly. According to Bishop Macedo, 'if Lula wins, the Catholic Church will give the orders' (*Jornal do Brasil*, 3 Dec. 1989). The details of the agreement between Macedo and Collor are uncertain, but all the versions agree that Macedo wanted to pray at the inauguration. It would mark the definitive entry into civil religion. By 1991, the UC was already 'disillusioned' with Collor and his 1992 impeachment was interpreted as God's judgement for not fulfilling the agreement.

The Four-Square did not officialise support for Collor in the first round, but recommended members not to vote for 'candidates of the left' whose ideology is 'totally opposed to the gospel'. Even the moderate social-democrat Mário Covas was included in the ban. This internal communiqué was reproduced in national newspapers on the eve of the election, probably paid for by the Collor campaign. To show the hierarchy had gone too far, one Four-Square church invited the leader of the Evangelical Pro-Lula Movement to speak. In the run-off, the hierarchy came out for Collor.

The AG did not support or prohibit anyone in the first round. Centre-left candidates even enjoyed some sympathy: the AG president professed friendship with Covas, and the Evangelical Pro-Brizola Movement was run largely by AG members. In the run-off, the hierarchy supported Collor. 'When we saw Lula was going to win, the AG got busy all over Brazil', the president says (Mariano and Pierucci 1992: 101).

The Evangelical Pro-Collor Movement was directed by an AG deputy and a pastor, although initially without official AG support. When Collor's lead diminished, he invested heavily in the pentecostals. He was not put off by the leaders' initial preferences for other candidates, and his investment paid off handsomely in the run-off. As a basically pentecostal movement, it did not appeal to ordinary members but to pastors who would then orient their flocks. Collor would combat corruption, support Israel and govern with the help of Protestants. He was the only candidate capable of beating the 'atheist' left. Like their Universal counterparts, AG leaders became disillusioned with Collor because, once elected, he forgot them.

Why did several pentecostal hierarchies support Collor? His anti-corruption theme was important, as was the promise of change and the 'anti-political' messianic posture (which attracted the social segments to which many pentecostals belonged). Another trump was his self-presentation as 'God-fearing', in contrast with the 'atheist' Lula. Pentecostals associated atheism with persecution of religion. Mariano and Pierucci cite examples of pentecostal concern and conclude: 'a wave of religious panic seems frankly out of place' (1992: 104). However, it is not enough for the social scientist to view the case from what he knows of Lula's intentions. He has to reconstruct the pentecostal plausibility structure. The basis of the latter is the treatment of Christians in Marxist countries. The presence of the communist symbol at Lula's rallies (the Communist Party of Brazil was in his alliance) evoked this history.

It may be objected that no democratically elected socialist government has ever persecuted religion. Against this, pentecostals have many stories, true or not, of supposedly discriminatory treatment from Workers Party local administrations: use of stadiums denied, open-air services prohibited, pastors treated with hostility. On the other hand, a dissident AG journal said rumours of persecution reflected a fear of auditing (*O Alerta*, Jan. 1990: 6). When I telephoned the Pro-Collor Movement before the run-off and asked if they were worried about freedom of religion, the reply was no, since that was guaranteed in the constitution.

However, while there was undoubtedly a degree of manipulation, there was also widespread genuine fear of a Lula victory. For many pentecostals, he represented a Catholic–communist alliance. The centre-left populist Brizola, closer to a lay tradition, did not face the same suspicion. *Pace* Mariano and Pierucci, the fear of persecution was not pure 'fantasy', but had a basis of plausibility. In several Latin American countries, according to a Catholic publication, the 'Catholic counter-offensive' to the 'Protestant sects', even in 'certain progressive sectors', includes the desire for 'government repression' (*30 Dias*, Oct. 1990: 48–55). In Brazil, a progressive Catholic close to Lula is reported as seeing the 'sects' as monitored from the United States to make the people resigned to their misery (*Diário do Povo*, 28 Apr. 1991: 20). Accusations of 'invasion of the sects' usually come from two quarters: the secular left and the Catholic Church. Not surprisingly, an alliance between them seemed threatening. The fear would only be attenuated by a much larger effort than the Lula campaign in fact made.

The Evangelical Pro-Brizola Movement was directed by an AG businessman and supported by some leading AG figures from Rio, including a leading televangelist.

The third Evangelical Movement, the most intellectually articulate, was the Pro-Lula. Its bases were mostly historical, with some pentecostals, especially from the AG and Four-Square. It contrasted with the Pro-Collor Movement in composition and strategy, being both of pastors and ordinary members, and appealing not to leaders specifically but to the individual citizen. The appearance of its leader on Lula's televised propaganda had wide impact. But the Movement only achieved this opening with difficulty. 'We were not listened to by the Lula campaign with regard to participation in rallies and on the media', its report complained. A request that Lula should address evangelicals on television is said to have been rejected under pressure from another religious group.

In the run-off, rivalry increased. Ecumenical Protestants, mostly pro-Brizola in the first round, came over to Lula. With their access to the media and relations with progressive Catholics, they marginalised the Evangelical Movement. The latter's leader no longer appeared on television; in his place was the Inter-Religious Pro-Lula Committee. From the point of view of evangelical votes, the strategy was probably counter-productive; a pronouncement by an 'inter-religious' group is unlikely to persuade pentecostals.

Even so, there were probably more votes for Lula in Protestant churches than in the Base Ecclesial Communities. With another 20 per cent of the Protestant vote, Lula would have won. While the Pro-Lula Movement suffered limitations from being situated mainly in the historical churches, the chief limitations came from the Lula campaign itself. The latter's secular leaders did not perceive the importance of the Protestant electorate, and internal religious rivalries caused strategic mistakes.

To what degree did pentecostal voters heed their leaders' injunctions? In Chile, ordinary pentecostals were more favourable to Allende than their non-pentecostal neighbours, whereas the pastors were much further to the right (Tennekes 1985: 106). Pastors judge parties more by the guarantees they offer churches; they do not want to criticise the social structure which has allowed their own upward mobility; and their on-the-job training socialises strongly in corporate interests.

We know little about how Protestants vote and why. To tip the close election, Protestants only had to divide seventy to thirty in the run-off; a plausible division, not only for religious reasons but for social characteristics. Pentecostals are disproportionately elderly, feminine, poor and unlettered, all factors which favoured voting for Collor. My research among 2,148 Protestant electors from diverse denominations shows it is quite possible that the Protestant vote was decisive in the run-off (Freston 1993a: 260–6).

However, Brazil is unique in Latin America in having an active and growing evangelical left wing. The most famous pentecostal politician in Brazil (who in 1992 almost became mayoress of Rio, and in 1994 was elected senator) diverges sharply from the corporate politics described.

As a leading member of the Workers Party, Benedita da Silva was an atypical pentecostal (by the mid 1990s, she had become Presbyterian,

Brazil

following AG dislike of her marriage to a non-evangelical). But, more than that, as a 'woman, black and shanty dweller' (as her campaign slogan says) in congress, she is an atypical Brazilian. What was pentecostalism's role in constructing this singular figure?

Twelfth of thirteen children of a construction worker and a washer-woman, Benedita worked as maid, street-peddler and nursing auxiliary. Finally, her salary as city councillor allowed her to do a university course in social work. Her political education was in the Catholic Church, through shanty dwellers' associations. Her religious trajectory was not untypical of the popular classes: from Catholic-Umbandista syncretism to pentecostalism. She joined the AG at twenty-four, adapting to the customs but not the aversion to politics. The official journal mentioned her candidacy in 1986 but omitted her party; criticised her on abortion and homosexuality but was silent on her social positions. Other pente-costal politicians treated her respectfully as a 'sincere believer'. In short, she was tolerated but had little space.

Evidently, she was not a political product of the AG. Her whole trajectory went against the *sectarian* mentality which discourages ordinary members from conquering positions in secular society. But her pentecostal faith and lifestyle probably helped to support her upward course. Only after 1989 does she widen her Protestant contacts through the Pro-Lula Movement and the Evangelical Progressive Movement. 'Our faith and political militancy is aligned with the spirit of the Lausanne Pact', she began to affirm, alluding to the 1974 international evangelical congress which made landmark statements on social questions. In 1990, her Protestant electorate, previously insignificant, increased considerably.

If Benedita managed to combine pentecostalism and successful left-wing militancy, there is no reason to suppose others may not do so, even if (due to her national uniqueness) without the same success. In fact, there is a small but constant flow of pentecostal candidates in left-wing parties. Many leaders of rural unions are pentecostal. Novaes (1982) describes a rural meeting of the Workers Party in which the organisers were Protestants and a member of the God is Love church agreed to be a candidate. There was debate with apolitical pentecostals; both sides quoted the Bible, but at no time did they concern themselves with the views of pentecostal hierarchies.

The caucus in the Constituent Assembly and the Protestant vote in the 1989 election stimulated the founding in 1990 of the Evangelical Progressive Movement (MEP). The MEP declares itself evangelical (affirmative of emphases on the Bible, prayer and conversion) and progressive (committed to structural changes in society). It is the work of a new evangelical leadership whose social concern was legitimated by the Lausanne Pact. Reacting against pentecostal corporate politics, it desired to change the political profile of evangelicalism. Other factors facilitated this: the two major anti-left arguments (the association with militant atheism and the Catholic Church) lost force with the collapse of communism and the weakening of progressive Catholicism. Parties of the left began to seek out new social bases. But the most important factor was democracy in the context of economic and political crisis. In the social asymmetry of Brazilian religion, it is democracy and not dictatorship (as in the Catholic case) that is more favourable to a Protestant turn to the left.

Typical of the new evangelical left is Wasny de Roure, a Baptist state deputy who became the finance secretary for the Workers Party administration in the federal district in 1995. A product of the evangelical student movement and the Latin American Theological Fraternity, he is distant from the old Protestant left of the 1960s and 1970s which was linked to ecumenical organisations and non-conservative theologies.

The MEP can grow in historical, and to some extent pentecostal circles, through debate and propaganda. But a wider penetration among pentecostals will depend on the growing institutionalisation of churches like the AG and the Four-Square, changing the criteria of leadership and allowing younger seminary-trained pastors to take charge.

Time-serving, vote-selling and even straightforward corruption have characterised Protestant politics since 1986, and are closely related to the model of official candidates. Corporate politics give access to resources which help to structure this vast popular religious field.

In 1992 President Collor was impeached for corruption. During the period following the publication of the congressional inquiry until the actual vote, the Protestant caucus was always considerably more 'undecided' (i.e. available for offers) than congress as a whole. Only when impeachment was virtually inevitable did many decide to abandon the president.

In 1993 another congressional inquiry led to corruption charges against many members of congress itself. In the case of *evangélicos*, the denunciations affected not only politicians, but also denominational leaders, social-work institutions and organisations supposedly representative of the Protestant world in general. The politicians were mainly

AG official deputies. One of them had negotiated (for a price) his own transfer to two different parties within a week. In the best known case, Manoel Moreira, a former member of the congressional budget committee, had acquired a fortune of eight million dollars.

Since the moralisation of public life had been a theme used by pentecostal leaders to justify entry into politics, the scandals could be expected to affect the corporate model. There were indeed questionings in the AG. An article in the official journal lamented that 'now what is sought is status, human glories... For the professionals of the pulpit, there are no ethics but only interests, "thrones" to be preserved at any price.' The editorial expressed the hope that, in the 1994 elections, 'services do not become the occasion for political campaigns. [The pastor] may not commit the vote of his flock in exchange for personal or collective benefits' (*Mensageiro da Paz*, April 1994). But in practice, the corporate model continued. Manoel Moreira's former father-in-law, head pastor in Campinas, tried to elect his daughter, and in doing so embezzled two million dollars from the church. Since her vote, although small, had prevented the son of the national president of the AG from being elected, the latter intervened in the Campinas church. A deputy from the Madureira branch of the AG, implicated in the scandals, was elected to congress in 1994 with 160,000 votes.

The class composition of pentecostal churches and their *sectarian* nature explain the limited effect of the scandals on corporate politics. The demand for political morality sprang largely from the middle class. The pentecostals, mostly lower class, were little affected by it; and their leaders, initiators and beneficiaries (as individuals and/or as pastors) of corporate politics, had no interest in heightening their awareness.

The 1994 elections were the first since the founding of two entities which claimed to speak for the whole Protestant community. Efforts to unite Protestantism have always been closely linked to politics. After the scandal involving the Evangelical Confederation in 1988, young leaders linked to the evangelicalism of the Lausanne Pact (a sort of Vatican II of world evangelicalism) started to articulate an entity which would be less dependent on political junctures. This crystallised as the Evangelical Association (AEVB) in 1991.

The AEVB's founders were from the political centre and left of the theologically conservative Protestant world. This was too narrow a base for a representative entity. Other sectors were successfully wooed. Within two years, the AEVB had won over the AG General Convention, several other pentecostal and charismatic groups and most of the historicals.

Initially, the Universal Church also made overtures to the AEVB. But realising he would not be able to dominate it and that the latter would adopt inconvenient positions regarding financial accountability and electoral ethics, Bishop Macedo decided to found a competing entity to reflect his new aspiration for hegemony within the Protestant world. He allied with Madureira, the dissident sector of the AG now structuring itself as an independent denomination, to found the National Council of Pastors of Brazil (CNPB).

The methods used illustrate the meaning of corporatist politics. Madureira was granted by the governor of the federal district an enormous plot of land for the CNPB's headquarters. One of the leaders of the governor's party (and since 1998, the same governor's deputy-governor) is a federal deputy belonging to Madureira. We see politics helping the CNPB and Madureira to institutionalise and strengthen their positions in inter-church competition.

The lines of the conflict between the CNPB and the AEVB were already drawn in the reaction of the latter's president to the former's inauguration: 'The AEVB fears the proclaimed objectives of the CNPB ... to elect a president of the republic identified with the interests of the evangelical community' (*Correio Braziliense*, 3 Sept. 1993: 9). As the political coordinator of the Universal Church said: 'we have been left out of governmental projects. Our leadership has been ignored... It is through the union of the evangelicals, of the evangelical leaders who elect the politicians [a significant phrase], that we shall demand the participation we deserve' (*Folha de São Paulo*, 27 July 1994: 1–8).

The CNPB grew to incorporate several other pentecostal and charismatic groups. Even one important figure of historical Protestantism was involved: Nilson Fanini, president of the Brazilian Baptist Convention and (from 1995) of the Baptist World Alliance. Fanini, for many years a public opponent of the Universal Church, had suddenly started defending it. Only later did the reason for this volte-face become known: the UC had bailed out his television station in a secret deal (the station could not legally be sold until it had been functioning longer).

A meeting with President Itamar Franco exemplified the CNPB's strategy. Among the many requests made were the following: a nation-wide radio programme on the official service; a daily slot of thirty seconds during the official broadcasts; diplomatic passports for Brazilian Protestant missionaries; and access to the inland revenue's list of churches (for the CNPB's mailing list). Even though unrealistic, these requests show what politics represents for the CNPB. Madureira's journal reported this meeting under the headline 'President of the

Republic officialises CNPB'. At first sight, this is a curious claim: in a country which lived for centuries under the Portuguese *padroado* (government of the Catholic Church by the crown), a group of Protestant leaders now grants to the temporal power the right to legitimate a pan-Protestant entity. But the real meaning is different: temporal power is a weapon in the struggle for intra-Protestant hegemony and for increased fire-power to propagate one's message. Far from being Erastianism (the supremacy of the state in church affairs), it is the appropriation of the democratic state by a self-confident *sectarian* mentality.

The 1994 election brought the rivalry between the AEVB and the CNPB to the boil. That year, the media projected onto the national scene the president of the AEVB, Caio Fábio D'Araújo Filho. Caio Fábio is a charismatic leader of elitist origin but self-taught after an adolescence spent in the drug culture; a Presbyterian pastor but with charismatic tendencies and wide acceptance in pentecostal sectors; director of his own parachurch organisation and television programme. In recent years, he had gained famous converts, including a well-known gang leader and the governor of the state of Rio, as well as starting a large social project. Caio criticised the UC's Bishop Macedo for the 'terrible visibility he has given to the *evangélicos* as a whole'. Unlike Macedo, who accused Lula, the left-wing candidate for president, of being 'the devil's candidate', Caio stated after the election that he had voted for Lula because 'I did not think of myself but of the millions of destitute people in the country' (*IstoÉ*, 25 Jan. 1995: 4–7). In 1994, the media gave national projection to Caio as an 'anti-Bishop Macedo'. The spectacular growth of the *evangélicos*, making them an important market and electorate, was the reason for the search for an 'anti-Macedo'.

But 1994 also showed there was now a Protestant force much more powerful than its rivals and able to create an unprecedented polarisation. The Universal Church has the power of its media organs, a reasonable political base, enormous financial resources and a theology (of success and prosperity) which is shared by broad sectors of Protestantism today.

The flashpoint in the conflict was the 'Ten Commandments of the Ethical Vote' produced by the AEVB. The Christian, it said,

should not deny his way of seeing social reality, even if a church leader tries to point the vote of his community in another direction... No evangelical voter should feel guilty for having political opinions different from those of his pastor... In the political sphere, the pastor's opinion should be heard only as the word of a citizen, and not as a divine prophecy… It is important that an evangelical candidate should want to be elected with larger objectives than merely to defend the immediate interests of a religious group.

The document brought to the attention of the whole Protestant community a criticism of the practices prevailing since 1986, thus making it more difficult to present the Protestants as a political bloc. In response, the CNPB defended a pastor's right to adopt political positions and indicate candidates. It also counter-attacked, saying the AEVB and its president Caio Fábio were in fact allied to the left-wing candidate Lula. Admitting he had regular meetings with Lula, Caio denied having instructed him on how to 'penetrate' the Protestant world.

In 1994, the pentecostal leaderships were, on the whole, more discreet in their involvement in the presidential elections. Various factors contributed to this: the disappearance of the spectre of atheistic communism; the fiasco of the Collor government; the AEVB's pronouncement on the 'ethical vote'; the greater concern of the left to court the *evangélicos*; and the lack of an anti-Lula candidate capable of galvanising Protestants as Collor had done. At first, Iris Rezende still attracted hopefuls. But he lacked support in his party, having to be content with the candidacy for vice-president offered to his wife, also called Iris. A housewife without political experience, her nomination as running mate by the PMDB candidate (who suffered from a poor ethical image) largely failed to ignite Protestant triumphalism.

Unlike 1989, the Lula campaign took the lead in organising support among Protestants. Contact was increasing between the post-Berlin Wall Brazilian left and a new evangelical left. Some evangelicals had joined the Workers Party (PT) or similar parties. The Evangelical Pro-Lula Committee found greater acceptance this time with the campaign's general coordination. The range of support in the Protestant community was also broader, but still over-concentrated in historical sectors.

Sectors of the Workers Party initially proposed an Inter-Religious Committee, similar to that which functioned in the second round of the 1989 election. The Protestants opposed this, saying it would be a liability in the Protestant world, which has a pluralist and competitive model of the religious field.

The Evangelical Committee proposed alterations to Lula's programme, especially in areas which might provoke open opposition from church leaders: freedom of religion (not only of worship but of propaganda and expansion); mass media (guaranteeing access for religious groups to use and ownership); abortion (opposition to its liberalisation); homosexuality (against legal recognition of homosexual unions); religious education (maintenance of optional instruction in public schools); and missions among indigenous peoples (especially rights of Bible translation and distribution).

The extension of the evangelical left into pentecostal territory brought changes in language. The committee in Rio used 'spiritual warfare' language dear to charismatics. 'Demons must be expelled from social life in the name of the vote, justice, organisation and democracy by the power of the name of Jesus... We desire a Brazil free from spiritual oppression such as hunger, misery, unemployment, inflation, corruption, organised crime... No demon can resist our faith.' In a more traditional vein, speaking of values rather than demons, the Campinas committee said: 'Lula has shown he defends Christian values of justice, peace, freedom and fraternity.'

The only repetition of the pentecostal anti-Lula campaigns of 1989 was in the Universal Church. When Lula was ahead in the race, the UC mobilised its media. There were several lines of attack: Lula's supposed intention to liberalise laws on abortion and homosexual rights (his programme had dropped initial proposals to do so); the anti-democratic nature of the Workers Party; Lula's visit to an Afro-Brazilian centre ('Lula, who has daily lessons from the pastor without a flock Caio Fábio ... promises to punish [evangelicals] who say candomblé and umbanda are religions of the devil'); the links between his party and sectors of the Catholic Church ('a new inquisition may be on the way against the evangelicals'). Macedo said the election was between 'the church of the Lord Jesus Christ and the church of the devil' (*Folha Universal*, 22 May 1994; 15 May 1994; 19 June 1994; 26 June 1994; 10 July 1994).

What motivated this campaign? Fear of a Lula government was probably connected with a question which could not be mentioned openly because of its particularistic nature: the media. The current policy had allowed Macedo to establish a media empire (TV Record, some thirty radio stations, newspapers). The changes proposed by Lula (democratising the process of awarding stations and enforcement of laws against oligopolies) would make this expansion more difficult.

It seems Macedo did not have an accord with any candidate, as he had had in 1989. He showed simultaneous sympathy for Orestes Quercia of the PMDB and Fernando Henrique Cardoso, opting for the latter when it became clear he was the only candidate who could defeat Lula.

In the end, the UC gave lukewarm support for Cardoso. On Cardoso's part, there was little desire for a close association. This was due not only to Cardoso's personal convictions and style (a leading sociologist, he was one of the inventors of neo-Marxist dependency theory in the 1960s), but also because Macedo had waited too long to commit himself; by that time, it was clear Cardoso would enjoy a comfortable victory thanks to the anti-inflationary Real Plan which had been his brainchild as Finance Minister.

In fact, the majority tendency among Protestants was unenthusiastic support for Cardoso. Although the latter now declares belief in God, it was well known that in 1985 he had lost the mayoralty of São Paulo by confessing himself an atheist. His party, the PSDB, has few links with the Protestant world, largely due to its elitist intellectual origins. The Protestant political class followed the national trend; those who had supported Collor in 1989 were now with Cardoso.

For many, fear of Lula and desire for power were mixed with frustration at having to support a former avowed atheist. The president of the AG received Cardoso in his church, introducing him as 'the man chosen by God to be the architect of this bold economic plan' (*O Estado de São Paulo*, 10 July 1994: A-11). But the same pastor affirmed in the denominational journal that there was no candidate 'after the heart of God'; that the most that could be expected was a president 'who doesn't persecute us but helps us'. The article concludes with reluctant support for Cardoso (*O Mensageiro da Última Hora*, July–Aug. 1994).

The historical churches showed little change from 1989. The Lutheran hierarchy made a cautious pronouncement, emphasising rural questions: 'the small farmer is being strangled by lack of assistance. Land concentration goes on, adding to the rural exodus' (*Contexto Pastoral*, Sept.–Oct. 1994: 4). This reflects the erosion by migration of the traditional social composition of the Lutheran church.

As in 1989, the Methodist hierarchy adopted a more left-wing posture than any other Christian church. The bishops described (just as their Catholic counterparts) three ideological axes in the election (neoliberal, democratic-social and 'organised capitalism'), insinuating a clear preference for the second without naming candidates. 'As Methodists we are called to adhere to the cause of the poor and oppressed.' The use of church space for debates is encouraged, but pronouncements on or by candidates during services should be avoided ('As Eleições de 1994', Pastoral Letter of the Episcopal College).

The journal of the Independent Presbyterian Church republished

Lula's 'Open Letter to Evangelicals' and criticised those who demonised him. The Presbyterian Church of Brazil and the Baptists were traditionally reticent; this time, without insinuating reservations about Lula.

How did all this influence the Protestant vote? A poll (Prandi and Pierucci 1994) concluded that, even after taking into account social and demographic factors which differentiate religious groups, religion itself is an important variable in electoral choice. Protestants voted slightly less than average for Cardoso and much less for Lula; somewhat more for the eccentric right-wing Enéas and for the centre-left populist Brizola; and considerably more for Quercia. There were also more undecided. But historicals voted for Lula in virtually the same proportions as the national average, and would give a smaller than average victory to Cardoso in a hypothetical second round. Pentecostals on the other hand, together with Catholic charismatics, gave Cardoso a much larger than average victory. When the effects of sex, colour and schooling are allowed for, historicals appear as a factor of strong rejection of Cardoso and moderate rejection of Lula; pentecostalism, however, does not militate against a vote for Cardoso but is strongly anti-Lula.

Thirty Protestants were elected to congress in 1994, maintaining the level which began in 1986. Of these, nineteen were pentecostals and eleven historicals. The two branches of the AG (General Convention and Madureira) had ten representatives, and the Universal six. The new caucus was very conservative: twenty in parties to the right of the main centrist PMDB, seven in the PMDB itself and only three in parties to the left.

The link with the media remained strong. The clearest example was Francisco Silva, who had by far the largest vote for federal deputy in the state of Rio de Janeiro (210,000 votes, eighty thousand more than the second-placed man who was a former Minister of Finance). His case illustrates the power of the media in structuring the pentecostal world.

Silva appears to represent the invention of religious identity for political ends. Of poor origin, he prospered in the pharmaceutical industry. Perceiving the growing evangelical music market, he started a recording company. In 1987, he bought an FM radio in Rio, gave it totally evangelical programming and was an instant success. It became his platform to politics. He won over pastors by announcing their birthdays on the air and allowing them free announcements, thus setting up his direct-mailing list for election time. In 1990 he was elected to congress with forty thousand votes, mostly from the AG.

Silva sometimes calls himself 'an *evangélico* of all the churches', but on other occasions he claims to belong to the Christian Congregation. This is curious, since the CC prohibits political activity and rejects the mass media. A leader in the church said he did not know of Silva. If the link is really an invention, it is very intelligent since the CC is the only church which would never bother to publish a denial. Silva seems to be a new type of politician: an entrepreneur with a totally evangelical market who invents a church affiliation to project himself politically. Protestantism offers a rapidly growing market relatively lacking in cultural resources. In addition, it has no institutional centre capable of drawing authorised boundaries, thus leaving it exposed to 'exploiters'.

But if Silva can be classified as such (as he is by many), he is not elected without the agreement of church leaders. This exemplifies the conflict felt by many pentecostal pastors because of their contradictory status, and the longing of a socially inferior community to see its symbols and values disputing a place in public life. It also shows the power of the religious media as intermediary between *conversionist sects* and public life, as an expression of their doctrinal, proselytistic and *sectarian* ethos.

In 1994 the would-be candidate for president, Iris Rezende, had proportionally the largest vote for senator in the country. But another Protestant stole the limelight: the left-wing pentecostal Benedita da Silva, who became the first black woman senator ever. Around 20 per cent of her two million votes in Rio de Janeiro seem to have come from evangelicals.

In São Paulo (the most influential state), Francisco Rossi got to the run-off election for governor. His campaign made intensive use of his evangelical identity. As the candidate of a party weak in São Paulo, Rossi surprisingly won a place in the run-off, in which he managed 43 per cent against the candidate of the president-elect.

We do not know what percentage of Protestants voted for Rossi and to what extent such heavy emphasis on a minority religious identity in an election for governor is worth while. It is true that Rossi spoke more of a generically Christian identity, but the whole style was Protestant, as the media realised. His campaign song was the traditional evangelical hymn 'Hold the hand of God'.

Sectors of the Catholic Church, traditionally close to the other main candidate, attacked the 'abuse' of religion. Cardinal Arns, valiant defender of human rights during the military regime, surprisingly said on television (*Opinião Nacional*) that 'religion should not be used for politics'. Even some Protestants complained of the use of the name of God in the campaign. The newspapers associated with a laicist position which

banishes religion from the public sphere called the appeal to religious
sentiments 'political underdevelopment' (*Folha de São Paulo*, 11 Oct. 1994:
1–2). Rossi replied that his strategy was determined by the nature of
televised campaigns: 'you have to say something which awakens the
collective unconscious. It's no use detailing plans for government' (ibid.,
23 Oct. 1994: 1–14). In fact, Cardoso obtained a winning lead for
president without presenting a programme.

The Universal Church did not support Rossi, despite triumphalist
expectations in many evangelical sectors. For the UC (surprised by
Rossi's success in the first round), the question of religious identity is
subordinate to its strategy for hegemony over the Protestant world. In
addition, it was courting the new federal government by supporting its
candidate for governor.

Rossi represented a new phenomenon in Brazil: a career politician
converting and continuing his career in a new evangelical style. A
leading politician since the 1970s, Rossi joined a charismatic church in
1993. As a politician turned evangelical, Rossi is closer to the
Guatemalan tradition referred to earlier.

The case appealed to Protestant triumphalism, the idea of a divine
right to govern. The president of the CNPB called on all Protestants to
campaign for Rossi. 'As spiritual beings, born again, we are the "cream
of society". The church is on a higher level to normal people . . . because
it has the answers the politicians seek . . . With the firm and effective
action of the church in politics, there will be a glorious future' (*O
Semeador*, Aug. 1994: 3).

In legislative elections, this triumphalism was expressed by the charismatic Baptist Lamartine Posella, a televangelist from a business family.
As Lamartine said: 'if we evangelicals are one day going to literally
dominate on earth, why can't we start taking power now, as a foretaste?'
This divine right to govern is linked to concepts of 'spiritual warfare', a
strongly dualistic world-view. 'The social, political and economic
chaos is due to spiritual curses lying on our country [idolatry,
spiritism] . . . The transformation of Brazil will begin with spiritual
restoration . . . God is raising up men full of the Spirit to take over the
positions of power' (*Integração Cristã*, 11 March 1994: 5).

Although triumphalism and corporatism are sometimes mixed, the
latter was still stronger, above all in the Universal Church. In 1994, its
members in congress increased from three to six, its state deputies rose
to eight, and for the first time it acquired a state secretariat and risked a
candidature for the senate. Its support for the winning gubernatorial

candidate in Rio included the state secretariat for work and social action. When a Universal deputy took up the portfolio, newspapers reported the main posts were being filled with Universal pastors and the UC was receiving privileged information regarding job opportunities.

The Universal candidate for senator was an elderly journalist with military links. Despite his somewhat elitist origin, he became a presenter of journalistic programmes on TV Record, and in 1994 joined the UC. Having many links outside the church, he was a wise choice as its first candidate for a post for which church votes would not be enough. He got half a million votes, 6 per cent of the Rio electorate. Though well short of election, this vote increased the bargaining power of the church.

We should not, of course, be deceived by the noise made by some evangelical groups in Brazilian elections. Noisiness is a sign that they are still relative outsiders. Catholic political activity is less visible, reflecting its traditional direct access to circles of power. The stridency of evangelicals reflects their status as an emerging force of popular origin rather than their actual fire-power. But by 1994 this fire-power was undoubtedly on the increase. One proof was the capacity to influence other political actors. An Afro-Brazilian religious journal said they now wished to elect their representatives, seeing 'other religions' elect more and more (*Correio Afro*, June 1994: 2). But they have difficulty in imitating Protestant strategy. In the 1991 census, only 0.4 per cent of the population identified itself as belonging to Afro-Brazilian religions, although a far larger number (most of whom consider themselves Catholic) make use of their services. Their influence in society is more diffuse. Since the community aspect of these religions affects very few people, they do not have a political presence compatible with their undoubted cultural influence.

Protestants also influence secular political actors. Even the left now searches for evangelical candidates who can add votes to their party list, and there are also cases of what look like self-interested conversions at election time, a custom previously restricted to other points of the ideological spectrum.

Pentecostal practices influence the historical churches. The latter feel uncomfortable with the new Protestant politics, either for ideological reasons or out of institutional jealousy, and become politically somewhat 'pentecostalised'. In 1994, the Methodist Church gave more space for candidates belonging to the church to divulge their names; the Presbyterian Church made a point of saying how many Presbyterians had been elected; and the Independent Presbyterian Church even chose official candidates, electing one state deputy. This is a significant divergence from the (socio)logic of the *denomination* type. Without pentecostal instigation it is hard to imagine it happening. At the same time, to compete with historicals in having an attractive public role, pentecostals are investing more in the social action which their theology has usually portrayed as irrelevant.

The 1998 elections represented another turning-point, almost as significant as 1986, in the history of evangelical politics, marked by a quantitative jump and a qualitative change. The leading protagonists were the Universal Church and the new governor of the state of Rio de Janeiro. In 1999, both were very much identified with opposition to the government of President Cardoso; but the future trajectory of both, in ideological terms, was far from clear.

Cardoso was re-elected by a comfortable margin and with similar lukewarm evangelical support as in 1994. There was no intra-evangelical clash such as that of 1994 between the AEVB and the CNPB. The AEVB had gone into crisis over its 1995 attempt to classify the UC as a non-evangelical church, and had subsequently gone into near-terminal decline as the career of its charismatic president, Caio Fábio, ran into difficulties.

The rift in evangelicalism exposed by the 1994 elections had deepened in 1995. The UC's TV Record, besides recovering its financial health and expanding its territorial coverage, had a solid social base. A mass church, whose resources can finance constant expansion, is a new route to media power. Concerned about this, the Globo network (Brazil's largest) decided to attack. It launched a soap opera called *Decadence*, which portrayed the ethically dubious rise of a pentecostal church. Although supposedly fiction, the text used verbatim extracts from interviews given by the UC's founder, Edir Macedo. Thanks to its own media empire, the UC was able to counter-attack. In the ensuing polemic, Caio Fábio came out strongly against the UC, saying Macedo was transforming 'his private quarrel with Globo into a dispute between evangelicals and Catholics'. Macedo had the 'belligerent, aggressive and theocratic spirit of the Islamic countries'; the growth of the UC would 'make any democratic project unviable in this country'. It was not an evangelical church but a new syncretic religion, mixing 'evangelical teachings, precepts of medieval Catholicism and Afro-Amerindian elements' (*Folha de São Paulo* 10 Sept. 1995; *O Globo* 20 Sept. 1995; documents of the AEVB).

This denial of evangelical status to the UC did not please many evangelicals, even some affiliated to the AEVB. Many believed the UC was being attacked solely because it threatened the interests of the Catholic Church and TV Globo.

The Universal reacted by paying for a Manifesto to the Evangelical People to be published in the secular press. For the Manifesto, it mobilised its allies in other churches (Baptist World Alliance president Nilson Fanini; dissidents from the AG; charismatic Baptists...). It accused Caio Fábio of being linked to Globo. It pointed out that a recent publication of Caio's organisation had called him 'informal advisor to TV Globo on evangelical affairs', and had claimed Globo was 'beginning to separate the wheat from the tares among evangelical institutions'.

In late 1995, the police discovered cocaine in Caio Fábio's social project in a Rio shanty. Before the case could be investigated, the state governor suggested the project might be closed. But the ease with which the police had found the exact location of the cocaine raised suspicions. There were demonstrations of support for the project by leading civic figures and opposition politicians. Even so, Caio continued to receive anonymous threats (*Vinde*, Apr. 1996: 23). The context for this is his criticism of the Rio police for its incompetence and corruption, and his friendship with the former governor who had converted to Presbyterianism. The then governor, on the other hand, had allied with the UC.

These incidents showed not only that evangelical divisions deepened the closer evangelicals got to real power, but also that the political strength of several evangelical segments already went beyond the mere election of representatives and provoked the active opposition of important social actors who felt threatened (TV Globo; the Rio state government).

The trajectory of the AEVB, the main force for containment of the UC within the evangelical world, mirrored that of its president Caio Fábio. Charismatic and personalistic, he at first made the AEVB surprisingly representative of the Protestant field, besides giving it a high profile thanks to his own projection in civil society, the media and among left or centre-left political leaders. But then the ambition to develop a media empire led him to develop contacts with large donors, some of dubious reputation, and tone down his left-wing stance. Finally, in the aftermath of the 1998 election, the story emerged of supposed bank accounts in the Cayman Islands to which the president, the governor of São Paulo and other leading government figures were diverting public money. Caio was accused of having attempted to sell the dossier to left-wing politicians just before the election. He denied the pecuniary element in the accusation, claiming he had been informed of the dossier in a pastoral confession and had wished to place it in the hands of opposition leaders rather than the police. As a result, Caio's social projects were boycotted by federal and local governments, and civil society and political leaders who had previously courted him felt too unsure of his connections to come to his defence. Months later, an extra-marital affair came to light which ended Caio's remaining influence in the evangelical community and obliged him to dismantle the ministries he had built up.

The 'Cayman dossier' involved an evangelical churchman playing an unprecedentedly key role in a major political affair, but it also illustrated the evangelical community's institutional fragility and worn ethical image. Caio's previous social projection was indeed the result of evangelical growth, but it was shown to be bereft of any institutional support capable of transcending his personal fate. Although both AEVB and CNPB still existed in 1998, neither retained much political importance; the AEVB had lost its charismatic president in 1997, and the CNPB had by 1996 lost the support of the UC, which with its own increasing power saw no further need for it.

Although the two main candidates (Cardoso and Lula) organised evangelical committees, the campaign failed to ignite passions. Since re-election was virtually certain, the leaders of some churches, notably the AG, pledged support and asked in exchange for a bigger slice of public funds for evangelical social projects and of the president's ear in decision-making. But the one-sided campaign left them with little leverage, and their position does not seem any stronger now than in Cardoso's first mandate.

The gubernatorial races were different. In the Federal District, the incumbent Workers Party governor came close to re-election. Evangelical Workers Party activists generally agree that the evangelical vote was important in the tight run-off and that the governor had unnecessarily lost evangelical sympathy by being insensitive to churches over bureaucratic questions and ignoring the left-wing evangelicals. Leaders of the charismatic Comunidade Sara Nossa Terra resurrected the old extreme anti-Workers Party posture, alleging links between the party and satanism, but the efficacy of such tactics now is uncertain.

In São Paulo, the early front-runner was Francisco Rossi, the evangelical who had finished second in 1994. His campaign was now less evangelical in tone, his previous experiences having dashed the illusion of a united evangelical electorate. His main rival, veteran right-winger Paulo Maluf, formed a Christian Front led by the Renascer Church, a largely middle-class charismatic denomination, which hoped to get the Welfare Secretariat in a Maluf government. Once eliminated, Rossi surprised everyone by supporting Maluf in the run-off, having previously lambasted Maluf's unethical political style. This volte-face was badly received by the media and, it seems, his own electorate.

The elections produced one evangelical governor and three deputy-governors, two of whom were women and two black. The key case was in Rio de Janeiro, where evangelicals became governor and deputy-governor. This represents the peak of evangelical electoral success so far in Brazil, and it is probably significant that Rio has the lowest proportion of Catholics in the country (little over half). Interestingly, this first successful all-evangelical slate is on the left of the political spectrum. The deputy-governor is Benedita da Silva, the black former shanty dweller, formerly of the AG and now a Presbyterian. The governor is also Presbyterian: Anthony Garotinho, a 38-year-old radio presenter who rose to fame as highly popular mayor of a large city. Garotinho had turned evangelical only four years previously, following a car crash during an unsuccessful campaign for governor. This time, uniting his regional vote with, it seems, a very high percentage of the evangelical vote, he won the run-off.

Garotinho had considerable support amongst Baptists and the AG. His Evangelical Committee brochure shows the two main appeals: 'partnership' between state government and churches in social programmes, and possible posts in government. In fact, in the first year or so of his government, a programme of assistance to poor families was carried out in large measure via evangelical churches, leading to accusations of religious favouritism. On the other hand, there were only two evangelicals in positions of importance in his government. One was an AG pastor who had led the Evangelical Committee; the other was the federal deputy Francisco Silva. As owner of important evangelical radio stations, Silva was vital in Garotinho's election, even though he was in the rightist PPB which officially supported the rival candidate. Garotinho stood for an alliance of all the left and centre-left parties, but Silva was rewarded with an important secretariat.

Although the president of the rival candidate's party was an evangelical deputy, and the UC sat on the fence, Garotinho very successfully mobilised the evangelical vote. A few months into his mandate, he made clear his presidential aspirations for 2002. As the first plausible evangelical presidential hopeful in a decade, initial enthusiasm for him amongst evangelicals was widespread. Unlike Iris Rezende, who had evangelical roots but scanty practice, Garotinho was a recent and highly enthusiastic convert. A main plank in his project was to make his name nationally known by means of the evangelical connection, and to that end he began, in late 1999, frequent trips to other states to preach in churches. Political reaction was swift; even the leader of his own party, a veteran *caudilho* unwilling to be eclipsed by his one-time protégé, criticised this 'obscurantist manoeuvre' and 'sinful association between faith and politics'. Garotinho, in reply, stressed that Protestantism was his personal religion and there was nothing opportunist in his preaching tours. Some evangelicals were concerned, however, at Garotinho's lack of evangelical socialisation (as with Guatemala's Ríos Montt at the time of his presidency), the role played by Francisco Silva in financing these trips, and the connections with AG leaders with a history of time-serving politics. The Universal, meanwhile, remained cool, tempering occasional praise with frequent criticism for the lack of evangelicals in government and his failure to stem the tide of violence in Rio. While Universal support for Garotinho's state government might depend on what slice of power he was prepared to give it, support for his presidential aspirations would hinge on larger institutional calculations. It is doubtful that the UC would support a major evangelical political project not fundamentally dependent on the UC itself. The oft-touted ideology of 'power to the evangelicals' would cede before evangelical rivalries; even when there is only one evangelical candidate in an election, some reason can always be found for putting in abeyance the injunction to evangelical political unity employed on other occasions. But in the last analysis, Garotinho's political future would be decided outside the evangelical camp, in the reputation of his state government and ability to build a broader party base. Although defining himself ideologically as capable of uniting the centre and the left, and favouring a policy of economic growth, his ideological future was far from clear, especially after the Workers Party withdrawal from the state government in 2000.

The other major outcome of the 1998 elections was a steep rise in number and composition of evangelicals in congress. Forty-nine were elected, and by February 2000 fifty-four were in office. Two-thirds were pentecostals and one-third historicals, reflecting the division of the evangelical population. It was probable that, by the end of the legislative term, over sixty would have taken seats, an increase of some 60 per cent. Evangelicals are more numerous than all but five parties. Unity is a chimera; but the opposite is true of the Universal deputies, more united than any party, making them effectively the ninth-largest party.

The distribution of evangelicals amongst the lower house's permanent commissions reflects their concerns, with heavy concentrations in the commissions responsible for the media and religious freedom. As for party distribution, twenty-nine of the fifty-three deputies are in parties which support the government; six are in the 'right-wing' PPB (ideological labelling of Brazilian parties is hazardous); nine are in parties to the left of the government; and ten are in a two-party bloc effectively controlled by the UC. Thus, evangelicals, who are 10.3 per cent of federal deputies, are only 8.4 per cent of pro-government deputies and only 8.0 per cent of deputies in the left-wing opposition, while they are 12.2 per cent in the right and 62 per cent in the Universal-led bloc.

As of 2000, there were four congressmen identified with the leftist Evangelical Progressive Movement (MEP). Coincidentally, all four were Baptists and had higher education. The evangelical electorate was vital for some of them, but only secondary for others; three also had trade-union connections. Three had occupied posts in state Baptist conventions. These deputies issued a manifesto in reaction to the UC's initial attempts to speak for all evangelicals in congress.

While left-wingers remain a fairly small minority amongst evangelical politicians, more and more people with a history of leftist or unionist militancy convert to evangelical churches and continue the same political activities. Any criticism from church leaders is laughed off, but without diminishing loyalty to the church in other areas. On the other hand, the increasing contingent of evangelicals in the Workers Party still complains of party attitudes, especially the leaders' inability to perceive evangelicals' social importance.

The MEP's reaction to the Universal illustrates a broader trend; the UC's rise has stimulated some denominations to raise the profile of their politicians and present them as more organically connected to the church. The Presbyterian Church took pride in its seven politicians elected in 1998, and talked of organised candidatures for city councillor in 2000 (*Brasil Presbiteriano*, Nov. 1998). The Four-Square devised a 'broad political project to give support to the church' (*Voz e Ação*, Aug. 1998). There have only been three Four-Square congressmen, but all of them, together with some state deputies and city councillors, have a characteristic which sets them apart from AG trajectories: they are all

top church leaders. Indeed, the denominational president is a federal
deputy. The church began as circus-tent evangelistic campaigns known
as the 'National Evangelistic Crusade'. The culture of the 'crusade',
with its lionising of miracle-working pioneer preachers, is still important, and the pioneer generation now unites bureaucratic power to
charismatic legend. This is a mixture that the older and more staid
Assemblies cannot emulate, its leaders preferring to elect relatives or
protégés instead of standing themselves. It is also different from the
UC's recent practice of electing pastors and bishops, most of whom
entirely lack personal charisma. The typical Four-Square politicians,
when young men, healed the blind, raised the dead and sometimes got
jailed. Now in command of large institutions, they convert their religious prestige into political capital.

The Four-Square's fire-power is small compared to the AG, but the
latter is running into difficulties. Of the original thirteen deputies elected
in 1986, only one was re-elected in 1994 for a third term, although
another was the son of a veteran. (Yet another, Benedita da Silva, was
now a senator; but her trajectory was unconnected to the AG hierarchy.) Six of the original twelve elected in 1986 as official candidates
had by 1994 fallen foul of scandals. In those twelve states, the corporate
project had run into the sand in seven. Only in two did it continue in the
same hands; but in one of those the deputy was only a substitute after
1994 and did a deal with the UC in 1998 to be re-elected. In another
state it had passed from father to son, and in two further states had been
maintained by a shift of allegiance on the part of the local AG hierarchy.
On the other hand, official candidates had been successful in three other
states, as well as a fourth where the initiative had passed from the
General Convention to Madureira, thus representing different interests
and a different electorate.

In 1998, the AG once again managed eleven deputies, but by this time
it had lost political leadership of the Protestant world to the Universal.
One of its new deputies illustrates the problems. Silas Câmara's brothers
control the AG in Amazonas and Pará, as well as the Boas Novas media
network, the largest evangelical media consortium outside the UC. Silas
thus represents the greatest concentration of ecclesiastical, media and
political power yet seen in the AG. Yet by early 2000 he was under
investigation for a range of accusations from drug trafficking and for-
gery to bigamy.

The 1998 polls marked the shift of Protestant political hegemony to
the Universal Church. It had elected six federal and eight state deputies

in 1994, but now even its own expectations were exceeded. It had penetrated smaller cities and even rural areas in virtually all states, and its media empire was practically national in extent. As a result, it elected fifteen federal deputies and twenty-six state deputies, besides three federal deputies from other churches supported by the UC. It is the denomination which most successfully mobilises the corporate electorate; in 1998 its candidates for congress received over a million and a quarter votes. The AG at its height probably never mobilised more than 40 per cent of its potential voters. The corporate vote is never automatic, depending on a relationship which has to be constructed and maintained with difficulty. Leaders of some middle-range pentecostal denominations have confidently tried for election and received only 10 per cent of the votes they expected. Nevertheless, this has not affected their continued success in the religious sphere, showing that the pentecostal electorate is capable of separating religious from political injunctions. All this shows how surprising is the success achieved by the UC. Even it cannot manage 100 per cent of members' votes; there are a growing number of members from left-wing parties, besides a constant stream of new attenders yet to assimilate church norms. As an educated guess, we can estimate the UC corporate vote at 70 per cent of its potential; allowing for votes from non-members, and for non-electors among the members, that would mean a membership of just over two million, which seems plausible.

What is the social profile of the current crop of UC politicians? Are they anonymous figures imposed on a passive electorate, as suggested by one of their own deputies ('our voters are faithful; we could get a lamp-post elected')?

An analysis of the church's fifteen congressmen nuances the picture, suggesting an evolution in which charisma of office (as 'our church's candidate') is complemented (not replaced) not usually by personal charisma but by personal qualifications and some degree of name recognition from ordinary members. The latter is achieved through pastoral work, social work and above all by presenting programmes in the church media. The most typical professional self-description of UC congressmen, especially the new ones, is 'pastor and media presenter'. Since the UC cultivates members' identification with its media (Fonseca 1997), this suggests that members may not be always voting for 'lamp-posts' but for someone they are familiar with and recognise as active in 'God's work'. In most cases this may happen through conscious initiative of the church (e.g. by placing a prospective candidate for a couple of years on its media programmes or as state director of its social work); but this itself is a recognition that the corporate vote is not automatic but needs to be maximised in various ways (uniting a sense of institutional defence against 'persecution' with a perception that 'so-and-so is a dedicated church leader whom I know and who will make a good parliamentarian'). Only a couple of older congressmen seem to be less connected to religious work.

That some identification between candidates and electorate is sought (and maintained through regular articles about deputies' activities) is only part of the explanation for electoral success. The main factor is the leadership's emphasis on 'persecution' suffered by the church, which only greater political presence will impede. The UC's relationship with society is tense enough to give this view coherence; and its parliamentary activities have been sufficiently successful thus far (and free of individual scandals) to make the suggested remedy plausible. But there is a limit; too much political success could weaken self-identity as a 'persecuted church', and thus be self-defeating.

Pentecostal politicians post-1986 included an above-average proportion from lower social backgrounds, with lower educational levels and darker skin. Post-1998 UC politicians are not especially dark, but in other respects are of exceptionally low social origin. Whereas 83 per cent of congressmen have university degreees, this dips to 62 per cent of non-UC Protestants and plummets to 38 per cent of UC deputies.

As with the official AG and Four-Square congressmen, all the UC ones are men, although four of their twenty-six state deputies are women. The fifteen federal deputies have been members of the UC for an average of fifteen years, and very few had been in other Protestant churches. Sixty per cent are now pastors or bishops. With one exception, all were unaffiliated to any political party until just before their election, showing that parties are little more than (legally obligatory) electoral vehicles.

The typical UC congressman is thus a white man in his forties, without higher education; a non-Protestant until converting to the Universal in the 1980s; a pastor and presenter of church media programmes, and possibly involved in church social work; now in his first legislature, with no previous political experience or party involvement.

The eighteen federal parliamentarians elected by the UC in 1998 are dispersed among parties of the centre and right, although after the election the church concentrated about half in two small existing parties, which now act as a bloc.

In addition, since the UC is rigidly hierarchical, its politicians, regardless of party, act as a solid caucus. Activity continues to revolve around protection of its media empire. In pursuit of this overriding aim, rigid discipline has prevented the individual scandals which have undermined the credibility of other pentecostal politicians. Without regional oligarchs like the AG, it has no localised corporatist demands to process, and individual ambitions, while impossible to abolish, can be restrained by the certain loss of UC institutional benefits, including the inevitable failure to gain re-election.

In party terms, the distribution of the eighteen federal deputies reflects the church's interests. As of February 2000, eight are in the major parties allied with the government; two are in a party to the right of the government, and the other eight are in the bloc of two small parties dominated by the UC. None are in the left-wing parties which oppose the government. The caucus is thus divided between pro-government parties (usually with little influence in them) and an independent front; a combination of autonomous ('Christian') politics and a pro-government stance which seeks to satisfy corporate demands, with leftist parties being ignored. In terms of parliamentary commissions, UC deputies are concentrated in the media and foreign relations (presumably due to the church's increasing investment in international expansion).

The relationship to the left may hold the key to future developments. Up to 1994 it was extremely anti-left, openly calling Lula a 'demon'. However, as I speculated at the time (Freston 1994a: 135), it was not obvious that this virulent anti-leftism would last. Concern about media interests seemed to be the key factor, and it was unlikely that the Cardoso government would grant it any special relationship. Besides, its prosperity gospel counsels members to become self-employed. Thus, in economic policy, it might be as well served by the left's proposals for strengthening the domestic market and small-scale enterprise as by a recessive neoliberalism which throws people onto the informal market but abandons them there.

After late 1995 the UC's anti-leftism waned. It began to court left-wing leaders, giving space to them in its media. Although UC candidates are still in centre and right parties, this is probably because the left demands greater party loyalty and would thus complicate the church's capacity to act as a bloc. Articles in the *Folha Universal* and speeches by Bishop Rodrigues, the church's political coordinator, became increasingly critical of the government's lack of a social policy. It remained to be seen whether this was a strategy for goading the Cardoso government into a closer relationship (especially with continuing problems from the inland revenue and the federal police over the purchase of TV Record and other media deals), or whether it stemmed (as Rodrigues himself claimed) from the new exposure to social reality triggered by the expansion of the church and its social work, leading to a realisation that 'in Brazil nothing works right, the country needs to change' (*Vinde*, Oct. 1998). In the end, the UC supported Cardoso's re-election in 1998, but only after giving equal exposure in its media to the various candidates, including Lula. This support was explained by Rodrigues as due to an agreement with the president to veto clauses in an environmental law which would levy fines on noisier churches. Whether a complete explanation or not, this points again to the corporatist dimension in its politics; in the end, institutional interests speak louder than the more universalist concerns increasingly present in the church's discourse.

Criticism of government recommenced soon after the elections, and the *Folha Universal* took on a more left-wing tone. As a Brazilian church with no affiliations (much less financial dependence) on foreigners, the nationalistic criticism of multinationals, the International Monetary Fund (IMF) and indiscriminate privatisation was perhaps not so surprising. Somewhat more so is Bishop Rodrigues' verdict that 'globalisation is the fruit of an economic policy dictated by the developed countries to expand their markets ... giving their citizens all the things they "steal" from ours. Globalisation is the domination of the underdeveloped countries' (*Folha Universal*, 17 Oct. 1999). Or the reconciliation of anti-neoliberalism with prosperity theology by Bishop Alfredo Paulo:

There is a Satanic trinity in capitalism: the great 'god' is the market, the great world religion is capitalism and the Holy Spirit is the IMF ... When we do a Prosperity Chain [meetings dedicated to obtaining prosperity] we are going against the elementary principles of the market, which include 'you are poor, you were born to be poor, you will die poor'. (ibid., 25 Apr. 1999)

Two incidents in February 2000 exemplify the current political stance. The first was a speech in congress (9 Feb. 2000) by Bishop Rodrigues, on the twentieth anniversary of the Workers Party (PT). The PT arose basically as a mix of unionism, Marxism and Catholic Base Communities. Rodrigues stressed that he spoke on behalf of his church 'that used to fight ferociously against the PT' because 'we didn't understand politics... We thought everything red was communist, that they would close the churches... But when we got to know Lula [and others, including evangelical PT congressmen] we saw our truths were lies, our fears were groundless'. Now, 'we realise you fight for the same thing as us', which is why 'my Liberal Party has followed the PT in 90 per cent of votes' in congress. 'At many times, your struggle for a more just and fraternal society . . . is the same as our religious struggle . . . Some nights I leave here frustrated because we, of the left, did not manage to defeat a proposal of the right'.

This speech, unthinkable from the UC of five years earlier and unlikely from the leader of any other pentecostal denomination even today, raises the question whether the UC, whose unique combination of mass popular membership plus institutional power (hierarchical organisation, political representation, financial wealth and media empire) is the secret of its strength, allied to its growing social work which it says makes it aware of the need for change, might not become a leading promoter of what some in Latin America are calling neopopulism.

However, the second incident from February 2000 shows the ambiguity of UC politics and the pragmatic limits on its leftward turn. Corporate interests seemed once again to take precedence over all else. With municipal elections imminent, the UC agreed to change the line of its media, and give its bloc in congress a more pro-government stance. In exchange, the government would show greater 'goodwill' in regularising UC media purchases and in the UC's revenue affairs under investigation (*Folha de São Paulo*, 18 Feb. 2000). Thus, despite signs of an evolution towards a more universalist and ideological politics, they are still subordinate to corporatist demands.

Presenting itself as effective defender of evangelical institutional causes and as strategist of a more efficient corporatist project, the UC seeks political hegemony in the Protestant world. The words of the president of the Baptist Convention of Bahia are probably representative of reactions amongst many denominations: 'We have reservations about some things they do but we cannot deny the importance of having spokesmen who really defend the interests of the people of God.' In a critique of corporatist politics as practised by other churches, the UC says that 'organised sectors of society normally indicate candidates and raise funds'. With evangelicals, the opposite occurs: candidates help churches rather than receiving help from churches. 'Imagine electing someone who goes to congress just to fight against gay marriage. We expect much more. We need government recognition of our social projects and equality [with Catholicism] in treatment of our institutions' (*Folha Universal*, 12 July 1998).

So Protestant political leadership, having passed through Presbyterians, Baptists and the AG, has not just passed to another denomination. UC politics is not only stronger numerically, but is rigidly
coordinated and backed up by unprecedented wealth and media
power. In addition, the highly centralised UC enjoys an advantage over
most denominations in that its organisational model is closely adapted
to the residual neo-Christendom model which still dominates the way
the Brazilian state expects to relate to the religious field. It is thus helped
politically by its similarities to, rather than by its differences from,
Catholicism.

How will this model evolve? One can anticipate problems of form
and content in the medium run. The UC needs institutional issues
(opposition to a law against noisy churches, or against proselytism on
community radios) to mobilise its own voters and to bring the evangelical field under its leadership. Such issues are not only safer (since
socio-economic questions might produce ideological divisions within
the church); they also loom large as the logical result of a mobilisational
model in which the ecclesiastical leadership chooses candidates and
controls its parliamentary caucus. Attempts at a less particularist politics
(inevitable if the UC develops its apparent project of becoming a
substitute national church) would reveal the limitations of this model of
political engagement in the modern world. As regards content, a more
clearly defined socio-economic position, besides being internally divisive, might harm its still vulnerable institutional interests, leaving it
hostage to pressures. Of course, over time the UC may become less
politically vulnerable and create its own 'tradition' of social teaching,
enabling more independent postures. But the resultant combination of
institutional and ideological concerns, and the direction of the latter,
while difficult to predict, will in any case have to take account of the
precarious loyalty of members of any church which functions in conditions of competitive religious pluralism.

Further comment on characteristics (some typical, others seemingly
unique) of the Brazilian case will be made after our survey of the three
continents.

PART TWO

Asia

Evangelical Christianity in Asia presents a complex picture. Only one country, the Philippines, can in any way be compared to Brazil, being the only nation-state with a Christian (Catholic) majority and a growing evangelical minority. Another country with a unique experience is South Korea (and the whole of Korea before division, and possibly the whole of it again when unification comes), being the only country in Asia where Protestantism has reached significant proportions and entered the national mainstream. Protestantism there is not a 'minority' religion in a sociological (rather than statistical) sense, that is, as lodged primarily in a politically and/or economically marginalised ethnic or caste group (as with Dalits and tribals in India, Chinese and indigenous minorities in Malaysia and Indonesia, tribals in Myanmar). Protestantism has achieved a remarkable relationship to Korean national identity, something still unthinkable for believers (even though not from ethnic minorities) in Taiwan and Singapore, still less in China itself.

If evangelicalism in Latin America relates to a traditionally hegemonic Catholicism, and in parts of Africa to Islam, Asia presents a more complicated religious field. Hinduism, Buddhism, Islam and Japanese religions have proved impermeable to Christianity, which (except in Korea) has achieved African or Latin growth only where those religions have not penetrated, and especially where oppressed tribal groups have shown interest in acceding to modernity by means of a world religion which is not that of their immediate oppressors.

Keyes (1996) stresses this dynamic. Early missionaries often met hostility from rulers, and converts were from the margins (uplands, outer islands, recent Chinese immigrants, lepers). Colonial governments later facilitated missions amongst the 'primitives' rather than amongst the core populations. Some peripheral peoples who converted in Indonesia and Burma later supported separatist movements during transition to independence. The Karen rebellion goes on, as does conversion in many places; independent governments made the state more intrusive, transforming life-worlds and indirectly encouraging adoption of a world religion different from that of the core population. However, space for this varies radically; while Indonesia was 4.8 per cent Protestant by the mid 1980s, Thailand was only 0.2 per cent. A non-ethnic conversion dynamic is at work in Singapore, where Christians grew from 10.3 per cent in 1980 to 18.7 per cent in 1988, largely due to evangelical expansion. Concern that religion might provide a platform for opposition to Singapore's authoritarian regime led to the Maintenance of Religious Harmony Law of 1990. In Vietnam, evangelicals apparently doubled in the decade after communist unification (ibid.: 287).

All this means different dynamics in politics from most of Latin America and Africa. The 'ethnic' nature of much Christianity introduces a range of different questions, for which works such as Hastings' provocative *The Construction of Nationhood* (1997), even though not mentioning Asia, could provide insights. What are the political dynamics of an evangelicalism which has become the religion of a sizeable minority (or even an almost established majority) amongst ethnicities which have failed to become nations? Likewise, works such as Cohen's *Global Diasporas* (1997) could help in understanding the political implications of evangelicalism amongst overseas Chinese in Indonesia, Malaysia and elsewhere. Questions of nation-building and 'civil religion' are most pertinent here. Ethnically diverse and even geographically dispersed states, sometimes new creations from colonial boundaries, develop ethnic and religious policies which sharply determine the space for conversion and for Christian politics.

CHAPTER 2

Korea

South Korea, like Brazil, is a key centre of evangelicalism in the Third World, both in numerical strength and missionary-sending importance. But unlike Brazil's position within Latin America, this regional Protestant 'superpower' has a unique history and is probably not a forerunner of developments in other Asian countries. This applies also to its evangelical politics.

Korea is the most important case where knowledge of a non-Western language might significantly increase access to worthwhile secondary literature. (English, Spanish, Portuguese and French, in roughly that order, are the key languages for Third World evangelicalism.) While works in English on Korean Protestant politics are more numerous than for other Asian countries, the quality is behind that produced on Africa and Latin America.

The most relevant is Kang's *Christ and Caesar in Modern Korea* (1997). It is very useful but, like some other works, better on the pre-1945 period (the rise of Japanese influence and the colonial period itself), when Christianity was smaller and less fragmented and the Korean political agenda was very clear. In the post-1945 world the religious and political fields become more complex and Protestantism's contribution to nationalism (emphasised in rather self-congratulatory fashion by Korean Christian historians) seems to become shipwrecked on the rocks of anti-communism, dictatorship and the chaebol (Korea's huge conglomerates like Hyundai and Samsung which have grown up under state tutelage). Kang's picture of Protestant politics becomes rather one-sided, as if nearly all Christians were 'progressives'. Perhaps that is the fate of a country on the front line of the Cold (and at times not so cold) War. As the early original ideological contribution is replaced by mere numerical force and fractured voices, so the picture offered by Kang and others becomes hazier, and what we do not know becomes more intriguing than what we do. We need to know more about the actual politics of the 'conservatives', even those claiming to be apolitical. Denominational institutional factors need to be taken more into account in explaining positions. Protestantism is very important in Korean politics, and has only been less so because of the long dictatorial interlude. Until 1997 the only two elected presidents in Korean history had been Protestants. Their careers are easy to scrutinise, but (as with Guatemala) we must not neglect other levels: the actual politics of the diverse church leaderships, the electoral behaviour of members and the characteristics of the many Protestant members of congress, for example.

South Korea is about 20 per cent Protestant. Some Protestant estimates talk of 29 per cent in 1993 (*Korean Torch*, July–Sep. 1993: 22). Government figures talk of only 19.7 per cent in 1995, up from 16.1 per cent ten years earlier. This contrasts with 6.6 per cent Catholics, 23.1 per cent Buddhists and 0.5 per cent Confucianists. Those professing 'no religion' are 49.3 per cent, down from 57.5 per cent in 1985 (Hong 1999: 136). The latter category is officialdom's way of hiding the massive presence of shamanism, or traditional Korean religion. Rendering 'invisible domestic religions from below while privileging world religions from above' is a typical practice of East Asian states (Rudolph 1997a: 17). There is, however, a slow process of adherence to world religions. Buddhism, learning from Protestantism, has reorganised and is growing again, possibly a factor in Protestant difficulties in the 1990s.

Protestantism is 62 per cent Presbyterian (in many denominations), about 11 per cent Methodist (rather less divided), 10 per cent pentecostal, 8 per cent Holiness and 7 per cent Baptist (*Korean Torch*, July–Sep. 1993: 22). However, Presbyterianism is considerably pentecostalised. Greater Seoul is home to twenty-three of the fifty largest megachurches in the world (Hong 1997).

After decades as the envy of the evangelical world for its rapid growth, Korean Protestantism is stagnating numerically. Government figures show a slowing growth rate since 1990 and an absolute decline of 4 per cent in 1993 (*Korean Torch*, Jan.–Mar. 1995: 8). Speculation is rife as to causes (economic success; redemocratisation; Buddhist revitalisation; the perceived social indifference of most churches). Although Korean evangelicals are in the enviable Asian position of not having to justify their very existence as Christians, this assured place in society does not guarantee them against the subtle danger of irrelevance. As for the pro-democracy campaigners of previous decades, their very success has made them less certain of their role (*Far Eastern Economic Review* –

hereinafter *FEER*, 30 May 1996). The political side, as in Latin America, can impact directly on the future of the church.

The Protestant trajectory in Korea is unique in Asia. Since arrival in the 1880s, it has enjoyed the comfortable position of representing modernity but not also a colonialist threat. On the contrary, it quickly achieved an association with emerging modern nationalism. Buddhism did not have a strong link with Korean identity, having been marginalised since the fourteenth century by neo-Confucianism (Grayson 1995). When the latter faltered in the late nineteenth century, Christianity offered itself as both 'Western Learning' and a civil religion for Korean revival. Although the missionaries arrived in the context of a Korean–United States treaty, the immediate imperialist threat was from Japan. Besides, Protestantism had arrived not only through missionaries but also (and firstly) through Koreans returning from China or Japan (In 1996: 16). The Nevius Principle of missions, emphasising participation, self-support and use of native cultural styles, was applied. And the simpler (but largely neglected) Hangul script was used for the Bible and Christian publications, popularising literacy.

The Toknip Hyophoe (Independence Club) was founded in 1896 with a significant Christian constituency; and the great revival of 1907 broke out in the context of national anguish over the abdication of the king under Japanese pressure. One of the leaders of the revival was Sun Chu Kil. From a noble family and steeped in the Confucian classics, Kil had passed through a Buddhist meditative sect before converting and becoming the first ordained Korean pastor. As head of the Central Presbyterian Church of Pyongyang, he was a leading nationalist and one of the signers of the March First Declaration of Independence in 1919. He was not just politically active, but developed a theology of Korean national messianism, with an eschatological flavour and based on non-violence (In 1996: 112–24). Of the thirty-three signers of the Declaration of Independence, sixteen were Christians, including eleven pastors (ibid.: 164, 180), even though Christians at the time were only 1 per cent of the population. The church network was crucial for this well-planned movement, and Kil's non-violence was included in instructions for participants: 'whatever you do, do not insult the Japanese, do not throw stones, do not hit with your fists, for these are the acts of barbarians' (ibid.: 165). Seven of the eight members of the Provisional Government formed in exile afterwards were Christians.

As In says, Protestantism inspired Koreans with its sense of freedom and justice (1996: 37). We can add that this was possible because in

Korea the exploited were not an internal class, forcing the church to make a class choice, but the whole nation. And because the missionaries were racially different from the non-Christian imperialists. In addition, Japanese colonial policies (direct rule, militaristic, suspicious of the church and, in the 1930s, shintoistic) further helped to make Christianity an ally of nationalism. But Janelli talks of a split in Korean nationalism in the 1920s between cultural and communist versions (1993: 78). It is here that existing Christian accounts seem to go silent. They just talk of Japanese rule, but not of what went on amongst the Koreans under it. Is this where Christian nationalism is derailed, allowing itself to become an anti-communist ideology after World War II? We need more nuanced analysis of the relationship between Protestantism and various versions of Korean nationalism in more recent times.

In the Japanese colonial period (1910–45), the church was traumatised by three major incidents: the 105 People Incident of 1911 (a crude atttempt to attack church leaders); repression after the 1919 Independence movement; and the Shinto shrine controversy which effectively lasted from 1936 to the end of the war. Most of the church in fact reached an accommodation over the latter, but a minority, especially of Presbyterians, held out and some fifty died in prison as a result. By the early 1940s the Korean church had been effectively reorganised as a branch of the Japanese church.

While the enemy was external, the church remained largely united organisationally and suffered little internal tension about its public role. But after 1945, and even more after the Korean War, the difficulties became internal to the country, provoking denominational schisms and political tensions. During the military regime from 1961, rapid industrialisation, urbanisation and social tensions led to a polarised church, blessed and cursed by its position on the Cold War front line. Reconstruction of the churches after 1945 enjoyed American support, aiding a proliferating denominationalism. In addition, Christianity had been largely northern before division. After 1945, and again during and after the Korean War, there was a huge influx of Christian refugees to the Seoul area.

The prestige of Christianity after World War II was due not only to its resistance to Japanese colonialism, but also to being the religion of the American liberators, which had proved more powerful than its Eastern competitors. Thus, of fifty officials in the Korean government in the American-occupied sector in 1946, thirty-five were professing Christians; of the ninety members of the Interim Legislative Assembly in

1946, twenty-one were Christians. In the Legislative Assembly of August 1948, Christians were thirty-eight out of one hundred and ninety (Kang 1997: 75).

The most prominent was none other than the first president, Syngman Rhee. Rhee was educated at a Methodist school, becoming 'an ardent nationalist and ultimately a Christian', as the *Encyclopaedia Britannica* revealingly puts it. In 1896 he helped to form the Independence Club; in 1898 he was imprisoned for six years, during which time he converted to Methodism. On release, he went to the United States and obtained a PhD at Princeton. After a time in Korea with the YMCA (Young Men's Christian Association), he returned to exile, becoming a spokesman for independence and, for twenty years from 1919, president of the Provisional Government in exile. As the only Korean leader well known to the United States, he was well placed to benefit from the outcome of the war. The Americans returned him to Korea before other Provisional Government members, and helped him build a mass organisation with strong-arm squads. Apprehensions about communism led US forces to deny the legitimacy of national political groups and establish their own military government, which employed many anti-communists and former employees of the Japanese state (Janelli 1993: 70–1). After the assassination of moderate leaders, Rhee won the 1948 elections. He was re-elected in 1952 and 1956, building up dictatorial powers and purging the opposition.

A National Christian Council of Korea publication describes Rhee as a devout Methodist who had prayer meetings before state functions. In 1952 Christians campaigned for the all-Christian slate of Rhee and Ham Tae-young. In 1954 Christians openly supported Christian candidates from the pro-Rhee party. In 1960 Rhee and his Methodist running mate pleaded for Christian support. But the rigged elections were greeted with protests leading to the aged Rhee's overthrow, and leaving the churches trying to shake off their identification with the corruption of his era (NCCK 1990: 30–1).

From 1961 Korea had a military regime which applied an export-oriented policy with strong state control of the economy and promoted rapid industrialisation with little social protection, for which it needed an increasingly authoritarian regime. Protestant churches split more and more between defenders of the regime (often using apolitical rhetoric) and opponents. The key role of church-based opposition movements is widely recognised, especially among the middle class and in support of labour activism (White 1995: 60). The literature talks much of

progressives' actions during this period, but little about what was going
on in the rest of the church and why. Simplistic dichotomies cannot do
justice to the multitude of intermediate positions, much less to effects of
the social composition of the rapidly expanding Protestant field on
public stances of hierarchies. As with the military periods in Latin
America, there is much to be done in the way of less partisan scholarship. Also, the correlation (or lack of it) between theological positions
and political action needs to be demonstrated more in empirical evidence. Did changes in socio-political postures in parts of the global
evangelical world from the 1970s impact on Korean Protestantism, and
did minjung theology affect some theologically-conservative Protestants
in a similar way to Liberation Theology in Latin America? What have
been the evolving political commitments of the greatest phenomenon of
post-war Protestantism, Yonggi-Cho's Yoido Full Gospel Church, a sort
of religious equivalent of the chaebol? Yoido owns a leading daily
newspaper, so it is no stranger to the public sphere.

Korea's democratic transition began in 1987 and was effectively
completed in 1992 with the election of a civilian president. White talks of
'the courage shown by, and the political impact of organisations of
students, workers and Christians' (1995: 62). The transition led to the
election of another Protestant president.

Kim Young-Sam, elder in a Haptong Church (the largest Presbyterian denomination), was first elected to the National Assembly in 1954
with Rhee's party. He became a leading opposition figure during the
military regime. In 1983 he staged a twenty-three-day hunger strike to
protest against government policies. His long-running rivalry with Kim
Dae-Jung, partly based (as so much in Korean politics) on regionalism,
split the opposition at key moments, culminating in the 1987 elections
which either could have won if the other had stepped down. Kim
Young-Sam finally merged his party with the ruling party in 1990,
guaranteeing a conservative coalition for the 1992 elections, which he
won with 42 per cent of the vote. His inauguration was regarded as the
return of full democracy, and early policies justified that. Besides his aim
of social welfare, economic revitalisation and political reform, there was
a moral element. He intended to root out corruption and end the
false-name financial system which allowed former rulers and others to
accumulate invisible fortunes. He made public his own assets and within
three months a thousand public officials had been arrested, fired or
reprimanded. He pursued a corruption probe in the armed forces,
denounced an illegal clique in the army and praised the Kwangju

uprising of 1980, brutally suppressed, as a pro-democracy movement (Luckham 1996: 220). He exuded 'a sense of mission to end corruption and put society on a righteous path', comment Lee and Sohn (*Asian Survey*, Jan. 1994: 8). The Christian magazine *Korean Torch* exulted about 'reform under a Christian president'. 'The main initiator ... is an elder of a Presbyterian church ... A majority of Christians ... joined together in earnest prayer for him during the campaign so that such reform could [happen]' (July–Sep. 1993: 4).

However, in 1994 things took a different turn. Kim's stance on democratic freedoms became more conservative. Restrictions on union-isation were retained, the National Security Law was not repealed, despite election promises, and was used against labour activists. Amnesty International estimated that political prisoners had more than doubled by 1995 (Moran 1996: 468). Breaking another pledge, unions were not allowed to fund political parties. Kim soft-pedalled on anti-corruption campaigns, since the chaebol were flexing their political muscles, freed from controls they had suffered under the authoritarian state. While economic liberalisation would slim down the chaebol (the Korean economy being one of the most highly concentrated in the world), the new demands of globalisation required them to be strengthened as the only competitive Korean companies in the world market. Thus, the impetus to political liberalisation which stemmed from civil society and had impelled his early moves in government gave way to a more accommodating attitude to the new hegemonic power in the state, the chaebol (ibid.: 477).

Soon, figures close to Kim were mired in scandal and his popularity rating dropped to 4 per cent in 1997. Under immense pressure, he apologised on television: 'I lower my head in shame for involvement of people close to me in the [Hanbo steel bribes-for-loans] scandal.' Later, his son and trusted advisor was arrested. But by then Kim was widely held responsible also for mismanaging the economy, fumbling on policy towards North Korea and failing to keep his promises. Although a former president was sentenced for corruption, it was widely felt that Kim himself, as the latter's successor and ally after 1990, could not be above reproach. Although business tycoons were convicted for bribing former presidents, none was imprisoned, poss-ibly because they had been leading fund-raisers for Kim's own presi-dential campaign.

Two telling verdicts on Kim both made reference to his religion. The head of the Samsung Economic Research Institute said: 'Kim set up a

Calvinistic agenda for the rest of the country but failed to police corruption in his own inner circles' (*FEER*, 13 Mar. 1997: 16). Yoon (*Asian Survey*, 1996: 522) went further: difficulties stemmed

from his initial failure to level with the public about his own failings as a politician during the past four decades. His trouble began as soon as he put himself above others as a paragon of virtue. As a participant in South Korea's distorted politico-economic system throughout his whole political career, Kim thrived in that environment. As a devoted Christian, he could have benefited from the biblical admonition to let him who is without sin be the first to throw a stone. A more wholesome approach would have been to concentrate on structural reform that will help prevent future wrongdoing.

An admonition not without relevance to some evangelical political projects in Latin America and Africa as well.

In the 1992 elections for the National Assembly, it is claimed that ninety Protestants were elected out of 299 congressmen (*Korean Torch*, July–Sep. 1993: 22). It would be good to know something about these congressmen, along the lines of research in Brazil. How is an 'evangelical politician' produced in Korea, and what does he really signify? This percentage, if correct, is above that of Protestants in the population, the opposite of the Latin American situation. This is a key difference; in Korea, Protestant political presence is often far greater than its numerical size, as if filling a gap in a historically traumatised country. It may also relate to the more urban middle-class composition of Korean churches, as against their more lower-class composition in Brazil and especially Chile.

This makes evangelicalism potentially important in democratic consolidation in Korea. As analysts (Moran 1996: 459; Han 1995: 15) worry increasingly about the power of the chaebol to prevent democratic deepening (and perpetuate corruption), the continuing role of civil society will be vital. 'International economic liberalisation can be portrayed as intrinsically undemocratic. The process centres on the state, and certain powerful economic interest groups such as large corporations with links to the global market' (Moran 1996: 463). Does Protestantism, proud of its cultural legitimacy and historical role, have as much to say to Korea at the beginning of the twenty-first century as it did at the beginning of the twentieth?

There are other political challenges. Can Christianity help to overcome the chronic regionalism manifested in extremely skewed voting patterns and increasingly uneven development? Could a truly national politics be one of the church's contributions? We need to know whether

Protestant voting also shows this accentuated regionalism. For example, in 1992 did Kim Young-Sam's Protestant affiliation actually annul regional preferences among church leaders and members? Does evangelical identity overcome these primordial ties based historically on Confucian values? We must at least doubt it, since major denominations still have strong regional bases, which may in part explain political postures, even when dressed up in theological justification.

The careers of Syngman Rhee and Kim Young-Sam would constitute interesting case studies, to be placed alongside Chiluba of Zambia, Ramos of the Philippines, and Guatemala's Ríos Montt and Serrano.

Protestantism has been in Korea just over a hundred years. Broadly speaking, for the first fifty it was under the shadow of the Japanese, and for the second fifty under the shadow of communism and the Cold War. Only now is it emerging into a third phase. Whatever this may hold, unification (and its consequences) will loom large on the agenda of evangelical politics. Protestantism was strong in the pre-1945 north, and many South Korean Protestants today are northerners or their descendants. Not surprisingly, Christians were prominent politically in the North before the hardline communist system solidified. Christian parties were created in 1945, such as the Christian Social Democratic Party and the Christian Liberal Party, organised respectively by a Presbyterian pastor and an elder. The CLP grew to half a million members in a few months (Kang 1997: 156). Since 1986 the World Council of Churches has organised meetings of Christians from South and North in neutral venues to discuss unification. Later, some Christian leaders defied the ban on contacts with the North (*FEER*, 30 May 1996). With unification, or even some liberalisation in the North, the history of Korean Christianity will enter a new phase (assuming Northerners to be riper for the gospel than for materialism, as in the less dramatic conditions of Eastern Europe), and evangelical politics will likewise be affected.

CHAPTER 3

Philippines

The only country in Asia with a Christian majority, the Philippines have much in common with Latin America. This extends to evangelical politics, which probably need to be studied more in Latin American than in Asian terms. Spanish colonial heritage, Catholic majority, poverty, American influence in the twentieth century (more directly in the Philippines), dictatorship in the 1970s and 1980s, democracy now consolidating and a Protestant community between 7 per cent and 15 per cent – all this is similar to Latin America. Philippine Protestantism is medium-strength by Latin standards, and with a similar growth pattern.

There are, obviously, specificities. The South-East Asian location may in the end prove fundamental. The economy just might become a tiger, but there is far to go, especially after the Asian crisis of the late 1990s. The Filipino experience of dictatorship was more similar to the minority Latin model (Somoza in Nicaragua, Duvalier in Haiti) of a personal ruler clinging to power and being toppled by popular revolt, rather than to the majority Latin model of military dictatorships disengaging through negotiated transitions based on elite consensus (Thompson 1996). This contributed to the troubles of democratisation, with no fewer than eight coup attempts during the first democratic government. The Philippines is regarded as having one of the worst structural situations of the new democracies outside Africa.

In religion, a distinguishing characteristic is the existence of powerful indigenous churches whose relationship to evangelicalism needs clarification. Johnstone's *Operation World* (1993), a mine of interesting but often methodologically suspect information, talks of 7.5 per cent Protestant and 8.4 per cent 'Indigenous Marginal' (an expression reminiscent of Barrett's awful 'indigenous non-white' category.) The latter comprise 282 groups of over five million people, but by far the largest is the Iglesia ni Kristo. Founded in 1914 by Felix Manalo and now led by his son, the

InK is a wealthy centralised organisation, 'neither Catholic nor Protestant but "evangelical"' (*FEER*, 7 May 1992: 20), famed for literalistic Bible interpretation and bloc voting. It is unitarian, presumably not in the rationalist New England sense but in the 'Jesus Only' tradition represented by large swathes of world pentecostalism. Avoiding Eurocentrism, the InK should probably come within our purview as much as, for example, the Zion Christian Church (ZCC) in South Africa.

This is highly relevant. The InK's support for Marcos was 'a factor in his longevity in power' (*FEER*, 7 May 1992: 20). In 1992 the InK openly supported Eduardo Cojuangco, business tycoon and former crony of Marcos, who finished third. Cojuangco's running mate was Joseph Estrada, the former film star who was elected vice-president on the split-voting system and then won the 1998 presidential elections. What has been the InK's role in all this? And what about its activity at other levels (congressional and local)? Their bloc voting reminds one of Brazil's Universal Church of the Kingdom of God.

Pace Timberman (1992: 120), 1992 may not have been 'the highwater mark of the involvement of religious groups in electoral politics'. But certainly the 1992 presidential elections, the first after transition (since the 1986 elections were actually held under Marcos, whose attempt to annul Corazon Aquino's victory led to the People's Power revolt and his overthrow), were marked by religious involvement. They were in fact the first real multi-party elections in Filipino history (ibid.: 112), signalling a 'quiet revolution in Filipino politics' (*FEER*, 7 May 1992: 18) – the rise of candidates relying more on personal qualities than on party machines, including many from outside the old oligarchic elite. Cardinal Sin transparently endorsed Ramon Mitra as the only reliable candidate from a Catholic perspective. He instructed Catholic voters to repudiate 'oppressors and plunderers' identified with Marcos (a swipe at Imelda Marcos and Cojuangco) and candidates 'who will oppose Catholic principles in their public acts' (aimed at Protestant candidates). Sin later renewed his attack on the eventual winner, the Methodist Fidel Ramos, concentrating on Ramos' past: a military man, he had been commander of the Filipino Constabulary and responsible for enforcing martial law under Marcos. The Ramos campaign said that he had only obeyed orders but had been quietly opposed to the dictatorship, and had made amends by leading the mutiny that opened the way for People's Power demonstrations. Sin replied caustically that supposed silent opposition only betrayed a 'deadening absence of moral convictions at a time when their expression was needed... Repentance now is unacceptable if no reparation is given ... [including] forsaking the ambition to govern the country' (*FEER*, 7 May 1992: 18).

Ramos, a Methodist described by a leading Filipino evangelical as 'more mainline than evangelical' and who 'does not wear his Protestantism on his sleeve', overcame the Cardinal's opposition and scraped home with 24 per cent of the divided popular vote. He had been secretary of defence in the Aquino government, and instrumental in blocking coup attempts. Although not nominated by the main party, he had Aquino's endorsement and support from business. His policies justified that support – his administration saw improved infrastructure and economic performance, as well as privatisation. The military seemed reconciled to democracy and the communist and Islamic rebel movements were weakened (Thompson 1996: 179).

Despite not wearing his Protestantism on his sleeve, his government saw conflict with the Catholic hierarchy. One reason was suspicion that he would change the constitution to allow a second term, or introduce a parliamentary system and become prime minister (*FEER*, 27 Apr. 1995: 20; 20 Mar. 1997: 29). But the main confrontation involved birth control, the probable target hinted at by Cardinal Sin in his election pastorals. As the government prepared to support the UN Cairo conference policies on population, Sin asked for mass protest, once again calling Ramos 'an obedient accomplice to Marcos' misdeeds' (*FEER*, 18 Aug. 1994: 17; 17 Nov. 1994: 12). But with the third-fastest-growing population in Asia, and Ramos determined on a policy from which even Marcos had shied away but which had the support of a significant majority of Filipinos (*FEER*, 13 Apr. 1995: 18), the hierarchy redirected its attack towards his secretary of health.

The other Protestant candidate for president in 1992 was Jovito Salonga, president of the senate. Salonga, lawyer and lay preacher of the United Church of Christ, was rather more left wing and reputedly worried US interests (during his presidency, the senate had abrogated the treaty on US military bases). His candidacy was based 'on his long record of public service and his leadership of the small but venerable Liberal Party' (Timberman 1992: 112).

The elections saw a flurry of Protestant candidates at other levels. The *Far Eastern Economic Review* prophesied that Catholic influence over government might soon be yielding ground to 'born-again' Christians (23 Apr. 1992: 16). The article mentions four born-again candidates for the senate, twelve for the House of Representatives, fifteen for mayoralties and four for governorships. It would be good to know more about these people, their social, ideological and ecclesiastical profiles. The article says the senatorial hopefuls all ran under the Nationalista Party. All are preachers, some televangelists. All seem to belong to new charismatic churches. Vincent Crisologo, a former power broker from north Luzon, heads the Loved Flock group, with a television audience of two million. Ramon Orosa, a banker, is a televangelist with the Body of Christ, and claims a three million audience. One notes their elitist origins and previous experience of political or economic power. Guatemala suggests itself as a comparison. But with what implications for evangelical politics in the Philippines? We need to know more about these levels to go beyond an impressionistic picture of evangelical involvement. Another question is the role of denominational and para-ecclesiastical leaders. What effect did a Protestant president, and one at times at loggerheads with the Catholic hierarchy and therefore tempted to appeal, albeit subtly, to evangelicals as a counterweight, have on the interface between evangelicals and the state? It seems a group of church leaders calling themselves the 'Elders of the Nation' emerged, professing to speak to state and society in the name of all evangelicals – a situation fraught with implications. Proximity to power has effects on internal organisation, structuring and power relationships in the evangelical world itself, which in turn react back onto evangelical involvement in national politics.

There are few specialist discussions of evangelical politics in the Philippines. Rose (1996) says apolitical and conservative views predominated among evangelicals during the dictatorship and the People's Power revolt. The Council of Evangelical Churches, generally supportive of Marcos, took no stance on the revolt. Tate (1990), however, says the Catholic Radio Veritas, essential in the revolt and expecting to lose its signal, urged listeners to tune into the international evangelical station FEBC (Far East Broadcasting Corporation); and 'Protestant lay persons ... participated prominently in People Power.' Lim (1989) nuances the picture. As in several countries, Protestantism produced two large organisations in the 1960s: the National Council of Churches (NCCP), and the Council of Evangelical Churches (PCEC). The former was more 'mainline' (which does not mean that some individual members were not evangelical). In 1962, says Lim, 10 per cent of congressmen were Protestants, largely from NCCP churches. In 1973, the NCCP became the first ecclesiastical body to speak against martial law, and in 1986 the first to proclaim the elections fraudulent. It was thus more consistently anti-Marcos than the Catholic hierarchy, even though the latter's political weight was in the end more important. At the other extreme, the InK was consistently pro-Marcos. The PCEC and its constituency were at various points in between. During the dictatorship, its institutional stance was critical of protests. In 1986, it adapted cautiously to reality, always following rather than leading events. Thus, just before the (fraudulent) election results were announced, it called for upholding the decision. But by the height of the revolt, it had concluded that civil disobedience was a Christian duty when a government ruled contrary to the will of God. Finally, when Aquino was already *de facto* ruler, it announced that 'on the basis of Romans 13 . . . our submission is to the actual [Aquino] government'. On the other hand, sectors of the PCEC constituency had taken their own course. The FEBC radio station had early discussed civil disobedience. Groups of evangelicals took to the streets in the revolt, the main one being the Konsensiya ng Febrero Siete organised by Melba Maggay, head of an evangelical think-tank.

Rose writes of the late 1980s and early 1990s, emphasising relations between 'fundamentalist' groups and the armed forces. Although she does mention Butch Conde, of Bread of Life mega-church, as being against the continuance of US military bases (1996: 349), the relationship is usually of mutual support. In 1989, the military supported the founding of the National Association for Democracy, involving conservative Christians and vigilante groups. One member organisation was Gavino Tica's Alliance for Democracy and Morality. Tica presided over International Baptist Ministries, a network of churches with links to US fundamentalist Jerry Falwell. Tica organised Value Formation Courses in the armed forces, in which several other new churches (Word of Life International, Living Waters Fellowship, Heaven's Magic, Christian Life Fellowship, Joshua for Christ) collaborated (ibid.: 342–3). A more important link, since it involves more 'mainstream' evangelicalism, would be PCEC membership in the Church and Defence National Committee, and above all the fact that the former general secretary of the PCEC and current head of the World Evangelical Fellowship (WEF), Agustin 'Jun' Vencer, was supposedly appointed by President Ramos as head of intelligence for the armed forces (ibid.: 328). This allegation by Rose, which would have obvious importance for understanding Filipino evangelical politics and intriguing implications for worldwide evangelicalism, is categorically denied by Vencer himself (personal communication, 23 Oct. 1999), while leading Filipino evangelicals are divided on the plausibility of Vencer having been recruited into the intelligence network. The vice-president of the WEF claims no knowledge of any military connections on Vencer's part (Key Yuasa, personal communication, 4 Nov. 1998). A recent article gives insight into the political stance of the first Third World head of the WEF (Vencer 1999). Vencer affirms Christian participation in politics, but eschews endorsement of candidates by churches. He rejects state relig-ions and the imposition of values in a pluralistic society. Democracy is affirmed, and a person need not be a Christian to be a good ruler. At the same time, Vencer sees nation-building as including 'spiritual warfare', citing approvingly Margaret Thatcher's address to the Church of Scotland. On economics and resistance to the state, Vencer is cautious. Capitalism is attractive because it encourages individual enterprise but repels because 'it seems to care less for the weak and poor'. The best ideology encourages positive traits of capitalism and socialism. In a phrase which illustrates how Liberation Theology has both influenced and been domesticated by mainstream evangelicalism, Vencer says 'the church must take the side of the poor, not necessarily against the rich per se but against oppression'. Civil disobedience is a last resort, but Christians are not to resist 'even the evil state, or to seek its over-throw'. In the context of a study of global evangelicalism, it should be remembered that these are Vencer's personal views rather than the official position of the WEF, which is in any case no more than a non-binding fraternal organisation uniting only a portion of the world-wide evangelical constituency.

CHAPTER 4

Malaysia

Once hailed as possibly the next Asian tiger, Malaysia is also a centre of Islamic renaissance, particularly in its intellectual form. Politics is defined by a mixture of religion and ethnicity. The very slight numerical advantage of the Malays has led to Islam's use as an ethnic glue for constructing a stable national ideology for this multi-ethnic and geographically divided state. Islamic resurgence owes as much to ethnicity and nationalism as to pan-Islamic influences (Eyre 1995).

The Bahasa Malaysia language, Islam and Malay culture are the official formative principles of national culture. The Malay-Muslim identity is materially reinforced (Malays who leave Islam lose social and political privileges). Non-Malays are religiously and politically fragmented, and most non-Muslim religions are not explicitly politicised. But since the 1969 race riots, the expression of non-Malay ethnicity via political symbols has become dangerous, channelling it partly into the religious arena (Ackerman and Lee 1988: 59–60).

Affirmative action for Malays glides into discrimination against non-Malays. But due to need for unity between Peninsular and East Malaysia, ethnicity and religion do not totally overlap. If Muslims are effectively a politically protected and advantaged category (prohibition of proselytisation of Muslims; linguistic limitations regarding Bibles and Christian literature; incentives to tribals to convert to Islam), there is also the politically and culturally advantaged category of *bumiputeras*, sons of the soil, some 10 per cent of which are tribals. A gap is thus opened in the battle for cultural legitimacy through which Christianity can slip. Christianity in Malaysia is largely Chinese (and Indian) or tribal. Chinese are urban and have economic resources, but lack cultural legitimacy. Tribals of Sabah and Sarawak, on the other hand, are usually poor and uneducated but enjoy cultural legitimacy and have some political involvement. At the federal level, this does not amount to much, but at the state level in the East it can do.

Johnstone (1993) talks of 5 per cent of Protestants; Eng (1992), however, places Christians at 5.1 per cent in 1985, of which under half were Protestants, although evangelicals enjoyed the quickest growth. But in Sabah, more Catholic, Christians are 30 per cent, while in Sarawak, more Protestant, they are 34 per cent. Even though Christianity is not the majority religion in any ethnic group (unlike parts of Indonesia, India and Myanmar), it has a significant presence. The heavily Christian Sabah United Party held state power for several years until 1994, and has seats at the national level. In Sarawak, where the main churches are Methodist and SIB (Evangelical Church of Borneo), Christians form the largest religious grouping but enjoy limited political influence. There, ethnonationalist consciousness ('Dayakism') has never been strong enough to take state power.

However, Malaysian Christians are still at a very basic level in a battle for political legitimacy and full religious freedom. The fusion of Malay and Muslim identity gives Islam an automatic majority. Christianity can only work (evangelistically and politically) at the margins, and its own ethnically determined base suffers bloodletting, as in the emigration of educated Chinese-Malaysians encouraged by pro-Malay educational policies. Official dialogue with Christians is denied them, to avoid giving *de facto* recognition.

Christianity in Peninsular Malaysia (and by extension, despite different local dynamics, in the East) still pays the price for colonial policy and ecclesiastical trends established in the colonial era. The British upheld Islam in the Malay states and discouraged mission amongst Malays. Evangelisation was directed to the Chinese, Indians, Eurasians and Europeans, usually producing ethnically divided congregations. (This was partly due to the lack of a strong evangelical tradition in Malayan Anglicanism (Northcott 1992).) Without roots amongst Malays, Christianity did not become associated with nationalist movements. Post-Independence legitimacy was thus weakened.

This has encouraged an unusual degree of ecumenism, and an inversion of political stereotypes often associated with theological currents. Increasing Malay-Muslim assertiveness made all Christian leaders view public unity as essential. This resulted in 1985 in the Christian Federation of Malaysia, including the old (mostly mainline Protestant) Christian Council, Catholics and the National Evangelical Christian Fellowship. They have 'together refined their ability to speak ... to the authorities... This is no game for amateurs' (Roxborough 1992: 299). However, 'those with links to the international ecumenical movement . . . have been more circumspect . . . On the Protestant side it has been left to some of those whose theology is said to debar them from thinking in other than a conservative mode to voice deeper questions' (ibid.: 300). The latter trend accompanied 'the rise of a social conscious-ness among evangelicals in the 1980s' (Hunt 1992: 351), although the authors cited do not explain the causes of this phenomenon.

While Peninsular Christianity is largely Chinese and Indian, urban and middle class, East Malaysian is heavily rural and tribal. For evan-gelical politics, Sarawak is the most important case. This least populous state, incorporated into the federation at independence in 1963, is the only one not to have adopted Islam as its official religion. Christians, although not a majority, are more numerous than Muslims. Their continuing difficulties illustrate the Malaysian dynamic; but their rising number points to a possible direct challenge to this dynamic, and makes this corner of Borneo of particular importance for future studies of evangelical politics in Asia.

In Sarawak Christians increased from 7 per cent in 1947 to 28 per cent in 1980 (Gabriel 1996: 105). The Muslim population, mostly the politi-cally dominant Malays and Melanaus, has been stagnant at around 26 per cent for decades, while tribal religions have declined. Before 1970 Christianity grew fastest among the Bidayuh and smaller tribes, and since then mostly amongst Chinese and especially Iban, the main ethnic group. As Gabriel says, one would expect demographic patterns to ensure Christians a much stronger political position than in the feder-ation as a whole, but this is not so. The Malay–Melanau alliance of Muslims dominates with federal help. Even though most Christians are *bumiputeras* and thus theoretically enjoy political legitimacy, they still experience discrimination (ibid.: 9). In addition, Christians are politi-cally divided by ethnicity. Tribal Christians are usually rural and with little formal education, leaving them distant from state-level political life.

Evangelical politics in Sarawak cannot be understood without the national context. The state's peculiar religious make-up has not been allowed much 'impact on questions of identity, culture and public life' (ibid.: 95). This has caused Christians frustration 'at being denied their rightful place in society' (ibid.: 102). One of the main state opposition parties is the Iban-led PBDS, whose manifesto reflects the caution necessary in Malaysia. While defending freedom of worship, it accepts Islam as the official religion of the nation and affirms Sarawak as an inseparable part of Malaysia (ibid.: 124–33).

However, Gabriel's book tends to analyse Sarawak ahistorically, neglecting the dynamism. Christianity has grown rapidly and overtaken Islam. This creates political tension, since it contradicts the Islamising intent of the federal government. Any future large-scale evangelistic success (possible amongst the 45 per cent who are neither Christians nor Muslims) could make the current political situation untenable. In addition, if conversion continues, Christianity could become the 'established religion' of some ethnic group, introducing a different political dynamic. Gabriel does not tell us who the opposition political leaders are, what role Christianity and the churches play in their activities, and what role politics has in the ongoing conversion of tribals and Chinese. Religion is politicised by definition in Malaysia, so the 'politics' of proselytism is part of evangelical politics.

Besides lessons on evangelicalism and ethnicity in the construction of nation-states, Malaysia would make a useful case-study of evangelicalism and politics in the Chinese diaspora, examining whether evangelicalism affects political postures in this 'trade diaspora' which traditionally practised 'sojourning' (and hence lack of commitment to local politics), and since independence has been politically marginalised as a threat to Malay supremacy (Cohen 1997).

CHAPTER 5

Indonesia

Indonesia is a key case for evangelical politics in Asia, and merits a deeper study than is given here. One of the most populous countries in the world, it is also significant in evangelical terms by Asian standards. Its place on the fringe of Islamic expansion (which, as Walls (1996) says, is 'progressive', spreading out from a constant heartland, unlike Christianity's 'serial' expansion involving jumps from one heartland to another) makes it a 'swing' case for the politics of Islam, and consequently of Asian Christianity as well.

Indonesia has similarities with Malaysia, but also striking differences. Once again, there is Christianity amongst the Chinese (fewer than in Malaysia) and small ethnic groups of animist background. There are some small-scale Christian societies, such as the totally Christian island of Kisar, evangelised by Indonesian missionaries since the 1920s. Irian Jaya is 60 per cent Protestant – a stark contrast with Bali's 0.5 per cent and Java's 2.5 per cent. Johnstone (1993) gives 9.3 per cent Protestant for the whole country, but Hefner estimates 6 per cent. As Hefner remarks, about 4 per cent of ethnic Javanese are now Christians. He cites a missionary author to the effect that this represents 'the largest group [in modern times] ever to become Christians of a Muslim background' (1993: 100). Battered by a revitalising Islam, some Javanists (adherents of the cultural mix made famous in the West by Clifford Geertz's studies) turned to Christianity, on the principle that if they were 'bad' Muslims they would rather not be Muslims at all (ibid.: 109).

The essential point is that in Indonesia religion is subordinate to religious nationalism, and thus an inherently political phenomenon. This again echoes Malaysia, but in totally different fashion. What is missing is the nervous ethnic closing off of religion. Thus, although Muslims are 87 per cent in Indonesia and only 52 per cent in Malaysia, Islam has not become one of the bases of the state. (Whether it will become so is another matter, and the fear that it might constitutes a key theme in evangelical politics.) Instead, despite fears of creeping Islamisation (a 1979 law prohibits evangelisation of Muslims, while Islamic propagation is state-financed), Indonesia still lives under the aegis of a unique religious nationalism. The nation-state has been constructed on Pancasila, or the Five Principles, the first of which requires belief in one Supreme Being, referred to as Tuhan (Lord) rather than Allah. It is thus not an Islamic state, yet neither is it secular. Having an *agama* (religion) becomes a necessity of citizenship, and not any religion but one of the state-authorised ones: Islam, Catholicism, Protestantism, Buddhism and Hinduism. Although articulated at Independence, this principle came into relief in the aftermath of the failed coup of 1965, when half a million were killed on suspicion of communist sympathies by a military-Muslim crackdown. As Spyer puts it, pagans and Chinese 'became Christians to save their lives' (1994: 176). On the eastern island of Aru, mass conversions in the 1970s involved persons stigmatised as 'not yet having a religion' and thus suspect politically. Local officialdom largely orchestrated the conversion – in reality, a double conversion, to a world religion and to Indonesian citizenship.

In Indonesia, then, conversion to Christianity is closely related to politics. That does not mean it always is, or that a conversion initiated in this way cannot go beyond it in terms of commitment (Hefner (1993) stresses precisely the opposite). In any case, as Willis (1977) points out, if political events after 1965 were the occasion of large-scale church growth, churches were only able to take the opportunity because they were sufficiently Indonesianised and had refused to take part in the anti-communist massacres. In addition, Indonesian-founded churches were more favoured in the rush to Christianity than foreign imports; and it seems the demand for conversion was actually greater than the supply of instruction and organisation offered by the churches. Willis detects two spurts of growth: at the height of the post-attempted-coup massacres of 1965–6, and in the wake of a renewed (non-governmental) Islamisation initiative in 1967–8. Most converts were from the *abangan*, the traditionalistic nominally Muslim rural population, and often went into churches of regional rather than national extension. These factors limit the political potential of this church growth: a plethora of localised denominations with an increasingly rural and mass-based constituency are unlikely to have much political involvement, especially during the socially demobilising Suharto regime hostile to suspected former communists.

In any case, Indonesia is not a religious state in the sense of prescribing a specific religion. But neither is it secular, since it assumes responsibility for ensuring that citizens follow an acceptable religion as an obligation of citizenship and as the 'sole basis' for all political parties (Spyer 1994: 181–2). Christians have had a certain space in this state, especially in the 1960s and 1970s, being an ideology of nationhood that gave more room to Christians than did the main competitors, communism and militant Islam. The most influential Christians in politics have been Catholics, but also some from the ethnically divided but nationally associated Reformed churches. At times, there have been a number of Protestants in parliament, reflecting their traditionally disproportionate presence in the professions and the military. Some leading advisors to Megawati Sukarnoputri, daughter of the first president and, since 1999, the vice-president, are Reformed Protestants.

As for non-Reformed Protestants, the crisis of 1998 triggered debates regarding an evangelical political party, to add to the hundred or so parties founded since the downfall of Suharto. Involved in this are intra-Protestant rivalries with the Reformed, as well as newly found political ambitions among sectors previously apolitical. Greater democratic space, plus the example of evangelicals in Korea and the Philippines, may point to more evangelical politicisation in the near future.

In addition, regional movements are vital. The separatist movement in Irian Jaya (or West Papua) merits deeper study, since this sparsely populated western half of New Guinea is nearly two-thirds Protestant. The Dutch, who administered it separately from other East Indies colonies, handed it to the United Nations in 1962. The latter turned it over to Indonesia in 1963, on condition that a plebiscite take place in 1969. The government began an Indonesianisation programme belittling Papuan culture, encouraging transmigration of Javanese and reserving the fruits of development for non-Papuans. No real plebiscite was held. The OPM (Free Papua Movement) guerrillas began operating in 1965, and the intermittent war ever since has killed about 10 per cent of the population. Occasional (West Papuan) flag-raising ceremonies have taken place; at one such in 1988, the thirty-seven people arrested included seven church leaders (Anti-Slavery Society 1990: 47).

Political Protestantism in West Papua probably shows continuity with its tradition of cargo cults, the mythical hero Manseren becoming synonymous with Jesus. Protestants reportedly predominate in the separatist movement, although the churches have been officially cautious. For Papuans, there are really only two forms of political expression available: through the OPM and through the churches (ibid.: 47).

Besides the native Gereja Kristen Injil, the Pacific Christian Church (an offshoot of the Unevangelized Fields Mission), Baptists and Adventists have considerable influence.

Voices as disparate ... as exiled Max Ireeuw (with a Dutch Reformed background) ... and Joshua Daimoi (a Baptist ...) have insisted on social justice for their people, in anxiety over Indonesian neo-colonialism (especially Javanese officialdom, military intervention, the transmigration of easterners to Irian Jaya and the 1994 decision of the Jakarta government to expatriate 200 foreign missionaries to allow more room for other faiths). (Swain and Trompf 1995: 217–18)

Until then, foreign missions (Protestant and Catholic) had effectively got along with Indonesian authorities (their planes facilitating movement of bureaucrats and military to remoter regions), in exchange for the possibility of providing services for Papuans and interceding informally with government to ameliorate excesses (Anti-Slavery Society 1990: 79). Although Protestant churches had generally been more loathe to criticise human-rights abuses than the Catholics, the Biak massacre in 1998 provoked church leaders into becoming more outspoken for independence.

With the 1998 economic downturn and the prospect of elections after Suharto's fall, the violence suffered (and at times perpetrated) by Christians throughout Indonesia increased abruptly. The Indonesia Christian Communication Forum claimed that two hundred and seventy-five churches were closed or destroyed between 1995 and late 1998. Fears of a more Islamising government and the effects of transmigration on older patterns of inter-faith cooperation led to much Christian–Muslim violence on Ambon. The Ambonese, like the Karen of Burma (Myanmar), had benefited from Christian education and risen within the colonial administration and army. In 1950, after independence, they proclaimed a South Moluccan Republic, eventually suppressed (Keyes 1996). In late 1998, violence against Ambonese in Jakarta led to violence against the Muslim minority in Ambon, religious identities being largely surrogates for struggles over internal colonisation, scarce resources and the very survival of the sprawling Indonesian nation.

Even further down the latter road was the case of East Timor. One of the few colonies the Portuguese retained in the East, it was never part of the Dutch East Indies. As the Portuguese empire tottered after 1974, East Timorese nationalist parties were formed, led largely by mixed-race army men, and independence was declared in 1975. Days later,

Indonesia invaded. Their rule never received UN recognition, and in the aftermath of Suharto independence was again mooted. The Portuguese heritage, including Catholic institutional strength, was mobilised by the freedom movement, putting Protestantism in a politically less advantageous position than in former Portuguese Africa. Catholicisation, only 28 per cent in 1975, is now 85 per cent, even though the church suffered pressures to Indonesianise during the occupation. It now seems that a predominantly Christian state (only the second in Asia) will be born in East Timor, and it may share the Philippine characteristic of a growing Protestant minority. The acting moderator of the main denomination, the Gereja Kristen di Timor Timur, was killed by pro-Indonesian militias following the 1999 referendum on independence, a tragedy which parallels that of many Catholic clergy and may have symbolic value in legitimising Protestantism in the new nation.

CHAPTER 6

India

If the study of evangelical politics takes serious account of the social base of the church, it must give priority to two groups in India's diverse population: the Dalits and the tribals, or in official terminology, Scheduled Castes and Scheduled Tribes. The Dalits ('untouchables') are important for evangelical politics as the majority of Christians, and tribal Christians are important as a majority of the total population in a few states.

Two contemporary questions are also relevant: the rise of Hindu nationalism, eroding the secular state created at independence; and economic liberalisation since 1991, with its accompanying social challenges and opportunities.

Webster's *The Dalit Christians* (1992) surveys the history of the Dalit political movement, stressing its origins in the so-called 'mass movements' of conversion to Protestantism by untouchables, mainly between the 1860s and the 1930s. These were localised grass-roots movements, initiated and led by Dalits, with foreign missionaries playing a secondary and often hesitantly supportive role. 'The history of Christianity in India became inextricably intertwined with the history of the Dalit movement', concludes Webster (1992: 39), an only slightly reductionist viewpoint.

Although mobility and change of status was a motivation for conversion, and was the social hope of the missionaries, only a minority achieved it. For all the personally significant transformations (recovery of dignity, overcoming of spiritual fear, etc.), not even large-scale conversion could overturn the caste system and the agrarian system (ibid.: 70). But mass movements brought the Dalit plight to the attention of Hindu reformers and nationalists when no other political force showed interest in them. Attention intensified after the Government of India Act of 1909 which established communal electorates and transformed conversion into a political issue. The phase of the 'politics of numbers' began, provoking Dalit political awakening. However, Dalit Christians were classified by constitution-makers as Christians rather than Dalits, and the Indian Christian elite were recognised as their spokesmen. Many Dalit politicians therefore rejected Christian conversion as weakening Dalit numerical force in politics.

Indian Christian political organisation also dates from the period following the 1909 Act. The All-India Conference of Indian Christians was established in 1914, being 'small, elitist and predominantly Protestant' (ibid.: 85). It petitioned Government for reserved seats on legislatures, citing its numerical strength and high literacy rate, and painting an idealised picture of its social structure. 'Drawn from all communities, classes and castes [and] helping obliterate class divisions', the church has done more than any community to uplift the untouchables. The Christian community may therefore 'represent their claims better than any other community in India'. The latter claim may not have been wholly mistaken, but it still revealed a patronising pre-empting of Dalit identity by the non-Dalit Christian leadership and foundered on its lack of contact with the realities of Dalit life.

For the converted Dalit to cease to identify himself politically as a Dalit, it would be necessary to find a casteless community in the church and for that community to be a force for political change. Failing that, in political terms their Dalit identity would remain primary. As the great Dalit leader Ambedkar noted when considering which religion to convert to, 'I have never noticed the untouchable Christians meeting in conferences for the redress of their social wrongs' (ibid.: 117), a critique often heard regarding Latin American pentecostals.

With the independent constitution of 1950, the politics of numbers gives way to compensatory discrimination within secular democracy and planned economic change. Legislative seats, educational places and government jobs were set aside for Dalits and tribals, and in many cases 'Backward Classes' as well. However, at federal and often at state level, religion is not a criterion for inclusion, but it is used to disqualify many who would otherwise qualify, thereby discouraging conversion. India's secular state is by no means a religious 'equal opportunity' one. A Presidential Order of 1950 ruled that no non-Hindu should be deemed a member of a Scheduled Caste. While in 1956 this was amended to include Sikhs, and in 1990 to include Buddhists, Christians are still excluded. Thus, religious equality is still lacking, and constitutes an important part of a Christian political agenda. Some states have laws which distinguish the right to propagate one's religion from the right to convert another to that religion.

However, the question arises whether the fight for equality in the reservation system is the best strategy. Religious equality (and abolition of the disincentive to conversion) could be achieved by the system's abolition as much as by its expansion. Christian political thinking which is truly universalistic and more than a defence of group interests must either reject the system or elaborate a defence of it in overall terms. This is especially pressing in view of the Hindu backlash.

For Webster, the reservation system once again left Dalit Christians in a bind. Their well-being was not a main item on the Christian elite's political agenda. Instead, the latter devoted itself to nation-building, doubtless motivated by theological considerations, but also by the need to overcome the image of a colonial religion in post-colonial times by emphasising national loyalty. The Christian elite was, says Webster, oblivious to the fact that the social base of the church was predominantly Dalit (ibid.: 130). The problem of Christian elites whose political projects are oriented more by concepts of nationalism than by the sociological composition of the church is not unique to India.

The Dalit movement has gone through mutations since independence, fragmenting and turning more to cultural and grass-roots action. Although some leaders are Christians, it has developed forms of Dalit identity which sit uneasily with Christianity. As the *Dalit Voice* says in 1990: 'Dr Ambedkar's works should be given the status of the Bible ... If there is a conflict between [Dalit Christians'] religion and Dalit identity, their choice should be the latter.'

Compensatory discrimination (implemented in a religiously discriminatory fashion) is blamed by Webster for the dramatic drop in Christian growth rates. Prior to 1951 the Christian population grew far above the national average. Since then, it has approximated the national rate. But Christianity has grown in the predominantly tribal states, since tribal Christians are not ineligible for benefits (ibid.: 171). Today, Christians (including Catholics) are around twenty-three million, some 3 per cent of the population.

In this situation, the politics of Dalit Christians includes the internal politics of Christian institutions. Excluded from many state benefits, do they find ecclesiastical compensation? Usually not, says Webster, since caste affects appointments in Christian institutions, and institutional priorities also reflect caste priorities. Thus, economic issues play a key role in Dalit Christian politics (ibid.: 180). However, in 1990 the All-India Convention for the Rights of Christians of Scheduled Caste Origin staged a massive rally to press for the same rights just obtained by Buddhists. The deputy prime minister retorted that 'the Christians should go back to Europe and America where they came from', revealing the hurdles still faced by Christians in Indian politics. In 1996, the government introduced a bill to include Dalit Christians in Scheduled Caste reservations, a move described by the Hindu nationalist BJP as 'anti-national'. Its passage was suspended by the ensuing elections. The reservations policy has reinforced caste identities by using caste rather than individual need as the criterion for benefits (Hardgrave 1993: 64).

Dalit Christian politics is thus forged increasingly in the interstices of the growing conflict between the Indian version of the secular state and Hindu nationalism.

The other significant sociological base of the church, from the political viewpoint, is the tribal societies of North-East India. As I once heard a Naga claim, independent Nagaland would be the only Christian nation in Asia outside the Philippines. He could have added that it would be the only Baptist nation in the world!

Perhaps 15–20 per cent of Indian Christians are tribals from the North-East (Downs 1991: 155). Conversion followed the consolidation of British power and the suppression of inter-tribal warfare and head-hunting, but did not depend on the presence of missionaries (Jacobs 1990: 194). This Christianisation is overwhelmingly Protestant, chiefly Baptist or Presbyterian, depending on the region.

Christianity, says Downs, helped the tribes retain their distinct identities (even though in modified form) and gave them tools and skills which ensured that power would not fall into the hands of outsiders (1991: 164). Moreover, it helped to create the very identities used today as rallying-cries. The Naga, for example, consist of numerous tribes with distinct languages and traditional political systems, ranging from autocracy to pure democracy. With poor communications, no common language and a history of intertribal raiding, there was not much to unite them other than Christianity and the experience of missionary education, though British administrators also helped in developing pan-Naga identity.

The conversion of the hill tribes is a classic case of adoption of a world religion distinct from that of one's more advanced and distrusted neighbours. Today, Christianity is a vital part of ethnic identity, distinct from the Hindus and Muslims of the plains and the central government. It infuses all political expressions: Naga separatist nationalism as much as Naga integrationist nationalism (ibid.: 152); the Mizo National Front, the Naga National Council, even the Maoist National Socialist Council of Nagaland (NSCN), as well as the Nagaland Peace Council and other peace initiatives in Nagaland and Mizoram, such as the Shillong Accord of 1976 and the Mizoram Accord of 1987; for this region has known little peace. Demands for autonomy or full independence have led to guerrilla movements and federal repression. To cultural, ethnic and religious difference is added their presence on the sensitive borders with China and Burma, where the spectres of subversion and drug trafficking raise their heads. Statehood was achieved by Nagaland in 1963, Meghalaya in 1972 and Mizoram in 1987. But peace has not resulted, although the NSCN and the federal government have agreed cease-fires since 1997.

All this raises questions about the role of Christianity. As Rao points out, political theology is conspicuously absent from curricula of regional seminaries, even though the political elites are all Christian and the churches are often called to intervene in politics. The proportion of Nagas who claim to be 'born-again' is one of the highest in the world, and regular mass meetings pray for the nation. It seems, however, that Christianity only served to create or preserve identities, but had little to say subsequently about political conflicts and the methods employed. The problems are enormously complex, involving the whole question of viable ethnic identities in the modern world, the role of the central government and possible development of 'narco-guerrillas' à la South America.

Naga nationalism is a classic case of ethnic 'invention' aided by religion – even perhaps as a union of the 'tribes' on the Israelite model (see Hastings 1997). Politics is beset by tribalism and revenge, and suffers from the lack of a pan-Naga lingua franca (Horam 1988: 22–9). Not only the divided Naga underground (the Naga National Council and the two factions of the National Socialist Council of Nagaland) but also above-ground politics are riven by tribal loyalties which criss-cross ideological ('pro-India' versus 'pro-underground') divides. The churches have been active in peace-making, although sometimes needing a prod from concern over Chinese interest in Naga affairs (ibid.: 105). The well-known Indian Protestant theologian M. M. Thomas, after two years as federally appointed governor of Nagaland, concluded that Naga churches have forgotten 'the victory of the crucified Christ over the demons of public life', and thus 'go along with people pursuing corruption, violence and mutual revenge' (1992: 150).

The need is great for a sympathetic and sociologically informed study of Christian politics in these marginalised tribes of India (and Burma). What is the role of Protestantism in these isolated Christendoms beset by violence (against the central governments and inter-ethnic, as for example between Kukis and Nagas in Mizoram) and by an almost frantic search for, and clash of, ethnic identities? The internalisation of conflict amongst the tribes shows an almost Yugoslav potential for blood-bath and ethnic cleansing. How does evangelical faith function within the guerrilla groups, increasingly fragmented (often on tribal lines)? What is its role not only in formal peace accords, but in ongoing initiatives and formation of mentalities and viable proposals? What is the role of figures such as Rochunga Pudaite, a leading Hmar evangelist now based in the United States, who has been involved in Hmar nationalism since the 1950s (*Frontline*, 5 June 1992)?

There are lessons here (many perhaps negative) for evangelical communities in the Third World who would love to be in the situation described by Hluna: 'Whilst the elites of the Great Rising of 1966 were all Christians [Baptists in the south and Presbyterians in the north], the peace movements have been initiated by the churches and the people who reject the separatism of the rebels are also Christians ... Christianity has become the "established" religion in Mizoram' (1985: 19). It penetrated tribes in the North-East in a variety of ways (in submission to or in rebellion against colonial government; subordinate to or independent of mission influence), and it would be interesting to know if these variations correlate at all with different political positions today. Nagaland is a fascinating case of almost a Baptist Christendom. The Indian magazine *Frontline* describes a 1992 attempt to bring all four insurgent groups to talks, with the help of churches and state governor Thomas. The process was scuttled by the central government, anxious to get local allies into power, and Thomas was dismissed for sticking to the constitution and delaying these designs. The state chief minister 'had enlisted the help of the church, which holds an almost complete sway over Naga society... The Baptists, under the banner of the Nagaland Peace Mission, and the Nagaland Christian Revival Church have set the process in motion' (30 July 1993: 29). *Frontline* comments that the Indian government

continues to treat the entire Peace Council (and indeed the Baptist Church, which has about 85% of Nagaland society under its fold) as sympathisers of the insurgents. The Church's influence in the State is all-pervasive and there is no real ... option other than doing business with the Council... A section of the Peace Council ... is sympathetic to the separatists, but another section is relatively moderate... These church leaders recognise that a tiny, mountainous State like Nagaland cannot be a viable economic unit. (19 June 1992: 50)

Rao adds that with the centre pouring in funds for pacification, corruption is rampant even in states with a Christian majority (1994: 5–6).

A photograph in Jacobs' book gives a fascinating insight into the role of evangelicalism amongst the guerrillas (1990: 177). It shows a gospel-music group run by the NSCN, wearing suits and ties, preaching to Naga villagers in a thatched hut on the Burmese side of the border. Christianity has been introduced into remoter Burmese parts of the Naga Hills by the guerrillas. We thus see a group of Asian socialist guerrillas spreading the evangelical message, and doing it in thoroughly Western dress! The surprises do not stop there. The founding manifesto of the NSCN (in Horam 1988: 319–31), in 1980, is imbued with a sense of mission and even takes church leaders to task for their lack of spiritual perception. The Indian government is intent on spreading Hinduism and 'supplanting the Christian God, the eternal God of the universe'. 'Preachers of the gospel ... are you prepared to resist these surging waves of the Hindu world upon our country?' Christian leaders fail to grasp the way evil forces work. They do not realise the significance 'defending one's national freedom has on the question of spiritual salvation'. Hindu doctrine may be beautiful philosophy, but 'the way to eternal life is not philosophy'. 'Come for Christ, come for Nagaland's freedom ... or go for India and Burma and their goddesses. There is no third way.'

Christianity and socialism are perfectly compatible. Even a Marxist view of history is embraced ('we are profoundly convinced of the course of human society to socialism, that is, the inevitability of socialism'), together with a Leninist doctrine of the vanguard ('to achieve the salvation of the people in socialism, the dictatorship of the people through a revolutionary organisation is indispensable'). The result is a mixture of socialism, democratic centralism, evangelical missionary fervour, a liberal doctrine of religious toleration and a profession of faith in guerrilla warfare.

The sovereign existence of our country, the salvation of our people in socialism with their spiritual salvation in Christ are unquestionable ... We stand for the sovereign right of the Naga people ... We stand for the principle of people's supremacy, that is, the dictatorship of the people through the NSCN and the practice of democracy within the organisation ... We stand for socialism ... We stand for faith in God and the salvation of mankind in Jesus, the Christ, alone, that is, *'Nagaland for Christ'*. However, individual freedom of religion shall be safeguarded and the imposition of this faith on others is strictly forbidden ... We rule out the illusion of saving Nagaland through peaceful means. It is arms and arms alone that will save our nation.

The manifesto finishes with a resounding 'Praise the Lord! We hold the promises of history.'

There are here several political challenges to the church, and themes for study. What happens when a church which inherits the Baptist tradition of church–state relations comes into a near-Christendom position? The sociology of religion and worldwide Christian political reflection would be enriched by a mature analysis of this Baptist state.

The contemporary changes which pose questions for evangelical politics are Hindu nationalism, reflected in the rise of the BJP, and the economic changes since 1991. The secularism and socialism of the Nehru era are being rejected. By 1999, the increase in anti-Christian violence was worrying even the allies of the BJP government.

CHAPTER 7

Myanmar (Burma)

Nagaland is not the only region where Baptist Christianity plays an overwhelmingly important role in politics. The same holds true for parts of neighbouring Burma inhabited by ethnic minorities such as the Kachin and the Karen. The national and religious contexts are, however, very different: instead of Indian democracy, the notorious Burmese military regime; instead of the Indian ethnic patchwork, one numerically dominant group (the Burmans) imposing an 'ethnocratic state' (Brown 1994); instead of Nehruvian secularism, an aggressively religious state which belies Buddhism's reputation in the West for 'tolerance'; and instead of a recognised Naga federal state contested by underground independence movements, an unrecognised independent Karen state in rebellion against the central government.

Burma (now known officially as Myanmar) came gradually under British colonial rule during the nineteenth century. In the lowland and more developed ethnically Burman areas, colonial administration was direct and the monarchy was abolished, creating a political vacuum later filled by resurgent monastic Buddhism. In the anti-colonial struggle, Buddhism became 'the most important element of Burman identity' (ibid.: 43). But as often in Asia, religion is intertwined with ethnicity in state-building. The non-Burman hill tribes were governed indirectly in the colonial period, and some became incorporated as lower-level civil servants and soldiers. Since independence in 1948, the Union of Burma has largely pursued an 'ethnocratic' agenda, in which the state acts as agent for the ethnic majority in promoting its own ethnic values as the core component of nationalist ideology. Ethnic minorities have been excluded from power and their languages, religions and cultures subordinated in the portrayal of the nation (ibid.: 34–8).

Unlike Malaysia, where Malay dominance has been pursued within a relatively open system, Burma has been under military rule since a 1962 coup brought in a socialist one-party state. Its pro-socialist isolationism until 1988 has been followed by the international isolation of a regime abhorred for human-rights abuses. A 1988 pro-democracy uprising was crushed by a new junta, which then refused to hand over to the National League for Democracy (NLD), overwhelming winner in the 1990 elections. The NLD had managed to include the Karen National Union (KNU) and other ethnic groups in conflict with the government. Its most famous leader is Aung San Suu Kyi, Nobel Peace Prize winner in 1991, daughter of an independence hero and Baptist mother.

One of the pillars of the regime is Buddhism. Although officially the state religion only briefly in the early 1960s, it has always been promoted by the state and its importance has increased since the late 1980s when assimilationist policies switched emphasis from ethnicity to religion. State-promoted revivals of Buddhism especially target ethnic minorities, including violent inducements to Burmese Nagas to renounce Christianity.

The state, bent on assimilationist policies (Burman language, Buddhist religion, administrative centralism), has been contested militarily ever since independence. The first insurgents were the communists, soon followed by the Kachin, Wa, Shan and above all (in longevity and numbers) the Karen, led by displaced or emergent elites inventing new forms of ethnic consciousness (ibid.: 34). They created a string of unrecognised independent states along the frontier. While the 'ethnocratic state' has been strong enough to disrupt the peripheral communities, it has never been able to control the whole national territory.

All Protestant missionaries were expelled in 1966, but as in many places Christianity, far from being a colonial relic, had acquired an essentially local dynamic. Johnstone's (1993) estimate of 5.2 per cent Protestant may be realistic, with the Baptist Convention (of American Baptist origin) being the largest denomination. Most Christians are from precisely the ethnic minorities which are (or have been) insurgent, and in some cases Protestants are now a majority amongst these groups. The national Baptist Convention has autonomous linguistic and regional sub-conventions, which probably contributes to the church's difficulty in aiding national integration but its facility in promoting ethnic separatism. There is of course no reason why this role should be judged negatively, in view of Hastings' (1997) caveats about the artificiality of post-colonial 'nationalism' and the way classical processes of evolution to nationhood were interrupted by colonialism and decolonisation. This would be true even if the Burmese state had not pursued 'ethnocratic' and 'Buddhist' policies.

One of the most Christianised groups is the Kachin, most of whom are Baptists, with some Catholics. The Kachin Baptist Theological Seminary produces sixty graduates annually, and the Kachin Baptist Convention is the main social organisation within Kachin state. Its executive secretary was instrumental in the cease-fire between the government and the Kachin Independence Army in 1996. This was one of many cease-fires between the regime and insurgent groups, reflecting a tilt in power towards the military and increasing isolation of the Karen as the last stronghold of opposition.

Of the so-called 'tribal' peoples of South-East Asia, says Smith, the Kachin and the Karen have been the most persistent in their dream of independence (Smith, M. 1991: 34); and evangelicalism has been central in both cases. Never under Burman control, the Kachin Hills were governed directly by the British from 1886. Despite the tradition of recruitment into police and army by the British, there was no immediate Kachin rebellion when Burma gained independence. The Kachin had been evangelised by Baptists since the 1870s, initially by Karen and later by Americans. After a slow start (less than 2 per cent in 1911), growth was quick, reaching 30 per cent in 1930 (Tegenfeldt 1974: 181) and probably over half the population today. The Kachin Baptist Convention was formed in 1951, with Baptist MPs such as Ugyi Htingnan playing an important role, and the government's expulsion of foreign missionaries in 1966 had little effect (although nationalisation of schools was more of a blow). All early heads of the Kachin State, except for the first, were Baptists, as were nearly all the Kachin MPs (ibid.: 346–7).

With growing discontent over treatment from the Union government and cession of some Kachin areas to China, the Kachin revolt against Burma began in earnest in 1961, sparked by the declaration of Buddhism as state religion. The Kachin Independence Organisation (KIO), founded in February 1961, forged a united movement despite linguistic divisions within the Kachin. The founders were largely students led by two pastors' sons, with the support of intellectuals headed by Brang Seng, headmaster of the Baptist Mission High School in Myitkyina (Smith, M. 1991: 192). This raises the question of the relationship between Baptist Christianity and Kachin political aspirations. Tegenfeldt, a former missionary writing in the early 1970s, is cautious. He says the insurgency, which spread rapidly and was repressed with a scorched-earth policy, hindered communication between churches in government-controlled and insurgent-controlled areas, leaving church personnel under suspicion from both sides. He admits that 'virtually all

Kachins sympathised with the insurgents, even though the majority opposed their methods'. He laments, however, that Baptist leaders 'remained largely neutral ... and did not openly shoulder their scriptural responsibility to be peacemakers' (1974: 249). There were Baptists on both sides, and leading laymen were detained on suspicion of aiding the rebels. Even so, church growth continued (ibid.: 250). The author may not have grasped (or for reasons of mission politics may not have wished to express) the depth of separatist feeling in the church. What it would be interesting to know is not just the effect of the insurgency on the church but the effect of the church on the insurgency, especially as the Baptist Convention is the leading institution in Kachin life. To what extent was opposition to insurgent methods caused more by their cost in repression than by a rejection on principle?

Given the geopolitical situation, all the ethnic insurgencies faced the question of relating to the also-insurgent Communist Party of Burma and to China. In all cases, this led to internal divisions and oscillations, and sometimes to war with the CPB. The KIO, initially viewed as radically leftist for its banning of the feudal village system in favour of a more democratic one, later fought the CPB and joined the World Anti-Communist League. But dissatisfaction with leaders' lifestyle, enmeshed in arms dealing for Kachin jade and opium, saw the rise to power of a new leadership under Brang Seng. A devout Baptist and able leader (Smith, M. 1991: 390), Seng was an intellectual without a military background. He led the KIO into a more sympathetic position towards China and the CPB. This resulted in new weaponry and the ability to maintain the uprising (at times controlling over half the Kachin state) for nearly another twenty years. But he kept the KIO ideologically free of Maoism, using Christianity and Kachin belief in their traditional existence as a nation to build a 'staunchly nationalist' movement (ibid.: 332). Seng died in 1994, just as a cease-fire was being agreed, the KIO having lost Chinese support in the late 1980s.

The Karen, although only a quarter Christian (Falla 1991: 18), have been important missionaries among other ethnic minorities. They are also the largest ethnic minority (over 6 per cent), as well as being found across the border in Thailand. Their long-running rebellion and historically ambiguous relationship to the British have assured them greater international limelight than the Kachin.

The evangelisation of the Karen is a far from unique instance of how evangelicalism can mesh with the politics of ethnicity. They have been fighting the lowland kingdoms for centuries: 'rebellion is part of their identity' (Falla 1991: xvi). In colonial times, Karen were numerous in the military and civil service. The invading Japanese, inciting the Burmans to rise against the British, also gave them a free hand against the Karen. The latter resisted valiantly. Subsequent British support for the Union of Burma and failure to endorse either a British Karen colony or an independent Karen state was regarded as a betrayal. The Karen National Union, created in 1947, declared Karen independence the day after Burmese independence. In 1949, fighting began in earnest. Initial Karen success led to the creation of the rebel state of Kawthoolei. At its peak in the 1980s, this KNU-run free state controlled considerable mountainous stretches and had forty thousand men under arms. But factionalism and a renewed Burmese offensive took their toll. Today, little is left of the free state and the Karen are increasingly isolated (fifteen other rebel groups have agreed cease-fires). In 1995 the KNU were driven from their capital Manerplaw and a group of Buddhist Karen (more numerous than Christians but less prominent) defected under the Democratic Karen Buddhist Organisation. From 1997 onwards, government troops systematically destroyed Karen villages, increasing the number of refugees in Thailand. Many other Karen live in lowland and urban areas of Myanmar.

Baptist Christianity has played a central role in all this since the missionary effort in the nineteenth century. Karen myths and indigenous religion played a preparatory role (though the degree of Christian reworking of them associated with the advent of literacy is uncertain; even if considerable, this itself shows evangelicalism's role in the development of an ethnic identity). The illiterate Karen were aware of writing amongst the Burmans. But the Karen version of the 'lost writing' myth includes a 'white younger brother' who removes the Karen book overseas. He will return, bringing with him the Golden Book (equated by Baptists with the Bible) and the Silver Book (education). It is thus not from the Burmans that the means of liberation will come. Stimulated by this, Baptist preaching made converts and indigenous missionaries. Autonomous mission demonstrates the strength of identity built up by the missionary elaboration of a Karen script, the translation of the Bible and the production of an indigenous literature, supported by a network of church-run schools. Baptist schools introduced a new concept into the loosely allied society of intermarrying villages, the idea of pan-Karen organisation (ibid.: 226). Even today, church and school are the most powerful strands of village life, unifying a people whose language and customs vary greatly. There are echoes of the Naga story: 'scholars sometimes suggest it was the missionaries and bureaucrats who created the Karen' (ibid.: 373); created, that is, a pan-Karen identity. The Karen saw education as the means to strengthen their position *vis-à-vis* the Burmans, and the Baptist seminary in Rangoon became virtually a Karen university (ibid.: 142). In 1881, Karen Christians founded the Karen National Association, forerunner of the KNU.

But Karen national consciousness is more than 'a product of literacy' (Brown 1994: 60). The meshing of Karen mythology and the Biblical tradition produced an ethnic theodicy in which Karen and Israelites are in parallel in a history of election, disobedience, servitude, liberation and promised land (Falla 1991: 230). This theodicy found carriers in the new Karen elite produced by Christianity, education and colonialism. This new elite was doubly marginalised: it did not have the local prestige of traditional leaders (whose power was being eroded by colonial and post-colonial change), nor could it achieve full recognition within the Burmese state administration. What it did have (and this is one of the classic contributions of churches to political life, especially in the Third World) is a link with the masses. Since the educated were not traditional leaders, their claim to a political role had to be based on the existence of a separate Karen nation (Brown 1994: 62), a pan-ethnic level which transcended village and dialect and was articulated around a biblically inspired notion of historical uniqueness.

There is thus a basic link between the Karen rebellion and Christianity. But it is strangely ambiguous, since Buddhists and religious traditionalists still predominate numerically, even though the KNU elite is largely Christian. Falla, who lived in the free state in the late 1980s, says the Information Department struggles to counter the impression of a purely Christian rebellion. Ideologically, Karen nationalism has gone through experiments in communism, capitalism and united fronts with other ethnic insurgents (Smith, M. 1991: 46). As the KNU retreated into the hills once its original uprising had failed, it came into contact with the CPB. This led in 1953 to a Maoist-style vanguard party called the KNUP, which for a decade controlled the KNU and made selective experiments with communist ideology. By the 1960s the delta was largely lost and the KNU in the mountains was split into a pro-CPB faction led by KNU president Ba Zan, a Christian socialist who professed admiration for Robert Owen, and a pro-Western faction under Bo Mya. The latter, unlike many Karen leaders, was a poorly educated military man of traditionalist origin who had converted to Adventism upon marriage. From then on, his political statements were imbued with references to the Bible and Christianity, as well as profoundly anti-communist. His rise was assisted by the government's new 'Burmese road to socialism' economic policies, which resulted in increased black-market trade with Thailand and gave guerrilla commanders a source of income. Consolidating his power with ruthless methods, Bo Mya managed to replace Ba Zan as president of the KNU in 1976. Bo Mya insisted that the KNU accept aid only from capitalist nations and rid the KNU 'national democratic' doctrine of any class implications (ibid.: 298). Falla, however, feels the anti-communism he saw was largely spurious, as was the pro-communism of earlier times, motivated by the need for allies against the Burmese state (1991: 105). In the 1980s Bo Mya's 'pronouncements have become increasingly interwoven with Christian sentiment and the KNU judicial system now reflects a distinctly Old Testament view of Christian morality' (ibid.: 393); the latter element presumably reflects Bo Mya's Seventh-day Adventism. Freedom of religion is, however, 'one of the most important articles of KNU faith' (ibid.), and the churches value their independence from the KNU since they try to work with Karen on both sides of the battle lines.

In 1994 a group of Buddhist Karen accused the KNU of religious discrimination. They were in turn accused by the KNU of being government spies and subsequently assisted the Burmese military in its offensive. KNU moderates attributed the problems to the aged Bo Mya's intransigence. Especially since the fall of Manerplaw in 1995, many young people have been studying abroad and founding organisations which reflect their experience of democratic pluralism. In a completely different direction, the KNU's defeats of 1997 saw the rise of a splinter group called God's Army, led by twelve-year-old boys and with beliefs reflecting Karen messianic traditions rather than orthodox Christianity. In 2000 Bo Mya was finally removed from the presidency of the KNU, although retaining command of the army. With the insurgency in tatters, the new president promised a more flexible approach and claimed to reject any pretension to independence, favouring a federal democratic Burma. Given the Karen's geographical spread and linguistic diversity which have always hampered nation-building aspirations, this is probably a more realistic goal for the foreseeable future, despite a resurgence of separatist dreams amongst South-East Asian minorities with UN intervention in East Timor.

What is the relationship between Protestantism and the Karen rebellion today? The Burmese government, for its own reasons, at times accentuates the supposed role of Christianity as a cause of insurgency

(Smith, M. 1991: 393). The worldwide church can provide an international link which the Karen need. Within Kawthoolei, Falla talks of Pastor Moses, 'the rock of the Baptist Church... He observed the tribulations and intrigues of the revolutionary leadership without participating directly – but his nod of approval counted' (1991: 40). More important is the educational and ideological role. Education in the Karen language is a cornerstone of revolutionary policy, and the system is dominated by Christianity, even though animist and Buddhist children also attend. 'Three forms of redemption go hand in hand: Christian faith, national liberation and salvation through knowledge' (ibid.: 142). In 2000 a Karen who left Rangoon for the refugee camps won the Baptist World Alliance human rights award for his work as principal of Kawthoolei Baptist Bible School. A far higher literacy rate among Christians helps to explain their dominance in Karen politics. Nearly all KNU Central Committee members are practising Baptists, and several others are Adventists. Christians also predominate amongst district leaders, although most village-level officials are Buddhists or animists (Smith, M. 1991: 393). Not for nothing, pastors from various minorities have been arrested, tortured and killed by the Burmese military (Smith, M. 1994: 108), and Burma is on the US State Department's official list of countries which practise religious persecution.

But when one compares the Karen with the Kachin or Naga, there are unexplained elements. Why has Christianity apparently stagnated amongst the former, at around 25 per cent, whereas it has become overwhelmingly predominant amongst the latter? The same favourable factors would seem to operate. One wonders whether the hardline Christian leadership of the KNU has adversely affected Christianisation; and whether this particular relationship between Christianity and the politics of ethnicity has not been unfavourable to the former's capacity to expand.

There are many unanswered questions regarding evangelicals and politics in Myanmar, but the difficulty in studying them cannot be underestimated. The Kachin and other smaller Christianised minorities need to be studied more; and the relationship between the KNU rebellion and the arrested Christianisation of the Karen needs to be elucidated.

CHAPTER 8

China

After diverse Asian political models, we come to the greatest surviving model of Communist Party monolithic rule. There have been variations in its religious implications over the years, and the return of Hong Kong introduces a further imponderable. What will be the role of Hong Kong evangelicals in the political future of China? The Christian community there is approximately 10 per cent, although in terms of China this is a drop in the ocean. Martin Lee, head of the Democratic Party which won most seats open for election (only a third) in the Hong Kong Legislative Council in 1998, has Catholic affiliations.

China offers considerable difficulties for research, but we have an excellent source in Hunter and Chan's *Protestantism in Contemporary China* (1993), on which the following is largely based.

In 1949 there were about one million Protestants, but by 1958 nearly all churches had been closed. After the Cultural Revolution, it seemed that religion had disappeared. But 1979 saw changes in policy and the beginnings of a remarkable revival of Protestantism, more so than of other religions (with the possible exception of folk practices). This revival is known in official publications as 'Christianity fever' (though they refer to evangelical Protestantism, rather than Catholicism). In sociological terms, Tu divides the new Protestantism into two: peasants converted by indigenous dialect-speaking preachers with a nativistic and anti-foreign streak; and students, professionals, social activists and executives who, in an urban context, perceive a natural fit between Christianity, science and democracy (1999: 91–2). In addition, religion gained a higher profile after 1989, when the Party perceived the role of the churches in Eastern Europe and introduced a somewhat tighter policy to prevent similar happenings in China. This highlights the political relevance of Protestant 'fever'. 'Evangelicals and politics' includes the reaction of other political actors to the mere existence of evangelicalism, however 'apolitical' the latter may consider itself.

Christianity in China is the subject of wild speculation. The official church claims five million registered believers and few unregistered. Some overseas evangelical sources talk of fifty or a hundred million. This is unlikely; inflated figures plague in-house estimates of evangelicalism in many countries. Hunter and Chan think a judicious estimate would be twenty million, mostly Protestant, making it even so one of the largest Protestant communities in the world. The vast majority fit the evangelical label, since 'pastors in both official and house churches generally adopt a conservative theology' (Hunter and Chan 1993: 77). A case-study of one official church reveals 'little to distinguish [it] from orthodox evangelical churches in Hong Kong' (ibid.: 185).

The changes facilitating 'Christianity fever' were not just in policy towards religion. They were alterations in the CCP's (Chinese Communist Party) relationship to society. In the countryside, there was a massive reduction in state power, as communes were abolished and family farming revived. In the cities, disaffection was widespread among intellectuals, some of whom showed interest in Christian thought. But, say Hunter and Chan tellingly, 'Christianity in China has yet to evolve an intellectual dimension equivalent to its spiritual life' (ibid.: 8) – a characteristic which, while not unique to China, will limit evangelicalism's political contribution if liberalisation occurs.

Protestantism is divided into two camps: the official church and the 'house' churches. Soon after 1949, all religions were required to found 'Patriotic Associations' under leaders effectively coopted. Before the Revolution, Protestants were 'never a united anti-communist force, unlike the Catholic Church' (ibid.: 113). Some were genuinely supportive and had experienced the 'United Front' strategy in communist-held areas after 1937. Others, however, were secret Party members sent to work with the churches – one leading figure of the official church in the 1950s was later discovered to be a 'plant'. In 1954, the Three Self Patriotic Movement (TSPM), the recognised Protestant church, was founded under the direction of the Religious Affairs Bureau. Its official journal emphasised, especially in the 1950s, the struggle to build socialism and hatred of class enemies.

From the late 1950s, policy was even tougher, and for twenty years religion ceased to have significant meaning in society. Only occasional reports of illegal activities persisted. But in 1979, the government recalled the old TSPM officials to oversee the reopening of churches. Religion was still given little attention by the Party elite, a sign that it lacked the influence it had in communist countries like Poland. There was no questioning of Marxism-Leninism, the very basis of CCP rule.

China had never had a tradition of inalienable individual rights *vis-à-vis* the state, and even now tolerance for social groups unsupervised by the Party is extremely limited. Religious groups are among the few permitted. The level of surveillance is still quite high, although active persecution is low. Some house church leaders have, however, been tortured in detention.

The theoretical basis for Party policy to religions is the 'united front'. The United Front Work Department formulates this, and the Religious Affairs Bureau implements it. The basic guideline to cadres dates from 1982: 'Marxism is incompatible with any theistic world-view. But in terms of political action, Marxists and patriotic believers can, indeed must, form a united front.' Religious activities which are not counter-revolutionary or foreign-run should be tolerated.

The official Protestant church consists of the TSPM, an overtly political organisation which oversees church policy, and the China Christian Council (CCC), which is more pastoral. The same man is president of both, and most leaders are now elderly. When the Party became nervous about religious involvement following Tiananmen, the official journal returned to 1950s' rhetoric, saying it was necessary to guard against bourgeois liberalisation as seriously as against Aids. The official church is regarded by intellectuals as timid in the political arena. But it is not totally subservient, nor could it be, on pain of losing all credibility.

The other part of Protestantism is the 'house-churches', which Hunter and Chan prefer to call 'autonomous Christian communities' – autonomous in relation to the TSPM, the government and foreign denominations. But many participate simply for spiritual satisfaction or geographical convenience, and not because they disagree with the official church's relationship with the state. Home meetings are not politicised. The Party document of 1982 comments: 'as for Protestants gathering in homes for worship services, in principle this should not be allowed, yet this prohibition should not be too rigidly enforced'. However, by 1992 the state-run press was warning that to avoid a repeat of the churches' role in Eastern Europe, it would have to 'strangle the baby in the manger'. Since then, hundreds of house churches have been closed and leaders imprisoned (Marshall, P. 1997: 80).

The leader of the official church, Bishop Ting, supported the protests in 1989 and defended the end of political control over religion. Hunter and Chan conclude: 'he has probably done as much as any person to promote freedom of religion in China and has argued far more vigorously for the rights of the house churches than have any of his colleagues' (1993: 90). This contrasts with a speech by another bishop, reported in the official journal, claiming house church leaders 'steal money, rape women, destroy life and health, spread rumours and destroy social order. Some even foment believers to oppose the leadership of the Party.' In this return to the rhetoric of the past, the ascending hierarchy of sins is revealing.

A Party orientation dating from 1991 is similar to the 1982 document, but emphasises reaffirming Party control, albeit without overt repression. In official rhetoric, foreign forces are blamed for Christian growth. This allows the Party to save face, but it also shows church growth itself is seen as a threat. That is so, even though 'the most characteristic theological position of Chinese Christianity is a conservative pietism ... free of the contamination of politics ... [This] accords well with mainstream tradition in China, in which religion [keeps] well away from political concerns' (ibid.: 136). Ironically, the TSPM is in a sense more Western. It is urban-based and relatively educated. It is centralised, liturgical and clerical. Its ministers are sometimes jealous of the popularity of house churches and ask authorities to suppress them. 'The official church tends to accept "this world" and argues for the preservation of the status quo and obedience to the government' (ibid.: 203), since it represents those who have achieved higher social status. But house churches are closer to indigenous religiosity, being of the poor and less educated, without professional clergy, and with experiential worship styles. The ironies affect politics too. The TSPM inherited a tradition of political thought which it had to abandon after 1949. There are few examples of Protestants in anti-government protests; the students at Beijing seminary voted not to go to Tiananmen. It is, in effect, a state church, but whose temporal master limits its expansion. The house churches, meanwhile, tend to an apolitical stance influenced by dispensationalist theology, but are obliged to operate semi-clandestinely, unwillingly becoming political deviants.

Various conclusions can be drawn. Firstly, evangelicals are in official and house churches, and the opposition between these must be relativised. Secondly, all evangelicalism is politicised by means of the CCP's attempt to control all religious activity. Thirdly, evangelicals and politics in China include the dynamic and fuzzy relationship between the TSPM, whose authority is based on state power, and the house churches. Rhetoric apart, the official and house churches live a symbiotic relationship. Neither would be what it is and able to do what it does if the other did not exist. Existence of house churches, and the possibility that tighter repression might backfire by making more believers go underground, means the TSPM has a greater margin of manoeuvre *vis-à-vis* the government than it would otherwise. And the TSPM's existence gains concessions for believers that house churches alone would not obtain.

Tu mentions sporadic reports of Christians being elected leaders in village and township enterprises, showing that Christianity is becoming accepted in parts of rural China (1999: 93). The future extent of this will depend, as he says, on how far China can return to the multi-ethnic and multi-religious self-conception which characterised certain periods of imperial history.

This section may be the place to mention religious persecution. Marshall's *Their Blood Cries Out* (1997) has brought the subject to attention again. Most of his cases of persecution or discrimination occur in Third World countries. He describes persecution of Christians today as 'worldwide, massive and underreported', usually intertwined with ethnic, political or territorial concerns. There are four main categories: (i) Islamic countries, whether from the state, communal violence or terrorists; (ii) the remaining communist countries, of which Cuba has eased but the Asian ones have worsened; (iii) religious or ethnic nationalism, mostly in Central Asia; and (iv) persecution of Christians by Christians, including indigenous evangelicals in Mexico. In 1999, the US State Department included China in a list of countries which practise religious persecution.

PART THREE

Africa

GENERAL INTRODUCTION

Compared to Asia, sub-Saharan Africa is relatively uniform socio-culturally and in its history of colonialism and independence. The South African experience, though, has unique features for our purposes. Another fault line runs between countries in which Christianisation is overwhelming and those in which Islam constitutes a formidable presence and where evangelical politics is largely constructed by that reality.

Fault lines also run between the colonial heritages, especially Anglophone and non-Anglophone. In general, Protestantism is stronger in the former. But sometimes the religious pluralism of British colonial policy and metropolitan reality diluted or overturned Protestant predominance; and anti-clerical governments in France and Portugal, and in the latter case the opposite extreme of a Catholicism at the service of the state, helped to give Protestantism a reasonable presence in some Francophone and Lusophone states. Angola is possibly as Protestant as Tanzania. However, in only one Francophone country, the Central African Republic, is Protestantism predominant (Baur 1994: 464).

In continental West Africa, Christianity is probably only a majority in Ghana. Islam and even African Traditional Religion are strong competitors in West Africa. According to Baur (1994), Protestantism has a majority only in South Africa, but is near one in Kenya, Swaziland, Namibia, Zambia and Malawi. Sub-Saharan Africa has about one hundred and twenty million Protestants, some 30 per cent of the population; a massive numerical base, much of it post-independence, and still growing (it is commonly asserted that six million Africans per year become Christians (Haynes 1996: 201)).

Given the greater similarities, it is easier to talk generically of the state, civil society and democracy in Africa (i.e. sub-Saharan Africa) than in Asia. After the high hopes of independence, when the new states inherited Congress of Berlin borders and parliamentary democratic systems, virtually the whole region had one-party rule or military regimes by the early 1970s. And by the mid 1980s, it was plain that economic development, the great legitimiser of these new political entities (states attempting to create nations, as Hastings (1997: 161) puts it), had not materialised.

Hastings (1997) is required background for consideration of evangelicalism and politics in Africa. He disputes the Hobsbawm–Anderson–Gellner thesis on the late genesis of nationalism globally, preferring to root it in the biblical culture and vernacular literature of the Middle Ages. The root of nationalism is not in post-Enlightenment modernity, but in 'the impact of the Bible [and] of vernacular literature ... in creating a politically stable ethnicity, effectively "imagined" by its members across a unique mythology'. In Africa, we see the beginnings of something similar, says Hastings. 'The nineteenth century Protestant missionary was, above all, a Bible man.' In translating, 'he was often to a considerable extent creating the language and, with it, a defined ethnicity', since the adopted form became normative and established a new kind of language community. However, the criteria regarding degree of difference which required a separate Bible translation were often unclear. Retranslation was right if one saw Christianisation as urgent. The alternative medieval pattern, defended by a minority of missions in Africa, needed time. Given that, it would generate genuine nations transcending dialectical differences. However, the Bible Society ideal is to have the Bible in every discoverable dialect, which diminishes the social significance of each translation, since the likelihood that a literature and educational system will ever develop in that language is reduced.

One would have expected, says Hastings, to see a twentieth-century Yoruba nation-state, or a Buganda one. But this nation-making process was stopped in its tracks by a different one which lacked ethnic foundations – the production of nations by imperial borders. Independence movements then became known as nationalist movements. As Hastings scathingly says, 'we talked of African nationalism ... but we linked it ... with European-created entities. [Other] movements ... related to some pre-existing people were regarded as tribal, reactionary ... This made very little sense in terms of the genus of nationalism ... [and was] almost bound to lead onto the huge political confusions of post-Independence Africa.' Hastings concludes that religion has not been a major factor in African national consciousness and nation-formation in the second half of the twentieth century, since 'the characteristic Christian approach to the enhancement of ethnicity [in the direction of nationhood] was undermined' (1997: 166).

Out of the failed experiments of the 1970s and 1980s in non-democratic systems, some unexpected transformations started in the late 1980s. These form the immediate context of current evangelical politics. More than half of sub-Saharan states made political reforms after 1989 (Joseph 1997) – this, despite the fact that democratisation was not supposed to happen in Africa, which was considered to lack the structural and cultural prerequisites. The rhetoric of pre-1989 authoritarian leaders was that multi-party democracy was a recipe for ethnic fragmentation; in fact the one-party states themselves often became *de facto* fiefs of a particular ethnic group.

However, democracy did not go as far as hoped. For one thing, it usually involved drastic economic reforms at the behest of international institutions, which hindered many features commonly associated with full liberal democracy (high participation, authentic political choice, extensive citizen rights) (ibid.: 377). Economic policies have been insulated from popular involvement, a process known as 'virtual democracy'. Secondly, power-holders have learnt how to hold on to power while satisfying international pressure. After the shock electoral defeat of Kenneth Kaunda of Zambia, African leaders started advising each other on how to hold elections and stay in power. They discovered the limits to which external agencies were prepared to go, and learnt to manipulate opposition parties by multiplying them, often on ethnic or personalistic lines. This was possible because the basic impulse to democratisation usually came from outside, from the power of international institutions over weakened economies, from the lower tolerance of the West for authoritarian regimes after the Cold War and from the weakening of African states by fiscal insolvency. Unlike Korea (strong state but also increasingly strong civil society, tipping the balance to democratisation), most of Africa had weak states but weak civil societies, unable to maintain momentum towards democratic consolidation. Even mainline churches, important parts of nascent civil society, suffer from weaknesses, being often divided and mutually competitive, with elitist leaders who prefer *ad hoc* rather than prolonged involvement in politics (Gyimah-Boadi 1996: 123–4).

Sanneh is more severe in his strictures; African Christians are novices at the game of state building. The inherited tradition of a secular state has no parallels in African traditional religiosity, still less in Islam. African Christianity must reflect on church and state, since religious toleration requires arguments that go beyond those of public usefulness. Against pressure for sharia (Islamic law), the utilitarian ethic of the secular state is utterly inadequate. The state as vehicle for tolerance and human rights must now be conceived in terms hospitable to claims for truth (Sanneh 1996).

In colonial times, freedom of religion was protected by the Congress of Berlin. Only Portuguese colonies after 1940 had a church–state relationship remotely similar to colonial Latin America. Although, as Hastings (1995) says, the tendency of missionaries to identify the church and the colonial state could be considerable, in the last analysis British pluralism and French anti-clericalism, plus the division of missions by denomination and nationality, made such identification impossible to sustain.

At independence, mainline churches feared the new states might turn to communism or African traditions, and were happy to accept requests for help in state-defined development. The state was seen as the key actor, and churches enjoyed precarious legitimacy. By the late 1980s all that had changed. The state's legitimacy was now in question, while the churches' had grown, accompanying numerical growth and Africanisation of the clergy. In addition, churches were now often the only important institutions in civil society, and their international connections were advantageous rather than a liability. So they came to be seen as key actors in the 'second democratisation'. By the late 1990s, however, it was clear how limited that process was. It was only of the hierarchies of mainline churches. There was little parish-level mobilisation, and little attempt to involve pentecostal and other churches. It was thus a very elite phenomenon.

We need to look beyond this level. There is often a jockeying for position, inside the religious field, in claims to be important in democratisation, or in claims that other groups were obstacles to the same. 'Democracy' can be a jargon and set of procedures available only to an elite. Gifford's writings often make dichotomous statements regarding 'mainline' and 'evangelical' churches. 'In general ... the mainline churches ... have challenged Africa's dictators; the newer evangelical and pentecostal churches ... have provided the support' (1995: 5). A large and varied category are lumped together as 'religions of the right'. But we need more empirical evidence, and also an awareness of selective appropriation by the grass-roots. In addition, African Independent Churches (AICs) are missing from many analyses since they do not put out written statements. As Maxwell stresses, the Apostolic Faith Mission of South Africa is numerically as strong as the Dutch Reformed Church; the Church of Pentecost is Ghana's largest church (1997a: 147). We need to take these churches seriously and avoid seeing the Christian field through the eyes of mainline churches. Gifford tries to include the 'born-again' movement, but in a manner, as Maxwell says, that is too one-dimensional and fixated with the American religious right. Kalu also pleads for its political methods to be taken seriously. Spiritual 'mapping' and marches to break covenants with Satan are unusual forms of nationalism, but they still emphasise the breakdown of ethnic identities in favour of commitment to national welfare (Kalu 1997: 30). And yet, one may add, while contributing to the creation of trans-ethnic communities (not least through inter-tribal marriages), they avoid the idolatry of the nation-state which has characterised so much official discourse in Africa.

Ranger also questions the common view of the churches' role. The international character of some churches helped them to be more effective in a moral crisis and political vacuum than internally democratic churches open to 'local subversion'. But democracy is easier to inaugurate than to consolidate, and while ecclesiastical iron cages might be needed to face down regimes, decentralised congregations were better at creating the values needed for democratic sustainability (1995b: 26).

It is unrealistic to expect churches of the poor, without foreign connections, to play the same role in opposition to authoritarian regimes as mainline churches. As we saw with regard to Lutherans in Brazil, a *church* (in the sociology of religion sense) is more protected in the adoption of politically risky postures, and more protected from the 'local subversion' factor. These are advantages stemming from social position and sociological type rather than theological factors.

The actual performance of mainline churches in Africa does not always reflect these advantages. The Catholic Church is more heavily missionary-manned and foreign-funded, and this is crucial for its socio-political influence (Gifford 1994b: 522). Yet it and other mainline denominations have usually needed a threat to their institutional interests before opposing regimes. And mainline churches have supported far more years of authoritarian rule in independent Africa than other churches. It was they who supported a century of True Whig rule in Liberia, who asked the United States to intervene militarily in 1990, who could not speak out against the regime in Monrovia because many of their members lived at the mercy of Charles Taylor, and whose generally fatalistic approach paved the way for catastrophe. Once the non-mainline churches have been appropriately nuanced, as in some more recent accounts (Marshall 1991, 1993, 1995; Maxwell 1995, 1997a), one wonders whether, *when all else is equal*, there is much to choose at the institutional level between them and their mainline brethren. And they may be better in their overall effect on democratic *consolidation*, even if less important for democratic *inauguration*.

But this is speculation about potentialities, a favourite pastime of authors on Africa and Latin America: new political language, new public space, new values and abilities which can be brought to public life. Non-mainline churches could, in Tocquevillian and Weberian fashion, become the *sectarian* prototypes of a democracy based on a hive of voluntary associations. The argument is logical – unlike so much that actually happens. The value of such arguments is limited when divorced from empirical demonstration of trends, but they should make us wary of equally non-empirical projections to the contrary.

Linden, reviewing Gifford's edited volume (1995), comments on a question the book never comes to grips with: can the churches move from conflict with autocratic governments into being schools for 'high intensity democracy'? The jury is still out on that, says Linden. There are a number of theologies working themselves out in practices, and a number of practices working themselves out in theologies (1996: 226).

As yet (and undoubtedly for many reasons), there has been no real corporatist electoral politics à la Brazil by mass evangelical churches in Africa. Whether there are moves in that direction is a topic for research. Generally, there is a need for more detailed country-level studies. The virtually simultaneous growth of evangelical religion straddles the two continents, but political involvement has been far from uniform in either. We should not now remain at abstract levels of explanation, but delve into national political contexts, the structure of national media and religious fields, giving body to, and showing the limits of, global explanations. Evangelical religion means different things to different people at different times, and holds different positions in society and in the religious field of each country. If Gifford's study of Liberia (1993), one of few in-depth country analyses, is critiqued by Haynes (1996: 209) precisely in terms of Liberia's uniqueness (highly Americanised, only one-third Christianised, settled by emancipated slaves and now in civil war), this points to the need to multiply such studies. If the 'long run' argument adduced by some authors on Latin America (that pentecostal-ism may in the end do more for political reform than mainline churches, by providing free social space in which to learn new notions of the self, new responsibilities and new independence) is a key debate today on Third World evangelical politics, it cannot be answered in the abstract, but only by national studies which cut close to the grain. Between anthropological micro-studies, and continent-wide generalisations, we need country-level macro institutional studies to understand how evangelical politics are actually developing, enabling us to move beyond conspiracy theories on the one hand (that the American right is influencing African politics via evangelical churches), and on the other hand general theories about the potential of evangelical religion based on historical analogy or on supposed essential characteristics of charismatic Christianity.

CHAPTER 9

Sudan

Sudan is estimated by Baur (1994: 525) to be 4.7 per cent Protestant, while Johnstone (1993) talks of 7 per cent. It is the only part of sub-Saharan Africa where Islam has become state ideology. Its Christians (and their animist kinsmen) have been at war with the government since 1955, with a break between 1972 and 1983. As a result, Sudan has the world's largest population of internally displaced people.

Islam in Sudan, unlike other sub-Saharan countries with Muslim majorities, is associated with Arabism, adding ethnic and cultural components to the religious divide. In the north, Christian kingdoms a thousand years old were overthrown in the sixteenth century, but even the Ottomans could not extend effective control over the south. The Anglo-Egyptian condominium from 1899 endorsed the traditional link between Islam and the state in the north, but in the south it permitted Christian missions. The evangelical Anglican Church Missionary Society (CMS) gained Equator Province and the American Presbyterians gained the east of Upper Nile. John Garang, head of the Sudan People's Liberation Army (SPLA), is a product of Anglican work among the Dinka, and the SPLA makes a point of describing him as 'a practising good Christian'. At independence in 1956, the south demanded federation, but the government was determined to Arabise and Islamise. The true conflict is Arab versus non-Arab, says Haynes (1996: 101); not exactly so, says O'Fahey (1995: 42). Although the first civil war (1955–72) was hardly articulated ideologically, that was the period when much Christian conversion took place. However, the current civil war is undoubtedly religious as well as ethnic, since sharia (Islamic law) was introduced in 1983. Sudan now figures on the small US State Department list of countries which practise religious persecution. In 1989 a coup brought in a new military-Islamic regime. Its main civilian component is the National Islamic Front (NIF) led by Hasan al-Turabi, which aspires to a state with 'one language, Arabic, and one religion,

Islam'. While the government claims it is waging a holy war against a Christian conspiracy to split the nation, the NIF was never able to come to power democratically even in the north, and has repressed Muslim as well as non-Muslim opponents. In 1995, an umbrella opposition movement was formed, including the SPLA and two northern Muslim parties.

The Sudan People's Liberation Movement (SPLM) and its armed wing, the SPLA, have been led by John Garang since their beginnings in 1983. The SPLM proclaims its aim to be a New Sudan, democratic and secular (i.e. with separation of religion and state). Officially, it hopes to keep Sudan united, but its strategy does not preclude (and in effect presupposes) the possibility of separation.

The government, besides encouraging cattle and slave raiding against non-Muslims, has maximised ethnic and other splits in southern ranks. Human-rights abuses and power struggles have prompted several prominent Dinka commanders to leave the SPLA and conclude treaties with the government. On the other hand, conflict between Dinka and Nuer led in 1991 to a breakaway (mostly Nuer) South Sudan Independence Movement, which in 1997 also made peace with Khartoum.

In this situation of civil war plus inter-ethnic and factional conflict within the south, Christianity has grown and acquired an important role. Conversions in previous periods were linked to education, offering a broader pan-tribal identity as well as values and skills which 'enabled southerners effectively to challenge the northern Sudanese claim to total superiority' (Deng 1995: 221). Since the 1980s the move to Christianity has become more mass-based, provoked by uprooting and the breakdown of traditional life. In distinct areas and ethnic groups, churches such as the Catholic, Episcopal (Anglican), Presbyterian, Africa Inland Church and the Sudan Church of Christ have grown rapidly, despite (or because of) the expulsion of foreign missionaries in 1964. The Episcopal Church is reputed to be the fastest-growing in the worldwide Anglican Communion. Anthropologist Sharon Hutchinson talks of 'one of the fastest-growing movements of Christian conversion in the world' amongst the eastern Nuer from the 1970s and western Nuer by the mid 1980s, where it takes the form of 'puritanical strains' of evangelical Presbyterianism (1996: 312–37). This is quite independent of missionaries, and predates any channelling of aid by Christian relief organisations in the 1990s to strengthen congregations (ibid.: 348). By the early 1980s, powerful Nuer families had endorsed conversion. Causes of this rapid growth include the politicisation of religious identities by the regime, which encourages forced Islamisation and regards traditional religion as devil-worship, making Christianity a politically attractive alternative; the saving of increasingly scarce resources represented by the rejection of cattle sacrifice (the cornerstone of traditional religion); the need for a new religious system among refugees in camps or northern towns, outside the cattle economy; and the trend, encouraged by dislocation, toward giving a larger role to the High God rather than to localised powers (Hutchinson 1996: 300–12; Nikkel 1991). Traditional identity and Christian and Western influence have combined in a modern southern identity of resistance, says Deng (1995: 205). For the oppressed and displaced, the church provides a rallying-ground in the face of the erosion of traditions and social structures, preserving traditional values and offering new opportunities. It also provides meaning in suffering, through contextualisation of Biblical accounts (such as Isaiah chapter 18) which are seen as foretelling their current tragedy and their ultimate vindication.

The relationship of this religious revival to the civil war is complex. Christianity can, of course, provide not only solace and meaning but also ties as global as those of the Islamic government. But the religio-military synthesis does not add up to a jihad, claims Nikkel, since the tone is pro-autonomy and not anti-Islam. Nevertheless, some SPLA commanders have declared themselves Christians recently, and chaplains accompany the rebel forces. Elite southern circles promote the idea that Christianity should be cultivated as a pivotal element in southern identity. This may not be advocated openly by the SPLA leadership, says Deng, but is an essential ingredient in the hidden agenda (1995: 222). Hutchinson recounts a fascinating incident in which a leading SPLA commander was approached by civilians wishing to convert to Christianity but without a minister to baptise them. He then summoned a pastor by military order. After a month, the pastor asked to return home for the planting season, but the commander ordered him to continue baptising while his soldiers did the planting. The same commander said many church songs had begun to sound like SPLA war songs, but that the rights of non-Christians were protected by the SPLA (1996: 334).

As for the institutional church itself, as so often in civil wars, it has to bear in mind that its constituency is on both sides of the battle lines (in northern towns and in 'liberated areas'), even if not, in this case, on both sides of the conflict. In the face of a deepening culture of violence (ibid.: 355), it has had a unifying and reconciling role in the intra-south conflict.

An example of this was the 1998 Loki Accord between the (largely Presbyterian) Nuer and the (heavily Episcopalian) Dinka, in which chiefs and church leaders met under the auspices of the New Sudan Council of Churches and agreed an end to years of bad relations marked by cattle raiding and abduction.

CHAPTER 10

Angola

Site of the ancient Catholic kingdom of Kongo and a Portuguese presence since the sixteenth century, modern Angola was a product of the Congress of Berlin, and 'in effect a confederation of three colonies in Portuguese West Africa ... Angola lacked a cultural, educational, economic and administrative unity on which the aspirations of black politicians could be focused. The south knew little of Luanda' (Birmingham 1992: 24ff.).

The Catholic Church was not able to provide that unity. It was very weak on the ground at the end of the nineteenth century, its missionary presence crippled by metropolitan policy towards the religious orders. In the early twentieth century, the Republic also pursued an anti-clerical policy. In addition, the Catholic Church came to be highly identified with the white settlers (as many as half a million) and, after the Concordat of 1940, with the Salazar government's policy of Portugalization.

Not surprisingly, it was from Protestant ranks that the leaders of all three independence movements (Agostinho Neto of the MPLA, Jonas Savimbi of Unita and Holden Roberto of the FNLA) emerged. But once again, geographical unity was lacking. The Protestant missions, established from the 1870s onwards, were in three separate groups, 'a division that was to have fundamental long-term consequences for the evolution of Angolan nationalism' (Birmingham 1992: 24). Methodists took the centre, Congregationalists the south, and Baptists the north. It is thus impossible to understand modern Angolan politics without taking Protestantism into account. 'Protestant missions, which provided the most important source of educated leadership, were thus to some degree responsible for the three-way partition that occurred in the national leadership' (ibid.). The Protestant old-school networks developed only sub-national cohesiveness.

Protestantism provided nationalist leadership not only because it educated, but also because it was considered semi-subversive by the Portuguese. As Henderson says, the anti-Protestant attitudes of the colonial government predisposed Protestants to be anti-Portuguese (1990: 321). In addition, church networks were vital in political organisation, and the lay democratic nature of the churches gave experience in organisation and administration. When guerrilla movements began in 1961, Protestant missionaries began to have their visa renewals refused, and six (mostly Methodist) were expelled from the country (ibid.: 309).

The tripartite division of the churches soon corresponded to a similar number of nationalist movements: Baptists with the FNLA in the north, Methodists with the MPLA in the Luanda-Catete-Malange corridor, and Congregationalists with Unita in the centre-south. Most of the northern population took refuge in Zaire and the Baptist church went with them. But the Methodists and Congregationalists became heavily involved in politics. Jonas Savimbi had studied Social and Political Sciences in Lausanne with a scholarship from the latter church, and several other leaders of Unita were church leaders. Savimbi's father had been the director of a mission, and Savimbi consolidated Unita's support among Protestants in the region, promising government support for educational and health projects. Unita needed the Congregational Church's network. Most pastors saw themselves as Unita's 'sponsors', and Unita saw the church as its 'conscience'. In the short-lived Popular Democratic Republic based in Huambo, pastors and elders took administrative positions, making this the only moment of Angolan history in which a government did not view Protestants with disinterest, suspicion or hostility (Schubert 1999: 407). Once the Unita republic had been overrun by the MPLA, the Congregational Church split between the 'city church' which sought a place in official Angola and the 'bush church' which retreated with Unita.

The relationship between the MPLA and the Methodist Church was not quite the same. Agostinho Neto, leader of the MPLA, was the son of a Methodist pastor, had had a Methodist education and been secretary to the bishop. He had since renounced Christianity, but even so the Methodist Church was the first to recognise the MPLA victory in the fighting which ensued upon Portugal's chaotic withdrawal in 1975, affirming full support and even echoing its Marxist language, declaring it to be the 'vanguard' of the people in the 'historically necessary' construction of socialism. As a result, it came to be seen as the 'state church' by other churches. The government saw the Congregationalists, on the other hand, as 'the church of Unita' (ibid.: 410). The government pursued a variant of a Marxist policy on religion until the late 1980s, requiring official recognition of churches and prohibiting new ones. In the 1990s, with the fall of international Marxism, religious policy was relaxed, but the civil war simmered at a lower intensity and peace eluded Angola. The 1997 integration of Unita into a government of national unity suffered a setback the following year, when its failure to disarm led to the ejection of its representatives from the cabinet and national assembly. However, if anything approaching a normal political life revives it will be interesting to see the role of Angola's numerically flourishing Protestant community in it.

CHAPTER 11

Mozambique

As with Angola, Portugal's hold on Mozambique at the time of the Congress of Berlin was precarious, and the Catholic presence minimal. In 1855 there were only four priests in the country (Helgesson 1991: 197).

Protestant missionaries from the 1870s went to the interior, still effectively under local chiefs. Protestants aimed especially at the south. The most significant influence was the Swiss Mission (Presbyterian) of the Free Church of Vaud, influenced by the *reveil* spirituality typical of much continental evangelicalism. The Mission formalised the Tsonga vernacular, generating a regional solidarity which became a taproot of nationalism (Birmingham 1992: 23). Cruz e Silva concludes that Presbyterianism helped the Tsonga resist Portuguese assimilationism; it also contributed indirectly to Mozambican nationalism through education, relatively democratic procedures and emphasis on Tsonga cultural values (1998: 236).

In addition, the Swiss Mission produced the founder of Frelimo, Eduardo Mondlane. Mondlane was educated by the Mission and worked as evangelist and mission school teacher. His studies in South Africa and the United States were paid for by Swiss Mission and Methodist scholarships, and there were hopes he might become general secretary of the Christian Council of Mozambique. Instead, Mondlane worked with the United Nations before founding Frelimo (Cruz e Silva 1998: 228–34; Helgesson 1994: 280). In Ngoenha's words, Mondlane converted his former Swiss Mission spiritual guides to his vision of a Mozambican identity, different both from the colonial idea of 'black Portugueseness' and the missionaries' idea of Tsongan-ness. The Mission founder's nephew, a member of the Mission board, transformed his office in Geneva into Frelimo's advance post in the Western world (1999: 435). But Ngoenha does not answer his own questions regarding how far the missionaries were capable of following Mondlane even into the armed struggle and the socialist camp. Nor do we read of the effect of Mondlane's death in 1969 on their relationship to Frelimo.

In Inhambane, Methodists played a somewhat similar role. A pastor opened the local branch of the African National Congress (ANC) in 1918, and Methodist youth fled in large numbers in the 1960s to join Frelimo forces (Helgesson 1994: 207, 342). In colonial times, there was a split among educated Mozambicans, between the Catholic-educated and Portuguese-speaking, and the Protestant-educated and vernacular-speaking. The early Frelimo was dominated by the latter, with the former sometimes mistrusted (Vines 1991: 103). As the war of liberation (1962–74) increased in intensity, many black Protestant leaders, especially Presbyterians, were arrested by the Portuguese. The president of the synodal council was later found hanged in his cell (Hastings 1991: 171).

If the reasons for Frelimo's post-independence anti-Catholic stance are easy to understand (since 1940 the church had worked under a Concordat by which it became an agent of Portugalisation), the doctrinaire opposition to religion in general is not. One reason is that after Mondlane had been killed in 1969 he was replaced by a more hard-line Marxist leadership under Samora Machel. Another factor is the weak Christianisation of Mozambique (only 10–15%) at independence (Vines and Wilson 1995: 133), which contrasts with the rest of southern Africa. Still another reason is suggested by Cruz e Silva (1995: 448). She talks of Frelimo's fear that Protestantism's denominational divisions could be dangerous for the project of national unity. This reminds us of Hastings' point that the exigencies of nation-building in artificial circumstances often led to state policies in which Protestantism's link with pluralism and the end of monolithic structures was a threat. The construction of nationhood in relation to Protestant institutional divisions is an important general theme in the continent. In addition to recent multiplication of churches, there is the heritage of comity agreements between the old missions, which often made each church regionally and linguistically limited, creating complex links between denomination and ethnicity which can still affect Protestant politics.

From soon after independence in 1975, when schools and hospitals were nationalised, until 1982, Frelimo was hostile to all organised religion. The Party was organised along Leninist lines, some churches were closed, and all denominations were barred from the new communal villages. The Methodists lost 40 per cent of their membership in this period (Helgesson 1994: 1–8). But Frelimo's opposition to religion declined as its own troubles multiplied. These related in part to the civil war against Renamo guerrillas. Frelimo's own policies, added to

economic dependence on apartheid South Africa and the latter's efforts
at destabilisation, combined to make Mozambique one of the poorest
countries in the world by the late 1980s.

The mission churches of the south had retained some relationship
with Frelimo and in the late 1980s they convinced it that it must
negotiate with Renamo. The conflict was not as it was painted in foreign
church sources. On the one hand, the World Council of Churches
(WCC) portrayed the war as entirely the result of South African and
Western destabilisation, with Renamo as a demonic puppet force.
There was no sense of the Mozambican dynamic – Mozambicans only
appeared as victims of 'apartheid terror'. On the other hand, right-wing
evangelical groups such as the Frontline Fellowship tried to convince
sponsors in white South Africa and the United States that Renamo was
fighting God's war against communism (Vines and Wilson 1995).

Vines (1991) nuances the picture regarding Renamo and religion.
Accentuating its difference from Frelimo's materialist ideology and
practical hostility to religion in the war zones, Renamo's external
propaganda reflected its largely Catholic-educated leadership. Its
leader, Afonso Dhlakama, was supported by some Catholic hierarchs
abroad, and the Mozambican Catholic Church angered Frelimo by
appealing for talks with Renamo. Mozambican Protestant churches, on
the other hand, denounced Renamo in terms similar to those of the
government, and Protestant aid organisations enjoyed a good relationship with Frelimo by the late 1980s. However, most of Renamo's
church-derived external aid came from Protestant sources. After 1985
some right-wing evangelicals in the United States (Christ for the Nations
Inc., Don Ormond Ministries, End-Time Handmaidens) campaigned
for Renamo, describing the zones it controlled as scenes of revival and
attributing some of its own massacres to Frelimo. The white Zimbabwean church Shekinah was given freedom to preach in Renamo areas.
Peter Hammond of Frontline Fellowship, a South African mission
specialising in recruiting evangelical soldiers, produced 'Eyewitness
Testimonies of Persecution and Atrocities', a centrepiece in Renamo
publicity. Christian, mainly evangelical, organisations were thus associated with Renamo in fundraising, publicity and intelligence activities.

From 1984 onwards, the Mozambique Christian Council, uniting
seventeen Protestant churches, helped in establishing a Peace and
Reconciliation Commission and gained permission from the Frelimo
government to have confidential dialogue with Renamo. By 1988
church-sponsored peace talks were under way. In 1990 one-party rule

ended, and a cease-fire was reached in 1992. The churches' role (including Catholic) had been as a social space that could represent popular will and secure participation of both sides. The erosion of state legitimacy led to churches providing virtually the only other 'national' institutional framework. They had credibility and relationships with actors on the ground, plus international contacts (Vines and Wilson 1995: 147).

In the 1994 elections, Frelimo won a narrow majority over Renamo, and the transition proceeded relatively well. All parties appealed for religious support in the elections, but the churches on the whole adopted a low-key approach. While contributing technical skills (civic education courses to raise voter interest; mediation in the crises which threatened to engulf the elections; prayer services for peace; bringing in international observers), most churches resisted the temptation to give open support to candidates. However, the fact of civic education increased the churches' representation amongst those who actually voted. In the outcome, religion and ethnic or regional factors are hard to separate; it would seem that Frelimo's victory was due largely to those areas where Protestantism or Islam are strongest, while Renamo's best showing was in more Catholic areas (Baloi 1995; Morier-Genoud 1996). It would be interesting to know more about Protestant candidates for deputy and their public role.

One church that seems to have a clear option is the Universal Church of the Kingdom of God. Mozambique is one of the countries where this Brazilian church has been most successful. Arriving in 1992, by the late 1990s it claimed over thirty churches, plus much social work. It has also achieved media power: a television network which retransmits TV Record from Brazil, besides several radio stations. It seems, says Morier-Genoud (1996: 10), to have made a deal with Frelimo before the 1994 elections, which allowed it to set up its radio and television stations and rent two floors of the Frelimo Central Committee building in Maputo. Since the UC had only just arrived in Mozambique and could offer few votes to Frelimo, it presumably offered money and future media and electoral support. In 1999 Bishop Macedo was received by President Chissano on a visit to Mozambique (Teresa Cruz e Silva, personal communication). If the UC's membership grows and its leadership becomes more Mozambican, its media power and financial wealth may help to make it a force in Mozambican politics.

The 1991 census points to the delicate religious balance in this secular state. In southern African terms, it is still little Christianised, even though Protestantism has grown apace, especially through Zionists and local pentecostal groups. Traditionalists are still 31 per cent, and Muslims 19 per cent. Catholics are 24 per cent and Protestants 21 per cent. However, only Catholicism has a really national presence; other religions are regionally concentrated. Protestants vary from 49 per cent in Maputo province to less than 1 per cent in Nampula. Presbyterians are concentrated in Maputo and Gaza, Methodists and Congregationalists in Inhambane; even the languages they use are different. The potentialities of this balanced pluralism, and the challenges of reconstructing a war-torn and impoverished country heavily dependent on foreign aid and foreign NGOs (non-governmental organisations, including Christian ones), will make Mozambique a fascinating case to watch.

Mozambique would make a fine case-study of the *de facto* political role of foreign evangelical NGOs in highly vulnerable countries. This would not be an 'American religious right' study, but more nuanced regarding intentions and actions of the foreign organisations themselves, and especially the way they are made use of by local actors of all persuasions.

CHAPTER 12

Zimbabwe

The conversion of Southern Rhodesia was slow by regional standards, perhaps due to the settler invasion. But Christianisation proceeded rapidly from the 1950s, and by independence in 1980 was well established, a factor in avoiding the sort of persecution adopted in Mozambique.

Hastings summarises church–state relations in the following way. The churches initially provided the colonial and settler state with validation. Even so, some churchmen defended African rights – notably Methodist John White and Anglican Arthur Shearly Cripps. The churches educated the black nationalist leadership, such as Catholic Robert Mugabe and Methodists Joshua Nkomo, Abel Muzorewa, Canaan Banana and Ndabaningi Sithole. In the civil war, church agencies, especially Catholic, were influential in documenting atrocities. For a while in the early 1970s, church leaders such as Muzorewa and Banana were able to substitute for the imprisoned politicians. But with the coming of black rule, black church leadership proved too limited in education and experience to have much to say to the government (1991: 184ff.).

The Methodist missionary John White, who viewed settler society as under the judgement of God as much as black 'traditional' societies, was mentor to Thompson Samkange, a leading figure in church and politics from the 1920s to 1950s. Samkange's Methodism, says Ranger (1995a), was enthusiastic, locally rooted, prophetic and political. As a pastor and as secretary of the Southern Rhodesian Native Missionary Conference, Samkange had a formidable reputation as evangelist and revivalist, and his prayers for the sick attracted large crowds. Some white missionaries expressed concern about his 'excess of evangelical fervour' (ibid.: 12). His pietism was accompanied by increasing political involvement, based on convictions 'deeply rooted in his religious beliefs' (ibid.: 1). Seeing the Methodist Church in Rhodesia as the outcome of initiatives and contributions from black and white, he was 'determined to accept no offence either to his church or his race' (ibid.: 5). The advancement of the latter had to be spiritual as well as material, and the black clergy, with their education and prestige, were fundamental in giving leadership. In 1943, Samkange was elected president of the Southern Rhodesian Bantu Congress, then the leading African political grouping. Although he represented an emerging black middle class whose grievances were remote from the masses, he sought to bring a broader constituency into the congress and demanded full democratic rights and immediate recognition of African trade unions. He left the presidency in 1948, and events later favoured a different sort of nationalism from Samkange's. 'Ideologically he was not really in sympathy with a "totalitarian" view of nationalism, in which a single movement organises the people's life' (ibid.: 120), such as the mass movement of the early 1960s which instructed people to spend Sundays at political rallies rather than at church. Samkange combined 'a fierce indignation against white racialism with an abhorrence of black racialist repudiation of whites' (ibid.: 160). But in the 1990s, his 'reluctance to see all associational life devoured by an engrossing nationalism' has found echoes in resistance to the one-party state and the revival of civil society; and his vision of a responsible and restrained (and Christian) elite seems as pertinent as ever (ibid.: 206).

The main churches in Southern Rhodesia usually had black and white members and could not afford to alienate their wealthy whites by being anti-government (Hastings 1991: 164). Even after UDI (the Unilateral Declaration of Independence by the white minority government) in 1965, the churches only really clashed with the state following the constitution of 1969 which affected the work of clergy among other races. On the Protestant side, the main political activity in the 1970s came from black Methodists. The ANC was established with Muzorewa as president and Banana as vice-president, to convince the British that the settlement it had negotiated was unacceptable to blacks. This brought Muzorewa to the centre of politics for the next decade. He combined leadership of the United Methodist Church and the ANC, being almost the only senior black ecclesiastic in the country. Later, the ANC became more moderate, with black middle-class support, and Muzorewa agreed to take office in 1979 as prime minister of Zimbabwe-Rhodesia in an 'anti-communist' government still controlled by the white Rhodesian Front. This sealed Muzorewa's political fate. After multiracial elections in 1980, he was left with only three seats in parliament.

Despite fears for the churches based on Mugabe's Marxist sympathies, there was in fact very little post-independence hostility. For Hastings, this was because of Christianity's social rootedness by this time. 'The advance of nationalism in rural Zimbabwe coincided with, rather than conflicted with, the advance of Christianity' (ibid.: 178).

However, tensions remained. Canaan Banana, who had transferred to ZANU during the guerrilla war, became president. He developed a Zimbabwean Liberation Theology in which the churches, in exchange for help with organisational restoration after the war, were expected to support state development plans for a socialist country. 'For all his rhetoric about a proletarian church of self-reliance, [Banana] was more interested in dealing with restored ecclesiastical hierarchies' (Maxwell 1995: 110). The Zimbabwe Christian Council, having initially supported Muzorewa's ANC, was taken over by another faction which adopted the state's definition of development, and remained silent on repression in Matabeleland until 1984 (ibid.: 113–14). (The minority Ndebele were shut out of government by Mugabe's Shona-based regime and repressed bloodily.)

In 1987, a unity accord brought the Matabeleland conflict to an end and changed the political climate. Popular demands for accountability in government led to greater openness to sectors of civil society. But Zimbabwe is a case of 'concession without conversion' (Joseph) in which former autocrats have ridden the storm of democratisation and remained in power. Even so, the changes have affected the balance of power within the Protestant field.

As part of Mugabe's opening up to society, the (mostly black) evangelicals organised in the Evangelical Fellowship of Zimbabwe achieved greater visibility and became more politicised, even petitioning against Mugabe's intention to introduce a one-party state (Maxwell 1995: 119). There is, it seems, a clear-cut divide between the Zimbabwe Christian Council and the EFZ, with no dual membership. As the president of the EFZ told the author in 1996, the evangelicals, and not just the Zimbabwe Christian Council and the Catholic bishops, were now also political actors. He even referred to the EFZ having been 'recognised' by government in 1990 and always being consulted since then. Economic woes forced the government to open up to Protestant groups other than the WCC-affiliated churches they had known since the liberation war. He said the EFZ was trying to include in the constitution a declaration that Zimbabwe is an 'Afro-Christian' nation 'governed under God'. This proposal was in fact made to the Constitutional

Commission of 1999, along with proposals for outlawing satanism, witchcraft, homosexuality and abortion on demand, but there was no consensus within the EFZ about this.

The greater openness to non-Zimbabwe Christian Council churches seems to have coincided with the political marginalisation of Banana (Maxwell 1995: 119). The political field, however, remains very restricted. In the parliamentary elections of 1995, the ruling party won all but two seats. In the presidential elections of 1996, both opposition candidates pulled out alleging fraud. Both were Protestant clergymen: Bishop Muzorewa and Revd Sithole.

However, little is known yet about attitudes and activities of a whole range of evangelical churches, especially large independent groups such as the Vapostori. Maxwell, who has done ground-breaking work on independency and specifically on the ZAOGA (Zimbabwe Assemblies of God Africa), sets the agenda for this. Zimbabwe intellectuals, he says, ignore the pentecostal, evangelical and independent churches which have the potential to restrain as well as legitimise the state. When sects refuse to participate in modernisation, they are striking at the hegemonic ideology of the state. 'There is a danger in a selective reading of just the "message" of pentecostal churches, for its overt political content, which misses other significant dimensions of their contribution to the democratisation movement' (ibid.: 122).

Maxwell (1998; forthcoming) has since developed his analysis of ZAOGA, the largest Protestant church in Zimbabwe. The church began in 1960 in Highfields where the nationalist movement was taking off, but there are no direct links. Despite asserting black autonomy, it cultivated pragmatic links with whites to obtain resources and government cover. One of the co-founders, Ezekiel Guti, used American links forged while studying in the United States to rise to undisputed leadership and operate a patrimonial system. By the time of the guerrilla war, which affected ZAOGA little because of its urban location, Guti was developing a personality cult. Independence threatened to disrail the trajectory, so the church showed its loyalty by cooperating with state-led development projects. But relations with the ruling party were not good: besides being identified with the Ndau ethnic group of rebel leader Ndabaningi Sithole, to whom Guti's wife was related, ZAOGA's leadership cult looked suspiciously political and its capacity for multi-ethnic mobilisation looked threatening. As in Mozambique (but in a milder way), the ruling party's main concern was that a church like ZAOGA might undermine its nation-building project.

All this changed after the Unity Accord of 1987. The ruling party's legitimacy waned, and the mainline churches distanced themselves. The ZAOGA leadership filled the gap amongst the elite and its patrimonialism. Mugabe's second wife is a ZAOGA member, as is his sister. In the 1995 elections, ZAOGA leaders told members to 'catch the cockerel before dawn', the cockerel being the ruling ZANU-PF symbol. In the 1990s, ZAOGA's prosperity gospel resonates with the regime's economic liberalisation, and its discourse of moral and spiritual renewal replaces discredited Marxist rhetoric. Good relations with government facilitate movement of money, personnel and equipment within and outside the country (ZAOGA having spread abroad). Archbishop Guti was handpicked by Mugabe to sit on the 1999 Constitutional Commission. Even so, one should not exaggerate ZAOGA's political clout; Guti was just one of 395 members of the commission, and as we have seen in Brazil the noisiest religious groups in politics are not necessarily the most powerful.

The result, says Maxwell, is tension between an increasingly authoritarian and wealthy leadership and the more egalitarian culture at the grass-roots of the church. Class, age and ethnicity are all involved in this tension. There is a growing perception that leaders have lined their own pockets and favoured the Ndau. Young pastors, mostly poor and dependent on the church, are drawn into local struggles for social improvement and resent the ostentation of the top few. At a different social level, young people have founded the Highfields Action Party to protest against leaders' wealth and ethnic favouritism, while university students and young professionals influenced by Western rights discourse have founded Think Progressive ZAOGA to expose corruption within the movement. Maxwell's nuanced work is a corrective to some previous work on Zimbabwe, such as Gifford's *The New Crusaders* (1991), which looks at Christianity through the activities of religious elites (NGOs, church councils, pastoral statements, conferences), with little research into how their discourses are received by ordinary believers, or even to what extent they correspond with those elites' own actions.

CHAPTER 13

Malawi

In Malawi, Ross (1995a, 1995b) says, Christianity and national identity grew up together. The arrival of Christianity predated Nyasaland as a political unit. In 1875, two Scottish missions were established: the Church of Scotland in Blantyre, in the south; and the Free Church of Scotland at Livingstonia, in the north. They thus preceded the British protectorate, which was lobbied for by the missions as the only way of preventing takeover by the Portuguese. The latter would be a disaster for the Scots' vision of a land set apart from white settlement (Portuguese or Rhodesian), a land of 'Christianity and Commerce'. As one of their missionaries declared in 1895, '"Africa for the Africans" has been our policy from the first.'

Thus, says Ross, Malawi began as a product of the missionary imagination. In colonial Nyasaland, two large churches developed: the Church of Central Africa – Presbyterian (CCAP – a fusion of the Scottish missions and a Dutch Reformed mission) and the Catholic Church. The Presbyterians educated the emerging black elite and were often critical of colonial policy, while the Catholics were mostly rural and politically conformist. The nationalist movement was predominantly Presbyterian; of 1500 people detained in 1959, 1200 were of that church. In the first cabinet after independence, eight of the ten ministers were products of Presbyterian schools. The church was, in short, too close to the government to maintain its tradition of social witness.

Within weeks of independence, national unity was shattered. President Banda, a Presbyterian elder, dismissed all northern and southern ministers and established the political hegemony of Chewa-speakers from the central region. Political control became ever more repressive, and the churches remained silent, as Banda ruled as life president until the early 1990s.

By 1992 times were changing in Africa. Neighbouring Zambia had had free elections and turned out the incumbent. The Malawian economy was battered by drought. But it was not the Presbyterians, who had a tradition of social criticism in Malawi, who took the bull by the horns, but the traditionally passive Catholics. With some encouragement from the international church, the bishops began the Malawian transition with a Lenten Pastoral Letter. Three months later, the Presbyterians had the courage to follow and go further. The situation had deteriorated in the meantime, since Western donors had suspended aid. Even so, the Presbyterians needed the support (and prodding?) of the international church in order to act. In June 1992 a delegation from the World Alliance of Reformed Churches visited Malawi and accompanied the church leaders to present an open letter to Banda, suggesting specific reforms.

Presbyterians needed the help, protection and perhaps stimulus of the World Alliance in order to overcome 'local subversion', that is, the subverting by local interests of the values of the worldwide church to which they belong, something which is much more common in less hierarchical churches such as Presbyterianism than in hierarchical churches such as Catholicism. Even so, the action caused deep divisions among Presbyterians, for two reasons: mission history and regionalism. The CCAP was really a union of three mission churches. The southern synod, of Church of Scotland origin, was historically close to the Blantyre-based government, and took a critical but conciliatory approach. The northern synod, of Free Church of Scotland origin, was more confrontational because it was situated in the disaffected north. But the central synod, of South African Dutch Reformed origin, besides having little tradition of social critique, was located in the heartland of Banda's power base. In fact, it stayed out of the public initiatives altogether. This regionalism was exemplified in the 1994 general election, when each of the three regions gave overwhelming support to a different party.

In this situation, Ross feels the CCAP can still be a custodian of national identity. Although not immune to tribal fragmentation, it has retained a Christian vision of the nation and a nationwide organisation. Malawi is thus an interesting case to investigate the nation-building power of Christianity in Africa, in the light of Hastings' sombre warnings. The CCAP has a strong evangelical component to it; but one would also like to know what the smaller evangelical churches are doing in this phase of democratic consolidation.

CHAPTER 14

Rwanda

Information is somewhat patchy on Rwanda as far as evangelical involvement in (unfortunately the word is probably correct) and reaction to the genocide of 1994 are concerned. The importance of Rwanda for our study is that it was the cradle of one of the great evangelical revivals, the East African Revival of the late 1930s and early 1940s. Ian Linden's *Church and Revolution in Rwanda* (1977) places the Revival in political context. There are two main ethnic groups in Rwanda, the majority and 'traditionally' subservient Hutu and the minority and 'traditionally' dominant Tutsi. The Tutsi court and aristocracy had become Catholic, so evangelical Protestantism, transmitted through the Anglican Church Missionary Society, inherited the mantle of the Nyabingi prophetesses as the Hutu dissident cult. The Revival, increasingly independent of mission control, was a translation of the CMS teaching on the radical sinfulness of man and of pagan society, plus an emphasis on the Holy Spirit, into the medium of witch-calling and Nyabingi shamanism.

The Revival, says Linden, was partly caused by social and political upheavals and by the Catholic monopoly of chiefly office. As the Belgian demand for forced labour mounted, the Protestant Hutu were discriminated against and beaten. For them, Catholicism was merely nominal Christianity and they alone had the true faith. 'Resentment engendered by discrimination became internalised as an intensified sense of personal wickedness' (1977: 205).

Today, Rwanda is about 18 per cent Protestant, amongst Anglicans, Presbyterians, Free Methodists, Baptists and Pentecostals. Longman, writing before the genocide, says Protestant church leaders remained silent during earlier ethnic violence (1995: 195). In fact, they were even more reticent to criticise the government than Catholics. The president of the Presbyterian Church was on the council of the then (Hutu) ruling party, and the Anglican archbishop strongly supported the government.

However, in 1991 Catholic and Protestant leaders formed an ecumenical council (including Adventists and pentecostals) to bring government and opposition together after the 1990 invasion by the Rwandan Patriotic Front (RPF), launched from Uganda where many Tutsis had lived since being ousted from power at the time of independence.

Nevertheless, Longman presciently said the churches were ominously silent about human rights, even massacres by practising church members. He described one Presbyterian parish where pastors and lay leaders were known to be involved in the right-wing Hutu nationalist group implicated in violent attacks. Within Protestantism, there had been substantial growth of theologically conservative, anti-political movements. The *abarakore*, the saved, generally preached against involvement in political parties. They saw Rwanda's crisis as foreshadowing the second coming of Christ, and thus impossible to oppose (1995: 203).

The coming crisis was not unforeseeable and certainly not negligible. A 1993 article in *Le Flambeau* stated that 'Rwandese fascists and their chiefs have decided to apply "the final solution" to their fellow citizens' (in McCullum 1995: 16). For some time, the government-controlled media had been inciting to ethnic hatred, urging citizens to kill all Tutsis. McCullum adds: 'to the best of my knowledge, no church leader ever spoke out against' these broadcasts (ibid.: 18).

On 6 April 1994, the death of the Hutu president, attributed to Tutsi rebels, was the signal to begin the genocide, which lasted for three months until the interim government was driven out by the RPF. Estimates of the number of dead vary from half a million to a million, with another two million going as refugees to Tanzania and Zaire (mostly Hutus terrified of the RPF's revenge, and including many organisers of genocide).

There are different versions of Christian involvement. One is favoured by many Christian Hutus, including those Anglican bishops who went into exile: it was a mutual genocide, church leaders in exile have to minister to exiles and it is dangerous to go back. Tutsi Christians usually give a different version: Christians did nothing to prevent the massacres, it was a failure of the church, and Hutu churchmen fled because they were involved with the Hutu government and even with the genocide itself.

The latter seems to tally better with existing accounts. McCullum talks of an 'almost deafening silence from churches' (ibid.: 28). The greatest blame must go to the Catholic Church, which claimed a 60 per cent allegiance and whose leadership was notoriously close to the government. However, Protestant churches 'had a disproportionate degree of influence right up to the office of the president'. Their statements during the genocide were 'inadequate and insignificant' (ibid.: 65). Eight of eleven Anglican bishops fled the country when the extremist Hutu government fell. The archbishop was 'unrepentant for his support of the extremists', with whom he maintained contact in the refugee camps. In a press conference in Nairobi in June 1994, when most of the killing had already occurred, he blamed the RPF and called the government 'peace-loving' (ibid.: 81). He even refused to assent to a document published on 13 May, more than a month into the genocide. This document, signed by four Catholic and four Anglican bishops, and the heads of the Presbyterian, Methodist, Free Methodist, Baptist and Pentecostal churches, apportioned blame equally to the RPF and the government, without mentioning genocide (ibid.: 69).

Longman goes further. 'Some clergy and many other church employees and lay leaders ... took important roles in organising the genocide.' One pastor oversaw organisation of the nightly death squads. Protestant and Catholic leaders remained silent, finally issuing a weak letter calling for peace in May, after the most extensive killing was completed. The population interpreted silence as endorsement. 'Many of the faithful interpreted the well-known personal dislike for the Tutsi of many national and local church leaders and the close association of church leaders with the leaders of the genocide as a message that the genocide was consistent with church teachings' (1998: 10). Longman tells of two Presbyterians from Kibuye. Amani, a Hutu, was a devout lay leader. He became local president of the Coalition for the Defence of the Republic (CDR), the virulently anti-Tutsi group that split from the governing MRND in 1992 and effectively took control after the president's death in April 1994. On that occasion, Amani directed the local 'self-defence' efforts. He encouraged Tutsi to gather at a church school, promising protection. Later, he personally led the gang that slaughtered all sixty of them. One of them was Géras, a Tutsi agronomist who ran a Presbyterian development project, whose life had been dedicated to empowering peasants and denouncing ethnic prejudice. As Longman muses, 'the mixed response of churches ... should give pause to those who view civil society in romantic terms as inherently democratic' (ibid.: 15ff).

McCullum also talks of Protestant martyrs, such as the Anglican dean of St Etienne cathedral, a Tutsi who refused to abandon his post and saved many lives before being killed. 'Small movements existed within the churches which did work for justice, peace, human rights and democratisation. [They] were early targets of the militias' (1995: 77). Some accounts wish to go further. Shenk says 'it seems that those committed to violence chose first to attack the revivalists, who were known everywhere as the reconcilers'. Shenk quotes a missionary source estimating that fifty thousand revivalists were killed (1997: 135–6). There is no indication of how this number was calculated, but it would mean about 6 per cent of genocide victims, not implausible since revivalists are a large part of the Protestant community of 18 per cent. However, it would also mean revivalists were not singled out. But most revivalists were Hutu, and it may be they were over-represented among the Hutu victims, or at least were one of the groups whom the organisers earmarked to be killed first.

Available sources do not seem to confirm Shenk's assessment. Prunier's list of those targeted first does not include revivalists, unless subsumed under another category. He mentions pro-democracy politicians, civil rights activists, some journalists, Hutu sympathisers of opposition parties, Hutu who looked like Tutsi, intellectuals in general, and, above all, every single Tutsi man, woman and child. Prunier estimates that about eight hundred thousand Tutsi were killed (some 85 per cent of all Tutsi in Rwanda), and between ten thousand and thirty thousand opposition Hutu, totalling 11 per cent of the population. Revenge killings by the RPF account for no more than 2 per cent of the total (1995: 267). So much for the notion of 'mutual genocide' put out by people such as the Anglican hierarchy in exile. It would also make the claim of fifty thousand Hutu revivalists being singled out for slaughter unlikely; Tutsi revivalists would, of course, be killed just for being Tutsi.

Most of the evidence regarding Christian stances concerns church hierarchies. Revivalists tend not to be among them, and are often at odds with them (Longman 1998: 13). McCullum says leaders of other churches were as unwilling as Catholic and Anglican leaders to take courageous stands; sources within churches suggest they had been bought off with presidential favours (1995: 80). This is plausible from what we know about many evangelical leaders elsewhere. It may still be that grass-roots Protestants, many of whom would be revivalists, did oppose the genocide and were disproportionately among those targeted; but this needs to be demonstrated rather than just affirmed, since the history of evangelicalism does not give solid grounds for presuming it was so.

In fact, as Prunier says, there was one important difference between Catholic and Protestant churches: an admission of guilt at a high level by the latter. He is referring to Roger Bowen, general secretary of Mid-Africa Ministry, part of the Anglican evangelical CMS. His 1996 article makes disturbing reading. It talks of 'close involvement of Christians' in the ethnic violence. 'For Anglican Rwandans, the evangelical heritage of the East African Revival, for all the blessings associated with it, failed to equip the churches to challenge the conditions which led to mass murder.' Revival, by and large, 'was unable to deal with the ethnic and power issues within the Christian community itself, let alone in the wider society'. Its combination of pietism and dispensationalism can lead either to withdrawal or to uncritical support of whoever is in power. Both reactions are discernible in Rwanda. Anglican leadership was exclusively Hutu. There were glorious exceptions to this triumph of ethnic feeling, and the stories have yet to be told of heroism by Hutu Christians who protected their Tutsi neighbours. However, as Bowen stresses, mere growth in numbers without costly discipleship is powerless to confront the pressures of evil. There is little awareness of the solidarities of sin in which we are all embedded as members of society. Sin tends to be simplified to that of the individual, while the corporate nature of man is lost to view and the full magnitude of evil most seriously underestimated. The Revival doctrine of sin underestimates the power and depth of evil. In addition, Bowen blames authoritarian church leadership and church teaching methods which discourage reflection.

Rwanda is thus a vivid example of the impotence and collusion of anti-political evangelicalism, of the price that can be paid for the lack of a theology of the public sphere. Whatever the ethnic dynamics in the original revival, there were decades of opportunity to teach about public dimensions of radical sinfulness. The genocide was not at all unforeseeable; there had been dress rehearsals without, it seems, a reading of the signs of the times. But many evangelical communities of other nations could scarcely throw the first stone.

CHAPTER 15

Uganda

The picture is little better in Uganda, also influenced by the Revival. Uganda, despite British colonisation, is predominantly Catholic, but Protestants are 30 per cent, the largest group being the (Anglican) Church of Uganda. 'The real life of the Anglican Church has for long been carried forward by the Revival Movement rather than by the establishment' (Hastings, in Baur 1994: 487).

Waliggo claims that neither Catholics nor Anglicans have developed, at the institutional level, a clear theology or pastoral strategy for challenging tyranny (1995: 206). This is crucial for Anglicanism, since 'from Kabaka Muteesa II to Yoweri Museveni, all heads of state in Uganda have had an Anglican background' – except for Idi Amin (Ward 1995: 103). Even assassination and exiling of bishops has not provoked such a theology or strategy. Ward asks whether the Church of Uganda could have done more to prevent the descent into barbarism under Amin. It suffered serious weaknesses: quasi-establishment tradition, factionalism, failure to confront human-rights abuses early enough, during Obote's first government, and Catholic–Anglican rivalries which were transferred to party politics (ibid.: 82).

This last point is crucial. Waliggo says that by 1892 the hierarchy of religions in Buganda had been set: Anglicans on top, then Catholics, then Muslims and lastly traditionalists (1995: 208). By Ugandan independence in the 1960s, 'the institutional Anglican Church stood for the status quo which would ensure the continued hegemony of its followers. The institutional Catholic Church advocated power sharing between its followers and the Anglicans. For both churches, Muslims and traditionalists were destined to be forever marginalised. This conception is at the root of the failure to promote genuine democratic governance' (ibid.: 209).

After independence, the Catholic Church became associated with the Democratic Party and the Church of Uganda with the Uganda People's

Congress. In addition, the leaders of the Kabaka Yekka, the Buganda party, were Protestant laymen. So politics was permeated by religion. The first African Anglican archbishop was a *balokole* (revivalist), uninterested in politics (Ward 1995: 74).

Under Amin, Anglicans and other churches suffered greatly. Archbishop Luwum was murdered in 1977; for Ward, his fate was essentially because of his Acholi ethnicity rather than his Christianity, though Pirouet says it was because of the joint Christian-Muslim protests against violence (1995: 251). With hindsight, Pirouet says interventions by religious leaders had come too late. 'Action had been needed when things first began to slip during [Obote's first government, 1962–71], or during the first two or three months of Amin . . . It is doubtful whether approaches that are not publicised [as church leaders reputedly made early on to Amin] can achieve much' (ibid.: 251).

The lesson was not learnt. When Amin was overthrown and Obote returned to power, violence and factionalism continued. In addition, old political allegiances reasserted themselves, making joint Catholic-Anglican action harder. Anglican bishops were divided in their response to the regime's barbarities, and the archbishop refused to blame the army, preferring to use private influence on the government (ibid.: 255).

There is another dimension in this. When the archbishop was murdered in 1977, four other bishops fled into exile. In only one case was there no ethnic factor. Festo Kivengere, a leader of the Revival, was also outspoken on human rights, even when his own ethnic affiliation was not at stake. He had preached powerful sermons warning government officials of their accountability to God and calling attention to the robbery, violence and killing. He returned to Uganda after Amin's fall, but was passed over for archbishop because colleagues wanted someone acceptable to the new Obote government, intent on courting the Anglican hierarchy. Kivengere said in 1983: 'We have a government [almost entirely] of members of our church . . . We are constantly appealed to by . . . government to take the lead in "spiritual rehabilitation" . . . This sounds tremendous but . . . words do not mean actions . . . When the government is putting us in this position of favour, speaking the truth becomes doubly difficult' (in Pirouet 1995: 254).

Kivengere's *balokole* commitment did not prevent him from transcending its apolitical limitations. This earned him the admiration of Yoweri Museveni, president since 1986 after triumphing in a guerrilla struggle. Museveni himself had been active in the *balokole* at school, and 'the training in leadership, intellectual debate and moral commitment which the revival gave him was important in his development as a politician' (Ward 1995: 99). But he had come to reject its unworldly pietism and apolitical stance.

Museveni is generally regarded as a marked improvement on all that has gone before in Uganda, even if Waliggo's account is too partisan. Waliggo stresses the innovative democratic nature of Museveni's government, even though multi-party democracy has not been reintroduced. Museveni's alternative is participatory democracy through Resistance Councils and other associations. This is supposed to be a movement system rather than a one-party system. A Constituent Assembly was elected in 1994, after an innovative process in which sectors of the public were heard for suggestions. According to Waliggo, all churches participated actively, including newer 'born-again' ones. Religious leaders topped the list of people whom the public wanted to be represented in the Assembly, but this suggestion was rejected by parliament. The Constituent Assembly voted to prolong the existing system for five years, but called for non-party parliamentary and presidential elections. Some of the southern and western kingdoms would prefer a federal government.

Waliggo adds an insightful addendum. The Joint Christian Council is made up of Anglicans, Catholics and Orthodox; other churches have not been invited. The new Christian groups feel marginalised. Democratisation depends on a genuine ecumenical spirit among Christians and a respectful dialogue with Muslims (1995: 223). Especially, we may add, when a 'movement' system is in place, which internalises political struggle within each sector.

Uganda, like Rwanda, illustrates the cost of apolitical evangelicalism, and of the inability to develop a theology and strategy of resistance. It also illustrates questions of ethnicity, nationhood and religion. As Hastings says, 'if there existed one nation-state in nineteenth-century black Africa, Buganda would have a good claim to be it... The Luganda Bible [and other early Christian literature] give the impression of carrying the Baganda across a line they had already nearly reached dividing ethnicity from nationhood' (1997: 155–6). But a Buganda nation-state, says Hastings, was not to be. Or could it still be, we may ask? Should colonial boundaries be sacrosanct for contemporary Christian politics? Either way, there are difficult problems, on which Africa's burgeoning evangelicalism (and especially that within 'mainline' churches such as the Church of Uganda) needs to reflect.

There is also the figure of Festo Kivengere to show that the Revival heritage can be combined with political astuteness, responsibility and courage. To what extent is his example taken up by *balokole* laity today? How did they participate in the constitutional debates of the early 1990s? What is (and should be) the churches' position regarding the Museveni approach to a different form of democracy for Africa? Is there any future in this model (beyond Museveni's personal integrity)? What contribution (in public and ecclesiastical life) can evangelicals make now to prevent a return to barbarism in post-Museveni Uganda?

New pentecostal churches have mushroomed lately. What are their political roles? They do not make public pronouncements like the 'mainline' churches. This paucity of academic knowledge is typical, and reflects a lack of adventurousness and innovativeness, or even elitist disdain. Gifford (1998) sees the plethora of new churches as a parallel to the Museveni era. Museveni sees himself as creating a 'new dispensation'. The Catholic and Anglican churches are of the old dispensation, whereas the 'born-again' movement is part of the reconstruction. It is often said that Museveni is surrounding himself with born-agains. In a tax-department retrenchment, no born-agains were dismissed; as a result, revenue nearly trebled immediately, such is the greater honesty of born-agains. In Museveni's Uganda, pentecostalism may be an opting-in rather than an opting-out (1998: 170). One would like to know more about how this supposed political affinity really functions. Gifford himself says that in 1990 pentecostal radio and television programmes were banned because the government was worried about the religious intolerance manifested (ibid.: 175).

CHAPTER 16

Ghana

Ghana is the most Protestant country of West Africa (33 per cent) (Baur 1994: 524). Its Protestantism is fairly pulverised, with traditional, pentecostal and new charismatic churches all strong. As in many African countries, the Christian elite spearheaded the independence movement, in 1957 becoming the first colony in black Africa to achieve freedom. At the forefront was the Presbyterian J. B. Danquah, an intellectual who in 1947 founded the moderate United Gold Coast Convention, rivalled later by Nkrumah's mass-oriented Convention People's Party. Danquah's contribution to the new constitution was great, but when he ran against Nkrumah for president in 1960 he polled only 10 per cent. Still attacking Nkrumah's dictatorial rule, Danquah was imprisoned and died in 1965.

For all Nkrumah's excesses, he stopped short of open confrontation with Christianity. From 1981, Flight-Lieutenant Jerry John Rawlings governed dictatorially, but in 1990 he permitted debate on a democratic system. The Catholic Bishops Conference and the Christian Council had active roles in the transition, making suggestions to government and mediating between it and opposition parties to ensure parliamentary elections in December 1992. The presidential elections of the previous month, won by Rawlings himself, were denounced by the opposition. But international observers from the Carter Center of Emory University, Atlanta, considered the elections ultimately fair. (The role of the Carter Center and of the ex-president himself can also be considered indirect evangelical involvement in Third World politics.)

Dickson notes that the Christian Council and the Catholic Bishops tried to involve Muslim leaders in these initiatives but not other churches. Dickson contrasts the former churches with the latter. 'These churches, not being members of the Christian Council, were not involved in the attempts to bring about a political dialogue in the interests of peace' – a seemingly damning indictment. But the same paragraph admits that 'no invitation had gone from the Christian Council ... to join in' (1995: 274).

The Dickson article is a classic example of not taking factors internal to the religious field into account in explaining political action. Gifford's article on charismatic churches highlights the importance of the omission. He stresses the rising status of pastors of these new urban, mostly middle-class groups. 'Gone are the days when mainline Protestant and Catholic churchmen were the acknowledged religious leaders, moving among the elites of business and government, with the pastors of independent churches excluded as uneducated nonentities' (1994a: 259).

Gifford portrays two pastors who give an idea not only of the new roles these leaders play, but of the dangers of lumping them together politically. Duncan Williams, of Christian Action Faith Ministries International, founded in 1979, has become a major figure in Ghanaian Christianity. In 1994, a national thanksgiving service was held for the first anniversary of the Fourth Republic, attended by Rawlings. The churchmen leading the service were the Catholic archbishop, the Anglican bishop and Duncan Williams. The first two were determined not to let the event become a celebration of Rawlings, but Williams was fulsome in his praise of the president. He thus received more coverage than the other churchmen in the state-owned media, while the free press criticised Williams' 'culture of sycophancy'. Gifford feels desire for respectability and material rewards is what motivates such attitudes.

It would be interesting to know how Williams, whose church is new and not among the largest, managed to achieve this public status. It is not just a question of desire for respectability and benefits, which is true of many religious leaders, but of the dynamics of his rise to public visibility. We suspect that, besides inter-church rivalries (in which newer and older leaders and institutions struggle for legitimacy and space), a dynamic more directly related to the political field may be at work.

But Gifford also talks of another charismatic leader with a different discourse. Mensa Otabil, of the International Central Gospel Church, preaches black pride as well as the gospel of success. He talks of providing leadership for Africa. The West plays 'political and industrial games', ensuring 'we will always be running but never catch up ... I get amused when we talk of breaking the yoke of colonialism and still use the blacksmith called IMF or World Bank to sharpen our tools' (1994a: 261). Otabil used to say the Third World had to learn God's economic system, that is, the laws of prosperity theology. But by 1994 he was stressing structures: 'We can get everyone in Africa saved, but that won't solve our problem... You can have a Christian president or whatever, but that may not change anything, because poverty is not spiritual... We have to build new structures to empower you'. Before you can be blessed you have to own your own land. 'The key lies in a work-conscious, ownership-conscious, skilled populace' (in Gifford 1998: 241–2). Of course, as Gifford says, all this ignores the difficulty of getting capital or training in Africa, and Otabil never mentions the role that Africa's own elite has played. He does not really have a theology of a just society, and certainly not a preferential option for the poor. Even so, we would love to know how this translates into political practice.

The largest Protestant church is the Church of Pentecost, not really examined by Gifford or Dickson. The numerically largest church cannot be omitted from an analysis of Protestantism and politics. The same goes for the National Association of Evangelicals – how does it relate to the Christian Council and the Catholic Bishops Conference? What has been its political stance, and what factors have influenced it?

Since the 1996 elections, Rawlings' vice-president is an evangelical, John Mills, a university professor from an interdenominational church. Another candidate for president was a charismatic who claimed divine revelation. In the 1992 election, Kwabena Darko, a wealthy farmer and vice-president for Africa of the Full Gospel Businessmen's Fellowship International, ran for president. There is room for a 'Brazil-type' analysis of these initiatives, as well as of politicians at other levels in (at least partially) redemocratised Ghana.

CHAPTER 17

Kenya

The *Guardian* of 8 July 1997 has a photograph which takes us immediately into the world of evangelical politics in Kenya. It shows pro-democracy demonstrators fleeing as police open fire. Amongst them are clergymen clutching Bibles. The police chased demonstrators into the Anglican Cathedral; later, the evangelical archbishop held a service to cleanse the cathedral from its profanation by the police.

Kenya is a predominantly Protestant country, in which the Anglican Church of the Province of Kenya (CPK) is the most important religious institution, and in which evangelical Anglicanism holds a crucial position. Politically, while avoiding African socialism and military coups, Kenya followed as long as possible the one-party model, and then practised 'concession without conversion' (Joseph 1997: 375). President Moi learnt to manipulate the opposition and make gestures to earn approval from foreign donors. Even though opposition votes in 1992 exceeded those for Moi, the latter won, thanks to opposition divisions. The semi-authoritarian model was consolidated at the 1997 elections.

Kenya seemingly follows Gifford's rule: mainline church leaders oppose one-party regimes, but 'evangelical, charismatic and pentecostal churches' support tottering dictators (1994b: 528). Moi, a member of the Africa Inland Church, plays the Christian card to advantage; the state media portrays him as God-fearing and shows him every Sunday in church. His attendance is reciprocated by the flattered church leader. When he attended the Redeemed Gospel Church in February 1992, while pressured to lift the ban on opposition parties, the preacher proclaimed: 'In heaven it is just like Kenya . . . There is only one party – and God never makes a mistake . . . We have freedom of worship. What else do we want?' More direct support was forthcoming at the Africa Church of the Holy Spirit, where over 1,200 people registered as KANU members during the service. The apotheosis came when Korean pentecostal Yonggi Cho, conducting a crusade, said in the presence of Moi that 'Kenya is a blessed country because it has a God-fearing leader.' Throup says that, under pressure from KANU, some of the less well-established churches (a significant phrase) decided it was wise to dissociate from the National Christian Council (NCCK). The African Independent Pentecostal Church, the Full Gospel Church, the Association of Baptist Churches of Nyeri and the United Pentecostal Church expressed support for the new 'queueing' (non-secret) electoral system (1995: 151). The Africa Inland Church broke from the NCCK in the mid 1980s and joined the near-dormant Evangelical Fellowship, making it a key pro-Moi group (Githiga 1997: 17). Only the major Protestant churches and, less so, the Catholic, resisted a more totalitarian political culture (Throup 1995: 169).

But in Kenya, the Anglican Church is largely evangelical. The East African Revival had great effect. Revival believers resisted Mau-Mau and the oathing campaign amongst Kikuyu in 1969. But another tendency was at play: increasing Erastian subordination to the state. Jomo Kenyatta's brother-in-law had been the first African CPK bishop. No church leader spoke out when the opposition KPU was banned. Writing at the end of the Kenyatta period, Lonsdale, Booth-Clibborn and Hake warned: 'The indigenous Kenyan tradition of evangelical Revival, clear-sighted in crisis and prophetic in its defence of Christian autonomy when need arises is, because of its very suspicion of hierarchy and organisation, peculiarly ill-fitted to perceive, let alone guard against, such routine envelopment' (in Throup 1995: 146).

Another reason for amicable church–state relations under Kenyatta was that the CPK and the Presbyterian Church were increasingly dominated by Kikuyu. But Kenyatta's successor, Daniel arap Moi, was not a Kikuyu, and he began to reduce Kikuyu influence, revitalising the only legal party KANU and giving it a new ideology.

From 1982 to 1991 Kenya was a *de jure* one-party state under the Nyayo ('footsteps') ideology (Benson 1995: 178). Moi claims that Nyayoism is derived from the African tradition of public affairs, Christian faith and pragmatism, and is summed up as 'peace, love and unity'. It is a doctrine of top-down mobilisation, suspicious of debate. Nyayoism 'treats the church as "part and parcel of the government". Church leaders are ... just leaders; and all leaders must be part of the leadership corps ... The church is not considered as an entity over against the state' (ibid.: 185).

Erastianism (the doctrine of state control over the church) was thus taken to new lengths. What resources did evangelicalism have for resisting it? The churches had a limited theology of secular power, but a well-developed tradition of evangelical biblical hermeneutics. Evangelicals in the CPK, says Benson, believed themselves obliged to measure any state's actions by the standards of the Scriptures and to compel the state to attend to the Scriptures by preaching. But they only critiqued the consequences and not the theory of Nyayoism. Archbishop Gitari believes the church cannot support one system of government against another; it must critically collaborate with any state which attempts to respect God's purposes. It may not develop a root-and-branch critique of any system not explicitly organised to do evil. The Revival gives anti-hierarchical teaching antithetical to the Nyayo doctrine of sacral leadership; but as the Nyayo state tottered in the early 1990s, the church had no coherent alternative to offer (ibid.: 191–5).

Significant contributions to defence of democracy and human rights came from individual church leaders rather than institutions. Unlike the Catholic tradition of collective pastorals, it was courageous individuals who spoke out, perhaps because of the Revival heritage of institutional suspicion, plus the CPK's position as an autonomous national church within the Anglican Communion rather than as a branch of the worldwide Catholic Church with an authoritative social magisterium. Three CPK bishops (Muge, Okullu and Gitari) and the prominent Presbyterian minister Timothy Njoya have been the main critics. Muge was killed in a mysterious crash in 1990; the others have suffered harrassment and been criticised by the state press and government. Even so, the fact is that for many years it was only possible to criticise government without risking detention or worse if one was a church leader. And even then, only if one's church had international connections which would make the government think twice before acting. The CPK and the Presbyterians 'have preserved close contacts . . . with the wider Christian world and can less easily be intimidated than the Kenya-based independent churches' (Throup 1995: 160). We see the importance of global links, and the cultural capital which usually accompanies them, in making possible resistance to oppressive governments. While theology is undoubtedly important in Christian political action, it is but one factor amongst many. Before we make generalisations about evangelicalism and politics, we must take into account variables such as ecclesiastical position and international connections.

Ironically Throup concludes that the churches' 'conservative ideology has . . . enabled them . . . to serve as one of the last redoubts for secular liberalism and democracy' (1995: 173). For Sabar-Friedman (1997), the CPK, Presbyterians and Catholics offered a primary challenge to Moi, generating a public discourse on democracy and change. This covered a definition of politics and legitimate exercise of power, as well as questions of corruption and local conflicts. Although Haynes says criticism of government must be vociferous and broad-based before senior churchmen add their weight to it (1996: 85), this hardly applies to some CPK bishops. It was often they who took the forefront. This was recognised by Moi when, seeking international credibility, he added a former Presbyterian moderator and a bishop of the Redeemed Gospel Church to the KANU review committee on the party system (Throup 1995: 166). (The clerics named, of course, were tame and did not play a prominent role.)

As transition to some sort of multi-partyism loomed, Bishop Okullu, close to fellow-Luo opposition politician Odinga Oginga, became chairman of the Justice and Peace Convention steering committee. The NCCK, and especially CPK and Presbyterian clergy, were often identified with the incipient opposition parties, and association with Kikuyu interests had not been totally overcome (Sabar-Friedman 1997: 46–7). As Githiga says: 'One can see tribal loyalty in the outspokenness of the church leaders. They did not only speak on behalf of their churches, but also on behalf of their ethnic group as elders' (1997: 100). Bishop Muge, assassinated in 1990, was from the Nandi sub-group of Kalenjin which felt excluded from the benefits of Kalenjin president Moi's government. 'Muge was seen by the Nandi as a leader who could fight for their rights', and not just as a church leader (ibid.: 164). While the CPK and the Presbyterian Church are dominated by the disaffected Kikuyu and Luo, churches in the Evangelical Fellowship tend to be Kalenjin and pro-Moi. Githiga concludes that a weakness of those churches critical of Moi is that they themselves have not achieved the inter-ethnic unity they demand of the state. The CPK failed to mediate between the divided opposition in 1992, allowing Moi to be re-elected with a minority vote (ibid.: 259, 322).

Nevertheless, in 1992 the NCCK, CPK and Catholic Episcopal Conference set up a National Ecumenical Civic Education Programme, to replace existing organisms such as the CPK's Education for Participatory Democracy. The study of these organisms and their effectiveness would be a profitable theme. As the first multi-party elections since 1963 approached, pamphlets were produced on a range of topics: Why

You Should Vote; Towards Multi-Party Democracy in Kenya; Issues to Consider in the Forthcoming Multi-Party Elections; and A Guide to Election Monitoring.

Njoya and Okullu have written on a theology of power and stand in the evangelical tradition (Benson 1995: 187), but more influential than either has been David Gitari, the most articulate representative of Kenyan evangelical hermeneutics (and, since 1997, archbishop), whose controversial sermons have been published. He is a product of the Third World evangelicalism which came to prominence at the Lausanne congress of 1974, a sort of Vatican II of world evangelicalism both in the new vistas it opened up and in the subsequent internal battles over its interpretation. Gitari, like some Latin Americans, represented a more thoroughgoing socio-political emphasis than much establishment First World evangelicalism was prepared to swallow for very long.

But if Gitari is a product of this international wing in evangelicalism, he also represents an almost uniquely direct and influential application of it to political reality. This is made possible by the degree of Christianisation of Kenyan society, the institutional position of the CPK and the discrediting of the political system. This combination of advantages is not common in Third World evangelicalism. But Gitari's own initiative and courage were also necessary, since not all CPK bishops have acted in anything like the same manner.

Gitari's sermons are direct, usually starting with exposition of a biblical passage which is then applied to recent political events, such as the introduction of a one-party system, the queueing system for voting, rigged elections or specific cases of corruption or violence. He is always diplomatic, often praising as well as condemning, and calling on Christians to pray for political leaders and 'give them a chance' to do good even if, for example, they have been 'selected' and not elected. He often uses *ad hominem* language, adopting the slogans of the government and making them mean what they purport to: 'Regardless of where they classify you, you remain a true Nyayo follower if you are working for peace in the spirit of love by struggling against all kinds of injustice' (1996: 89).

However, Gitari is direct in his denunciations. In 1982, he preached on Esther chapter 4 ('who knows but that you have come to your position for such a time as this? Only do not keep silent!') to criticise MPs' docility towards the bill making Kenya a one-party state. On another occasion, the story of Naboth's vineyard, appropriated by king Ahab, 'urges us to know our fundamental human rights and to defend those rights at whatever cost. The story also serves as a warning to all land grabbers ... we cannot be mere spectators watching a few rich people and politicians grab as much land as they want ... Was there no Naboth to say "no" [on the city council]?' (ibid.: 105).

As Gitari and other outspoken clerics are often called troublemakers, he uses King Ahab's reference to the prophet Elijah ('is that you, you troubler of Israel?') to ask: 'Who are the troublers in Kenya? They are the land-grabbers, the election riggers, the councillors who ... participate in wrong decision-making ... [who] wish queueing method of elections ... [who] organise thuggery and raiding of people's homes ... who refuse to improve our human rights record' (ibid.: 109). Similarly with Ezekiel chapter 34 ('you are doomed, you shepherds of Israel'): 'The leaders in Kenya today are no different from the leaders of Israel ... in caring for themselves ... African leaders keep millions of dollars in foreign banks' (ibid.: 112). And 'we have in this country been building a tower of Babel [KANU] ... The idea was that by speaking a "one party language", Kenyans would be united in accordance to the wishes of "Nimrod" [a favourite biblical symbol for Africa's rapacious rulers]' (ibid.: 118). Departing from biblical analogies, he compares the treatment of a political detainee with that given to Steve Biko by apartheid South Africa (ibid.: 114).

Gitari bases this preaching on 'the Church's heavy responsibility to remind a nation ... of the standard of righteousness and justice which alone can exalt that nation'. Christian leaders 'must come out of their ecclesiastical ghettos and ivory towers to lead the citizens ... in giving active practical moral support to the state when it upholds the standards of righteousness ... If, however, those in authority depart [from such standards], the Church should follow the footsteps of the prophets and the apostles in declaring boldly the righteousness and judgement of God' (ibid.: 14). To the traditional Revival arguments that politics is a dirty game and that believers' duty is just to pray, Gitari responds that this 'leads to prayer without commitment ... We have to cooperate with God in bringing about a just, united, peaceful and liberated nation ... Isn't a game made dirty by players who are themselves dirty? Politics is about the welfare of the people and it is ridiculous for the politicians to expect Church leaders to ... merely spectate ... We are sailing in the same boat' (ibid.: 32). 'Politics is so important in human life that it cannot be left to professional politicians alone' (ibid.: 76).

The Kenyan case thus illustrates many points regarding evangelical politics in the Third World. An ecclesiastical institution may become involved in opposition to a dictatorial state because of its own institutional interests, or because of its own ethnic base, or because it is led into such a posture by a universalistic understanding of the gospel. In the latter case, there are several possibilities.

The first is the typical Revival posture which, as in Korean opposition to Shinto worship, sets non-negotiable limits to the state in its totalitarian aspirations when the latter encroach on religious loyalties. Kenyan examples are Mau-Mau and the 1969 oathing crisis. This is a reactive, not pro-active, politicisation, and the Revival tradition is second to none at it. One must ask, as with pentecostalism in Latin America, what its potential is for creating a democratic political culture.

The second possibility is the evangelical biblical hermeneutics position. Kenya is one of the few cases in Africa in which church leaders have gone beyond mediation to direct contestation (Joseph 1993: 247) – and this was done under evangelical aegis. Kenya thus shows that evangelicalism, given the right institutional location, can support a contestatory role. Kenya is thus a key case for showing the possibilities and limitations of such evangelical politics in the most favourable circumstances as far as location in the religious field is concerned. The lessons could illumine much for evangelical political militancy in other parts of the Third World. Are there intrinsic limitations to such politics under the auspices of an evangelical theology, even in the best of circumstances?

If Kenyan leaders had worked with the third possibility, a theology of power on the lines of Liberation Theology or South African black theology, would they be better placed to make a more integral contribution to politics? And would institutions similar to the Catholic Justice and Peace Commissions have helped?

Many other questions, some familiar from other cases, suggest themselves. How can (and does) Christianity help to consolidate democracy in a multi-ethnic state without a democratic tradition? The relationship between faith and ethnic identity is a key theme for assessing the political impact of the churches in Africa. What do church leaders actually do, not just to speak out in crises when other channels are lacking, but to educate and empower the laity for ongoing political roles? How do churches' internal structures aid or hinder this? We need to know more about how the CPK grass-roots behave politically, and more about the other bishops who do not speak out. And above all, we need more certain knowledge of what happens in the non-mainline churches, beyond the impressionistic evidence which litters the literature, taking seriously not only different traditions of political theology but specific locations within the religious field and society, and the presence or absence of international connections. Finally, it would be useful to have a sociologically and theologically informed case-study of Archbishop Gitari's ongoing role, as an evangelical leader with a national prominence to which many Third World evangelical leaders (for varied reasons) aspire.

CHAPTER 18

Zambia

Zambia is central to the study of evangelicals in politics, because it has a charismatic evangelical president who has brought public visibility to his faith. It is thus a laboratory for studying some typical tendencies in a certain kind of evangelical politics in action in highly favourable circumstances.

Northern Rhodesia became independent in 1964 under Kenneth Kaunda, a former lay preacher of the African Methodist Episcopal Church. His UNIP became the only legal party in 1971. The copper mines (which earned 80 per cent of foreign exchange) were nationalised in the late 1960s, making the state the largest employer in the formal economy. Soon after independence, Presbyterians, Methodists and Paris Mission joined to form the United Church of Zambia (UCZ). This corresponded to Kaunda's call to overcome imported denominations; to the political 'One Zambia, One Nation', the religious 'One Church' should correspond. Desire for ecclesiastical unity was thus mixed with desire to please the new state. The government certainly did not want a plethora of autonomous religious groups (the buzzing civil society which Tocqueville saw as the seed-bed of American democracy), especially in a land that had seen strong anti-statist groups during the colonial period, such as the Watchtower and Alice Lenshina's millenarian movement. The UCZ has at times been almost an established church; in 1980 the synod noted that 'most people in Parliament belong to the UCZ' (Baur 1994: 433). It is described by Johnstone (1993) as having a 'growing evangelical witness'.

Kaunda's one-party regime was one of the least repressive in Africa. He labelled his political philosophy 'humanism' and the churches enjoyed a special position. Some of his closest advisors were clergymen. Later on, however, his closeness to other religions caused tensions with those Christians who 'wanted a monopoly of all matters religious' (Sichone 1996: 123). Especially attacked were his links with the Maharishi Mahesh

Yogi, whose project to make Zambia 'Heaven on Earth' was televised just before the 1991 election (Gifford 1996: 1), and with his spiritual advisor Dr Raganathan. In 1991 the opposition affirmed that Kaunda was not a Christian. The head of the Evangelical Fellowship told the author that 'Kaunda declared himself a follower of various religions, so evangelicals turned against him.' Sanneh's concern to establish acceptable arguments for separation of religion and state (1996: 137–41) is clearly pertinent in Zambia. Kaunda, of course, also wanted church support for his regime, and is said to have received it from the Apostolic Faith Church (Gifford 1996: 3).

Kaunda's successor arose out of the trade-union movement, one of the strongest in Africa due to the Copperbelt. The Zambian Congress of Trades Unions (ZCTU) had always fought to retain a certain autonomy from the official party. Even after 1985, when the government banned the check-off system to undermine it, workers voluntarily paid their dues because they viewed the ZCTU leadership as free of corruption.

Much credit for this goes to ZCTU chairman Frederick Chiluba. A Zambian Lech Walesa, Chiluba was an employee at a mining company, rising to credit manager before being elected president of the ZCTU in 1974. He took secondary-school examinations by correspondence in 1988. But despite his lack of formal education, he had ample exposure to international unionism and International Labour Organisation (ILO) committees. From 1980, Chiluba led the ZCTU more into a directly political role as *de facto* opposition. In 1981 he was imprisoned for four months. Writing at the end of the Kaunda period, Hamalengwa says: 'The labour movement has ... earned the notice and respect of the majority of Zambians for their consistency in progressive criticism of government' (1992: 119). In late 1989 Chiluba declared that Africa should get rid of one-party rule since Eastern Europe had done so. He helped to organise the Movement for Multi-Party Democracy (MMD). When he won its nomination for president, he resigned from leadership of the ZCTU.

A UCZ member, Chiluba had a born-again experience while in prison in 1981. After release, most of his speeches contained biblical references. Later, he received the gift of tongues at a Reinhard Bonnke crusade (Gifford 1996: 2).

The Zambian economy had been in decline since the mid 1970s with deteriorating terms of trade for copper. The Zambian state was the epitome of the African dilemma, dominant but weak, trying to regulate everything but controlling virtually nothing (White 1995: 66). A

Structural Adjustment Programme (SAP) was started in 1986 but abandoned when it provoked food riots. Another SAP in 1989 sparked off similar unrest, this time presaging Kaunda's end.

If these problems were typical of Africa, less typical were Zambia's relative strengths: its degree of urbanisation (51%), employment in the formal sector and unionisation. This gave it a strong civil society by African standards; but still too weak to establish a coherent political order (ibid.: 69). The MMD was a coalition of unionists, students, businessmen, commercial farmers and religious leaders. The last 'played a particularly cardinal role not only in calling for democratisation but also in brokering the dialogue between the regime and the opposition' (ibid.: 68). Since the daily newspapers were all state owned, Christian newspapers, especially the weekly *National Mirror* (owned jointly by the Catholic Episcopal Conference and the Christian Council), played a crucial role in Kaunda's last days, popularising multi-party democracy (Sichone 1996: 123).

For the October 1991 elections, a monitoring committee was formed by several groups, including the Christian Council and the Evangelical Fellowship (Panter-Brick 1994: 242). Gifford says some UCZ pastors campaigned for Chiluba and the MMD from the pulpit. The 'born-again' churches particularly were thought to be pro-MMD, although some high-profile charismatic preachers were seen as campaigning for Kaunda. But the whole of Gifford's text at this point, despite being the main work on evangelical politics in Zambia, shows how little is really known about the churches' role beyond the *leadership* of the *mainline churches*.

In the end, Chiluba beat Kaunda by a comfortable margin, and the latter conceded defeat. It was the first time that a former British colony in Africa had changed a president through democratic multi-party elections (Chikulo 1996: 31). It seemed a new era had dawned, not only for Zambia but for Africa.

The high hopes were not to be realised. In the opinion of many, a golden opportunity was lost. It was true that Chiluba faced a difficult task in meeting expectations. The coalition of business, unions, students and churchmen could not last. The size of the MMD parliamentary victory (83.4 per cent of seats) meant there was no credible opposition. (The role of a credible opposition is essential in a democracy, and the *de facto* opposition role that some churches have played in dictatorial situations may need playing also in some *de jure* democracies.) Voter turnout, only 43 per cent in 1991, fell to 15 per cent in the 1994 parliamentary elections.

Above all, the critical economic situation and the need for radical reforms to please international donors meant that 'paradoxically, many of the social forces which organised the transition [ran] the risk of being weakened by the actions of the new regime' (White 1995: 69). As Nolutshungu says: 'Political reform was not always, if ever, identified with the unlimited opening of national economies to foreign penetration, the reduction of public expenditure on social welfare, or the large-scale privatisation of national assets' (ibid.: 70).

The government became increasingly dominated by business interests, but divided between more reformist and more cronyist elements. Reforms have made a narrow elite close to the MMD hierarchy extremely rich (*Africa Confidential*, 21 June 1996). Only ministers and their business colleagues have gained from privatisation, says public belief (ibid., 14 Feb. 1997). The MMD acronym took on other meanings in popular parlance: Make Money and Depart (but they have not departed), or Mass Movement for Drug-Dealers (Gifford 1996: 8). No ministers linked to corruption have been sacked (*Africa Report*, Mar.–Apr. 1994: 60).

Election promises have not been kept, such as the commitment to sell off the public media (now a mouthpiece of the MMD) (Gifford 1996: 11), and to abolish the one-industry-one-union policy. The latter betrayal has cost Chiluba much union support (Mihyo 1995: 211). Tribal favouritism, a blight of Kaunda's latter years, has returned under Chiluba, this time favouring his own Bemba (who at one stage held twenty-two out of twenty-five cabinet posts). Zambia is an example of what Horowitz calls a 'severely-divided society', in which multiethnic parties tend to decompose. Just as Kaunda had had multiethnic support against the British and then lost it, so had Chiluba against him; but in little over a year, the cycle restarted. All the tactics of a virtual one-party state reappeared. A year after taking power, Chiluba decreed a state of emergency in order to detain leaders of UNIP.

It is said that Kaunda's defeat sent shock waves across Africa and persuaded the old guard of dictators that they needed to learn the ropes of making superficial concessions while retaining effective power. But it seems Chiluba himself has also learnt from the Zambian case, and discovered how to maintain power as efficiently as the veteran dictators. After Kaunda had announced his candidature for 1996, Chiluba made a botched attempt to deport him to Malawi. Main opposition leaders survived strange road accidents (*Africa Confidential*, 1 Dec. 1995). Finally, Chiluba had the constitution changed so Kaunda would be excluded from running; a candidate must have been born in Zambia of Zambian

parents, a criterion Kaunda cannot meet. Safely re-elected, Chiluba
began to talk of regulating all non-governmental organisations and the
press. The Home Affairs Minister said 'people cannot be allowed to talk
anyhow against the state' (ibid., 14 Feb. 1997).

Once the 1996 elections were over (Chiluba 82 per cent; MMD 130
out of 150 seats), police invaded the offices of election monitors, the
leaders of the second-placed party (a schism from the MMD) went into
hiding and Chiluba placed the security forces on alert (ibid., 29 Nov.
1996). At the end of 1997 a supposed coup attempt gave Chiluba reason
to detain many opposition leaders, including Kaunda himself.

All of this happened within a unique relationship between evangelicalism and national politics. The MMD 1991 campaign manifesto had
said that it 'accepts that Zambia is a Christian country which is tolerant
of other religions... The MMD acknowledges the particular significance of churches and religious communities [and] shall welcome
criticism, ideas and practical cooperation from religious groups' (in
Chanda n/d: 78). Several ministers in his first cabinet (as well as some
provincial governors) were evangelical pastors, including the Minister
and Vice-Minister of Information and Broadcasting Services (one re-
members Brazilian evangelicals' concern for media questions). The
Minister, the Revd Stan Kristafor, banned Muslim radio programmes.
But he did not last in his post; as a white Zambian and wealthy
businessman, he was dismissed from government for alleged racist
treatment of employees (Gifford 1996: 6). In 1996 the head of the
Evangelical Fellowship claimed 'about five born-again ministers'.

After Chiluba's 1991 victory, the three Christian bodies (Christian
Council [CCZ], Evangelical Fellowship [EFZ] and Catholic Bishops
Conference) combined for what was almost, according to Gifford (1996:
4), a coronation service in the Anglican Cathedral. Then, on 29 December 1991, Chiluba proclaimed Zambia a 'Christian nation'. Saying 'a
nation is blessed whenever it enters into a covenant with God', he
repented on behalf of the people of Zambia

of our wicked ways of idolatry, witchcraft, the occult, immorality, injustice and
corruption... I submit the Government and the entire nation of Zambia to the
Lordship of Jesus Christ. I further declare that Zambia is a Christian nation
that will seek to be governed by the righteous principles of the word of God.
Righteousness and justice must prevail in all levels of authority, and then we
shall see the righteousness of God exalting Zambia.

The announcement took people by surprise, and its implications were
unclear. The Catholic hierarchy (ECZ) and the CCZ had not been

consulted. Even the EFZ had not been consulted as a body, says Gifford. The idea was either Chiluba's (denied by the head of the EFZ in 1996) or that of Brigadier General Godfrey Miyanda. Miyanda was Minister without Portfolio, and later vice-president. (In 1997, when favourite to succeed Chiluba in 2001, Miyanda was removed from the vice-presidency.) Gifford also suggests that a group of Danish Apostolic Church missionaries on the Copperbelt may have had something to do with it, though he does not clarify how. 'Chiluba may have contacted officials of the EFZ, who may have been reluctant to bring in the other bodies, probably because they saw this as their hour, having in the past felt themselves overshadowed by the ECZ and the CCZ' (Gifford 1996: 5). So many 'may haves' and 'probablys' in one sentence shows how little we really know about the evangelical role, although Gifford may be right to detect intra-Protestant rivalry. The CCZ may have not only 'overshadowed' but looked down their noses at the EFZ, if 'religious centre versus periphery' relations in other countries are anything to go by.

Gifford assesses the reception of the pronouncement by various Protestant sectors. He says, plausibly, that even some who approved the idea were put out by not having been consulted. In a (presumably incomplete) list of those leaders in favour, we find heads of the World Baptist Evangelistic Association, the United Church, the African Methodist Episcopal Church and the Reformed Church – hardly a collection of upstart 'born-again' churches. Yet Gifford suggests a dichotomy between 'mainline' and 'born-agains'. 'The rank and file of the born-again community was euphoric' (ibid.: 5), he says, without any indication of how he found that out. Statements in the press are usually from leaders, not grass-roots members, and (if Brazil is any guide) press material must be used with caution.

This is not to deny that Old Testament theocratic ideas have wide currency in some evangelical circles (and history would lead us to expect some such reading to be popular among the less sophisticated), but we need more evidence. What we do know is that the EFZ, CCZ and ECZ issued a joint statement weeks later. It praised Chiluba's intent to conduct government by Christian ideals, but warned against compromising social cohesion and the secular state (ibid.: 5). If that is all it says, it is theologically shallow. In any case, the EFZ was associated with it. But Gifford insinuates, without evidence, sincerity on the part of the CCZ and ECZ and duplicity on the part of the Evangelical Fellowship.

At the same time, Chiluba established diplomatic links with Israel, and in 1993 severed links with Iran and Iraq. Gifford attributes this (correctly as far as theology is concerned, though one can imagine other political motivations) to dispensationalist Christian Zionism, the view that a nation can only prosper if it is pro-Israel.

In 1996, the preamble to the new constitution included the declaration of Zambia as a Christian nation. This was at Chiluba's behest, going against the review committee which had said it was not desired by most Zambians. A joint letter by Catholics and Christian Council argued it would create second-class citizens, would not foster authentic religious practice, could lead to abuse and bring discredit, and that Zambia would become a Christian nation not by declaration but by Christians living their faith.

Whatever the truth about whose idea it was and who was consulted, it is clear that the internal dynamic of the Chiluba government must be analysed separately from the power struggle within the Protestant world. The major corporate actors (government, CCZ and EFZ) interact in complex and unstable fashion, each with their own agenda and, possibly, their own internal conflicts. The latter may be especially true of the EFZ, which has to balance diverse theological interpretations regarding temporal power, as well as an institutionally fragmented constituency with diverse projects for visibility in the religious and political fields. A study of the internal processes of the EFZ would be illuminating.

The declaration of a Christian nation seems to have been politically empty, since it did not introduce new substantive laws or establish any church. It was purely symbolic, in tune with much charismatic political theology which talks of benefits accruing mystically from such acts. Chiluba himself, on the fourth anniversary of the declaration, said that 'because Zambia has entered into this covenant with God, God is blessing this nation to the point where we shall stop borrowing; we shall lend instead' (in Gifford 1998: 233).

Chiluba has personally invited leading evangelists to come for crusades. One was the American Ernest Angley, with whom he seems to have a connection since 1981. Chiluba spoke at his closing rally. However, when the president invited him the following year, the evangelicals who had formed the organising committee declined to do so again. Richard Roberts, of Oral Roberts Ministries, was also invited, but evangelical leaders responded that such invitations should be through the churches and not the government (Gifford 1996: 7). The reaction is significant: a partisanly 'evangelical' government ends up dividing even the evangelicals themselves, besides alienating others. There are two main reasons for this: the rivalries of the evangelical field, which such a government will find it impossible to mediate; and the undetermined border between what should properly be church initiatives and what should be done by an 'evangelical' government. This border problem would be especially acute, the more a government is regarded as having a duty to govern in favour of the evangelicals. Illustrations of this can be seen in the invitations to controversial evangelist Benny Hinn by the Deputy Minister of Finance, Dan Pule. Hinn came in 1994 and 1995 and pledged money for Chiluba's re-election campaign. Similarly, Zambia's most famous evangelist Nevers Mumba denounced media criticism of Chiluba in his crusades. 'Chiluba is part of the household of faith. His victory is our victory.' Speaking at a Mumba rally, the president said problems had arisen in Zambia because the Christians had stopped praying and started grumbling.

A clear example of evangelical aspirations from an 'evangelical' government came in a meeting chaired by vice-president Miyanda. This man, a member of the Jesus Worship Centre, seems to be the gatekeeper between government and churches, and is possibly the initiator of the more overtly religious measures. Miyanda rejects the idea that Chiluba should have carried out a public consultation before the 'Christian nation' declaration, on the grounds that 'any Christian who condemns the declaration, I question whether they are for Jesus' (ibid.: 12). Anything with a supposed biblical mandate need not be subjected to democratic procedures; a view of the political function of the Bible we have already seen in Brazil. Many possible interpretations of the declaration were mentioned by Christian leaders at the meeting: that pastors should have positions in government; that the religious education syllabus should be replaced with the Bible; that churches should be given land to build on; that the building of mosques should be halted.

The reaction of evangelicals to the Chiluba government is little understood. An article in *Christianity Today* a year after his election says, with perhaps a dose of *naïveté*, that 'evangelicals have distanced themselves from the party in power in order to continue to correct and admonish rulers'. An EFZ statement says 'the church should maintain a reasonable distance from the government' (9 Nov. 1992). In fact, the EFZ is probably torn, as can be divined from Gifford's article. On the one hand, we see EFZ officers flanking the chairman of the CCZ as he makes a public denunciation of the government in late 1994 (Gifford

1996: 11). In November 1995 the EFZ, CCZ and ECZ issue a joint pastoral statement deploring intolerance, supporting the poor against the ravages of structural adjustment and promoting human rights. The impression is that the EFZ has at least partly broken the old elitism and gained some recognition as equal partner from the other representative Christian organisations. On the other hand, Gifford also talks of a split among evangelicals. Many leaders are embarrassed at their 'Christian' government because scorn for it extends to them as well. This suggests only a self-protective, rather than a principled, distancing from government. But Gifford also suggests (and we have seen this already in Brazil) another reason for some evangelicals' dissatisfaction: a feeling that 'their' government has not brought them the access and influence they expected. Some wanted a Ministry of Christian Affairs, or pastors among the ten MPs appointed by presidential nomination, or at least unlimited access to the president's ear. Bishop Mambo of the Church of God said 'Pagans must not be voted for . . . The church must . . . run the affairs of this country' (ibid.: 14). Yet Chiluba seemed periodically to change his confidants among the clergy (probably wisely, since he did not owe his presidency to the churches), and the EFZ leadership came to be marginalised.

It is, of course, not only EFZ leaders whose actions may partly be motivated by resentment at such marginalisation; CCZ and ECZ leaders are also human and have suffered a certain marginalisation. But for some evangelicals, the disappointed hope of a career boost is compounded by a theology of hierocracy: that God's agents on earth are basically church leaders and that government of the nations by the people of God, promised in the Old Testament, is to be exercised through the direct political power (whether by holding government posts in person or through proxies) of evangelical church leaders. Lacking is any idea of diverse ministries of the people of God, including lay people involved in politics in subordination to the word of God but not to ecclesiastical hierarchies. In this context, it is interesting that Nevers Mumba, the evangelist who in 1994 was still denouncing all criticism of Chiluba, formed a National Christian Coalition in 1997. Widely regarded as a surrogate party with an eye to the 2001 elections (when Chiluba cannot, under present rules, run for re-election), it met with a cool reception from government and Evangelical Fellowship. The government withdrew his diplomatic passport and had his television programme stopped. Mumba replied that his movement was not anti-government, but that it was not good enough merely to have a president and vice-president who are Christians. All political positions, said Mumba, should be occupied by God-fearing people.

The mass evangelicalism of the Third World thus demands a re-examination of the trajectory of separation of religion and politics in the West. Is the Third World's problem that it has not been educated in the implications of this normative trajectory, or is it that this trajectory is not normative and needs to be reformulated? Sanneh (1996) could be a useful starting point here. In any case, empirical study of the emerging (sometimes intriguing, sometimes disastrous) alternatives in today's global Christianity must feed into such debate. A phrase from an opposition politician goes to the heart of Zambia's dilemma: religion and ideology as papering over ethnic cracks. 'Last time our country was proclaimed a one-party state. Now it is a one-religion nation. Who knows, next it could be another dangerous clown proclaiming a one-language country or a one-race country' (in Gifford 1996: 13).

An article by an evangelical MP, Inonge Mbikusita-Lewanika (*Transformation*, Oct.–Dec. 1994: 21–5), says the EFZ should exercise a prophetic role, educate people in democracy and human rights and be open to working with the CCZ and the Catholics, as it is the latter who have mostly stuck their necks out and defended the people. This plea does not seem to have been heard. We read nothing about the churches' mediating or protesting the bar on Kaunda in 1996, although we do hear of such attempts by other sectors in civil society (*Africa Confidential*, 1 Nov. 1996).

There is much more we need to know about Zambia. Who are the evangelical government ministers and provincial governors? What are their careers? How do they act in government? How have ordinary evangelicals' attitudes evolved over the years towards Chiluba? How exactly do the churches function at election times? What do pastors say and do, and what effect does it have on members' political behaviour? Since Chiluba is originally from a mainline denomination, how much charismatic socialisation has he had and what do his politics really mean in relation to the political rise of the born-again community? The case of Guatemala's two charismatic presidents counsels caution in drawing conclusions.

In addition, how do leaders and members of the New Apostolic Church behave politically? This church, a non-pentecostal group with links to Germany, may be the largest Protestant church in the country in active members. An EFZ survey of 1994 in Lusaka showed Sunday attendance of 10.4 per cent at Catholic churches, 3.6 per cent at EFZ churches and 1.7 per cent at CCZ churches. The New Apostolic, however, had 2.6 per cent. An adequate discussion of evangelical politics must take this church into account.

As Gifford says, often in Africa 'Christianity is considered an unalloyed good; to describe something as Christian is to forestall all criticism' (Gifford 1996: 15). Is there, then, a possibility that political phenomena such as Chiluba will hasten a future weakening of Christianity due to its poor public performance?

Chiluba was, it seems, a good union leader but 'went wrong' in government. Why? Of course, he faced a hard task, but could have done much better. His evangelical connections do not seem to have helped him much. Evangelical leaders will, of course, dissociate themselves from him and will say he went wrong because he did not listen to them. But that is unconvincing; what did they have to say that would have made him a better president for Zambia, and not just for evangelical institutional interests?

CHAPTER 19

South Africa

The outline of the South African case (the unbanning of the ANC and other movements in February 1990, the first democratic multiracial elections in April 1994) are well known and will be presupposed here. South Africa has perhaps the strongest national tradition in the study of religion and politics in the Third World. But one of the darkest corners is 'what positions the wide array of ... evangelicals have taken' (Hale 1993: 41), and this despite the fact that 'South African history has been profoundly shaped by evangelical Christianity' (de Gruchy, in Hale 1993: 45). Indeed, it could be argued that this is the most strongly evangelical country in the continents we are examining.

Evangelicals 'brought to South Africa a wide array of legacies [in politics, from] Calvinist theocracy ... through the Lutheran notion of the "two kingdoms" to a British nonconformist insistence on the separation of church and state' (Hale 1993: 55). This is especially important when contrasted with Latin America where, although representatives of all these traditions arrived, the common condition for many years of tiny Protestant minorities in Catholic societies did not fully allow the distinctive traditions to flower.

A good place to start is with the composition of the Protestant field. Hendriks (1995) surveys the census results from 1911 to 1991 and alerts us to where an inquiry about evangelicals in politics needs to be directed.

In 1991 nearly 75 per cent of the population are Christians. Of course, demographical data on South Africa only make sense when disaggregated racially. Of the racial categories used during apartheid, Asians are only 12 per cent Christian, coloureds are 64 per cent, blacks 77.2 per cent and whites 77.9 per cent. Probably blacks are now more Christian than whites, since the former have increased steadily while the latter (plus the coloureds) have been de-Christianising since 1980. In 1991 there were twenty-one million black Christians and only eight million non-black. The future of Christianity, above all of evangelicalism, lies with the black community.

Of white Christians, half are in the various Afrikaans Reformed Churches. These are also the largest group among coloureds (26%), but rivalled by the independent churches (22%). Among blacks, however, independent churches account for 44 per cent, followed at a distance by Methodists, Catholics and others. Amongst blacks, these independent churches are nearly all what are often called African Independent Churches (AICs). The latter are now 36 per cent of the black population and 25 per cent of the total population. Independent churches as a whole are 38 per cent of all Christians.

Hendriks says the AICs are becoming the new 'mainline'. Their percentage of the population is higher than that of pentecostals in any Latin American country. Recent growth of AICs has been tremendous. Although divided into some four thousand groups, there are very large ones, especially the Zion Christian Church (ZCC), which vies with Methodists and Catholics for second place in the population as a whole.

The mainline churches, meanwhile, are in decline from desertion of white and coloured members to small-group oriented churches or to secularity, and from the shift in their black membership to AICs. It follows that AICs and other independent churches must be key elements in a study of evangelical politics. Although AICs are often regarded as outside the evangelical category, we must remember observations made in the introduction regarding their evangelical origins, their pentecostal phenomenology ('a good many of the classical AICs can rightly be called pentecostal' (Gifford 1998: 33)) and the need to avoid a Western-centred definition of evangelicalism.

Many other independent churches in Hendriks' survey are charismatic. He suggests that whites leave mainline denominations seeking refuge from collective guilt (1995: 43). This seems a priori unlikely, since the trend is global. There is a lot of stereotyping about charismatics' politics. Hexham and Poewe critique Morran and Schlemmer for relying on media reports and a limited questionnaire. The latter concluded that white charismatics were reactionary neurotics. But, say Hexham and Poewe, 'people who on survey questionnaires look "insecure" and "neurotic" are optimistic and creative when one studies their life histories'. Many started small businesses with blacks, or multiracial ministries. In the violence of 1985–6, they fasted together and created artworks to envision a new South Africa. Charismatics consistently came out somewhat more liberal politically than their neighbours.

Everyone interviewed was against apartheid, but also against violence and corruption (Hexham and Poewe 1994: 56–7).

Hexham and Poewe's reappraisal is more plausible than the extremes they oppose, but they may be too positive. Multiracial initiatives were not typical of white charismatics, most of whom, while denying racism, did not actively oppose apartheid. Some 'Third Way' positions examined later seem to fit many quite well.

The main white church is the Dutch Reformed, a quasi-state church under apartheid. It is often claimed that 'Calvinism' gave theological support to apartheid, but this is misleading. Firstly, Calvinistic churches in South Africa are varied and include black and multiracial ones. Secondly, it was a specific form of Calvinism, the neo-Calvinism of Dutch theologian and politician Abraham Kuyper, that was used by apartheid theologians. And thirdly, Kuyperianism was distorted from its original theological and political meaning, even though it can be argued (e.g. de Gruchy 1984: 109) that some basic theological weaknesses laid it open to this.

Kuyper's doctrine of sphere sovereignty (that each sphere of life has an autonomy which must be respected) was a doctrine of civil liberty in Holland. But in South Africa, a theology that limited the state became an idolatry of the *volk*, and civil liberties turned into 'separate development'. For Kuyper, social spheres take precedence over the state because they are given in creation, whereas the state is introduced after the Fall. In South Africa, the *volk* became a separate sphere grounded in divine ordinances, permitting the creation of an Afrikaner civil religion (de Gruchy 1984: 110–11; de Klerk 1975: 257).

Kuyper, in fact, has been popular recently amongst politically-involved evangelicals of a Reformed bent, but for different reasons. Although invoked by defenders of apartheid, he was also an inspiration to resist it. According to him, Christ, the apostles and prophets 'invariably took sides *against* those who were powerful and living in luxury, and *for* the suffering and oppressed' (in de Gruchy 1984: 108).

The idea of apartheid dates from the 1930s, and the Dutch Reformed Church (DRC) supported it from the start (Kinghorn 1990: 63). But in 1950, with the National Party beginning legislative implementation, the DRC felt obliged to pioneer a reinterpretation, the only time when it was ahead rather than behind. It initiated the idea of separate development, an implicit recognition that full racism was untenable in Christian dogma. The formula was that all people are equal, not as individuals, but within their particular nationhood. The notion of race was absorbed into that of nation, which is why the DRC has never felt guilty of racism. The reality of apartheid was substituted with a fantasy (ibid.: 67–8). In 1986, the General Synod recognised that some elements of apartheid policy were mere racial discrimination. But these were already on the way out, and the principle of apartheid itself was not questioned. Since the government had abolished the prohibition of mixed marriages, the DRC abolished its prohibition on non-white members. But it did not decide to unite with its coloured and black 'daughter churches'. This, says Kinghorn, is the crux: since church structures had been separate since 1881, contact on equal footing between Afrikaners and blacks had been virtually impossible long before apartheid (ibid.: 80).

The exegetical basis for apartheid theology was the creation narrative, Genesis chapters 10 and 11, Deuteronomy 32:8 and Acts 17:26: a slim base with no Christological element. It is a classic case of 'local subversion', in which local contextual factors in church practice overwhelm the universal heritage of the church. The chances of this are greater in less hierarchical churches which allow local autonomy. Although hierarchical churches can also suffer local subversion (especially during the *patronato* or *padroado* in which Iberian monarchs enjoyed considerable control over the Church in their dominions), it is harder to maintain in the long run. The DRC, of course, is not the only example of local subversion involving conservative Protestant theology. It is a constant danger for increasingly fragmented Third World evangelicalism. Being a decentralised faith, the globalisation of evangelicalism may lead more and more to a splintering of political perspectives unable to dialogue with each other.

The DRC case should be relativised. Firstly, its direct influence was never that great. It was not a state church, and being non-hierarchical it had difficulty in functioning as a pressure group (ibid.: 78). Secondly, many other churches which cannot appeal to ethnicity (Afrikanerdom) and history (persecution by the British Empire) as the Afrikaner Reformed Churches can, cannot throw the first stone; the Anglophone Baptist Union, for example. The Baptist tradition of separation of church and state did not prevent it from playing a 'protective ethnic function' (Hale 1993: 52) and identifying with British nationalism, without adducing a biblical basis for its positions. Although official publications occasionally criticised policies after the Union of 1910, it was a long time before racial separation was explicitly rejected. Only in 1976 did it resolve that its local congregations should integrate; and only in 1985 did it send an open letter to government urging an end to apartheid as 'in conflict with the Bible'. Even that led to internal controversy over 'becoming political'. Hale concludes that the Baptist Union showed a tendency to mirror (with a time lag) popular protest movements among whites, and there were 'pervasive secular determinants' to its positions (ibid.: 52ff.); so much so that in 1987 the mainly black Baptist Convention separated from it, alleging the latter's unwillingness to listen to its views (Walker 1994: 43).

The case of pentecostalism is illustrative. Pentecostalism began in the southern United States among blacks. For a brief time, it lived an inter-racial existence which was highly unusual, but within a few years segregation reasserted itself (Anderson 1979: 189). The South African trajectory was similar. Maxwell (1997b) says pentecostalism was non-racial for about a year and a half, perhaps aided by the drastic situation of Afrikaners after defeat in the Boer War. But 'local subversion' soon followed. The Apostolic Faith Mission decreed that 'baptism of natives shall in future take place after the baptism of white people'; then that 'baptism of whites, coloured and natives shall be separate'. In the 1950s its vice-president was a pro-apartheid senator. As Cox says, 'the great temptation facing pentecostals today is to forget or minimise the circumstances of their birth' (1996: 262).

It is difficult for most Third World pentecostals to find anything normative in their history (assuming they know it), since what matters to them is the recovery of the charismatic phenomena and not the socio-historical context in which this happens. But this docetic approach is occasionally overcome, as by the South African group Relevant Pentecostal Witness (RPW), which began in 1989. One of its leaders cites the primitive pentecostal experience in the United States, that 'the colour line was washed away in the blood of the Lamb' (Horn 1994: 28). Yet few churches are integrated. Writing in 1994, he describes the decline of RPW, divided by the post-1990 situation. This is a classic case of political involvement *in extremis*, which is left orphan once the unifying non-democratic enemy has been overcome and 'normal' politics is restored. But RPW's role was symbolically vital, as a counterweight to the pentecostal/charismatic Christian Action for South Africa which encouraged the government to maintain the ban on the ANC only a few months before it was lifted.

An increasingly common position among white evangelicals as the crisis of apartheid deepened was what Balcomb (1993) calls the 'Third Way'. Third Way theologies involved seeing the liberation movement as a mirror-image of the state: both were ideological options based on violence. The church had to be above ideologies and power struggles. Both the DRC's 1986 Church and Society document and the 1985 Kairos document influenced by Liberation Theology represented the coopting of the church by political agendas. The Third Way rejected violence and sought a specifically Christian contribution in reconciliation.

A key moment for this was the National Initiative for Reconciliation, organised by Africa Enterprise in 1985, when a state of emergency had been declared. It was rent by divisions, largely between black and white. A proposal by Desmond Tutu for a six-day stay-away was whittled down to a one-day 'pray-away' (ibid.: 86). Even that had to be packaged carefully for Africa Enterprise's corporate sponsors. For Balcomb, this Third Way became increasingly identified with National Party policy. Rejection of violence became a way of not really opposing the system, unlike the active non-violent resistance of leaders like Tutu (ibid.: 92).

A black-evangelical evaluation of Third Way theology (Molebatsi and Ngwenya 1994) portrays it as a white revulsion against apartheid, but a disagreement with the strategies of liberation movements, based on certain common beliefs: violence must be ruled out, the economy must not be destabilised, law and order was a lesser evil and reconciliation was a biblical requirement. For the authors, the Third Way meant 'seeking first the economic kingdom'; white evangelicals preferred law and order because they were not recipients of the system's brutality; their paternalism caused resentment; and there is no reconciliation without justice and no justice without restitution.

Perhaps the greatest mistake of the Third Way was not theological but sociological: they did not realise times had changed. Hastings points to the 1978 election of Tutu as general secretary of the South African Council of Churches as a symbolic turning-point. Until then, church–state struggle had been predominantly between whites. But with the banning of Beyers Naudé's Christian Institute, the history of white minority Christian protest effectively ended. It continued, of course, but had gone as far as it could. It had never won over most white Christians, and its role of defending blacks became less important as the latter increasingly spoke for themselves. The centre of gravity in the churches had moved to the black majority, whose leaders had a huge constituency. And those leaders learnt the lesson from Muzorewa's downfall in Zimbabwe: not to join a 'Christian' multiracial anti-'communist' alliance (Hastings 1991: 181). This latter project seems to have been an underlying interest of the Third Way.

It was not, however, a concern of an increasing number of black evangelicals. We have mentioned the Baptist Convention, which split from the Baptist Union. In 1985–6 black evangelicals from Soweto produced a statement on 'Evangelical Witness in South Africa', disillusioned with 'evangelicalism's normal identification with the status quo . . . We realised our theology was influenced by . . . missionaries with political, social and class interests . . . contrary or even hostile to both the spiritual and social needs of our people' (Concerned Evangelicals 1986). These 'Concerned Evangelicals' were concerned less with the things that worried the Third Way than with the evangelical 'track record of supporting and legitimating oppressive regimes'. Instead of issuing an 'evangelical response' to the (Liberation-Theology influenced) Kairos Document, they addressed 'the kairos evangelical Christians were going through . . . Black evangelicals are facing a crisis of faith [since they are] oppressed and exploited by people who claim to be "born-again".' The document was signed by members of thirty-five denominations and agencies, ranging from pentecostal to Calvinist, from Anglican to holiness.

Concerned Evangelicals were instrumental in starting a new Evangelical Alliance in 1995, with the hope that it would not be 'sidetracked into fundamentalist agendas'. Evangelicals, say Molebatsi and Ngwenya, need to earn the right to speak in the new South Africa (1994: 18).

One person who does not is Frank Chikane. A pentecostal from the Apostolic Faith Mission, the white denominational leadership cut off funding for his congregation because he was 'involved in politics'. Visits to members in prison led eventually to his being arrested and tortured for six weeks by a white deacon from his own denomination. Chikane signed the Concerned Evangelicals manifesto, as well as being general secretary of the Institute for Contextual Theology (which produced the Kairos Document). He was later general secretary of the South African Council of Churches, as successor to Desmond Tutu, during which time attempts were made on his life (SACC deposition to the Truth and Reconciliation Commision, 1997). In 1996, he was elected vice-president of the Apostolic Faith Mission, and has long been a leading advisor to Thabo Mbeki. He was elected to the National Executive of the ANC in 1997, and since Mbeki's election as president in 1999 has been directorgeneral of the Office of the Presidency.

Between 1990 (unbanning of the ANC) and 1994 (first multiracial elections), the white evangelical community had a chance to review its positions and participate in ongoing negotiations. In late 1990 a remarkable meeting took place at Rustenburg, with representatives from ninety-seven denominations, including the DRC, Baptist Union, Apostolic Faith Mission, several AICs and the charismatic Rhema Church. All agreed that apartheid was a sin which required repentance and restitution. Those who had not opposed it confessed misuse of the Bible. The need for a just economic order, affirmative action and a popularly elected Constituent Assembly was stressed.

One figure who came to prominence in this period was Ray McCauley, head of Rhema and of the charismatic International Fellowship of Christian Churches (IFCC). Horn says McCauley's role in reconciliation and peacemaking was seen as opportunist by some in Relevant Pentecostal Witness (1994: 25). A cynical reading of Rustenburg is possible: now that a church's previous attitude to apartheid could ruin its credibility, everybody suddenly became convinced it was a grievous sin. Indeed, McCauley's task during the stalemate of 1992, to draw Inkatha into dialogue (Walshe 1995: 89), could also be interpreted as a ploy to save something of white privilege through black allies. But other interpretations can be adduced (that he was salvaging the negotiation process), and McCauley and the IFCC eventually surprised sympathisers and critics alike by joining the SACC as observers (Horn 1994: 25).

If some or all AICs are included in the evangelical label, it is vital to study them. Their political role is ambiguous. There was some political activism in the early days. Schoffeleers says that between the Natives' Land Act of 1913 and the National Party takeover in 1948, the prophets' themes were often a protest against land policy, mission domination and white culture (1990: 4). In 1921 one hundred and eighty members were killed in a confrontation with police. In 1925 a government inquiry into independent churches recommended a policy of toleration (Claasen 1995: 18). With apartheid, the movement from mixed churches into AICs was seen even more positively by government. While Jean Comaroff stresses the protest character of AICs, albeit implicit, Schoffeleers (1990) emphasises 'massive cooperation and even collaboration with the apartheid regime'. Any protest was cultural and did not exclude political cooperation. *Pace* Balandier's interpretation, the healing churches are not instruments of resistance but tend to political acquiescence. Separatism and nationalism are antipodal reactions, says Schoffeleers, and not complementary reactions as Daneels prefers.

Along these lines, Schoffeleers interprets one of the most controversial incidents in the apartheid era: the visit by President Botha to the headquarters of the Zion Christian Church in 1985. This occurred during the annual gathering at Zion City, Moria, Northern Transvaal. Two million members of this, the largest AIC, received Botha with enthusiasm. The invitation had come from the bishop, Barnabas Legkanyane, grandson of the founder. Botha addressed the multitude, citing Romans chapter 13 about obedience to those in authority.

The church was heavily criticised by all opponents of apartheid. The government gained mileage out of the visit, using the ZCC to challenge the legitimacy of religious critics of the regime such as Tutu. The ZCC is the largest independent black church in the world, and has enjoyed phenomenal growth. It is prosperous, owning the Mt Moria complex, a fleet of buses and other enterprises. Its leaders radiate economic success, more extravagantly than is usual even among the newer prosperity gospel preachers. The ZCC star worn on the lapel is valued in the labour market, since the church grew after the 1960 Sharpeville massacre when the ANC rejected non-violence and the ZCC, in contrast, reaffirmed its commitment to non-violence. It represented 'a desire on the part of a large section of urban blacks to stem the tide of violence' (Schoffeleers 1988: 11). Unlike many AICs, it is pan-ethnic.

However, violence could be opposed without blessing the apartheid system. So why did the ZCC make a public display of support? Because, says Schoffeleers, African Zionism is itself a separatist system (ibid.: 4). It has no need to militate against apartheid; it organises its own separate system under its own leaders. It is not surprising that a room at the Moria headquarters has portraits of white South African politicians and a replica of the supreme symbol of Afrikanerdom, the Voortrekker Monument. The ZCC made this tacit support more explicit because it was prodded to do so by a government mindful of its size and concerned at growing opposition from other churches.

It was a mistake by the ZCC leadership. It tarnished its public image, equating it with the tame homeland leaders. ZCC members were humiliated in the townships afterwards, and even attacked. The bishop back-pedalled, saying the visit had not indicated support for the regime, but even so, more members started to question the bishop's leadership, something unheard of before.

The unexpected transformations thus constituted a severe challenge to the ZCC's image, politics and practices. Bridges had to be built with the ANC, helped by the fact that the latter could no longer simply criticise it as a dead-weight in the freedom struggle, but would need to treat it as a weighty participant in democratic politics. It seems the ZCC

in the end supported the ANC in 1994. However, the implications of the
unitary and non-racial state for the ZCC's world-view would also have
to be assimilated. The ZCC's evolution is thus a key theme in evangelical politics, especially in any future rearticulation of the party system.

In the new openness to the world, it is possible that the AICs may face
challenges from other Third World evangelical phenomena. The Brazilian Universal Church of the Kingdom of God has arrived with striking
success.

The post-1994 era has been full of new phenomena for evangelical
politics. Questions such as religious pluralism and the secular state,
abortion, homosexuality and the death penalty have politicised some
Christians who condemned political involvement against apartheid
(Villa-Vicencio 1995: 73). Their involvement thus faces accusations of
inconsistency and lacks legitimacy in the face of the new-found legitimacy of those who opposed apartheid. The head of the Evangelical
Alliance criticises evangelical moral outrage over homosexuality and
pornography for avoiding structural issues. There has been no nationwide Damascus experience for whites, he says, so the demons of racism
have not been expelled, they have just regrouped. Churches do not have
to integrate, raising the spectre of their becoming a rallying point of
racial sentiment – a grim future indeed for the most evangelical country
in the Third World.

An article on Christianity in the parliament makes a survey of the uses
of the Bible in politics ('Theological Reflection . . .' 1997). The tradition
of theological debate in parliament established by leaders of the Afrikaans Reformed Churches such as Malan and Verwoerd is continued in
the revamped National Party's Programme of Principles, which states
that the Party strives to 'develop our nation in accordance with Christian norms and values, with explicit recognition of freedom of religion'.
But such norms and values can be variously interpreted, since this
tradition is also used by others. Thus, some ANC MPs (such as B. N.
Mtuli and Lutheran minister T. S. Farisani) try to claim the moral high
ground by affirming it is their party that really understands the Bible.
And, in a new departure for South Africa, an evangelical party has
arisen, the African Christian Democratic Party, led by a charismatic
pastor Kenneth Meshoe. The ACDP's two MPs in the 1994–9 parliament often claimed divine authority for their positions. As Meshoe says,
the ACDP is based on biblical principles; 'for us it is not what the caucus
says, but what the scriptures say' (ibid.: 82). The party is described by the
authors as 'fundamentalist', suspicious of religious pluralism, critical of

legislation on abortion and homosexuality and favourable to the death penalty (ibid.: 86). The party itself claims to be in favour of religious freedom, a market economy, 'family values' and a federal system. It is very concerned to be tough on crime. The names of its candidates in the 1999 elections show a certain ethnic mix; it elected six MPs, while the United Christian Democratic Party elected three.

All the above examples use evangelical rhetoric (whether Calvinist or charismatic) in their public discourse; but there are also believers in parliament who do not see the need for or advisability of doing so.

In 1997, the Truth and Reconciliation Commission (TRC), presided by Archbishop Tutu, requested the churches to make submissions regarding their experience under apartheid. This semi-obligatory public reassessment offers rich reflection for the burgeoning evangelical communities of the Third World. South Africa illustrates, albeit extremely, certain typical relationships between evangelicals and politics, now repented of by some, shamefacedly excused away by others, or denounced by their erstwhile ecclesiastical opponents.

The denomination with the most sanguine opinion of its role is the United Congregational Church of Southern Africa (UCCSA). It claims the heritage of missionaries Philip, Moffatt and Livingstone and its membership is half black and half coloured. Former ANC president Albert Luthuli was a deacon. When the regime developed its Bantustan policy (nominally independent 'homelands'), the UCCSA called on its ministers who had taken public office in the homelands to resign. When coloureds and Indians were allowed a separate chamber of parliament, two former denominational chairmen led the coloured Labour Party in agreeing to participate; the UCCSA dissociated itself from them and removed them from their ministers' roll. It supported conscientious objection (by white draftees) and sanctions, defended the Kairos Document and encouraged non-violent opposition. It gave pastoral care to liberation movements and had contact with banned groups. It admits, however, doing little to order 'its own life and worship so that it could be a sign of the Kingdom'.

Other denominations not regarded as bulwarks of the regime are more self-critical. Even the South African Council of Churches, led at the height of the struggle by Desmond Tutu (and which allowed him freedom to speak without first consulting member churches), concedes that it 'was re-active rather than pro-active ... This allowed the government to set the agenda.' It also confesses a lack of programmes to prepare people for democracy.

The Anglican Church, Tutu's denomination, in which blacks and whites participated, also refrains from too rosy a picture, remembering the variety of stances in the church and the use of clergy as army chaplains. Another racially mixed body, the Methodists, admits it did not always 'live up adequately to its prophetic vocation [due to] fear of the consequences of radical action, sensitivity to the views of its economically powerful white constituency, insensitivity to the aspirations of the black majority and undue respect for the institution of government'.

The Reformed Presbyterians, a black church, understood resistance in the light of the 'just war' theory, but admits it only took an unflinching stand thirty years after apartheid's introduction. The Uniting Reformed Church, union of the black and coloured wings of the Dutch Reformed, also only rejected the homelands policy in 1978, and did not in general reject the Prohibition of Mixed Marriages Act. Indeed, through its chaplaincy, 'the church contributed to gross human rights violations'.

Two denominations admit to allowing their international tradition of social concern to be blunted by the context. The Quakers, largely white middle class, 'failed to protest'. The Salvation Army

chose to remain silent, a sin of omission . . . While we did care for body and soul, we ought more strongly to have attacked the evil which wrecked both bodies and souls in the first place. Professing an apolitical stance, we used this to avoid the kind of protest for which the early Salvation Army was known . . . [Today, we still] want to uphold the principle of not being involved in party political issues. We will endeavour, however, not to hide under this umbrella as an excuse for silence . . . on matters of injustice.

Two of the largest denominations, the Dutch Reformed and the Zion Christian Church, despite diametrically opposed constituencies, both had to come to terms with an uncomfortable reputation in the new South Africa. The ZCC says nothing about its relations with the apartheid government, especially the 1985 visit by Botha. However, it does mention that, among its activities aimed at 'the economic independence of the African people', the bus company was running at a loss until government subsidies began in 1985. In an indirect answer to critics, it affirms that, since 1948, its youth had been free to participate in 'African political movements' as long as these did not 'conflict with the practices of the church'. With soaring crime rates in the new South Africa, it calls 'unashamedly on the government to reinstate the death sentence'.

The DRC details its 'journey with apartheid'. It recognises that, before 1948, 'in a sense, the DRC took the lead in establishing the apartheid concept', understood as a Scripturally based idea that 'the

Lord wished separate peoples to maintain their separateness ("apartheid")' in every aspect of life. Even some theologians who did not see apartheid as a biblical imperative, accepted it as a practical arrangement. The DRC had pressed for the prohibition of mixed marriages since 1915.

Apartheid, the document says, 'envisaged the wellbeing of all involved', but 'was allowed to degenerate into an ideology which had to be put into practice at all costs' and became an 'oppressive system'. It is, however, 'disappointing that the misery caused by the application of the policy was not the subject of critical inquiry' in the DRC. It judged apartheid 'too abstractly and theoretically'. Presumably, the lack of criticism was not due to (as was revealed in 1978) the DRC (and other bodies) having received government funding to publicise pro-apartheid views; the funding was a result, not a cause, of the strong identification between church and state.

In 1986, when much 'petty apartheid' had been abolished, the DRC similarly recognised that Scripture did not forbid mixed marriages and declared membership open to all races. It would be, however, 'unfair to allege that ... the church was merely falling into line with what the government ... had already done... Certain convictions were arrived at more or less simultaneously at various levels of the Afrikaans community.'

Not surprisingly in view of this document, the DRC in 1997 was still suspended from the World Alliance of Reformed Churches. A separate submission to the TRC by the Belydende Kring (BK), a dissident group established in 1974 within the DRC 'family' of churches, claims that the 'daughter churches' (for blacks, coloureds and Indians) were 'held hostage theologically and financially' by the DRC during apartheid, and that the situation 'has not changed much'. The DRC document 'is pregnant with obfuscation and controversy', still refusing to condemn 'the theology that created conditions where many perpetrators [of human-rights abuses] could operate with innocence and joy'. The BK said the DRC should suffer expropriation of part of its properties as compensation for unjust treatment of many ministers and members of the DRC 'family' of churches.

In their depositions, more self-critical postures were adopted by evangelical mainstream groups. The Presbyterian Church of Southern Africa (PCSA), which claims a range of theologies from Liberation Theology to charismatic, never practised racial separation at the presbyterial level. It even voted in 1981 to defy the Group Areas Act, the

Mixed Marriages Act and the prohibition on the quoting of banned persons, and in 1985 proposed chaplains for the armed wings of the ANC and the PAC (Pan Africanist Congress). However, it 'never took a radical enough stance on the issue of military service; too many of its members were taken in by the propaganda about [communism. It] never thought of joining in any of the early demonstrations against apartheid . . . The leaders of the church were white and conservative.' In 1984, it rejected union with the non-white UCCSA. 'It is tragic that the PCSA was unable to move into a united black majority church ahead of the democratisation of the body politic.' The document confesses an 'almost complete failure to give a lead in matters of a political nature [through fear of accusations of] "bringing politics into the pulpit" [as well as] apathy, fear, indoctrination and an unwillingness to forgo privilege'.

The international evangelical parachurch organisation Scripture Union has held multiracial camps since 1977. The experience led some into politics or conscientious objection. It chose a black director in 1988. But 'we failed to confront the system . . . [especially] detention without trial of children and teenagers'.

A more complex situation prevails among Baptists. The largely white Anglophone Baptist Union said it had 'on numerous occasions condemned the wrongs of apartheid'. However, the black Baptist Convention, which until 1987 was in the Union, has a different estimate of the latter's record, which it labels 'institutional racism'. This is credited to the Union's 'conservative evangelical' theology, whose 'separatist laager mentality' expected black Baptists to embrace white minority fears regarding 'communism'. Criticisms of government that were made resulted from pressure by black members. The latter express

disgust and dismay with the white Baptist Church for its complicitous and sometimes explicit role in the perpetration of gross human rights violations . . . The greatest pain on our people was not inflicted by the marxist-communists . . . [but] by fellow Christians . . . in military and police uniform – also known to us on Sundays as 'brothers in Christ' . . . The white Baptist Union has contributed substantially to upholding the apartheid killing machine.

The Baptist Convention's analysis of the causes of this situation is ambiguous. It talks of 'the lack of a common memory/understanding of what constitutes Baptist theology and praxis'. But it also claims that the Baptist Union was 'immobilised by its choice of theological framework (basically conservative evangelical)'. The document, however, recognises individual exceptions among white Baptists and that the worldwide Baptist heritage is on their side. It concedes that the Baptist World Alliance put pressure on the regime, although it 'did not do enough'. It thus seems that their identification of the main problem as 'conservative evangelical theology' is unlikely. While elements in such a heritage reinforced contextual tendencies, it was the latter which set the tone, as they did with many South African Christians of other theological traditions. This book provides many examples of how an evangelical framework does not necessarily 'immobilise' its defenders; the reality is that 'evangelicalism' itself is far from uniform, and that 'local subversion' can take place in any Christian tradition, even though not all are equally susceptible in every area of life.

This can be seen from testimonies presented by charismatics and pentecostals. Hatfield Christian Church of Pretoria condemns both apartheid theology and Liberation Theology, and says the link between the ANC and the Communist Party clouded the issues, but admits to a 'naive acceptance of some aspects of society that should have been challenged in our teachings'. The Apostolic Faith Mission admits that many members held top positions in the government and that it 'failed in its duty to question the system more'.

The most revealing testimony is from Ray McCauley, pastor of Rhema Church, which is singled out for criticism in the 1986 'Concerned Evangelicals' manifesto for its flying of the old South African and American flags, and which in 1987 denounced black strikers as 'striking for Satan's purposes' (Jones 1990: 110). McCauley's subsequent evolution has already been mentioned. In his submission to the TRC as leader of the International Federation of Christian Churches, McCauley confesses to having 'often hid behind our so-called spirituality and ignored the stark reality of the apartheid age . . . Paralysed by a false respect for government authority most of our white charismatic and pentecostal church followers were simply spectators.' At the Rustenburg conference, McCauley tried to persuade other pentecostal leaders to join him in confessing failure, but only one group did so. McCauley goes on to 'seek the forgiveness of those who were willing to bear the scars of rejection, humiliation and persecution for their campaign to isolate through sanctions a minority government', and adds that 'restitution or reparation has to happen. There is hardly a white person in South Africa who did not benefit from apartheid.'

Finally, the new Evangelical Alliance, comprising thirty-one denominations, confesses 'the complicity of evangelicals by commission and omission', which it attributes to a 'failure to develop a theology that took adequate stock of social reality', thus making evangelicals 'easy prey to the forces of conflict'.

South Africa is in a new moment, in some ways similar to Latin America: formal democracy and relatively vibrant civil society in the midst of extreme inequalities. Some of the ways of studying evangelical politics in Latin America could be applied in South Africa. But other features are unique.

One such is that it is the only part of the world where a significant European diaspora has eventually come under non-white political rule. This could lead to cultural interaction between the West and Africa on historically unique terms, and this in a context strongly infused by evangelicalism. Thus, a unique historical chance is given to South African evangelicals, black and white, to contribute to the direction and meaning of this interaction. The effects of all this on evangelicalism will also be interesting to see.

Besides the AICs and new charismatic churches, the new South Africa is full of fascinating potential studies.   Right-wing organisations of evangelical inspiration, such as the Christian League of Southern Africa (surreptitiously funded by the government in the 1970s), United Christian Action (lead by Ed Cain, a former missionary in Mozambique), Christian Forum (led by Martin Badenhorst of Full Gospel Church, some of whose white ministers were members of the right-wing Afrikaner AWB (Jones 1990)), Gospel Defence League and Frontline Fellowship, need a sober analysis now that their national and regional importance has diminished.

What post-apartheid role has the Concerned Evangelicals sector had? It may well identify with evangelical movements in Latin America which have a similar per-capita income level and disparities. They are more familiar with the peace without justice which may be the price of the South African transition. The Evangelical Alliance, a black initiative, is a key organ and its political role should be studied.

CHAPTER 20

Nigeria

Nigeria is Africa's most populous state and its estimated 24 per cent of Protestants (Baur 1994: 524) represent a significant portion of African Protestantism. Catholicism is perhaps as large, but exact proportions of religious communities are unknown, and for good reason. Nigeria is the front line between modern Africa's main religions: Christianity and Islam. Since they are probably evenly balanced, and the country is the regional superpower, the political prize is tantalising. Clashing religious visions of the nation have become prominent, giving Nigerian evangelical politics a different dimension from the African cases already studied. Nigeria has one of the most important Muslim–Christian political clashes in any nation-state today.

Muslim and Christian political projects have arisen against a background of economic and political failure and ethnic rivalry. Oil wealth at first kept hopes of rapid development alive, but since the early 1980s the economy has plummeted. In addition, Nigeria has had military regimes rather than one-party civilian governments, and, after a 'feigned conversion' (Joseph 1997: 375) to democracy in the early 1990s, the military fended off international pressure and maintained a repressive system.

Regional and ethnic questions simmer near the surface. In the 1960s the largely Catholic Igbo in the east tried to break away as Biafra. The Igbo, the (predominantly Protestant or Muslim) Yoruba in the south-west and the Muslim Hausa-Fulani in the north together make up two-thirds of the population. The 'minorities' which make up the rest, many inhabiting the Middle Belt and traditionally subordinate to the northern Islamic elite, have been converting from African traditional religions to Christianity as part of their assertion of political autonomy. The ratio of Christians to Muslims has been transformed: in 1931, there were 6 per cent of Christians to 45 per cent of Muslims; by 1963, the proportions were 35: 47. The ratio is now about 45: 50 (Peel 1996: 608).

Within the Christian bloc, charismatic evangelicalism has grown apace since the 1970s.

Thus, Nigeria's religious situation makes it globally unique in terms of evangelical politics and accentuates aspects only dimly perceived elsewhere.

Islam reached the north in the eleventh century. In the early nineteenth century, a jihad set up a caliphate with sharia (Islamic) law. British rule in the north from the early twentieth century was always indirect, and in some ways strengthened Muslim predominance. Northern Muslims have risen to dominance in national politics since independence in 1960. Centralisation was aided by civil war in the 1960s and the oil boom in the 1970s. With Christianity growing rapidly, the late oil boom years saw the beginnings of a radicalisation of political perspectives on both Muslim and Christian sides.

For Igwara (1995), religion has merged with the emotional force of nationalism to produce 'holy nationalisms'. 'Apocalyptic visions of the nation' have emerged. Some authors explain this politicised religion as elite manipulation. Others see it as fanaticism. Yet others believe it a response to poverty, or to limited political opportunities after parties were banned in 1984. But for Igwara the explanation lies in the sacralisation of Nigerian identity. Citing Juergensmeyer regarding religious nationalism, she says the ultimate goal is conversion of Nigerian nationalism into holy nationalism, in which definition of the state in secular terms is rejected as morally empty.

This is clearest on the Muslim side. Since the late 1970s, militant Islam has aimed at purifying religion from syncretic practices and from the unrepresentative Hausa-Fulani establishment which has favoured the few. Militant Islam is concentrated in the north, whereas Yoruba Islam shows greater potential for coexistence. But while militants' desire for a theocratic order has grown, it has become increasingly unfeasible demographically, and even Muslim-controlled military regimes have delivered only symbolic gestures (Peel 1996: 609). While militants claim that Nigeria is 85 per cent Muslim, Muslims were a minority in the 1979 and 1988–9 Constituent Assemblies (Kenny 1996: 360). Their shrillness seems to reflect awareness of danger to their hegemony.

It was the 1979 proposal to create a Federal Sharia Court of Appeal that made religion a conflictual political issue (Igwara 1995: 334). The aspiration was for parallel legal codes, but in which local Christian minorities could not aspire to political leadership or proselytise Muslims, whereas local Muslim minorities could (Enwerem 1992: 270). Since the early 1980s, Nigeria has witnessed several religious riots, nearly all in the north.

In Nigeria, therefore, politicisation of Christianity has been primarily a reaction to the Muslim agenda (or to Christian perceptions of that agenda). The popular Christian belief is that colonialism strengthened the Muslims, who have increasingly dominated government and military since the 1970s and that government policies are discriminatory. As commonly happens, real grievances are intertwined with conspiracy theories; and, if comparisons with Latin America are valid, genuine concern is probably mixed with opportunist manipulation of the 'Muslim threat' for personal or corporate projects. Igwara (1995: 327) sees Muslim militancy as having a divisive effect within the Muslim community but an increasingly unifying effect within the Christian community.

Different perceptions of the state are the nub of the problem. Christians perceive the state as pro-Muslim, despite its supposed secularity, while Muslims see it as secular and therefore reprobate. Rival projects make proselytism important for both sides. They may also end up making it impossible, since conversion becomes tantamount to political treason.

A series of events has helped to produce a new Christian radicalism. The 1979 attempt to extend the jurisdiction of sharia courts was repeated in the 1988–9 Constituent Assembly. It created such tension that the military government withdrew the Assembly's jurisdiction over the issue, leaving sharia courts still as private religious courts (Kenny 1996: 349). But federal and some state governments were perceived as supportive of Islam through funding mosques and pilgrimages to Mecca, through kid-glove treatment of anti-Christian rioters, through restrictions on public evangelism and bureaucratic difficulties for building churches, and perceived marginalisation of Christians at top government and army levels. Above all, the secret decision in 1986 to make Nigeria a member of the Organization of Islamic Conference (OIC) sharpened Christian political awareness. As Igwara says, intense reactions will not come from the south, where religious co-existence is established. The major confrontations have been in the Middle Belt where religion is increasingly a proxy for ethnicity. The secretary of the Middle Belt-based Evangelical Church of West Africa claims 'the north–south dichotomy is dead. Religion is the new dichotomy' (Igwara 1995: 342).

The new anti-Islamic politics is articulated through the 'born-again' movement and through the Christian Association (CAN) (ibid.: 339).

CAN was founded in 1976 and initially comprised Catholic and main-line Protestant churches. The president during its most politicised phase since 1988 has been a Catholic archbishop. The federal government under the Christian general Obasanjo (the only military president to have handed power to a civilian government) encouraged the birth of CAN in 1976, as a way to combat growing radicalism on both Muslim and Christian sides (Enwerem 1992: 177). But by 1988 CAN embraced almost every Christian church and had become so politicised it was almost an unofficial opposition to the regime (ibid.: 193). The Organisation of African Instituted Churches and the Pentecostal Fellowship of Nigeria (PFN) had joined. However, Catholics and older Protestant churches retained 40 per cent each of voting power (ibid.: 209). The pentecostals were anxious for membership, whether for political respectability, as Enwerem supposes (ibid.: 303), or for greater protection. But they had no illusions about the position they were expected to occupy within CAN. In 1985, the Catholic archbishop, soon to be president of CAN, had even appealed for government assistance to curb the number of churches, lest there be a religious war (ibid.: 302).

CAN is thus caught between the threat of Islamisation and the threat of losing hegemony within Christianity to pentecostals. Talk of a 'threat' of religious war can be a weapon for maintaining the status quo within the Christian world.

CAN is criticised by Kukah (1995: 226–7) for poor understanding of national politics, which it interprets in terms of an Islamic takeover plan. When protesting against sharia in northern states and other perceived examples of bias, CAN curiously demands that the federal government restore diplomatic relations with Israel and set up pilgrim welfare boards for Christians as well as for Muslims; that church leaders who settle disputes between Christians be paid from public coffers, like Muslim qadis; that ecclesiastical courts be set up at government expense; and that in legal and political systems Christians be separated from Muslims (Kenny 1996: 349). Assuming such requests were not made tongue-in-cheek to demonstrate the absurdity of Muslim pretensions, one can only conclude that Islam is providing the model for Christian politics, just as traditional Catholicism has provided the model for much evangelical politics in Latin America. While protesting against Islamisation of the country, these Christian leaders have ceded to the Islamisation of Christianity. Their requests would freeze Christianity as a communal interest group, which is the death-knell for any hope of social transformation through peaceful evangelism.

Enwerem concludes that, although 'when CAN speaks, even a military government pays attention', the organisation suffers from political *naïveté* and partisan concerns. It also lacks alliances with non-religious groups working for change. However, Enwerem also sees a danger of 'fundamentalism', even within the mainstream churches (1992: 338).

As Peel (1996) says, Christian 'fundamentalism' means mostly the wave of neo-pentecostal or charismatic churches since the early 1970s, colloquially known as the 'born-agains'. But the born-again phenomenon now extends into the Christian mainstream, and the idea of rebirth is readily applied to the nation.

While independent churches known as Aladura date back to the 1920s and 'holiness' (traditional pentecostal) churches to the inter-war years, the 'pentecostal' (more middle-class charismatic) groups date from the 1970s (Marshall 1991). Ojo (1988; 1995) prefers the term 'charismatic movement' and traces its origins to evangelical student groups. The most famous figure is Benson Idahosa, later president of the Pentecostal Fellowship. His Church of God Mission International has American links and preaches prosperity. In 1990, when redemocratisation seemed close, he resolved to 'encourage the active mass participation of all Christians in the new political process' (in Hackett 1995: 206). The self-image of these groups can be seen in the advertisement published by the Pentecostal Fellowship in a national daily in 1997 and signed by Idahosa. Protesting against a campaign of calumny in the press (money-raking, charlatanism and ritual murder), inspired by the devil, the PFN claims that 'in only thirty years the population of born-again Christians in Nigeria has grown from almost nothing to more than sixteen million'. Not only does the PFN deny the specific charges, but it stresses the social and diplomatic role of born-agains. The church has a social responsibility. Nigerian missionaries carry national culture all over the world (*The Guardian* (Nigeria), 30 Jan. 1997). It seems, however, that Idahosa spreads not only Nigerian culture, but sometimes specific government objectives: in 1995, after the execution of writer Ken Saro Wiwa had brought international repudiation, Idahosa went to London as part of General Abacha's charm offensive (Gifford 1998: 324).

Much of this is similar to Latin America, but the difference (apart from the need to distance themselves from the Aladura's unacceptable concessions to tradition) is the presence of Islam, an irreducible obstacle to pentecostal growth and political aspirations. Despite this, they seem to aim not merely at preserving a non-confessional state, but at a specifically Christian one. Until the late 1970s politics was considered

unchristian, but the founding of the Christian Students' Social Movement of Nigeria (CSSM) in 1977 helped to change that. At first, the
emphasis was on spiritual warfare – the political arena is controlled by
spiritual forces and can be set right if Christians pray for the nation. The
CSSM's prayer bulletin is full of prophecies or prayer points relating to
socio-economic conditions which may be due to 'forces of darkness'.
'Let us ask God to move Nigeria out of OPEC.' 'Let us plead with God
to forgive our government for the expulsion of illegal aliens. NOTE. God
does not allow the maltreatment of strangers whether they are good or
bad.' While the former request is presumably anti-Islamic, the latter is
notably divergent from conservative Christian politics elsewhere (Ojo
1995: 118). In 1991 the PFN national conference discussed born-again
politics in the impending democratic transition (Marshall 1991: 35). And
in 1993 the PFN president proclaimed:

God expects us to reach a situation whereby we will decree that there will be no
rain in Nigeria [and it will not rain. As Proverbs 28:2 says] "when the righteous
are in authority, the people rejoice" . . . And how are we going to get someone
who is righteous in authority? . . . Thieves will never vote for a policeman . . .
Only the righteous will vote for the righteous. So . . . it is by winning the masses
to Jesus . . . PFN will become PFA . . . We will take over the whole of Africa. (In
Marshall, R. 1997: 15)

Apart from the lack of a theology of common grace ('only the righteous
will vote for the righteous') and the contradiction between that phrase
and the quote from Proverbs, one notes the nationalistic missionary
identity – a prophetic calling of Nigeria to be responsible for Africa. The
Christianisation of the Nigerian state, so problematic because of its
position *vis-à-vis* Islam, thereby acquires a missionary dimension.

A leading scholar of Nigerian pentecostal politics is Ruth Marshall.
Her writings (1991, 1993, 1995, 1997) evolve towards a less sanguine
evaluation, as the reality of political action by leaders highlights the
ambiguous way different levels interact. As Marshall says:

To have representation as a group within the 'political nation' means to enter
the high politics of the state . . . Prebendalism is the form of this engagement in a
civilian regime . . . Whatever the power of the moral vision of civic virtue, the
uses to which it is put in the high politics of the state rob it of its radical
potential, a process of narrowing and flattening of identity. (1995: 252, 258)

This is what I call corporatism, and the Brazilian case could partly
illuminate what may happen in Nigeria if non-religious conditions are
favourable. Marshall speaks of the totalitarian potential in allowing the

identity of the 'saved' to become the basis of political power. At the same time, she says, the inner logic of pentecostalism is radical enough to outlive this short-circuiting and the new political language can be turned back by the discontented within the community into a critique of their churches' own politics (ibid.: 260), something discernible in sectors of the Assemblies of God in Brazil and ZAOGA in Zimbabwe.

More recently, Marshall suggests there are even greater dangers in pentecostal politics in Nigeria: both pentecostalism and the new Islamist movements threaten national unity. Pentecostalism attempts to colonise the national public space. Its discourse of 'winning Nigeria for Jesus' is a new form of political mobilisation with repercussions for the integrity of the nation-state (1997: 3). Pentecostalism is a 'moral ethnicity' (Lonsdale) which seeks to link power with virtue. As one born-again writer puts it: 'what is it that we sow that could be responsible for the unfavourable conditions in this country?' The answer is not simply individual sins but 'sins of the fathers'. As every Nigerian knows, says Marshall, occupying a high position is itself evidence of ties with powerful spiritual forces. While mission Christianity failed to develop a discourse to address the reality of the forces expressed through these cultural forms, pentecostalism faces the issues behind power. As a speaker at a pentecostal conference on territorial spirits said: 'Many African leaders seem to have [a hunting spirit]. It's not necessarily poverty only, there's a spirit behind it' (in Marshall, R. 1997: 10).

As old forms of community prove unreliable, says Marshall, pentecostalism has provided new networks, an alternative 'tribal' history (in the Bible), a sense of belonging to a global movement and a challenge to the state's monopoly over the material fortunes of its citizens. It aims at material and political autonomy from the state. In a life-and-death battle, Islam is demonised and competition in the religious field is transferred to the political. As one pentecostal book says: 'We Christians in Nigeria want the peace and unity of the nation. But on no account shall we compromise our religion for any of them' (ibid.: 16).

The last phrase is important. Pentecostalism is 'nation-building' in Nigeria because it transcends ethnicity and values the nation-state, but in the last analysis it subordinates 'national unity' to a religious vision which is ultimately incapable of reconstructing the state in its own image because of the enormous presence of Islam. They wish to convert their adversaries and 'save' the state – but if the attempt destroys the state before that, then so be it. There is no sign, however, that they are in the business of physically eliminating adversaries. The way to power is 'winning the masses to Jesus' and getting the ever more numerous 'righteous to vote for the righteous'.

After 1989 Nigeria went through an aborted transition to democracy and a prolongation of dictatorial rule with a worsening human-rights situation. In 1989 the government itself created two parties, the NCR (more northern and Islamic and 'slightly to the right'), and the SDP (more southern and Christian and 'slightly to the left'). In 1993, presidential elections finally took place. Both parties presented Muslim candidates, but the NCR's was a Hausa from the north, and the SDP's was Chief Abiola, a Yoruba. Religion surfaced, however, in the vice-presidential debate. The NCR's candidate was an Igbo Catholic, who claimed his slate was 'balanced'. The SDP's was a northern Muslim who disclaimed he was running as a Muslim. Kenny describes how Christians watching the televised debate with him cheered the latter man and considered the Catholic a stooge (1996: 362).

Kukah (1995: 231ff.) asks what had become of all the talk of a Christian president. He answers that it had largely reflected the interests of ruling cliques in the south; calls for a Christian president had masked the quest for a southern president. In a controversial statement, the president of CAN said there was no problem with a Muslim–Muslim slate. Christians, it is thought, voted massively for Abiola. When it became clear that Abiola was winning, the government cancelled the result. Heads of CAN and the Anglican, Methodist and Presbyterian churches all appealed to the military to hand over power (Kukah 1995: 233–4).

Politics after that was dominated more by the divide over dictatorship than by religion. But results in other 1993 elections were allowed to stand, and there was Protestant participation. The Evangelical Church of West Africa, a strongly evangelical church based in the Middle Belt, encouraged members to run (*Christianity Today*, 9 Nov. 1992: 38–40). According to Kukah, priests, deacons, prophets, apostles and evangelists emerged as governors, deputy governors, local government chairmen and councillors. The Revd Nyame was elected governor of Taraba State in the north, and Bamidele Olumilua, an evangelist, became governor of Ondo State in the south (Kukah 1995: 236). One would like to know more about these people: their origins, trajectories, political bases, ideologies and performance in office.

In March 1999 further parliamentary elections and then presidential elections were held. The Christian general Olusegun Obasanjo, a Yoruba and former president who had handed over power to a civilian government in the late 1970s and had later been imprisoned by the Abacha regime, was elected president. Obasanjo is a Baptist who went through a revitalising spiritual experience in prison. He has made no secret of his Christian commitment, and has built a chapel in the presidential house (Cyril Imo, personal communication).

Diamond and Plattner's talk of the danger of religion polarising Nigeria in a way even ethnicity does not, and of the need for responsible leadership which eschews the mobilisation of religious issues for short-term gain (1994: xxv), seemed prescient in the sharia conflict which erupted months after Obasanjo's election. Leaders of several northern states indicated they wanted to introduce sharia, and the state of Zamfara actually did so. When Kaduna, with a larger Christian minority, prepared to do so, peaceful demonstrations turned into a blood-bath in which many Christians died. Rioting spread to other regions, with Muslims as victims. After hundreds of deaths, northern governors agreed not to press for sharia.

Obasanjo, democratically elected and a born-again Christian, had to walk a tightrope. Sharia is an emotive issue at the disposal of populist politicians in Muslim areas, and could destroy national unity. The secretary-general of the Anglican Church said any declaration of sharia was a secession plan, and CAN lobbied the president to take a strong stand. Obasanjo, however, was more circumspect than these leading ecclesiastics, preferring to use behind-the-scenes influence to defuse the situation. Placing blame on both sides, he condemned all religious violence not only on pragmatic grounds (as unpatriotic, since it squandered the new international goodwill towards Nigeria) but also on religious grounds. 'Islam by name is a religion of peace and Christianity was established by the Prince of Peace'; it was therefore foolish to promote either by violence (*The Guardian Online*, 24 Feb. 2000). It will be interesting to see whether Muslim religious leaders may actually have more respect for a president who has equally deep but opposing religious convictions than they would for politicians who combine a basic religious indifference with occasional opportunistic use of religious themes.

Nigerian evangelical politics is thus a crucial case. From Latin American experience, we can expect redemocratisation to lead to a flowering of pentecostal political ebullience in all its ambiguity. Marshall's articles are instigating but paint a somewhat uniform picture. We need to study differences between churches, as well as cases of pentecostal political actors. Nigeria is similar to Guatemala in its high-profile politicised middle-class charismatic churches, and yet it is reminiscent of Brazil in the conscious planning for action in the aborted return to democracy in the early 1990s, in its political use of the language of religious conflict (with Islam taking the place of Catholicism) and in its plethora of candidates. Whether this will lead to corporatist electoral politics at the parliamentary level remains to be seen.

However, Nigeria also defies comparison with Latin America or even with other African countries. Even where a Catholic 'threat' can be made plausible in Latin America and equality has not been totally achieved, there can be no comparison with the obvious political challenge represented by Nigerian Islam. Whether adopting the traditional defence of a religiously neutral state (interpreted as a 'Christian' doctrine by Muslim activists), or dreaming of a Christian theocratic counterpart to the Islamist ideals of their opponents, there is no way Christians can avoid the gauntlet thrown down by Islamist politics. In addition, the only way the huge Muslim population can be opened up for conversionist activities is through political action. With the diminution of the population adhering to African traditional religions, this is an increasingly urgent task.

A theme for comparative study is the political role of graduates of evangelical student movements. Nigeria seemingly contrasts with Brazil and Peru where graduates of movements related to the International Fellowship of Evangelical Students (IFES) have played a different political role.

PART FOUR

Spanish-speaking Latin America

GENERAL INTRODUCTION

Latin America falls in the medium range of Third World per-capita income levels – there are no tigers, but most countries are above all our African nations except South Africa. There is comparative cultural homogeneity, due to common Iberian colonisation, independence in the early nineteenth century (except for some Caribbean possessions), followed by economic dependence on Britain and later the United States.

'Latin America' is a French invention in the mid-nineteenth century, reflecting French aspiration for cultural (and even political) hegemony. The name is culturally but not ethnically justifiable. Anthropologist Darcy Ribeiro divides Latin America into three categories. The Witness Peoples are the modern representatives of ancient civilisations with which European expansion clashed, represented by countries where the Amerindian element is greatest: Guatemala, Bolivia, Peru, Ecuador, and to some extent Mexico. The New Peoples are a mix of disparate ethnic matrixes. Chile and Paraguay mix European and Amerindian elements; the African element is added in Brazil and Colombia. The Transplanted Peoples are overwhelmingly of European immigrants. Argentina and Uruguay are the main examples, but southern Brazil is also included (Ribeiro 1983: 58).

Decolonisation is a dim memory, unlike in Asia and Africa, and occurred in a different way, with criollo (native-born white) elites taking power and often still holding it. The nation-states are thus fairly solid and national identities secure, despite a recent rise in indigenous aware-ness in Andean and Mayan regions. Latin America is 'underdeveloped' but it is also, broadly speaking, 'Western' and 'Christian'. It is the poor part of the Western world, and its closest kin in some ways today is the European portion of the former socialist bloc. This ambiguous position is often cited as a reason for the emergence of Liberation Theology. There is no chance of taking refuge in a pre-modern non-Western culture, in an anti-Western reaction or a return to pre-colonial roots. This is only marginally possible in countries with a large indigenous population, as in the Mexican Revolution's cultivation of pre-Columbian themes. But for the New and Transplanted Peoples, it is not an option. Their whole history is irredeemably linked to Western expansion, experienced largely as frustration. There can be no cultural or religious refuge in Hinduism, Buddhism, Islam or a tribal past.

The economic crisis, while less severe than in most of Africa, is marked by startling inequalities. The informal economy is often huge. A highly concentrated landholding structure in most countries is often given as a reason for inability to follow the Asian tigers; another is minimal public spending on education and health. Since the early 1980s, foreign debt is a huge millstone on the region's neck. The 1980s became the 'lost decade' in which development hopes were shattered. The 1990s have seen a trend to neoliberal policies in most countries.

Nevertheless, civil society is stronger than in Africa, and some countries have had greater experience of multi-party democracy. The military regimes of the 1960s and 1970s ceded to a wave of redemocratisation from the mid 1980s, and there is currently formal democracy almost everywhere. However, Latin America has been here before – witness a 1961 book called 'The Twilight of the Dictators'! Democracy is not consolidated in many countries. The large-scale evangelical entry into politics has occurred in this context of redemocratisation.

Latin America has an older mass Christianisation than any African or Asian country discussed (except the Philippines). With exceptions such as secularised Uruguay, it remains a profoundly religious continent. However, this religiosity is in flux. The Catholic monopoly of colonial and early post-independence times, and even the secure hegemony of the first half of the twentieth century, are under threat in most countries. The traditional Catholic claim to be an essential part of Latin American identity has lost plausibility as pluralism has increased and Protestantism become deep-rooted. Modernisation and urbanisation have not been favourable to Catholicism, whose institutional structure remains too tied to a rural Christendom mentality. The chronic shortage of national priests in most countries highlights the gap between 'official' churchly Catholicism and 'popular' or 'folk' Catholicism, often syncretic, which dominates the masses and has only a marginal relationship with ecclesiastical structures. Liberation Theology and the Base Communities, important from the 1960s to 1980s but now on the wane, are in part attempts to revitalise the church at the grass-roots in the face of new challenges. The Catholic Charismatic Renewal, often larger than Base Communities, is another example of this. Afro-Brazilian religions (far from limited to blacks and now exported) also compete for followers, while the main new religious phenomenon among the middle class is, as in the developed West, esoteric and extra-institutional.

In this context, Protestantism has become prominent. Religious competition is different from Asia and Africa, and this can affect political stances. There are no non-Christian 'world religions' to contend with, nor vast reserves of followers of 'primal religions'. Protestant identity was forged in relation to the dominant religion, Catholicism. This produced a more 'adversarial' Protestantism than in Africa. All Protestants are usually called 'evangélicos' in Spanish and Portuguese, and evangelicals in the English-language sense are in fact overwhelmingly dominant in the Protestant field. There is no equivalent of the category of 'African Independent Churches' (although recent large-scale conversion by indigenous peoples in the Andes, Central America and southern Mexico may yet produce something similar), but pentecostalism virtually plays that role, being the main focus of local denominational creativity.

Whereas Protestantism entered Asia (except the Philippines) as a new religion *vis-à-vis* huge non-Christian faiths, and entered Africa in a variety of situations according to the colonial power, it entered Latin America (mostly in the second half of the nineteenth century) as an effectively sectarian variant of the dominant religion, but in tandem with the political and economic liberalism brought by the Anglo-Saxon powers. Until recently, growth was far slower than in many African countries and Korea. This meant that most Protestant churches had scant possibility of playing the role of surrogate oppositions to repressive military regimes in the 1960s and 1970s, as the Catholic Church sometimes (but not always) did. It also means it is sociologically worth trying, for example, to count the number of evangelicals in congress, an exercise that is of doubtful value in Anglophone Africa. In some countries there is still discrimination at certain social levels against evangelicals as individuals, as well as legal discrimination against churches. Although official separation of church and state, effectuated in some countries in the nineteenth century and in others only in the 1990s, is now almost universal (only Bolivia, Argentina and Costa Rica still have an official religion), there are countries where evangelical churches do not enjoy the same legal rights as the Catholic Church. One recent example from a country we shall not look at will suffice. In 1998 in Bolivia, the Ministry of Foreign Affairs and Cults announced a controversial regulation obliging non-Catholic churches to present lists of members with their identity card numbers, prohibiting collections of offerings and subjecting all public evangelistic activities to control of the authorities (*Servicio de Noticias ALC* (hereinafter *ALC*), 29 May 1998). Even where tolerance and freedom of worship are secure, there is often some way still to go before the practice of full equality takes hold in public life and civil society. In various countries one still finds state subsidies to the Catholic church, state funding only to Catholic universities, or restrictions on non-Catholic missions in indigenous areas (Sigmund 1999: 6–7).

There are probably some forty-five million Protestants in Latin America today, about 10 per cent of the population. The highest percentage is probably in Guatemala, with estimates between 19 and 30 per cent. The lower figure is probably closer, and percentage growth seems to have stagnated after being rapid in the 1970s and 1980s. Chile (perhaps 16% to 18%) and Brazil (between 12% and 15%) have had steady growth since the 1950s. Nicaragua is now 15 per cent. At the other end of the scale, Uruguay and Venezuela are still at 2 or 3 per cent. The middle range embraces the Andean countries at the top end and Argentina, Mexico and Colombia at the lower end. Martin (1990: 59) gives as a rule of thumb that Protestantism's chances of growth have been higher where the Catholic Church was politically weakened by liberalism in the nineteenth century but the culture remained unsecularised. Where secularisation took hold, or where the Catholic Church retained great political power, growth has been slower.

Perhaps 60 to 70 per cent of Latin American Protestants are pentecostals, and this percentage is increasing. Protestantism is most pentecostalised in Chile (perhaps 80%) and least in the Andean countries (under half).

In most of Latin America, Protestantism (especially pentecostalism) is associated disproportionately with the poor and less educated. Founders of major pentecostal groups include proletarians, independent artisans and lower-middle-class white-collar workers. Rare are the founders of higher social origin. Most pentecostal churches (unlike their historical counterparts) were founded either by Latin Americans who broke with an existing Protestant denomination or by independent missionaries, and only rarely by a foreign pentecostal denomination (Freston 1998c).

One major theme in Spanish-speaking Latin America, which we have scarcely come across in Asia, Africa or Brazil, is that of evangelical political parties, more than twenty having been founded in recent years.

CHAPTER 21

Argentina

A relatively developed country in the early twentieth century, Argentina started to decline economically, alternating between military and populist governments. For different reasons, the populist governments of Juan Perón and the brutal military regime of 1976–83 have marked not only modern Argentine politics but the trajectory of Protestantism as well.

Protestantism was for long associated with immigrant minorities. This was true even of pentecostalism. Although it started among Italians, it was for decades 'more readily accepted in mainly Indian communities or amongst central or northern European immigrants. The greatest resistance was met where there were most first-generation descendants of Italian or Spanish immigrants . . . [who did not want to] risk foregoing that which made them sense that this new Catholic country was indeed their own' (Saracco 1989: 69–70). Slow growth has to do with this identification with immigrants. According to D'Epinay (1975), it also has to do with Peronism's capacity to court the new urban masses with the quasi-religious cult of Evita. Only following the failure of Peronist populism in the 1950s did pentecostalism gain ground among the urban poor, and it reached new heights after redemocratisation in the early 1980s had left the Catholic Church shaken by its association with militarism (Saracco 1989: 140). By the late 1980s, Protestantism had achieved unprecedented projection, thanks partly to high-profile neo-pentecostals such as Omar Cabrera, Carlos Annacondia and Héctor Giménez. A survey of the evolution of churches in Buenos Aires shows that the pentecostal explosion dates from the return of democracy in 1983 (Saracco 1992).

However, the traditional position of the Catholic Church was not to be surrendered so easily. In 1993, a bill in congress sought to 'avoid the excessive number of registrations of groups with no roots or representativeness'. The bill required five years' existence in a location and a certain number of members for registration, as well as professional accounting of finances. The financial support which the state is constitutionally required to give to the Catholic Church grew fivefold between 1989 and 1998, reaching nearly ten million dollars.

Numerical growth and continued discrimination encouraged the formation of pan-pentecostal representative bodies (Evangelical Pentecostal Confederation; Federation of Autonomous Pentecostal Churches; Confederation of Pentecostal Churches of the Argentine Republic) and of political parties. The first evangelical party was the Movimiento Cristiano Independiente (MCI), which sprang from sectors traditionally reticent about politics. Many leaders were Baptists and Brethren, and it initially had the support of Héctor Giménez, a controversial neo-pentecostal leader. The MCI made its electoral debut in the congressional elections of 1993 in the province of Buenos Aires, but failed to elect anyone. It then contested elections for the Constituent Assembly in 1994 in the same province, while another evangelical party, the Movimiento Reformista Independiente (MRI) ran in Córdoba. Unlike 1993, the MCI candidates in 1994 were well-known church leaders – of the Association of the Church of God (pentecostal), the Evangelical Pentecostal Conference, the Baptists and the Brethren. In their own words, they were not seeking election as 'politicians but as servants of God'. But even though the MCI doubled its 1993 vote, it again failed to elect anybody, as also did the MRI in Córdoba (Mallimaci 1996).

After this second disappointment, some former members of MCI launched another party, the Movimiento Reformador (MR). The MR defines itself as opposed to the neoliberal model of the Menem government. The slimming of the state and indiscriminate privatisation generate an exclusionary model which concentrates wealth, it says (*Evangelicos, Politica y Sociedad*, June 1997: 5).

There was one Protestant elected to the Constituent Assembly in 1994. José Míguez Bonino, Methodist Liberation theologian and former leader of the World Council of Churches, now has a close relationship with the Latin American Theological Fraternity. He defines his current position thus: 'I have been catalogued as a conservative, revolutionary, Barthian, liberal, catholicising, moderate and liberationist. Probably all of this is correct. [But] what "comes from within" is that I am an evangelical' (Míguez 1995: 5). Míguez was elected by the Frente Grande, a centre-left coalition. He defended this choice because it allowed him to stand without a party affiliation, and because the Frente Grande's proposals were convergent with those fundamental to his evangelical identity. He criticised evangelical parties for 'confusing different levels: sacralising political themes and being superficial about religious convictions' (in Mallimaci 1996: 276). In the Constituent Assembly, the requirement that the president be a Catholic was abolished but state 'support' of the Catholic Church was not.

The degree of evangelical unity is closely related to its political clout in many Latin countries, and in this respect Argentina seems better placed than most. A month before the 1999 presidential elections, the Consejo Nacional Cristiano Evangélico organised a rally which brought an estimated 280,000 people from a broad range of denominations. This calculated show of strength included a 'Message to the Nation' which refused to accept the social situation as 'unchangeable, abandoned to the fortunes of the market or to the sinister fate of corruption'. Although the recipe for change was limited to an appeal for businessmen and industrialists to redouble efforts to 'overcome the dynamic of income concentration', it was significant that the organisers had told the presidential candidates (who in the end did not come) that they would not be allowed to address the crowd (*ALC*, 10 Sept. 1999). Such a posture is by no means typical in Latin American evangelicalism.

CHAPTER 22

Mexico

Mexico is the second most populous country in Latin America and the only one with a land border with the United States. Its history is exceptionally dramatic: the site of great Amerindian civilisations, culminating in the Aztec empire conquered by the Spanish, it attained independence in 1821 but lost much of its territory (Arizona, western Colorado, Nevada, Utah, Texas, California and New Mexico) to the United States in 1848. Identity is thus caught up with the indigenous and Spanish past (60% of the population is mestizo and 30% Indian) and with proximity to the United States. Not surprisingly, nationalism has been important in Mexican history, and from 1910 Mexico staged the first great Latin American revolution of the twentieth century, whose institutional outcome, the Partido Revolucionario Institucional (PRI), and secular tradition still dominate politics.

The relationship with the regional hegemonic power, the United States, which happens to be Protestant, has influenced Protestantism's chances of achieving a positive association with national identity, *vis-à-vis* Catholicism (still the nominal religion of nine out of ten people) and revolutionary secularism. Two major themes in current evangelical politics are how it relates to this secularist tradition and recent incipient transformations, and how it relates to the most startling phenomenon in Mexico in the 1990s, the Zapatista guerrilla rebellion in Chiapas.

In the 1990 census Protestants were only 4.89 per cent, but in the south, especially among rural mestizos and Indians, the percentage was much higher, transforming what had originally been a predominantly northern phenomenon. Both historical Protestantism and pentecostalism can point to autonomous origins. In the case of pentecostalism, there were Mexicans present at the famous revival meetings just across the border in Azusa Street, Los Angeles, in 1906. The founders of most pentecostal denominations were Mexicans converted in the United States.

The origins of Protestantism in Mexico are unique in Latin America. The independent country's early years were turbulent, including two monarchical experiments, defeat in war with the United States and the capture of the capital twice by foreign forces. The conflict between liberals and the Catholic Church was correspondingly fierce. The Church owned immense portions of the land and enjoyed enormous privileges. The Reform Laws under President Juárez in the late 1850s restricted Catholic privileges, but led to a civil war, during which Juárez adopted openly anti-clerical measures (nationalisation of Church property, suppression of male orders) and introduced freedom of worship. In this context, the government went beyond anti-clericalism and encouraged a religious revolution. At first, this took the form of supporting an independent national church, Catholic in doctrine and ritual but separate from Rome, known as the Church of Jesus. Short of funds and without bishops to ordain new clergy, this church requested support from the Episcopalian Church in the United States, though help only arrived several years later. With the failure to create an autonomous church, the liberal government opened its doors to Protestant missions as the only way of creating a viable alternative to Catholicism. Juárez declared that 'the future prosperity and happiness of my nation now depend on the development of Protestantism' (Bowen, K. 1996: 25). By the early 1870s some fifty non-Catholic congregations existed, mostly without foreign links, and many people from these early groups joined the Protestant denominations which arrived in those years (ibid.: 25–6).

The origins of Protestantism are thus largely national and allied to political turbulence. Mondragón talks of Juan Amador, the founder of a non-Catholic church and editor of an evangelical newspaper, in which he writes in 1873: 'We accept socialism as the sublime ideal of the transformation of society through peace, justice, equality and universal fraternity' (1991: 64).

With these origins, it is not surprising that Protestants played a disproportionately large role in the Mexican Revolution. They constituted only 0.5 per cent of the population, but were concentrated in the north, along railway lines and among the emergent lower-middle class (Bowen K. 1996: 27). They were 'a striking and voluble minority in the liberal press and clubs that emerged in the 1890s to condemn [President] Diaz's fraudulent elections and his conciliation with the Catholic Church' (ibid.: 30). They supported Madero's revolt against Diaz in 1910 to such an extent that mission statesman Samuel Inman wrote: 'when the Mexican Revolution broke out, the Protestant churches rallied to it almost unanimously'. Later, missionaries such as Inman and Mexican Protestant leaders undertook propaganda tours in the United States against the interventionist policies of sectors of the American government (Mondragón 1991: 71).

The Revolution was prolonged and complex, and Protestants did not have a uniform role. Bastian (1983) summarises the situation thus: the role of Protestant rural schoolmasters in interpreting the Revolution to the masses was fundamental. Most Protestants wanted reform of the oligarchical capitalist society to introduce a democratic regime, space for popular and moral education and land reform favouring small peasant properties. Their ideal was a social capitalism, and Venustiano Carranza (president from 1914) answered to their aspirations. But a minority wanted more than that, such as the evangelical Pascual Orozco who took armed control of most of Chihuahua in 1912 (Bowen K. 1996: 31), or the two Methodists (a pastor and a schoolmaster) who were in General Emiliano Zapata's general-staff, one of whom (Otilio Montaño) wrote Zapata's plan for radical land reform (Mondragón 1991: 68).

The Carranza government gave considerable space to Protestants. Presbyterian pastor Gregorio Velázquez was head of the Office of Information and Propaganda. As a leading ideologue of the regime, he promoted many Protestants to strategic jobs. Carranza practically left organisation of public education to Protestant intellectuals, especially the Methodist Andrés Osuna (ibid.: 71). Three state governors were Protestants, and there were ten Protestants in the Constituent Assembly of 1917. Osuna became governor of Tamaulipas; Presbyterian Aaron Sáenz was in charge of the Federal District and later governor of Nuevo León; his brother Moisés was Minister of Public Education. This was the high-water mark of Protestant political involvement in Mexico, and was without precedent in Latin America as a whole. It was due partly to the origins and early social role of Mexican Protestantism. It was also a strategy by Carranza, who realised the Revolution needed trained cadres like the Protestants who could not threaten the state, since unlike the Catholics they were a divided minority (Bastian 1983: 144).

The 1917 constitution contained anti-clerical clauses, which poten-tially affected Protestants as well. Churches were barred from maintain-ing schools and the clergy from being schoolmasters. No church could own land, and services could only take place inside church buildings. Only native-born Mexicans could be ministers of any religious body. Ministers could not vote or be elected for political office, and religious publications could not comment on national politics (Scott 1991: 40–1). The number of ministers of each religion could be regulated by state governments.

In practice, such articles were not often aimed at Protestantism, although its school network was soon broken (Bowen K. 1996: 37). In the late 1920s and early 1930s, during the most anti-religious phase of the Revolution, several states prohibited all religious services. In the 1940s certain governments, interested in détente with Catholicism, raised difficulties in registering Protestant churches and were tolerant of locally inspired attacks on Protestants (ibid.: 44), but this ended in the 1950s and Protestantism settled down to a comfortable relationship with the state. At the same time, Protestant presence in public life waned, due, says Mondragón, to loss of schools, abandonment of the liberal-radical heritage and lack of a holistic theology of salvation (1991: 75).

By 1940, revolutionary radicalism had run its course, and an authoritarian system developed. While formally democratic, the Partido Revolucionario Institucional (PRI) was practically monolithic. By the late 1980s this system was running out of steam. In the 1988 elections, only 22 per cent of the potential electorate voted for the new president. Massive abstention and accusations of fraud revealed a lack of confidence in the system.

In this context, Mexico requested entry into the North American Free Trade Agreement (NAFTA). Needing a more democratic image and greater legitimacy, the government initiated a less militantly secularist policy. President Salinas met Protestant leaders for the first time ever, and in 1992 restored full diplomatic ties with the Vatican.

That year also saw reform of the constitutional articles relating to religion. Churches may now possess property, hold events outside their premises and get involved in education. The right of the states to restrict the number of clergy and services was removed, and the clergy regained voting rights. However, evangelical fears centred on two aspects. Firstly, the perpetuation of state control over important aspects of religious life. Churches could own property 'indispensable' to their religious endeavours; the definition of 'indispensable' lay with the Ministry of the Interior. In addition, churches had to register, for which they had to prove they had been active in Mexico for five years and possessed 'sufficient property to satisfy church needs'. This was tantamount to declaring Mexico a closed market to all new religious movements. Political parties which allude to a religious creed are still prohibited, and clergy cannot participate in campaigns or openly support a candidate

(Blancarte 1993: 557; Limón and Clemente 1995: 179–80). Clergy who wish to stand for election must renounce their church position and wait for five years (Metz 1994: 76–7).

Thus, the new law not only retains excessive state interference in religion, but also restrains free competition in the religious field (Blancarte 1993: 565). However, there is another cause for evangelical concern: increasing Catholic influence. The hierarchy pressed for preferential space for the Catholic Church. This was justified by the Vatican representative on the grounds that justice is not 'giving the same to everyone... An elephant does not eat the same way as an ant' (ibid.: 563). It was the hierarchy which demanded that religious associations be prohibited from controlling electronic media. Fear of evangelical competition made the bishops renounce their own use of such media (ibid.: 567). There was a spate of unfortunate statements regarding evangelical churches: 'you do not have dialogue with bandits' (Bishop Lozano); 'the sects, like flies, have to be removed', being 'rapacious wolves' (the Vatican representative); 'we will defend ourselves from these imposters who wish to root out the faith and buy it with dollars' (the bishop of Cuernavaca) (Bowen K. 1996: 164, 249; Metz 1994: 72–3; *Revista del Instituto Rutherford*, 8, 1993: 7).

This leads to interesting reflections in the light of Hammond's 1980 article on whether there is a 'civil religion' in Mexico on the lines of that in the United States. He concludes not, since there is no transcendental ideology independent of both church and state. There is certainly nationalism, but it is secular and remains the domain of the state. There is also vast cultic activity surrounding the Virgin of Guadalupe, a dark-skinned Mary venerated since the seventeenth century on the site of the former temple to the Aztec mother of the gods. Bowen says evangelicals' rejection of this tradition has been an obstacle, since it is a core element in national identity (1996: 129). As Hammond says, this cult symbolises the mestizo nation, but it is not 'civil' or political. For a civil religion to arise, this cult would have to merge with secular nationalism. That it has not, has been due to conflict between church and state since the 1850s, making the church withhold its symbols from a joint venture with the state (1980: 51–7). Whether the changes initiated in the 1990s could move Mexico in the direction of such a civil religion remains to be seen.

How have evangelicals behaved amidst these upheavals? Scott (1991) studied evangelical voting in Mexico City in the 1988 presidential election. Traditionally, evangelicals are presumed to have voted heavily for the PRI, in part because it is felt to have secured basic liberties for evangelicals, and also because the other main parties are seen as associated with Catholicism (PAN) or with the atheistic left (PRD). This position was still supported in 1988 by leaders of the pentecostal Church of God (ibid.: 146). But Presbyterians and Baptists were abandoning the PRI by 1988; especially the Presbyterians, 48 per cent of whom in Mexico City voted for the PRD, against 37 per cent for the PRI and 14 per cent for the PAN. Baptists voted less for the PRD (34%) and more for the PRI (41%) and PAN (25%) than the Presbyterians. The Church of God was overwhelmingly PRI (64%) and anti-PAN (7%), giving the PRD 29 per cent (ibid.: 193). However, all three denominations were more loyal to the PRI than the general population in Mexico City (official results, presumably tilted to the PRI, gave it 27%, PRD 48% and PAN 22%). Evangelicals may thus be a bastion of support for the old monolithic PRI. Nevertheless, across the denominations voting is correlated to income levels: support for the PRD has a clear inverse relation to income, while support for PAN rises steeply with rising income (ibid.: 163).

Bowen also has figures from a nationwide sample. He cites the general superintendent of the Assemblies of God: 'Better the old for being known, say many of our faithful. This is why we are going to vote for the PRI; in spite of everything the system has guaranteed religious liberty' (1996: 205). This is borne out by Bowen's sample of evangelicals: 39 per cent voted for the PRI, considerably more than the national result. Slightly more evangelicals voted for the PRD than the official national average, while only 2 per cent voted for the pro-Catholic conservative PAN (ibid.: 204). This is one of many cases in Latin America where anti-Catholicism pushes evangelicals into a more leftist pattern than the general population, despite media and even academic perceptions of them as conservative. However, one must beware of attributing the same motives to ordinary evangelicals and to church leaders. The importance given to religious liberty and equality by church leaders, a concern of their professional status, may not be as great for lay people. We really do not know much about how ordinary evangelicals vote and what motivates their political choices. And since the evangelical community is presumably not a faithful replica of Mexican society in its social composition, we need to know to what extent its voting patterns are reducible to strictly religious factors rather than to social, educational, economic, regional and gender locations.

It seems there are now more evangelical politicians at the national level than in previous decades. Examples include the Baptist María de los Angeles Moreno, a former Sunday School teacher and childhood friend of former president Salinas. An economist, she was federal deputy from 1991 to 1994 and senator since then, having held top posts in both Houses. Regarded as a feminist, she was for some years president of the PRI. Another evangelical senator is Pablo Salazar, a Presbyterian lawyer who later joined the Nazarenes, well known for his legal work for the Indians, who gained space when the PRI courted Chiapas evangelicals. Other examples are deputies Porfirio Montero and Humberto Rice (the latter a northern Congregationalist who has been general secretary of the PAN). A Church of God pastor, Domingo López, was a candidate for deputy with the left-wing PRD. One interesting case is Evangelina Corona, a Presbyterian elder and reminiscent of Brazil's Benedita da Silva. A former domestic maid, she became leader of the seamstresses' union which she helped to organise. From 1991 to 1994, she was federal deputy for the PRD, and was nearly elected mayor of Ciudad Netzahualcóyotl (*Agenda Teológica*, Fraternidad Teológica Latinoamericana, April–June 1997).

The openness of the state to rethinking church–state questions, and the danger of Catholic pre-empting of this, has encouraged the multiplication of 'representative' evangelical bodies. To the Evangelical Confraternity of Mexico (Conemex) have been added the National Forum of Christian Evangelical Churches of Mexico (Fonice) and the National Confraternity of Christian Evangelical Churches (Confraternice) (Limón and Clemente 1995: 181–2). In the discussions on constitutional change, the historical churches were initially prominent, but pentecostals later exerted superior numerical power. But Bowen's verdict is that none are yet organised pressure groups in party politics, capable of negotiating privileges for votes. 'In the 1990s, as always, evangelical leaders were still primarily concerned with more immediate issues of self-defence' (1996: 162), a stark contrast to several Latin American countries.

Another distinctive feature of Mexico is the role of evangelicalism in the crisis in the southern border state of Chiapas which has led to the most famous guerrilla movement in contemporary Latin America, the Zapatista National Liberation Army (EZLN). Evangelicals are 16 per cent in Chiapas; in some highland municipalities, they are over 30 per cent. The real percentage may be higher, since many Indians tell census takers they have no religion, out of well-founded fear of reprisals (Martínez 1996a). In Mexico, the percentage of Protestants among

Indians is twice as high as the national average, and this is due to endogenous initiatives rather than foreign or mestizo missionaries (Martínez 1995).

This is a phenomenon of growing importance. In the Andean region and especially in southern Mexico and Central America, Protestantism has made headway among indigenous peoples. What is its appeal, and is it harmful or beneficial for indigenous cultures?

Earle's (1992) portrayal of a highland community in Guatemala is typical of one interpretation. With the decline of community-wide authority and increase in social discord, Protestantism exploits conflict, creating more division and facilitating capitalist penetration. New male wealth is spent on clothing and drinking, not on nutrition and children's education. 'People go from worship and collective defence of their land to a pliant acceptance of its commodification and a desire to obtain a *patron* in this world to build and guard a vacation bungalow for in order to receive their own from a parallel *patron* in the sky after death', concludes Earle (1992: 385). He portrays a community already undergoing differentiation and sees Protestantism as accelerating the break-up, offering nothing positive. Other analyses, however, present a different picture.

While recognising that Protestantism reinforces individualist tendencies in detriment to communal identity, Annis (1987) claims that what we call Indianness is less a relic of a glorious past than a cultural package that solidified Spanish control. According to Rapaport, the idea that missions hinder indigenous peoples from forging their own destinies neglects the way Indian evangelicals filter missionary teaching. The Páez and Guambiano of Colombia, where whole villages are pentecostal, 'resoundingly reject the political orientation of national and foreign missionaries, and they legitimate political activity oriented to self-determination' (1984: 112). After missionaries left, evangelical participation in land reclamation campaigns intensified. The Páez, while breaking with traditional ceremonies which legitimated their territory through worship of saints and drinking, developed evangelical alternatives. Two aspects were crucial in this: the similarity of evangelical millenarianism to their traditional messianism; and pentecostalism's reinforcement of ethnic identity by allowing a cult without non-indigenous intermediaries.

Returning to Mexico, Bastian sees indigenous Protestantism as defence of identity. 'With the penetration of capitalist structures into the countryside and the destructuring of traditional social relations, the *caciques* [traditional leaders] themselves broke the meaning of the traditional fiesta. It no longer serves to burn off excess or to renew the symbolic power of the people; it serves the political control of capitalist accumulation' (1983: 230–1). Popular Catholicism is thus deflected from its redistributive function. Conversion to Protestantism enables poor farmers to disentangle themselves from an exploitative system; they are then accused of destroying traditional community and culture. But 'one must analyse the instrumentalisation of the collective system by the *caciques*... Is it really true, as a *cacique* affirms, that they destroy "our culture because they no longer drink or get so ill, no longer fight so much or go to the faith-healer, no longer use candles or incense ... and prefer to pray to solve their problems"?' (1983: 238).

Garrard-Burnett says Protestantism is not so much a transition to modernity, as often claimed, as a means of asserting ethnic differentiation. They do indeed establish micro-communities, but that is only possible because the traditional community is already fractured. Protestants emphasise native-language use, far more than any other religion including traditional practices. What these Protestant movements mean for indigenous identity is not clear. They are prepared to identify themselves as Protestant even when the price is community division, persecution or expulsion. To what extent they are product or source of community disintegration is still controversial, but it is clear that these new identities are locally constructed. While sharing characteristics of other social movements, they also offer a dimension of meaning, forming not merely a movement but a moral community (Garrard-Burnett 1996a). The question also arises whether they do not have a right to contribute to the disintegration of tradition if that is what they want. Is not the right to change harmful or outworn traditions a basic human right, as with indigenous women who protest against gender-oppressive aspects of indigenous custom (Martínez 1996b)?

In short, indigenous Protestantism, as in mestizo society, has many faces. Its initial context is often the breakdown of old communities (though it does not usually provoke such breakdown). It may deepen existing divisions or create new ones; or it may reconstitute community (although not in the old monolithic form: as Martin (1990: 100) says, Protestantism logically implies division, creating voluntary networks in place of inevitable ones). As pluralism increases in the indigenous context, the role of Protestantism tends to be more integrative and less 'destructive'.

A key factor among indigenous communities throughout Latin America is the possibility of escaping mestizo domination at least in the symbolic realm. Even though a majority of highland Indian evangelicals in Chiapas are officially linked to the Presbyterian Church, they are organised in a separate presbytery. Their Presbyterianism is also highly pentecostalised. Converts have faced consistent hostility and violence for the last thirty years. The opposition goes from social pressure, through ostracism and threats, to violent expulsion and even murder. More than thirty thousand Indians have been expelled from their lands by the local *caciques* (Limón and Clemente 1995: 189). Sometimes they are presented with a choice: renounce evangelical faith or sign a document saying they are 'voluntarily' abandoning their land and belongings. No other group in Mexico has suffered such prolonged persecution, says Martínez (1996a); it is not 'politically correct' to defend their cause. They are victims of a double discrimination: as Indians from a remote region, and as evangelicals, and therefore proselytes of an 'anti-Mexican' creed, 'followers of anti-national sects which divide the peoples'. Many Mexican social scientists see them as a threat to cultural cohesion, but do not mention how this culture was constructed and is sustained. This is a racist and paternalist attitude which implicitly sees Indians as incapable of re-elaborating their own identity. They talk as if there were, for all time, only one way to be a genuine Indian. No one mentions that popular Catholicism also came from abroad and was historically constructed. Defence of indigenous tradition thus leads to the defence of islands of authoritarianism opposed to equality, freedom and social justice. Corporate rights are considered more important than individual rights. Religious diversity, which the same social scientists and human-rights activists would presumably defend for Mexican national society, is considered harmful to indigenous cultural unity. This unity is assumed to be an unquestionable good. That it may not always be so can be seen in the words of one indigenous deputy from the Chamula tribe: 'All the Chamulas, in assembly, have decided to be Catholics and support the PRI.' A government advisor says those converts who return to Catholicism go through 'a long and painful process of reincorporation, which demands humility and discipline, loyalty and respect. They fulfill the offices they are given [in the Catholic cofradias] and they recover . . . their lands and rights.' As Martínez says, this inquisitorial mentality robs the Indians of the rights which other Mexican citizens take for granted (Martínez 1994; 1995; 1996a; 1996b). As to the unsubstantiated presupposition that foreign religious and political forces are behind the growth of indigenous Protestantism, Bowen remarks caustically: 'Behind such conspiratorial notions . . . lies a naive contempt for indigenous peoples that assumes they were and are unthinking pawns, duped into betrayal of their traditional culture by a few "gringos" after four hundred years of resistance to mestizo culture and oppression' (1996: 171).

It is precisely in the most evangelical municipalities that the Zapatista guerrilla movement erupted on 1 January 1994. That was the day the NAFTA treaty entered into force, and the Zapatista movement is, amongst other things, a protest against exclusionary globalisation. The relationship between evangelicalism and the Zapatistas is ambiguous, but there is clearly considerable support and some participation. Limón and Clemente say support varies with the region, being higher in areas where expulsion of evangelicals has been more acute. In addition, many indigenous people trained in Liberation Theology while lay pastoral agents in the Catholic Church become pentecostal pastors because of the greater scope for indigenous leadership, and this led to an increase in pentecostal participation in the EZLN (Limón and Clemente 1995: 194); this trend seems to have decreased subsequently.

In any case, violence has not been totally eschewed by evangelicals. Even before the Zapatista insurgency, evangelicals had occupied the office of indigenous affairs in the state capital. In 1994 a mayor was kidnapped by evangelicals who exchanged gunfire with would-be rescuers. In 1996 in another locality, evangelicals resisted expulsion, leaving six dead (Martínez 1996a). As in a few parts of Asia and Africa, this raises the question of political violence by evangelicals in the Third World. The feeling that indigenous causes have only been noticed since the Zapatista rebellion would be one factor in evangelicals' justification of such actions.

Thus, an important question in evangelical politics is the struggle of indigenous evangelicals to get their case discussed at the national level. The Evangelical Church Committee of Alto de Chiapas and the State Committee of Evangelical Defence have been interlocutors with government and Zapatistas. The former petitioned the EZLN to have the question placed on its list of petitions, speaking of 'our decided support for the just causes of peace and social justice which you represent with dignity' (in Limón and Clemente 1995: 191). The Zapatistas included the question. However, the 1996 San Andrés Agreement between EZLN and government made no mention of religious tolerance (Martínez 1996c: 12–13).

Evangelicals in Mexico are still more often victims of intolerance than would-be or actual perpetrators of intolerance, as in some Latin American countries today. We still need to know more about the actual politics of large sectors of the Protestant world. Examples would be the Iglesia Cristiana Independiente de Pachuca, a large pentecostal denomination; or the idiosyncratic Luz del Mundo, the nearest parallel to an African Independent Church, with its semi-divinised founder and centre of pilgrimage in Guadalajara; and above all, the evangelical organisations in Chiapas, such as the Comité Estatal de Defensa Evangélica de Chiapas (CEDECH), the Organización de los Pueblos Evangélicos de los Altos de Chiapas (OPEACH) and the Consejo Indígena Campesino Evangélico de México (CICEM). As the only Third World country in an economic bloc with traditionally Protestant and developed neighbours, Mexico's evangelical politics will be of special comparative interest.

CHAPTER 23

Chile

Until the 1973 coup, Chile was one of the most stable democracies in Latin America. The highly repressive regime of General Pinochet lasted until 1990. His economic policies were neoliberal, unlike the South Korean military's state-led development. Chile failed to achieve comparable progress (although it is one of the more successful Latin American economies in macro-economic terms, despite a high social cost) and failed to broaden its political base. But controlled redemocratisation has left deep institutional traces by which the military keep a tutelary role (Luckham 1996: 222). These include non-elected senators, an electoral system which gives considerable power to the second-largest party and inhibits smaller parties, and Pinochet's right to appoint the first five directors of the central bank. Pinochet himself remained as head of the armed forces until 1998, before becoming life senator. His economic model and partially redemocratised political system have thus been hard to erode.

Chile (with Brazil) has the oldest mass Protestantism in Latin America. Significant growth dates from the 1940s. Protestantism is overwhelmingly pentecostal and accentuatedly lower class. Unfavourable electoral systems, the institutional power of the Catholic Church and a fairly rigid society with a social ceiling beyond which evangelical penetration is virtually non-existent, have led to the almost total absence of Protestants from formal politics in democratic periods. There are currently no Protestants in congress, and there seem to have been only four ever, compared to nearly one hundred and fifty in Brazil.

Pentecostalism achieved notoriety for alleged proximity to the military regime. There are grounds for this, but the picture must be nuanced by an understanding of its social composition, of differences between denominations and of the internal politics of the largest denomination. In addition, it is important now to understand Protestant participation since the restoration of democracy.

Chile is a partial exception to Martin's (1990) rule that Protestantism grows most where the Catholic Church was weakened but the culture was not secularised. Although tolerance of Protestant worship dates from 1865, Catholicism remained official until 1925. Even disestablishment did not mark, as in many countries, the triumph of radical anti-clericalism. Rather, it was negotiated with the Vatican (by that time adopting a more flexible stance about separation) and retained legal privileges for the Catholic Church, which alone enjoyed public legal personality (Smith 1982: 70–8). Only in 1999 was a law passed granting legal equality to other churches, despite the Catholic hierarchy's opinion that it might 'damage national life' (*ALC*, 18 June 1999).

This belated recognition of numerical reality was in part a reflection of social composition. The 1992 census gave 13.3 per cent of Protestants, although a 1990 survey had shown 16 per cent (Fontaine and Bayer 1991). The latter revealed a marked correlation with social class: only 1.6 per cent of the upper class were Protestants, as opposed to 12.5 per cent of the middle class and 24.8 per cent of the lower (and disproportionately among self-employed and those with unstable employment). Growth remains high, but there is a new phenomenon: a high percentage of non-practising pentecostals. Rural areas and coal-mining towns of the south have been central to growth, while Santiago and Valparaíso have a lower percentage than the national average.

Chile has the most pentecostalised Protestantism in Latin America, around 75–80 per cent. Unlike elsewhere, the historical–pentecostal divide corresponds to a missionary–nationalist one. Historicals never made a serious impact. In the late nineteenth and early twentieth centuries the peasants were very dependent and the upper class firmly allied to Catholicism (Willems 1967: 62), making Chile less permeable than Brazil to religious dissent. In Brazil, historical churches cut across class lines; in Chile, Protestantism has been more lower class, and therefore more pentecostal (ibid.: 253–4).

The pentecostal schism in the Methodist Church marked the break between missionaries and nationals, between a foreign mentality and local sensitivity to the extraordinary, between middle class and popular cultural forms (D'Epinay 1970: 53). Chilean pentecostalism is thus accentuatedly national in origin, a fact of which its leaders are proud (Lagos 1988: 53–4). Although foreign groups are present, they are small. Pentecostalism consists basically of the two churches into which the original schismatic National Methodist Church of 1909 split in 1932: the Pentecostal Methodist (IMP) and the Pentecostal Evangelical (IEP); and subsequent smaller divisions from these, such as the Apostolic Pentecostal, the Pentecostal Church of Chile and the Mission Pentecostal (the latter two being members of the World Council of Churches).

The Chilean trajectory is thus unique: its Protestantism is more pentecostal, and its pentecostalism more national, than anywhere else in Latin America. Distance from the United States and absence of large immigrant groups helped in this. Pentecostalism is also characterised by vertical, centralised structures, even compared to pentecostalism elsewhere; the Methodist rather than Baptist or holiness origin is an important factor in this.

Certain aspects of pentecostal history have had an enduring effect on political postures. Although the first pentecostal church was led by Methodist missionary Willis Hoover, he had broken with his mission under pressure from his flock.

The Chileans felt the missionaries had tried to prevent the free expression of the Holy Spirit. Chilean pentecostalism owes its dual character of nationalism and spirituality to the Chilean reaction against every attempt to control the expression of the Spirit according to the insights of the foreign missionaries, coupled with an exuberant desire for the Spirit to express Himself freely in the local situation. (Kessler 1967: 127)

However, a conviction that human guidance was after all necessary led Hoover to emphasise obedience to pastors. This has led, says Kessler (ibid.: 289), to the dominating and even dictatorial position of pastors in Chilean pentecostalism.

Hoover's principle of freedom of expression in services plus authoritarian church government proved a success while a superintendent remained who did not grasp after power, but was a temptation for leaders without Hoover's training who had risen from the lowest social strata (ibid.: 300). According to Kessler, Hoover did not hand over his authority to Chileans but tried to place both himself and Chileans without distinction under the authority of the Holy Spirit. The result was that, without seeking it, he gained such authority that for years he remained undisputed leader. When elderly, Hoover became disturbed at the ambitions of certain leaders and tried to cling on to power, contributing to the schism of 1932 between the majority which remained with Hoover's heir apparent, Manuel Umaña, in the Iglesia Metodista Pentecostal (IMP), and the minority loyal to Hoover which founded what was later called the Iglesia Evangélica Pentecostal (IEP).

Umaña had been in latent conflict with Hoover for years, and had appealed to nationalism as a means of gaining full control. After his takeover, he decreased the IMP's isolation from national life. This included organising members' votes so that politicians would be obliged to take note of pentecostals (ibid.: 309). But experience with Hoover had made the denomination wary of one man remaining so long in power, insisting instead on a rotating superintendency. So although Umaña became life pastor of the main IMP church in Santiago, known as Jotabeche, it was only in 1950 that he achieved his aim of becoming the IMP's only (and lifelong) bishop.

The effects of this system can be seen in the 1963 accusations by a communist newspaper (never denied by Umaña) that many church properties were in his own name and that, in return for organising members' votes, he had since 1960 received considerable government subsidies for social activities, some of which did not exist (ibid.: 312). This was during the government of Jorge Alessandri, whose family seems to have had political links with pentecostals since the 1940s (see ibid.: 307).

In 1964 Umaña died, having maintained his position despite damaging personal and political revelations. But IMP leaders had concluded that it was mistaken to allow the pastor of Jotabeche to be the denominational bishop. When Javier Vásquez became pastor of Jotabeche, the annual conference appointed Mamerto Mansilla from Temuco as bishop. It was only during the military regime that Vásquez succeeded in becoming overall leader of the IMP and, in effect, full successor to Hoover and Umaña. Vásquez' notoriously public alliance with Pinochet must be understood in the context of these ecclesiastical struggles.

Potential for allying with the military regime differed markedly among pentecostal denominations. The other large church, the IEP, had a less centralised system in which local pastors had to be approved by the annual conference. It was thus autocratic at the local level but democratic at higher levels. In addition, it retained Hoover's posture of 'separation from the world' and even from cooperation with other denominations. This made it harder to achieve concerted political action at the national level, and impeded participation in trans-denominational organisations with political aims. Resembling somewhat the Christian Congregation in Brazil, their rigorous *sectarianism* protected them from political 'adventurism' at the time when numerical success began to open doors in public life.

The numerous breakaways from both IMP and IEP are considerably smaller. Two main ones are the Iglesia Pentecostal de Chile (IPC) and the Misión Iglesia Pentecostal (MIP). The IPC broke with the IMP in 1947, and the MIP split from the IEP in 1952. For various reasons, neither followed the IMP in support of the military regime. Both were dissatisfied with Hoover's socially isolationist legacy and sought pan-Protestant cooperation and some form of social ministry. They both joined the World Council of Churches in 1961, which gave them different alliances (and theological interlocutors) and influenced reaction to the military government.

This excursion into Chilean pentecostal history has been to show that an understanding of evangelical politics is considerably enhanced by taking internal factors into account. Chilean Protestantism is overwhelmingly pentecostal; this pentecostalism is overwhelmingly national and branches out from a single trunk, the IMP. The IMP has inherited a highly centralised organisation, and its internal power struggles have helped to shape the common perception of 'pentecostal politics in Chile'. The other main denominations, emphasising other aspects of Hoover's heritage or reacting against them, have followed different routes which have also shaped their own (diverse) political postures.

How does all this translate into political involvement? Sepúlveda (1996) insists that pentecostalism's relationship to politics must be understood in terms of the political situation of the masses, the *bajo pueblo*, as a whole. This leads us to relativise the idea of pentecostalism as a 'haven of the masses' and engaged in a 'social strike', images made famous by D'Epinay's (1970) groundbreaking study of Chilean pentecostalism in the 1960s. This was done precisely when the Christian Democratic (PDC) government was engaged in radical social engineering to change the life of the *bajo pueblo*. Until then, the latter had been generally excluded from political and labour organisations, since even the Communist and Socialist Parties were of the skilled proletariat in the small industrial sector. 'Refuge of the masses', says Sepúlveda, is perhaps an adequate image until the early 1960s, but is misleading if taken to mean that pentecostalism prevented participation in social organisations. For the *bajo pueblo*, such organisations did not exist. But from 1964 the PDC government, intent on reform without revolution, aimed to integrate those on the margins: agrarian reform, rural unions, neighbourhood committees, and so on. With the election in 1970 of the revolutionary alternative, Unidad Popular under the socialist Salvador Allende, politics became all-absorbing and divisive.

How did pentecostals react? Between 1964 and 1973 (Frei and Allende governments) there are no grounds for thinking pentecostalism acted as a bloc against social participation. In rural areas, pentecostals often became leaders in the new organisations thanks to their organisational experience in churches. This happened less in urban peripheries, where churches held almost nightly services and restricted members' participation in other organisations. Since the PDC was identified with Catholicism, it probably received little support from pentecostals. The anti-clerical Radical Party allied with Allende in 1970, so the latter probably received considerable pentecostal support. Sepúlveda concludes that pentecostal preferences probably differed little from the *bajo pueblo* in general, except that anti-Catholicism made them shy away from the Christian Democrats towards greater support for the left (1996: 311).

Pentecostal support for the Socialist Party was not new. One smaller denomination has a curious history of left-wing activism. The Misión Wesleyana Nacional was founded in 1928 by pentecostalised Methodists. But two aspects made possible a different socio-political trajectory from most of pentecostalism. The split was not from the IMP but directly from Methodism and thus unaffected by the Hoover-IMP legacy. And the schism occurred in the southern town of Lota, dominated by coal-mines and highly politicised.

The originator of the split (reluctantly, since he was a devout Methodist) and leader until his death in 1969 was Victor Mora. A former miner, he had studied in the Methodist seminary where several teachers were influenced by the social gospel, and in 1933 he was a founder of the (Marxist-influenced) Socialist Party in the coal-mining region. 'I think religion with my heart and Marxism with my stomach', he used to say. He was involved in unionism (being imprisoned for a few months in 1936) and in founding cooperatives. Mora taught that a worker should identify with his class, saying (with a left-wing pastoral authoritarianism which mirrored that of the right): 'I would never allow a worker to be in the church and to be a member of a conservative party' (in Palma 1988: 95). Similarly, 'the Wesleyan pastors may never go against the workers and if anyone does he will be immediately suspended'. For him, helping to organise the 'disoriented union movement' was part of what it meant to be 'the light of the world' (Ossa 1990: 65). In 1937, Mora became regional leader of the Frente Popular of Socialists and Communists. He was a city councillor in 1940–1, replacing a fellow-member of the Frente, believing 'it is necessary to defend the working class, to encourage them to organise and defend themselves' (in Sierpe 1993: 86). According to Ossa, as a politician Mora did not use 'moralising or religious arguments, but his ethical posture was born of a desire to avoid the moral and human degradation of the population', and was characterised by flexibility and realism (1990: 111–12).

Mora's control of his denomination was no less autocratic than that of conservative or apolitical pentecostals (Ossa 1990: 36; Palma 1988: 92); and that may explain the gradual loss of left-wing vision after his death. The leader in the 1970s had been a socialist candidate in the 1960s; he says he asked the party for help but told them he would campaign as pastor rather than as party militant (in Palma 1988: 86–7). But already this man's refusal to applaud the military regime was not approved by second-level leaders. After 1980, leadership passed to retired armed forces men, with very different political postures (ibid.: 106).

Pollitt's (1981) study of pentecostalism in the coal-mining region during Allende sees it as complementary rather than competitive with the Communist Party, the dominant force locally. She sees pentecostalism and communism as critical responses both to 'dominant' upperclass culture and to 'traditional' peasant culture.

Communists and socialists were allied in the Allende government. While there is no solid evidence, it is often assumed that the evangelical vote was quite favourable to the winner. Allende asked for the traditional Te Deum to be no longer purely Catholic but ecumenical, including evangelicals and Jews; whether this was a way out for an atheist president, or a response to evangelical support (as Sierpe (1993: 90) thinks), is unclear. Tennekes (1985: 41–53) discovered that 77 per cent of surveyed pentecostals in Santiago voted for Unidad Popular in the municipal elections of 1971, against only 66 per cent of their nonpentecostal neighbours. Only 19 per cent of pentecostals voted for the Christian Democrats and a mere 4 per cent for the right-wing National Party. The same survey showed that although pentecostals were much less likely than non-pentecostals to be members of political parties (5% versus 15%) they were more prone to think the rich were wealthy because they exploited the people (68% versus 56%), and to think left-wing parties trustworthy (83% versus 69%).

As opposition to Allende mounted, especially within the military, a few pentecostals responded with outright support. The pentecostal group Acción Popular Evangélica Unida declared that 'we, the poor pastors, are constantly praying to God that the road which our people have undertaken may continue straight and firm; and that, through the unity of the people, the obstacles imposed by those who see their privileges threatened – privileges founded on the misery of the great majority of our brothers – shall be removed' (in Pollitt 1981: 342).

However, most pentecostal leaders who bothered to take up a public position were not at all so favourable to Allende (which does not necessarily mean they hoped for a highly repressive military regime such as that which in fact took power). The main analyst of Protestantism during the military regime, Humberto Lagos, can even say that 'evangelical practices [before the coup] were consensual and expressed through ideologically charged "prayers for peace" opposed to the Allende government' (1988: 184).

However, the fiercely repressive military regime soon created a tension between acceptance of the 'necessity' of the coup and horror at its consequences. The very next day, the Methodist Church demanded humane treatment of the detained. Weeks later, a group of Protestant leaders had an audience with the junta. While recognising 'the will of God' in the coup, they requested authorisation to help prisoners and agile mechanisms of appeal. This group included Lutherans, Methodists and Baptists, as well as some pentecostals such as José Gómez of the IEP and Alfredo Ramírez of the IMP (ibid.: 129–30). It would be useful to know more about the relative ecclesiastical weight of these leaders. The existing literature does not allow a nuanced evaluation of what many actions (critical or favourable to the government) represented in terms of overall evangelical stances.

Soon afterwards a Committee of Cooperation for Peace, in defence of human rights, was initiated. It had the support of the Catholic cardinal but the initiative was Protestant, through Lutherans Helmut Frenz and Augusto Fernández (Sierpe 1993: 94–5). It is significant that they had to ally with the Catholic Church for such action; they would need Catholic institutional protection, nationally and internationally, against repression. For such an alliance, certain internal and external conditions were necessary: churches with a strongly anti-Catholic stance would be unwilling to attempt it, and churches distrusted by the Catholic hierarchy would be unlikely to receive its support.

While one sector of Protestantism helped victims of the coup, another sector moved towards unconditional support of the regime. This became the new fault line in Protestantism. But it can only be understood when two non-Protestant actors are taken into account: the Catholic hierarchy and the government. Smith (1982: 287–305) divides the Catholic bishops' stance into three periods: (i) moral legitimacy for the regime (until March 1974); (ii) cautious criticism (April 1974 to April 1976); and (iii) episcopal prophecy amidst mounting attacks on the church (May 1976 to December 1980). In this light, it is not surprising that sectors of Protestantism were invited to have a closer relationship with the regime by mid 1974. Lagos says two sectors were responsive: pentecostals and some Lutherans. The latter (prosperous descendants of German immigrants) were motivated by class position, whereas pentecostals were motivated by their theology which values order and is anti-Marxist. Unconsciously they were also motivated by the possibility of taking over Catholicism's privileged position (1988: 137–8). Lagos' account is deficient. Firstly, he speaks generically of 'pentecostals', even though they constitute three-quarters of Protestantism, with internal divisions which must be recognised as much as those of historical Protestantism. And secondly, he sees the pro-regime Lutherans as self-interested, but the pro-regime pentecostals as ideological captives.

By late 1974 the regime had opened up to Protestants, something previously unthinkable in Chilean politics. The main Protestant figures were Javier Vásquez of the IMP, Pedro Puentes of the Independent Presbyterian Church, Ricardo Ramírez, superintendent of the Iglesia de Dios, and Hermes Canales of the Iglesia Unida Metodista Pentecostal. Puentes, the only non-pentecostal, soon faded from the scene due to tensions with the others (ibid.: 197). Ramírez and Canales were from small pentecostal denominations. Vásquez, Umaña's successor at the IMP's main Jotabeche church, was the key figure.

Vásquez was finishing a new building (for which he adopted the un-pentecostal name of 'cathedral') and invited Pinochet to the inauguration. Pinochet reputedly replied: 'give me a reason for going'. This is the background to a gathering at government headquarters on 13 December 1974, when 2,500 Protestants from thirty-two denominations participated in a show of support for the regime. Unfortunately, the existing literature does not analyse the group. It seems some attended in ignorance of the purpose of the gathering; and one suspects a large percentage were ordinary members of Vásquez' church, mobilised for numerical impressiveness. In Pinochet's presence, a declaration was read by Pedro Puentes. For the first time, it said, the evangelical church was being 'valued' by a head of state. 'We recognise the Armed Forces as the containing wall raised up by God against atheist impiety', promising evangelical support in its 'courageous fight against Marxism'. It repudiated the international condemnation of human-rights abuses, saying the regime was based on 'Christian humanism' and was 'God's response to the prayers of all believers'. It asks God to guide Chile's rulers, 'who are also believers' (ibid.: 156ff.); an extraordinary affirmation from normally anti-Catholic evangelicals.

The organisers had requested support from other churches, including the Baptist Convention, whose president had agreed to send a representative, without appreciating the import. He sent his vice-president, who was asked to make the public reading of the declaration. On seeing it, he refused, characterising it as 'theologically heretical, ecclesiastically Constantinian and historically biased'. Immediately after the act, various churches, including some pentecostal, withdrew their commitment to the declaration (ibid.: 164).

Pinochet rewarded Vásquez by attending the inauguration of Jotabeche cathedral. Negotiations began for a new supposedly representative Protestant organisation to be the official interlocutor with the government. The Consejo de Pastores was founded in July 1975 with fourteen affiliated denominations and missions. Lagos describes these as pentecostal and popular urban (ibid.: 188), an insufficient analysis for our purposes. Significantly, tensions soon led to Puentes' withdrawal (ibid.: 197). Whenever a government starts to pay attention to an institutionally divided minority sector, there will be internal battles for leadership of that sector. At the very time that 'unity' becomes concretely rewarding, its achievement becomes harder than ever. As in Zambia, government favour deepens intra-evangelical divisions between the contented and those who feel relatively or totally left out. We need a closer analysis of the Consejo de Pastores to know to what extent it was little more than a vehicle for Vásquez and the IMP.

For the government, the main function of the Consejo de Pastores was to give 'supplementary legitimation' (Lagos) to the regime, partially compensating for the Catholic hierarchy's withholding of the legitimation it traditionally granted rulers. The culmination came annually, from 1975, in the 'evangelical Te Deum' in Jotabeche cathedral. The idea of pentecostals celebrating a *Te Deum* in their *cathedral*, in the presence of the head of state, shows how far the IMP had come (presumably the main impression on those present); but it also showed how dependent it was on the Catholic model of church–state relations, and how tributary it was to the military's project. Even though undisputably the second religious force, it offered no alternative model of how religion and society might relate; instead, it could only see itself as a second-string actor waiting in the wings and substituting the main star when the latter was indisposed.

The Catholic Te Deum to commemorate independence had been expanded at Allende's request into an ecumenical one. This had been suspended since 1973, a gap which the evangelical version was to fill.

After the first one in 1975, the Association of Evangelical Churches of Chile (AIECH), founded in November 1974 by historical and a few pentecostal churches and rather more representative than the Consejo de Pastores, protested against the Te Deum and its presumed official status in the Protestant world. The AIECH statement was signed even by some churches which had signed the December 1974 declaration of support for the junta (ibid.: 194; once again, Lagos does not tell us *which* churches).

Even though Catholics restarted the ecumenical Te Deum as soon as the government had solicited the evangelical one, the government incorporated the latter into official protocol on the same level. At the 1977 celebration, Vásquez claimed that 'an important general is a member of the Evangelical Cathedral' (ibid.: 200). One would like to know who, and what mediating role he might have had between Vásquez and Pinochet. More generally, we need a study of the internal workings of the IMP and the repercussion of Vásquez' postures in the denomination.

In 1978, the preacher at the evangelical Te Deum was the president of the Lutheran Church of Chile, a schismatic Lutheran group formed in 1975 and linked to the Consejo de Pastores. One member of the junta was in this church. By the 1980s, however, although the Te Deum continued, it had lost importance. The turning-point was in 1981, when Cardinal Silva agreed Pinochet's request for an extra Te Deum to commemorate the new constitution, on condition that no evangelical Te Deum take place as well. Pinochet's acceptance shows that evangelical legitimation was needed only while the Catholic hierarchy was resistant to the regime. The government was not ready to risk a deeper break with the Catholic Church by promoting real religious equality. The continuation of the evangelical Te Deum after redemocratisation shows it was not designed, from the evangelical side, to support a particular government, but was a statement of their new place in society (Sepúlveda 1996: 312–13).

In the mid 1970s, the Consejo de Pastores obtained certain concessions from government to strengthen its position in the evangelical field. One was the easier granting of legal personality to churches (Sierpe 1993: 97). Another was free medical treatment for pastors' families if they had a Consejo de Pastores ticket. This prompted an AIECH protest. Such protests, and ultimately the mellowing of relations between regime and Catholic hierarchy, prevented the Consejo achieving its aim of evangelical hegemony. Unlike Catholicism, unifying organisations in Protestantism are often contested in their political role, and their legitimacy is effectively negated, making them of limited use to governments. However, they can be effective in shifting the balance of power within the evangelical field and in channelling official resources.

In 1984, a new Confraternity of Churches was formed, replacing AIECH. In 1986, as the regime came under fire, it published an open letter to Pinochet demanding democracy. Amongst the signatories were the leaders of the Iglesia Pentecostal de Chile, the Misiones Pentecostales Libres, the Misión Iglesia Pentecostal, the Misión Apostólica Universal, and the Iglesia Wesleyana; an impressive array of smaller- to medium-sized pentecostal churches. For the October 1988 plebiscite (in which the 'no' vote triggered redemocratisation), an Evangelical Pro-Democracy Committee was formed.

What can we conclude from the history of Protestant politics during the military regime? It is not enough to speak indiscriminately of 'pentecostals' or to look only at the regime's motivations. More notice must be taken of ecclesiastical competition between and within denominations; in particular, we need a history of how Vásquez sought to strengthen his own position within the IMP, and the IMP's position within the religious field, by means of an alliance with Pinochet. More actors in the story need to be located ecclesiastically, and other important denominations such as the IEP must be studied. Which pentecostal churches, besides the IMP, really supported the regime? Were they just smaller groups (or splinter groups within denominations) with leaders anxious for some public recognition and available for a political mobilisation subordinate to the IMP?

Vásquez today owns a fleet of buses, a concrete reward at the personal level. But already in 1988, when democracy was coming, Lagos could say that 'since 1986 the IMP has been in tension and even divided because of the fanatical and uncritical support of . . . Vásquez to general Pinochet' (1988: 145). In fact, of the four largest pentecostal churches, only the IMP allied with Pinochet. The IEP remained isolated. The IPC and the MIP were in the WCC and affected by human-rights concerns. The head of the MIP in the late 1980s said: 'In general I have always voted for left-wing candidates ... simply because I was from the people ... To vote for the right is to vote for capitalism and to vote for the other side is to vote for the people' (Pastor Arturo Palma, in Palma 1988: 237).

Evangelical politics since redemocratisation has been little studied.

Vásquez, having supported the right's defeated candidate in the first presidential elections, realised he needed to adapt. The Consejo de Pastores, while continuing to exist, joined a new broader forum known as the Coordinación Evangélica. Vásquez himself sought reconciliation with the new government and the evangelical world through a new relationship with the Baptist sociologist Humberto Lagos, formerly one of his main critics. Lagos, a member of the newly formed Party for Democracy (PPD), was a Special Advisor on Religious Affairs in the first democratic government. If the IMP was to accede to direct electoral participation, it would have to be via someone with political weight within one of the main parties. Unlike many countries in Latin America, the system did not favour corporate ecclesiastical candidates without previous political involvement. In many ways, the Chilean style of democracy is less favourable to the corporate exercise of political weight by minority churches than was the military regime.

There have been no evangelical members of congress since redemocratisation. In fact, there seem only ever to have been four (all in the lower house). The first one was the Baptist Roberto Contreras, Partido Radical deputy from 1948 to 1952 and government minister in Radical governments of the 1940s and early 1950s. The Partido Radical, anti-clerical, also reportedly had a pentecostal deputy in the 1960s, Francisco Poblete. During the Allende years, two evangelicals reached congress with his Partido Socialista: the Methodist Daniel Salinas and the pentecostal Oscar González. The latter was a miner and unionist from Lota, and member of the Templo Universal, a breakaway from Victor Mora's Iglesia Wesleyana. He was elected in March 1973, having campaigned as 'Christ's candidate'. His election was a surprise, and represented a protest against the entrenched power of the Communist Party in the region (Pollitt 1981: 272).

It is possible that further research will uncover more congressmen from the pre-coup period, but the number is still extremely low for such a strong Protestantism. Key elements in this are the strong party traditions, with a fairly stable core of ideologically defined parties, and the electoral system. The current system is 'majoritarian binomial' (Munck 1994: 11): each district elects two members, but for one party to win both seats it would have to obtain double the vote of its closest rival. Electors vote only once, which means each party or coalition generally presents only one candidate. The system favours two-party politics in congress, and gives unduly large representation to the second-largest bloc, which is currently the right, thus helping to perpetuate the heritage of the military era. Independents face great difficulty in being elected, as some evangelicals have discovered.

Many other posts are elected indirectly (regional councillors) or appointed (regional *intendentes* and provincial governors). It is to the municipal level that one must look to get a broader idea of evangelical participation in formal politics. The municipal electoral system is more favourable to evangelical participation (with municipality-wide voting of party lists): there are a reasonable number of evangelical municipal councillors and a few mayors (usually the councillor who received the largest popular vote). An example of the latter is Benjamín Soto, mayor of the small town of Cunco, in the south. A former Baptist now in a charismatic church, he owns an evangelical FM radio station. This enabled him to gain election as the most voted councillor. He is provincial vice-president of the PPD, but says the choice of party was merely 'conjunctural'.

An example of a different type of involvement is the Baptist lawyer Alvaro Rodríguez, a product of the evangelical student movement GBU (Grupo Bíblico Universitario) and the Latin American Theological Fraternity. He is president of the PPD in the 9th Region and on the national directorate. The PPD seems to have the largest number of evangelicals in positions of relative influence. However, the evangelical mayor of Puerto Montt is socialist.

Unlike many Latin American countries, Chile is not propitious for evangelical parties. An attempt in 1992 did not flourish. The electoral system is unfavourable and the main parties are not as discredited as elsewhere.

However, evangelical loyalty to existing parties is lower than among the general population. A 1990 survey (Fontaine and Bayer 1991) found practising Catholics and evangelicals virtually indistinguishable, except that the latter were more inclined to independents. That does not mean they are disguised rightists, since their image of Pinochet is worse than among non-evangelicals, and they are positive towards democracy. But it does mean they are a voluble sector, depoliticised but potentially mobilisable in campaigns which interest them specifically.

In recent years, the social bases of the main parties have weakened, and they have tried to reconnect with society through what are known as *referentes*, groups organised around particular social identities, including that of evangelicals. The *referente evangélico* in the PDC, for example, is led by a Baptist pastor. It is not part of the official structure, but has a consultative function (David Muñoz, personal communication).

Mention of the (traditionally Catholic) Christian Democrats is significant; after decades of concentration in the anti-clerical Radical Party, evangelicals are now active in all parties, from communists to right-wing UDI. This shows greater social and legal acceptance, allowing greater dispersal for non-religious reasons.

In the close-run presidential elections of 1999–2000, evangelicals achieved unprecedented visibility. Many analysts felt the run-off was decided by evangelicals. The candidate of the centre-left governing coalition, the socialist Ricardo Lagos, and his right-wing opponent Joaquín Lavín, both courted the evangelicals. In the first round Lavín built on a protest vote against government economic policies and his image as a religious man. However, as his links with the conservative Catholic Opus Dei became known, evangelical opposition grew. Lagos gained support from sectors previously silent, seeing him as heir to the anti-clerical tradition. Despite Lavín's protestations that evangelicals were fellow-believers and that he would promulgate the law on religious equality, his evangelical acceptance was limited. His most prominent supporters were Vásquez and Bishop Salvador Pino Bustos, both of whom talked of shared 'Christian moral principles'. Pino was the leader of a charismatic church and had attempted to run for president himself, alleging divine revelation. His support came mostly from the newer crop of charismatic preachers, many of whom own radio or television stations. Baptist churches in Santiago repudiated his intention, calling him 'manifestly unprepared'. In the end, Pino's candidacy was barred for not meeting requirements for registration.

There remains a lot to study. Almost nothing is known of evangelical electoral behaviour, and little of the postures of hierarchies. An additional area might be the politics of the growing movement of indigenous Mapuche evangelicals.

CHAPTER 24

Colombia

Colombia has already had more Protestant congressmen than Chile, although it has historically had one of the weakest Protestantisms in Latin America. In a country torn apart by drug trafficking and guerrilla warfare, and where the Catholic Church has massive institutional power, elections for a Constituent Assembly in 1990 were the catalyst for involvement, coordinated by the Evangelical Confederation. Since then, with a slight weakening of the two-party system, the new parties formed around special interests have included several evangelical ones, sometimes little more than vehicles for the political ambitions of leaders of charismatic mega-churches.

Colombia is one of the most violent countries in the world. Two phenomena contribute to this: guerrillas and drugs. The conflict between guerrillas, paramilitaries and the Armed Forces claimed six thousand lives in 1997 (*Folha de São Paulo*, 31 May 1998). Some of the current violence is reputedly by paramilitaries paid by foreign companies to clear peasants off desired land. The two main guerrilla groups, the FARC and the ELN, control a third of the country. The famous drug cartels constitute another parallel power. Colombia produces 80 per cent of the world's cocaine, and drug money helps to finance the guerrillas. Not surprisingly, it also finances much conventional politics: President Samper was elected in 1994 by a tiny margin, with contributions from cartels.

Political history has been characterised by the stable hegemony of the traditional Conservative and Liberal parties which date from the mid nineteenth century. As in many countries of the region, Conservatives broadly favoured strong central government, protection of the Catholic Church and its social prerogatives, and defence of traditional landowners, while Liberals advocated federalism, disestablishment of the church, and the defence of commercial interests (Martz 1992: 90). But in most of Latin America, these traditional parties disintegrated, whereas

in Colombia they endured, attenuating their rivalry in a system sometimes called 'oligarchic democracy'. After a virtual civil war between
1948 and 1958, known as La Violencia, Liberals and Conservatives
agreed parity in representation and alternation in power. This Frente
Nacional lasted officially until 1974 but effectively until the late
1980s. Even in the 1990s, elite two-party dominance continues, through
the personalistic leadership of regional bosses and often through inherited family allegiances. Both parties operate on 'patron–client' lines,
and not as European-style mass parties; and both enjoy multi-class
support under upper-class auspices (Medhurst 1984). A summary of
Colombian reality in the 1990s talks of the elite's continued reluctance to
relinquish formal power; the inability of the opposition, including the
guerrillas, to produce an alternative project; the endemic violence of
petty criminality; and the organised brutality of drug-related and drug-
financed paramilitary organisations (Gold-Biss 1993: 218). However,
with drugs producing an important proportion of national income
(Martz 1997: 271), the economy has done reasonably well by Latin
American standards.

Conservatives held power from 1880 to 1930, with negative effects for
Colombia's incipient Protestantism. The constitution of 1886, in force
until 1991, treated Catholicism as one of the foundations of national
unity (Moreno 1996: 74). While guaranteeing religious freedom, it del-
egated vast privileges to the Catholic Church. The 1887 Concordat
granted large powers in education, and made the church virtually a
parallel state apparatus in the 'mission territories' (one-third of the
country), where it was the only legal religious institution. Colombian
Catholicism has a peculiar position in Latin American terms: the clergy
are numerous (resembling Catholic Europe more than the New World),
national (few foreign clergy) and from relatively high social levels (Medhurst 1984). As Daniel Levine commented in the early 1980s, 'it is easy to
imagine the Colombian Church favouring more equal income distribution, agrarian reform and the like; but it is considerably harder to
envision its leaders willingly turning over to others . . . the moral authority to develop norms in these areas without reference to the Church' (in
Martin 1990: 81).

Protestantism's start was late and slow. By 1900 only one denomination, the Presbyterian, was established (Bucana 1995: 60). Until the
1930s it was the weakest Protestantism in South America. Protestants
sympathised with the Liberals as less hostile to them (Moreno 1996:
76). In La Violencia, when traditional partisan 'hereditary hatreds'

(Medhurst 1984) degenerated into near civil war, Protestant identification with the Liberals made them the target of attacks by Conservative mobs. In addition, this being the beginning of the Cold War, Protestantism was often regarded as a near-relation to communism. President Rojas Pinilla declared in 1956 that 'the Protestants are united with the Communists to destroy Colombian national unity' (Bucana 1995: 131). The 1957 agreement between Liberals and Conservatives which put an end to La Violencia declared that one of the bases of national unity was 'recognition by the political parties that the Catholic religion ... is that of the nation and that as such the state will protect it' (ibid.: 134). The agreement engineered a power-sharing formula which perpetuated the exclusionary exercise of power, of which the continued inability to break the guerrillas' control of huge areas of the country is the other side of the coin.

Conservative government after 1946 and violence after 1948 encouraged Protestants to form the Evangelical Confederation (Cedec) in 1950. Cedec calculated that between 1948 and 1956, forty-six churches were destroyed, seventy-eight believers were killed for their faith and two hundred schools were closed by the government (ibid.: 147). The difficulty of establishing its right to existence helped Protestantism achieve considerable unity (unusual in Latin America). Although a rival organisation arose in the 1970s, the two merged in 1989 to form the Evangelical Confederation (Cedecol). By that time, in very changed circumstances, Cedecol was willing to repudiate the position taken by Cedec in 1952: 'the Evangelical Church is outside partisan conflicts, national and international' (in ibid.: 236).

A Constituent Assembly in 1990 was the spark for effective evangelical participation in formal politics. Cedecol took an official role, in a way so far unique amongst Latin American evangelical councils of churches. According to a key protagonist, it wrote to all affiliated denominations asking if a coordinated effort should be made to elect evangelical representatives, receiving a unanimously positive answer. From dozens of prospective candidates, Cedecol chose six, of whom two were successful: Arturo Mejía Borda, a lawyer and university lecturer, and Jaime Ortiz Hurtado, of whom more on page 231. The electoral campaign was conducted through the local pastors' associations.

The vote in Colombia, unlike most of Latin America, is optional and the abstention rate was 75 per cent. The heterogeneity of those elected impressed observers, including 'Indian tribal elders and disarmed guerrilla leaders, along with two Protestant evangelicals (much to the dismay of the Catholic church)' (Martz 1997: 293). But although elected with 110,000 votes, 'they did not stand out for their active participation. Their focus was the dismantling of Catholic hegemony ... [but on] the economic situation they did not present projects' (Helmsdorff 1996: 81). The new constitution improved the Protestant position with regard to freedom of worship and legal equality of religious confessions.

The new constitution also brought about, in the words of Martz, 'the elimination of the two-party system that had long restricted political participation' (1997: 296). This may be overstated, but it did make candidatures open to 'parties, movements and groupings'. A plethora of new parties arose, representing specific sectors, and in the 1998 presidential elections an independent candidate finished a close third. But it is premature to talk of the end of two-party rule; congressional elections in October 1991 saw the Liberals and Conservatives receive over 90 per cent of the votes.

As with Brazil after 1986, evangelical participation, initially mobilised for a Constituent Assembly, was unlikely to disappear afterwards. The provisions of the constitution have to be regulated by normal legislation, an added reason for continuing the electoral effort. On this basis, three evangelicals (two senators and one representative) were elected in 1991, and four (two senators and two representatives) in 1994. However, the united effort of 1990 gave way predictably to fragmentation. The main Cedecol-linked group was in the Movimiento Unión Cristiana (MUC) and still harboured hopes of a united front. But such hopes were battered, first by the Partido Nacional Cristiano (PNC), based on leaders of charismatic mega-churches, and later by divisions within MUC itself.

The creation of several evangelical parties in the 1990s reflected in part a broader frustration with the traditional parties. There was a pulverisation of the political scene amidst a plethora of new actors and movements. But other factors affected evangelical actions. One was awareness of growing strength allied to a perceived relationship between the two main parties and the Catholic Church. As society became more open, as the legal position of churches improved and as evangelical strength increased, the Liberals no longer satisfied their aspirations. Evangelicals were no longer dependent on liberalism for their survival; but they were not yet strong enough notably to increase their space within it. However, what began as a unified Protestant effort whetted appetites and fragmented into diverse projects for channelling part of the Protestant vote. Unlike Brazil, it was not the older lower-class pentecostal denominations which took the lead, but the new urban charismatic mega-churches, better placed to capitalise on party fragmentation in a situation of non-compulsory voting and massive abstentionism.

The leading figure in MUC was Jaime Ortiz, elected to the Constituent Assembly in 1990 and to the senate in 1994. (The members of the Constituent Assembly were ineligible for the 1991 elections.) Trained as a lawyer and Presbyterian pastor, Ortiz established a broad Protestant base as rector of the Biblical Seminary of Medellín and as twice president of the Evangelical Confederation. He is an articulate defender of evangelical politics with echoes of Dutch Reformed (Kuyperian) themes: MUC, he says, is based on a Christian world-view of the temporal order, and a specifically Christian party is legitimate because every party is confessional in the broad sense of having a world-view. But the Bible does not give us a political programme, only general principles. MUC prefers lay people in politics; if pastors are elected, they should leave their ministerial work. (This has not prevented MUC from treating the active pastor Colin Crawford as virtually its representative in the lower house.)

Ortiz was MUC's only congressman after 1994. Previously, it had had two: senator Fernando Mendoza, a lawyer from the charismatic church Puente Largo and linked to the Haggai Institute, and representative Viviane Morales. But in mid 1995 MUC claimed fifty-six municipal councillors throughout the country, as well as two departmental deputies in peripheral regions (one from the Venezuelan border and one from the San Andrés Islands in the Caribbean which have a large black Protestant population); and two mayors of small towns (*Nueva Alternativa*, July–August 1995). It also has a theoretically democratic structure which seeks to reflect evangelical power structures; directors of missions, confederations of churches and evangelical media organisations have *ex officio* voting rights (ibid.). But it seems the practice is more hierarchical (Helmsdorff 1996: 83). The president of MUC, Héctor Pardo, a charismatic pastor, is also a leading figure in the Latin American Evangelical Confederation (Conela). Pardo, Ortiz and Claudia Castellanos of the PNC, attended the 1995 meeting in Miami of evangelicals in Latin American politics, organised by conservatives linked to Pat Robertson's Regent University. Pardo says the objective was to establish 'a strategy for taking political power with a view to extending the Kingdom of God'.

Former MUC representative Viviane Morales took issue with this strategy. She was re-elected in 1994 as an independent. Her lack of space in MUC was articulated into a critique of the idea of an evangelical party, although the price of independency was a closer relationship with the Liberals. Of middle-class Catholic origin, she was converted to the pentecostal Iglesia de Dios (Cleveland), of which her husband is now denominational head. Even if he does not manipulate the church politically, as she says, it helps her political career in evangelical circles to be the wife of a senior ecclesiastic. Viviane has a Master's degree in law from the Sorbonne, and is the best prepared intellectually of current evangelical politicians. She attributes her election in 1992 (with MUC) exclusively to the evangelical vote, whereas her re-election as an independent in 1994 was only partly through evangelicals. Viviane supported the Liberal presidential candidate, Ernesto Samper, as 'the lesser of two evils', citing not only his greater distance from the Catholic hierarchy but his better record on human rights and greater wariness of neoliberal economic policies. For Viviane, Colombia is the victim of American hypocrisy with regard to drugs; the resources for fighting the narco-war would be better used as social investment to undercut the appeal of the narco-economy.

Two other parties of evangelical inspiration have achieved parliamentary representation. One is the Compromiso Cívico Cristiano con Colombia, known as C4, of senator Jimmy Chamorro. Its base is a split, led by Chamorro's father, from Campus Crusade. Although generally perceived as evangelical, it has adopted a non-adversarial position *vis-à-vis* the Catholic Church and has supported the Conservative Party. The other party is the Partido Nacional Cristiano (PNC), linked to more mainstream charismatic evangelicalism. Pastors of Bogotá's megachurches have been key actors in the evangelical entry into electoral politics. As the vote is optional, a large congregation of relatively educated members can be mobilised to elect its own leader to congress, such as the Misión Carismática Internacional of César and Claudia Castellanos, and the Iglesia Filadelfia of Colin Crawford.

The PNC belongs to an ecclesiastical 'family business', the Misión Carismática Internacional. The Misión, started in the early 1980s by César and Claudia Castellanos, soon acquired a radio station. In Colombia, there are no evangelical television channels or even programmes; but Claudia ran for president in 1990 to gain time on state-run channels. If MUC at least tries to be democratic on paper, the PNC has no such pretence. It revolves around three family members: César and Claudia, and Claudia's father Alfonso Rodríguez, former city councillor in Bogotá with a trajectory in the Liberal Party. The PNC has acquired a reputation for vote-buying; it is said to have given household appliances to pastors on the Atlantic Coast who persuaded their members to support it (Helmsdorff 1996: 83).

Claudia, elected senator in 1991, was not re-elected in 1994, but the PNC retained a congressional presence through the election of Colin Crawford, previously a councillor in Bogotá, to the lower house. His case is perhaps unique in evangelical politics in the Third World. A naturalised Colombian born in Scotland and educated at the Bible Training Institute in Glasgow, he worked as a Brethren missionary in Colombia before becoming charismatic and founding his own church in 1974. He now has eight churches in Bogotá and four more in other regions. On this basis, and in alliance with the Castellanos, he was elected city councillor in 1992 and representative in 1994. He later distanced himself from the PNC and allied with MUC, which was bereft of a representative.

Crawford is a vibrant preacher who speaks Spanish, even after more than thirty years in Colombia, with a strong accent, which probably adds to his political appeal. He still teaches in his denomination's seminary; when I interviewed him in his office in the congress, he was using a book by Torrey to prepare an examination for his students that night. He professes a conservative ideology, sympathising with the Tories in Britain and the Republicans in the United States, and gives cautious approval to the New Christian Right. But, as he hastens to add, in Colombia the Partido Conservador is off-limits, being the preserve of the Catholic Church.

What has been the performance of all these evangelical parties and dissidents? One aspect has to do with religious freedom and legal equality with the Catholic Church (juridical personality, tax exemption, etc.). In 1995 President Samper regulated various clauses of the constitution regarding religion; the MUC's efforts (so its own publication says) brought the law into force five years earlier than planned and made it easier for the government to celebrate accords with non-Catholic religions (*Nueva Alternativa*, July–August 1995). In February 1998, with elections approaching, an accord which gained the epithet of Evangelical Concordat was celebrated, granting certain denominations the same privileges as the Catholic Church with regard to the legal status of their marriage ceremonies and access to prisons, hospitals, schools and military installations. Cedecol was part of the accord, thus benefiting its member churches, but eleven denominations (including some in

Cedecol) opted to be specified separately. Apart from the Seventh-day Adventists, concerned about legislation respecting Saturday, these churches were all pentecostal. The Concordat was criticised by other evangelicals. Some were unhappy because lack of open discussion had meant some interested groups were left out. Others were unhappy with the extension of the traditional Colombian model of state-negotiated privileges, instead of the adoption of a universalist model of rights for all religious groups (Moreno 1998: 18).

Another focus of both MUC and PNC, according to Helmsdorff, has been 'to obtain privileges and advantages for the expansion of the churches' (1996: 81). Sometimes, the *raison d'être* is even more restricted: resources are obtained for the social projects run by the politician's church, which in turn help to enlarge that church and support the politician's political career.

Virtually all evangelical politicians have supported the Liberals in presidential elections and key legislative debates. Samper's promise of fiscal equality for churches is said to have tipped the balance towards support for his presidential campaign in 1994 (Helmsdorff 1996: 83; Martz 1997: 286). After winning the election by 0.4 per cent, his presidency was overshadowed by the revelation that he had been financed by the drug cartels. Both evangelical representatives (Colin Crawford and Viviane Morales) voted against his impeachment, amidst the inevitable rumours of pay-offs. Whatever the truth, the political dimensions of the case (involving populism and nationalism) were more complicated than a judgement regarding Samper's personal responsibility.

What of broader concerns? While emphasising proposals related to the family and sexuality, economic themes are very tangential for evangelical parties (Helmsdorff 1996: 82). This straitened perspective, typical of much evangelical politics in the Third World, sits uneasily with the (also typical) traces of triumphalism, exemplified by senator Ortiz's phrase in a 1995 meeting: 'Colombia accepts us and wants us and needs us! As people transformed by the power of the Holy Spirit, we have much to contribute.' Or as his advisor said on the same occasion: 'We are very special people, and this automatically makes us a political alternative.'

It is true that evangelical politics contains diverse currents, not only amongst independents, MUC and PNC, but also amongst members of historical churches, especially Mennonites, who have 'worked with various tendencies in favour of freedom of conscience ... seeking benefits for the whole of society and not privileges for the churches' (ibid.: 84). But the majority tendency follows a different logic. In the run-off for president in 1998, pastors were bombarded with appeals from both candidates. Even the Conservative swore he would see to full implementation of the 'Evangelical Concordat' (*ALC*, 18 June 1998). *Pace* the triumphalists, it is not as 'special people' but as an electoral force that evangelicals have achieved visibility in politics.

In the 1998 congressional elections, there were shifts in the evangelical balance of power. Two were elected to the senate (Viviane Morales and Jimmy Chamorro) and two to the lower house (César Castellanos and Nelly Moreno). Viviane has become the key figure: her non-confessional movement Frente Esperanza (FE), linked to the Liberal Party, elected not only herself but the recently converted television actress Nelly Moreno (a member of the charismatic Casa Sobre La Roca church). Viviane is now on the national directorate of the Liberal Party, a position she acquired not only for her elegant defence of Samper in parliamentary debates but as part of Liberal strategy to court the evangelical vote. Having rejected the 'evangelical party' strategy, she has acquired far more real power than any other evangelical politician. Her elevation to the Liberal top ranks provoked an angry reaction from the Catholic archbishop (Moreno 1998: 20).

The PCN's fortunes were mixed: Claudia was defeated for the senate, but César was elected as a representative. MUC was the big loser: Ortiz missed re-election, as did Colin Crawford. Without any congressional representation, MUC's only prominent legislator was now Eduardo Cañas, city councillor for Bogotá and former president of the Assemblies of God.

Colombia in the 1990s has exemplified the virtual impossibility of unified evangelical politics once evangelical civil rights have been achieved. The tendency seems to be for each large denomination to present its own candidates, who will be more susceptible to denominational interests than pan-evangelical politicians. The Cedecol-MUC project will be hard to sustain. Some denominations will find it easier to elect a senator (since the vote is nationwide) than a representative of the lower house; a curious inversion of the rule in most countries.

The Colombian experience shows that in a context of pulverisation of the political world, it is easy for 'evangelical parties' to become little more than personal vehicles for ambitious ecclesiastics. The process of formation and subsequent internal procedures are often not democratic, and the interests defended are often particularistic rather than universalistic. In addition, behind the façade of independence, these parties are often linked to clientelistic practices which enable them to channel concrete benefits.

Although reflecting a broadening of democracy, their practices contribute little to this process. Their durability is questionable, since to a large extent they are not based on an ongoing universalist project with mass support, but on the personal strategies of ecclesiastics which, once achieved, tend to run into the sand. The price of relative independence from traditional parties may be precisely the tendency to play down the major themes of normal politics and concentrate on evangelical specificities; whereas the apparently more realistic and successful C4 (of Jimmy Chamorro) and FE (of Viviane Morales) have opted for closer links with Conservative and Liberal parties respectively.

In the late 1990s the physical safety of evangelicals became an increasing concern. FARC guerrillas, especially, assassinated tens of pastors (mainly from the Assemblies of God and the Iglesia Pentecostal Unida) and warned all pastors to leave the occupied zones, stating that they helped the armed forces or the paramilitary squads, and discouraged evangelicals from participating in meetings to discuss local problems. In early 2000, evangelical leaders met with representatives of the main guerrilla groups to try to end the hostility. The ELN were the more receptive, offering two posts on the coordinating committee for their upcoming national convention (*ALC*, 31 Jan. 2000). On the other hand, the paramilitaries have also killed evangelicals, especially those active in universities, as part of their attempt to prevent all organised student activity (*ALC*, 30 July 1999). As peace talks have faltered, civil society has become more active in peacemaking, and evangelicals have sought representation in the talks through a new Fraternity of Christians for Reconciliation and Peace, formed under the auspices of the Colombian branch of the evangelical development NGO World Vision (*ALC*, 27 May 1999).

CHAPTER 25

Peru

If Colombia is characterised by evangelical parties, Peru is characterised by the massive entry of evangelicals into congress through a single newly formed secular party. This was in 1990, after a traumatic decade for Peru. Declining real incomes, enormous unemployment and rampant inflation were compounded by guerrilla warfare. The brutal Maoist Shining Path was combatted equally brutally by the army in the Andean emergency zones, largely inhabited by the Indians who make up over half of the population. After a military regime between 1968 and 1980, unique in Latin America for its left-leaning nationalist ideology, civilian democratic governments in the 1980s were unable to bring peace and development and were increasingly perceived as discredited and corrupt. The narco-economy was also gaining importance.

In 1990, the political outsider Alberto Fujimori formed a new party, Cambio 90, and ran for president. Against all predictions he won, with considerable support from Protestants, estimated at 7 per cent of the population. From Fujimori's side, the interest was access to the indigenous vote. With their presence in areas where state, parties and Catholic priests are absent, Protestants were an alternative route to mass politics; and with their fame for honesty, they seemed to be a hope for preventing social disintegration. Nineteen Protestants reached congress, all but one with Cambio 90. The head of the National Evangelical Council, a Baptist pastor, was elected second vice-president. The fact that a pastor with no political experience could become second vice-president testifies to the disintegration of public life in Peru. His complete marginalisation subsequently by Fujimori, with no significant reaction, shows how dependent on outside forces was this precocious politicisation of Peruvian Protestantism.

Although Peru was one of the birthplaces of Liberation Theology, through Gustavo Gutiérrez, it also has a very conservative Catholic hierarchy. Opus Dei has an unusually high profile and claims half the episcopate (including, from 1999, the archbishop of Lima). Protestant-ism only established a foothold at the end of the nineteenth century, and *de jure* tolerance was only achieved in 1915. Separation of church and state came with the 1978–9 Constituent Assembly.

A characteristic of Peruvian Protestantism is an unusual degree of unity. In most Latin American countries, there are no strong representa-tive organs, or there are several competing ones. The Concílio Nacional Evangélico del Perú (Conep), however, was founded in 1940 and has retained allegiance of nearly all the Protestant field, incorporating the rising tide of pentecostal and charismatic groups. Conep expanded especially during the nationalist military regime, which gave an incen-tive to nationalisation of denominational leaderships and recognition of Conep by the state.

Peru has one of the least pentecostalised Protestantisms of Latin America. One reason is the strength of Seventh-day Adventism among the Indians; another is the relative strength of 'holiness' churches (the milieu in which pentecostalism started). Yet another factor is that, unlike Chile, pentecostalism did not start spontaneously but was introduced by American missionaries. The history of the main church, the Assemblies of God, is punctuated by nationalist conflicts. The first AG missionaries (1919) occupied the region assigned to them by a Committee of Cooper-ation, the northern Sierra, where linguistic difficulties and religious intolerance limited expansion (Zavala 1989: 69–79). In 1937, the Spring-field headquarters sent a representative with 'the express intention of organising and centralising authority' (ibid.: 82). The first Board of Directors was exclusively of missionaries, and soon affiliated to the newly formed Evangelical Council (Conep). Peruvians only effectively took over leadership after the nationalist military regime came to power in 1968. But conflicts have been endemic, leading to numerous national-ist schisms, a contrast with the absence of such schisms in the Swedish-influenced Brazilian AG.

The position of Conep helped to make possible two types of political action in the 1980s and early 1990s: the entry into electoral politics with Fujimori, and Conep's Paz y Esperanza (Peace and Hope) Commission which defended evangelicals against human-rights abuses in the zones affected by guerrilla warfare and counter-insurgency.

Paz y Esperanza has been analysed by López (1997). It represents the most significant defence of human rights by a strictly evangelical (as opposed to more liberal ecumenical) group in Latin America. While officially part of Conep, Paz y Esperanza was largely the initiative of university-educated evangelicals linked to the IFES-related student movement AGEUP (Asociación de Grupos Evangélicos Universitarios del Perú) and the Latin American Theological Fraternity (FTL). The two main directors of Paz y Esperanza, Pedro Arana (1984–6) and Caleb Meza (1987–92), had both been heads of AGEUP.

The context was the Shining Path guerrilla insurgency since 1980, and the increasingly violent army repression which was to lead, by the early 1990s, to some twenty-five thousand dead, hundreds of 'disappeared' and the forced migration of thousands of peasants. The immediate spark for Paz y Esperanza (PyE) was a massacre of evangelicals, dragged from worship at a Presbyterian church and shot by marines in August 1984. Since PyE is unique in Latin American evangelicalism, it requires explanation.

One factor is the longevity and institutional strength of Conep as the representative Protestant organ, capable of underwriting such action without fear of being undercut by a rival entity. Another is that, as often with Catholic initiatives also, violence against members of one's own religion was necessary to bring home the intolerableness of the situation. Massacres of evangelicals at worship meant that Romans chapter 13 (in which the apostle Paul exhorts believers to obey the authorities) could scarcely be used any longer to justify passivity. In addition, the conservative nature of Peruvian Catholicism meant it had not pre-empted the theme of human rights to the point of making anti-Catholic evangelicals steer clear of it.

Two other factors were vital. The Peruvian situation was one of extreme violence plus democracy. Outside the emergency zones, there was democratic space. This unusual conjunction of human-rights abuses and democracy was important for the involvement of a fairly poor religious minority in such risky activities. The final factor was the ascendancy of an articulate trans-denominational minority within Conep, mainly of people whose understanding of evangelical faith had been formed largely through the student group AGEUP and the Latin American Theological Fraternity. The autonomy enjoyed by the national movements related to the International Fellowship of Evangelical Students, of which AGEUP was a part, meant it was free to assimilate the militancy and deadly seriousness of the Peruvian university world of the 1970s and produce a generation of militant young evangelical leaders in the 1980s.

PyE's effective remit was defence of human rights of evangelical citizens. It was thus more restricted than Catholic organisations in many countries, which have usually not limited themselves to Catholics. Presumably, differences between a *territorial church* and evangelical groups which in Latin America are (in sociological terms) *denominations* or *sects*, may partly account for this. PyE did, however, take part as observer (not full participant) in the National Coordinating Committee on Human Rights. Resources came largely from overseas Christian organisations, especially European ecumenical and evangelical ones (WCC, Tear Fund, Christian Solidarity International, Bread for the World).

Since, by the early 1990s, opposition to PyE had curtailed its operations (although not abolished it), we have to ask why opponents went along with it for several years. The theological perspective of the AGEUP-FTL group never became widespread in Conep. While for this group, PyE represented a chance to implement an integral part of their view of mission, for the majority of Conep affiliates it seems to have been more a pragmatic question of corporate defence. The armed forces had overstepped a limit beyond which even very 'apolitical' evangelicals can take a strong stand against the state (as illustrated by Shintoism in Japanese Korea). Defence of 'human rights' may have been more a particularistic concern for religious freedom for evangelicals than a universal and permanent concern related to theological anthropology. Protestantism is stronger in rural areas, the hardest hit by the emergency. Churches have grown quickly in the emergency zones: Ayacucho went from 3 per cent evangelical in 1981 to 10 per cent in 1993, and Cangallo from 4 to 20 per cent; in rural zones of those regions the figure may be nearer 40 per cent (Markus Osterland, personal communication). It is said that two-thirds of leaders of the 'peasant patrols' formed to protect local communities from attack were evangelicals. This was an important part of the strengthening of civil society which contributed to the defeat of Shining Path. The latter was not only defeated militarily by the army, but by its ultimate incapacity to fulfil its strategy of creating a social vacuum into which it could step after banishing the state, the Catholic Church and the army from the areas of insurgency (ibid.: 4).

From 1992, however, when Fujimori closed congress and governed undemocratically, bolstered by his military victories against the guerrillas, PyE's space became more restricted within Conep. But for internal reasons as well the ascendancy of the AGEUP-FTL group within Conep was precarious. Nearly all human-rights movements are led by middle-class intellectuals, and an official defence of human rights would open up space for the leadership of such people within the evangelical community. Resistance to a continued emphasis on such aspects could be seen as a fight for 'turf'. If the 'holistic' approach to mission were admitted, some evangelical leaders would lose their comparative advantage and jeopardise their pre-eminence. The 'mission of the church' has to be what I have expertise in, not what I am completely at a loss in. It is probable also that the rise of charismaticism helped to change the balance of power and weaken Paz y Esperanza by bypassing the discussion over holism in mission. The popularisation of a charismatic world-view which 'decongested the discussion about evangelism and social action' by means of a re-enchanted world-view which saw spiritual warfare as the recipe for both, occurred not just in FIPAC (International Fraternity of Christian Pastors), a charismatic connection for groups outside Conep, but in Conep circles as well (Amat y León 1996).

By 1996 the directorate of Conep was made up of six pentecostals and three from holiness churches; a very different composition from a decade before. Even so, PyE severely criticised the Amnesty Law for military and police perpetrators of human-rights abuses in 1995. Dozens of evangelicals, including pastors, were still detained; and Conep and the Catholic human-rights organ jointly published a booklet 'Campaign of prayer and solidarity for those unjustly detained for terrorism', containing graphic testimonies of torture.

As for formal politics, Protestants had traditionally supported the main anti-clerical party. From the 1920s this was APRA (Alianza Popular Revolucionaria Americana), a centre-left grouping founded by Víctor Raúl Haya de la Torre, a young radical thinker who taught at a Protestant college and was friendly with the great Scottish missionary John Mackay. Haya exemplifies several great Latin American political figures who were educated in Protestant institutions or associated with them, without ever becoming Protestants. This reminds us faintly of the more important role such institutions played in Africa in educating the independence leaders. In Latin America, Protestant schools run by missionaries could only represent innovative methods and emphases, and greater educational opportunities for some middle sectors, but not the indispensable route to modernity that they signified in colonial Africa.

Haya was deported from Peru in 1923, having protested against the government's dedication of the country to the Sacred Heart of Jesus. He was the most important political figure for the next half century, although thwarted by military force and electoral fraud from becoming president. Protestant support for APRA was largely unbroken until the

1960s, and it was through APRA that a Protestant reached congress for the first time.

This was José Ferreira, a dark-skinned descendant of Brazilian immigrants in the Amazon region, and elder of the Iglesia Evangélica Peruana, the denominational result of the British mission EUSA (Evangelical Union of South America). Ferreira was elected as deputy when democracy returned in 1956, and as a senator in 1962. A coup in 1968 denied him probable re-election (Romero 1994: 7).

When the military began redemocratisation by calling a Constituent Assembly in 1978, Ferreira was too ill to run. APRA offered his place on the slate to a Protestant of his choice. The first person invited was Samuel Escobar, a leading thinker in the Latin American evangelical world. Escobar, together with Ecuadorian René Padilla, had had an important role at the 1974 Lausanne Congress on world evangelisation, an evangelical 'Vatican II' in the sense of opening up to the modern world and legitimising social concern as part of mission. When Escobar declined, another Peruvian who worked with the Latin American movements of the International Fellowship of Evangelical Students (of which AGEUP was the local affiliate) was invited: Pedro Arana, Presbyterian pastor and APRA militant. Arana had published *Providencia y Revolución*, strongly influenced by Reformed thinking, defending evangelical participation in secular parties based on a theology of common grace. He has also written about his participation in the Constituent Assembly (Arana 1987). In it, he defends his Aprista affiliation, since both the university circles in which he laboured and the periphery in which his church was located tended by then to feel that APRA's day was over. 'Many brethren from marginalised areas of the city had more sympathy with the Marxist left than with Aprismo. A strong evangelical sector was to vote in 1983 for the first socialist mayor of Lima' (ibid.: 23–4). Family ties and the influence of Mackay's writings had led him into APRA, which he saw as an option for social revolution by democratic means, and as having 'evident affinities with the evangelical movement' (ibid.: 17).

He was supported by the Conep secretary general and in the Constituent Assembly referred to himself as Conep's representative. But (unlike many evangelical politicians in the Third World) he was a convinced party man. The only other evangelical in the Constituent Assembly, Arnaldo Alvarado, a famous racing driver and new convert to the Christian and Missionary Alliance, was also in APRA.

Arana received eight thousand votes, placing fourth nationally in the

APRA list. Even so, he only spoke three times in Assembly debates. Religious freedom, and not a broad political project, was still the key issue. The main objective was achieved; separation of church and state was introduced, although the state still recognised 'the Catholic Church as an important element in the historical, cultural and moral formation of Peru' (Klaiber 1992: 353).

Democracy was restored in 1980. José Ferreira returned to the senate with APRA, but a more conservative Frente Evangélico, of leading pastors and laymen, also tried to elect candidates, without success. It was a sign of growing political dispersion, and growing ambition. In 1985, when APRA won the presidency, Ferreira narrowly kept his seat, while nearly all parties presented evangelical candidates. A Protestant grouping AMAR allied with a conservative coalition to present candidates, again without success (Arroyo and Paredes 1991: 92).

There was little sign that Peru was about to become the third Latin American country (after Guatemala and Brazil) to have a sizeable evangelical parliamentary representation. By 1990, economic crisis, guerrilla war and corruption had discredited APRA. Ferreira retired and endorsed Arana as candidate, but he was unsuccessful. Only one evangelical aprista was elected.

The route was to be a totally new party, organised by non-evangelicals but into which an important group was incorporated at an early stage. The organisers were a nucleus around the former chancellor of the National Agrarian University, Alberto Fujimori, the son of Japanese immigrants, and a group of small business owners led by Máximo San Román. Initially, the intention was to elect Fujimori to the senate. But when the fifty thousand signatures needed to register the party, Cambio 90, turned into two hundred thousand, it was decided to try for a bigger prize.

Cambio 90's take-off is often credited to the third force allied with it: evangelicals led by Baptist pastor Carlos García. A law graduate, García had been president of the Baptist Convention and of the paraecclesiastical social agency World Vision. Since 1988, he had been leading a group exploring the possibilities of a Protestant party. In 1989 this group, largely Baptists, Methodists and pentecostals (Romero 1994: 9), threw in its lot with Cambio 90.

Besides García, the key figures were Pedro Vílchez (an independent Baptist influential among churches outside Conep, especially in the interior, and who was the initial contact with Fujimori), Pablo Correa (also an independent Baptist and member of the Conep board) and

Alejandro Rojas, pastor of the Iglesia Pentecostal Misionera. These four had influence in diverse evangelical sectors.

Protestants were allotted sixty places among the one hundred and eighty congressional candidates, and García joined Fujimori's slate as candidate for second vice-president. The slate was unprecedented also in racial terms, being made up not of the usual white or whitish politicians but of a 'Chinaman' (as Fujimori was popularly called), a 'cholo' (San Roman being the typical mestizo Andean) and a 'black' (García having Afro-Brazilian ancestry).

Two months before the election, García was elected president of Conep. This was obviously fraught with danger: a vice-presidential candidate who is also the head of the representative organisation of the Protestant world. It is true that no one expected Fujimori to win; in fact, García was so little confident that he was abroad when the first round took place! It is also true that he then took leave of Conep in order to campaign for the run-off. But the impression of institutional linkage to a political project remained.

Fujimori campaigned in opposition to all that his rival, the novelist Mario Vargas Llosa, represented. Fujimori would defend Peruvian identity, the domestic market and the enormous informal sector. He would be the honest outsider untainted by the system. This discourse appealed to evangelicals; and their support added their own reputation for honesty. The evangelical grass-roots network is credited by many analysts with an important role in the surprise victory. The *Washington Post* talked of 'an unpaid army of evangelicals disseminating his simple message through remote valleys and dusty shanty-towns ... Evangelical volunteers went door-to-door in the shanties and village-to-village in the mountains' (in Arroyo and Paredes 1991: 97). There was also the racial factor; poorer, darker people were more inclined to vote for the 'China-man', and the evangelicals were strong among those sectors.

The result was that, besides García as second vice-president, there were nineteen Protestants in congress (four senators and fifteen deputies), all but one with Cambio 90. In fact, evangelicals comprised eighteen of their thirty-nine congressmen. There is no detailed analysis of this caucus in terms of social composition; some were from 'deep Peru' and the group probably represented a lower social level than the rest of congress. None had previous experience in elective posts, and some had no relevant experience at all. The denominational composition provides a contrast with Brazil. At least half were independent Baptists, that is, groups outside García's Baptist Convention. The Iglesia

Evangélica Peruana had three; there was one each from the Presbyterians, Methodists, Wesleyans and Pilgrims. The only pentecostals were two from the Iglesia Pentecostal Misionera. The absence of the Assemblies of God, the largest pentecostal group, is striking.

Electoral material of some candidates gives an idea of the varied motivations. One pentecostal candidate writes: 'Vote for your brother; don't vote for the godless.' A Baptist gives reasons to vote for a 'brother': 'After ten years of restored democracy, congress has passed two thousand laws, in very few of which the evangelicals have been favoured or treated equally with the official Church wrongly so called.' He then lists his intended projects: creation of National Bible Day; status of 'ecclesiastics' for pastors; status of faculties for evangelical seminaries; participation of pastors in official inaugurations; evangelical participation in the state media, and so on.

Victor Arroyo, graduate in sociology, member of the Iglesia Evangélica Peruana and former staffworker with AGEUP and World Vision struck a different note, in style and content. The professed concerns are more universalist: 'our evangelical faith cannot remain indifferent in the face of growing unemployment, lower salaries, administrative corruption, drug trafficking and violence'. The causes are historical and spiritual: 'we know there are structural and spiritual roots deep in history and the human condition which explain these evils'. The solution is evangelical involvement in alliance with others: 'the problems of the country are too complex to be solved by isolated efforts'. Echoing other evangelical politicians, Arroyo says priority should be given to those in whom God has a special interest. But for him, this does not mean the evangelical community, but the poor: 'the nation should structure its economic, social, political and cultural life around the interests and needs of the majority'.

Euphoria at success was short-lived as Fujimori marginalised the evangelicals who had helped him to power. Second vice-president García was given no facilities or responsibilities. Already in the run-off, Fujimori had downplayed his alliance with evangelicals in the face of Catholic reactions. The archbishop of Lima issued a pastoral letter 'in defence of the greatest treasure of our Peruvianness: our Catholic faith'. Once in power, disappointment with Fujimori grew as he abandoned campaign promises, refusing to communicate with the guerrillas and implementing the economic shock measures he had sworn to avoid. In late 1990, Conep issued pronouncements criticising Fujimori's policies (Arroyo and Paredes 1991: 98).

García, bereft of power in the decorative post of second vice-president, was unable to avoid complete political marginalisation. The evangelical congressmen of Cambio 90 were soon divided. Some remained loyal to Fujimori, whether because they saw him as Peru's best hope or because of concrete benefits he could provide to evangelical segments ready to join a different alliance, no longer as one of three equal partners but as a subordinate religious minority. Others left Cambio 90, some on principle (objecting especially to Fujimori's order to vote against prosecuting former president Alan García for illegal accumulation of personal wealth), and some because of disappointed corporatist aspirations.

The ease with which Fujimori could go back on his alliance without provoking any politically troubling reaction from evangelicals was because there had been no mass movement of evangelical political awareness equipped with its own project and capable of exerting pressure outside electoral periods. In addition, while Fujimori certainly disappointed many evangelical leaders who had joined his campaign, we do not know to what extent he disappointed ordinary evangelical voters who did not expect personal reward and were probably as alienated from the political projects of church leaders as they were from politics in general.

The alliance had undergone strains even during campaigning, not all of them related to Fujimori's need to avoid alienating Catholics. García had reputedly agreed to join the slate only because he thought there was no chance of winning, and had tendered his resignation a few weeks before the election and left the country. The resignation was too late to remove his name from the lists; but when news of victory in the first round reached him, he still took a week to return to Peru. When Fujimori denied him any part in government, he may have been over-revengeful but he was not being ungrateful to a faithful running mate.

Marginalisation may have been a blessing in disguise. The public image of evangelical integrity, badly shaken now in some Latin American countries, was preserved, at the cost of being seen as politically naive and inept. A document published by García and half of the former Cambio 90 congressmen after Fujimori's 'self-coup' puts the best gloss on the matter (*Participación de los Evangélicos en la Vida Política del Perú*, September 1992). Our involvement, they say, was not organised by our churches, but was purely individual (one wonders whether the same would have been said if they had been incorporated into a successful government). There were positive aspects, but basic weaknesses: lack of proposals, organisation, cohesion. Proposals for the future, however, are slim: seminaries should include courses on faith and politics and pastoral support should be given to believers in politics. Concretely, this grouping which had seemed to be a significant new actor in politics in 1990 had little to suggest for the country.

A Conep document (*Evaluación del Proceso Electoral Nacional 1990*) is more detailed. It stresses the opportunism without political vocation or preparation; the relativisation of the Bible's authority; the shameless use of the pulpit; the personal ambition and nepotism; and the lack of political culture and of knowledge of the country's problems. It recommends not only theological reflection on politics and pastoral help to politicians, but the need for academically qualified professionals and for training of church leaders in knowledge of national problems.

In April 1992, Fujimori closed congress, suspended the constitution and governed undemocratically in what came to be known as a self-coup. He had the backing of the army and widespread popular support, based on perceived victory over guerrillas and inflation. From the evangelical angle, there was a revealing sideshow. Congress met clandestinely and voted to depose Fujimori. Since the first vice-president was abroad, García was sworn in as 'president in clandestinity'. But, as he told me,

that night I thought: what do I do? I have no social base, no money, no car. So a politician advised me to seek asylum in the Argentine embassy. I stayed ten days there. I continued articulating with political leaders to restore democracy, but the US and the Organisation of American States were lukewarm. So I decided to leave party politics and go back to ministry.

García later headed the Peru branch of Campus Crusade.

Only a handful of evangelicals, all pro-Fujimori, won seats in November 1992 elections to the revamped congress. In the 1995 elections, amidst massive abstentionism, there were many candidates in opposition groups but none were elected. One group, the Movimiento Presencia Cristiana (MPC), which included former senator Arroyo, attempted to run independently, but later joined the Unión por el Perú, led by the former general secretary of the United Nations Javier Pérez de Cuellar. The movement's publication adopts a centre-left posture: 'What modernity is this which denies the right to work?' The government has imposed an inhuman economic policy, with 65 per cent of the economically active population unemployed. The president of Conep, Juan José Rivas of the AG, is quoted as saying that the 'government's labour legislation, presumably following IMF guidelines, is unjust and inhuman ... imposing the dictatorship of capital' (*Presencia*, Oct.–Dec. 1995). While recognising that Peru is a mestizo country, the journal exalts its Indian past, characterised by solidarity, responsibility and hard work (*Presencia*, Sept. 1994).

However, the only evangelicals elected were five pro-Fujimori candidates: one Presbyterian, one from the Iglesia Evangélica Peruana, one independent Baptist, one Wesleyan and one from the AG. The denominational spread suggests planning by the Fujimori camp. In 1999 one of these was being accused of pocketing government money destined for the victims of terrorist attacks (*ALC*, 2 July 1999).

Protestants are still occasionally the object of legal discrimination: in 1998 a Lima municipal tax on non-Catholic churches obliged some sixty to close down, before the law was overturned (*ALC*, 28 May 1998). The congressman who overturned the law was a Catholic. All this is a far cry from the exalted hopes of 1990. Brazil's corporatist denominational projects have had far more staying power than the pan-Protestant projects that arose in Colombia and Peru in 1990.

Peru would be interesting for a comparative study of the political role of evangelical student movements, in comparison with countries such as Brazil and Nigeria. The involvement of members of the Latin American Theological Fraternity (FTL) has also been greater than elsewhere. Peru would make a useful case-study of the political strengths and weaknesses of this grouping, which has equivalents in Africa and Asia. One theme might be the lack of reflection on the question of power, which stems in part from the reality of evangelical marginalisation until recently but is reinforced by strong Anabaptist influences within the FTL.

However, the key figure in evangelical politics in Peru is the non-evangelical Fujimori. Evangelical parties have been toyed with, but with little success (although Fraternidad Nacional, led by a lawyer from the Biblical Baptist Church and accused of being a stooge of Fujimori, elected twelve mayors in 1998). Fujimori has pre-empted such initiatives, polarising politics. We need to explain better why only pro-Fujimori evangelicals have reached congress since 1992 (despite Conep's condemnation of 'inhuman neoliberal policies' (*ALC*, 10 Nov. 1998)). We need analysis of such figures as the Quechua congressman Miguel Angel Quicaña; Gilberto Siura of the Iglesia Evangélica Peruana, who has had an important and controversial legislative role (*Presencia*, Jan.–Mar. 1996); and Pedro Vilches, the independent Baptist deputy who made the initial contact between Fujimori and evangelicals.

In 2000, Fujimori's constitutionally dubious attempt at a second re-election met with outspoken rejection from Conep, in which people of AGEUP-FTL origin had recovered something of their ascendancy. Conep called on Christians to prevent re-election, invoking a 'moral obligation to disobey governments when they lack legitimacy'. This was not just for legal reasons; Fujimori's rule was characterised by the absence of values such as truthfulness, justice and solidarity. The state of law had been eroded, poverty and unemployment were up, corruption was rife. 'The time has come to say No to the silence of complicity' (*ALC*, 21 Jan. 2000). This strong declaration provoked protest from some evangelical sectors, notably the rival FIPAC (comprising mostly charismatic pastors), which said Conep should restrict its political comments to areas of consensus amongst evangelicals (*ALC*, 28 Feb. 2000).

CHAPTER 26

Nicaragua

Nicaragua is remarkable for its recent experience (1979–90) under the revolutionary government of the Sandinistas, itself unique amongst Marxist-inspired states. This is now in the past, and evangelicals (who grew rapidly during the Sandinista period) have emerged as important players in politics in the 1990s.

Nicaragua became a large exporter of coffee in the late nineteenth century. Attempts to diversify foreign investment and develop a more national capitalism led to American interventions and occupations. For most of the period from 1912 to 1933, Nicaragua was occupied. The end of this period saw the famous guerrilla war of Augusto César Sandino, whom the marines were unable to crush. The creation of an American-trained National Guard Nicaraguanised the conflict, but it also created a new power in politics. In 1936 the head of the National Guard, Anastasio Somoza García, removed the president and established the Somoza 'dynasty' which ruled until 1979. The Somozas amassed a huge fortune by all possible means, the diversion of international humanitarian funds after the 1972 earthquake being just the most scandalous example.

This created the potential for popular revolt. But by the early 1970s the Somozas had begun to be a threat to other business elements as well. By the middle of the decade, the Catholic hierarchy and much of the commercial and industrial elite were opposed to the regime. But this bourgeois-led opposition failed to overturn Somoza. In 1978–9, the leadership of the opposition fell to the guerrilla forces of the Frente Sandinista de Liberación Nacional (FSLN). The dictatorship fell in July 1979, after a civil war in which 2 per cent of the population died and opposition factories were bombed by Somoza's air force.

Protestantism, now about 15 per cent, is strong on the isolated Atlantic Coast among the indigenous and black communities, where the Moravian Church has been established since 1847. In the more densely populated (and Spanish-speaking) Pacific side, the Protestant presence results from American missionary efforts after the Liberals took power in 1894. Subsequently, a Conservative reaction deprived Protestantism of state protection and enabled the Catholic Church to go on the offensive. In the 1930s the Mexican Assemblies of God missionary Manuel Bustamante, harried by Catholic-inspired and state-tolerated persecution, successfully appealed to Sandino for protection; their acquaintance dated from the latter's exile in Mexico (Zub 1993: 25–6). Today, AG and Baptists (from the northern American Baptist mission rather than the Southern Baptists as in many Latin countries) are among the key churches.

The first Protestant politician seems to have been Alfred Hooker, a Moravian from the Anglophone Atlantic Coast who was a Liberal deputy in 1911 (Zub 1996e). He was followed by the Baptist pastors-cum-military officers José Mendoza and Ramiro Cortés Largaespada. In fact, direct participation seems to have been largely Baptist until the 1990s.

Traditional Protestant support for the Liberals carried over into a fair degree of support for the Somozas, since the latter usurped the banner of liberalism (Miranda 1991: 78). We hear of two Baptist deputies, Luciano Astorga and Fernando Delgadillo, in the 1940s, and of three in the 1970s: Armando Guido, Napoleón Tapia and Rodolfo Mejía (the last-named an anti-somocista Liberal dissident). In the late 1960s a rapprochement between regime and church re-established Catholic religious education in schools, leading to a concerted effort by Protestant denominations against the measure (Zub 1996b: 33). But by the revolution, Protestants were only around 5 per cent and only possessed one important organism with a public presence: CEPAD.

While retaining the acronym, CEPAD has been through different incarnations. It began life as the Evangelical Committee for Helping the Victims (of the 1972 Managua earthquake); then became the Evangelical Committee for Development, and finally the Council of Evangelical Churches for a Denominational Alliance. It was founded by Baptist pastor and doctor Gustavo Parajón, and achieved prominence through refusal to assist official relief efforts involving large-scale diversion of international donations (Miranda 1991: 77). CEPAD became effectively a council of churches and had a privileged relationship with the Sandinista government. Pentecostal political activity has been constrained by the projection of CEPAD.

The relationship between evangelicals and Sandinistas was a subordinate chapter of relations between Sandinismo and religion in general, and the Catholic Church in particular. The FSLN had fused the Marxist revolutionary tradition with Sandino's nationalist struggle. It was not, on the whole, anti-religious, and Christians participated. Radical clergy had helped the guerrilla struggle and after the takeover in 1979 several entered government, notably the Cardenal brothers, Ernesto and Fernando, and the Foreign Minister Miguel D'Escoto. However, by mid 1980, the hierarchy had decided to be more openly critical towards the Sandinistas and called on priests in the government to resign. The latter were eventually allowed to remain as long as they did not exercise priestly functions, but it was ironic that the pro-Catholic Somocista dictatorship had prohibited clergy from participating in any sort of political propaganda whereas the Marxist-leaning FSLN was pleading for priests to be allowed to remain in their government.

The FSLN's Official Communiqué on Religion, of October 1980, said that Christians were an integral part of the Revolution and construction of a new society. 'Our experience demonstrates that when Christians . . . are capable of responding to the needs of the people and of history, their very beliefs impel them to revolutionary militancy.' This was clearly at odds with traditional Marxist doctrine, but still left many things undefined. The Episcopal Conference, in its reply, said that while the Sandinistas recognised the validity of religious motivations in the overthrow of Somoza, 'today they deny such beliefs any influence in shaping the new revolutionary structures'. Totalitarian systems, said the bishops, 'deny to the church all qualitative participation in public affairs'.

Nicaragua thus represented a new departure for regimes of Marxist inspiration: instead of totally excluding believers from public life and attacking or at least marginalising religion, the Sandinistas used religion as an added source of legitimation and encouraged Christian involvement in its project.

Were evangelicals persecuted in Sandinista Nicaragua? Not in the strict sense, says Stoll (1990: 260). Accusations in the international press centred largely on the treatment of indigenous Moravians on the Atlantic Coast. While many aspects of this reflected badly on the government, considerations of territorial security and national integration were the cause, rather than a desire to persecute believers. As for the Miskitu, Moravianism had become a mark of their ethnic identity. Although church members were under half the regional population, it was the 'expressive vehicle and institutional means' of Miskitu mobilisation (Hawley 1997: 111). The three main leaders, of Baptist, Catholic and Church of God origin, all joined the Moravian Church and asserted a

Christian Miskitu nationalism. The main leader, Steadman Fagoth, helped to form the first 'contra' units in Honduras in 1981. The group that carried out the first raids into Nicaragua was led by a pastor who had been head of the Moravian youth wing. His group was divided into two units called the Seven Evangelists and the Troops of the Cross; a church service was held every night and Moravian hymns were sung into battle (ibid.: 129).

On the Pacific side, tension had a broader cause. Many middle-level Sandinistas were orthodox Marxists little disposed to tolerate a well-organised and close-knit community largely unenthusiastic about participating in Sandinista organisations and which seemed to have some links to the world power which was encouraging armed opposition. In 1982–3, several church buildings were arbitrarily expropriated and there was a campaign of disrespect for pastors and believers on the part of the ubiquitous Cuban-style Sandinista Defence Committees (Zub 1996c).

On the whole, the leadership was not involved and never adopted an anti-evangelical position (Miranda 1991: 82), although Stoll cites one of the nine *comandantes* of the National Directorate, Luís Carrión, as alleging, without evidence, that 'an enormous quantity of ex-National Guardsmen are now evangelical pastors' (Stoll 1990: 233). On the other hand, Tomás Borge, also of the National Directorate, claimed an experience of Christ through the Full Gospel Businessmen's Fellowship International. Through Borge, the government requested eight hundred thousand popular language New Testaments, to be used by those who acquired basic reading skills in the 1980 Literacy Crusade. Borge said: 'I believe that between Christians and Sandinistas there should be a true integration ... to move the revolutionary process forward and to reconstruct ... the morality of the Nicaraguan man.' In addition, no Nicaraguan president before the Sandinista Daniel Ortega had had such a close relationship with Protestants, on many occasions attending evangelistic campaigns by evangelists Yiye Ávila and Alberto Motessi. Some churches gained permission for evangelistic work in prisons. And Gustavo Parajón, president of CEPAD and pastor of the First Baptist Church of Managua, was nominated by Ortega as one of the 'Notables' on the National Committee for Reconciliation. More Bibles were distributed than ever before, the government facilitated foreign funding through CEPAD, and pastors and seminary students were excused military call-up to fight against the anti-Sandinista 'contras', leading to a boom in seminary enrolment (Zub 1993: 70).

The main problem was deeper than persecution as such. It was not just that the FSLN did not yet perceive the political importance of evangelicals, as they did in the 1990s. As Stoll says, 'at stake was the right of evangelicals to refuse to participate in the Sandinista revolution' (1990: 260). The FSLN's centralised mobilisational politics was a major determinant of negative evangelical responses to the revolution. Influenced by the Leninist concept of the vanguard, they tried to create the mass mobilisation that did not exist. The struggle against Reagan and the contras seemed to require the politicisation of large areas of life. As the government demanded ever-larger sacrifices, more evangelicals became opponents. Perhaps the main difficulty was not that the Sandinistas were left-wing, but that they were mobilisational and politicising. There is a peculiar incompatibility between virtually all forms of Protestantism and a long-term mobilising revolutionary movement (even of the right). There are perhaps two sources for this: the classic 'Protestant principle' (Tillich) of a stubborn individualism, obeying the voice of conscience; and what one might call the 'Anabaptist principle', *sectarian* in the strict sense of 'cut out of' society, and the free associational model it implies. What really mattered in relations between the Cold War Left and Protestants was that the latter were anti-corporative, averse to all vanguards and unified revolutionary organisations.

How did this affect positions within Protestantism? It produced some curious reversals of usual positions. 'Left-wing Christians were using the language of revolution to justify conformity, and right-wing Christians were using their old language of spiritual escapism to justify political dissent' (Stoll 1990: 261). Since the regime was open to a form of clientelism with religious groups, struggle for control of the Protestant field became acute. In Stoll's words, 'dissidents had become the establishment, the establishment had become the dissidents, and neither side was accustomed to its new role' (ibid.: 261). To put it slightly differently: a minority was aligned with government, and the majority was either wary or actively opposed; the insistence on mobilisation tended to make would-be neutrals into adversaries. This put pro-Sandinista evangelicals in a difficult situation: a minority in their own religious field, aligned with a mobilising government which virtually co-opted them as their 'bureau of Protestant affairs' and therefore effectively transformed them into the 'established church'.

A few Protestants, especially Baptists, had been enthusiastic supporters of the FSLN since the early 1970s. By the revolution, one organisation was solidly aligned with the Sandinistas: the Ecumenical

Axis, led by Baptist pastor José Miguel Torres. But the Axis lacked a popular base, and its hegemonic aspirations made it unpopular (the Axis delegate to the Council of State warned that if churches failed to obtain their incorporation papers through his organisation, he would not be able to vouch for their integrity [Stoll 1990: 240]). The government soon realised it would have to mediate its relations with Protestantism through a more representative entity. Although not enjoying the government's complete trust, CEPAD became that entity. It had been evolving in that direction. At a meeting just three months after the revolution, attended by an estimated half of the Protestant pastors in the country, a declaration was produced which thanked God for the FSLN as the instrument of liberation from the Somoza regime, and appeared to give unequivocal support to the government (Freston 1983). One can presume that concern about Cuban-style anti-religious measures, opportunism and traditional views about biblical demands for obedience to the authorities all played their part in producing such a remarkable statement. That very little national theological reflection underlay this position can be presumed from the almost total absence of Nicaraguan Protestant authors from the CEPAD volume *Reflexiones Sobre Fe y Revolución*, produced in 1980. Initial caution from some denominations gave way gradually to open disaffection; some pro-Sandinista pastors were expelled from the AG in the early 1980s (Stoll 1990: 240).

While pro-Sandinista evangelicals were able to participate openly in social and political life, they also became trapped in the role expected of them by the FSLN's vanguard philosophy. As the politics of austerity and the demands of war against the 'contras' escalated, so resentment increased at CEPAD's privileged mediatory role. Although CEPAD tried to be selective in its defence of the revolution, in deference to the conservatives amongst the affiliated churches, it was still perceived as manipulative. A leader of the more conservative pastors' organisation Consejo Nacional de Pastores Evangélicos de Nicaragua (CNPEN) said 'we want more respect for the use of the term "the evangelical people"' (ibid.: 244). This is a case of the boot being on the other foot, since in most Latin American countries it is the counterparts of the groups associated with CNPEN which have been guilty of usurping the right to speak in the name of 'the evangelical people'.

CEPAD's claim to represent the evangelicals was based on its mediatory role with government and access to foreign funding. A pastor complained: 'If we want something, we have to go to CEPAD and Sixto [Ulloa, Baptist development worker elected a congressman in 1984 and

CEPAD's liaison between government and churches], who is lord and master of all the evangelical field' (ibid.: 244). It does not matter whether resentment of CEPAD was also motivated by ideological opposition, some of it fanned from the United States. The point is that the Sandinista's relatively tolerant model was still locked into a vanguard philosophy, which turned CEPAD into a semi-official organisation locked into an invidious intermediary role which created a backlash. Instead of the traditional Marxist model of a 'bureau of Protestant affairs' manned by a Party functionary, a religious organisation was co-opted and made to play something of the same role. The result may be greater cushioning, but it still creates resentment and loss of a prophetic voice. Patronage power through access to major foreign funding in a poor country, plus the favour of the political rulers, helped to polarise the Protestant field and heighten competition for power.

By the later Sandinista years, it was clear that evangelicals were growing phenomenally. The FSLN made no attempt to restrict this growth, and seems to have recognised that it was a non-counter-revolutionary interest group that needed to be included in consultations (Lancaster 1988: 119). Perhaps they intuited what Lancaster's 1988 book spelled out: that although only a minority of Protestant clergy (as indeed of Catholic clergy) was 'with the revolution' in a consistent manner, evangelicalism still made a contribution to their revolutionary project in its own way. As a religion of the marginal poor, its relation to the revolution was indirect. It unselfconsciously exemplified certain revolutionary values. Whereas Liberation Theology's relationship to the revolution was primarily ideological, evangelicalism's was primarily sociological. It radically reordered and regulated the lives of the very poor. It combatted the culture of despair by causing the poor to lead more exemplary lives. *Sects* of radical personal salvation thereby opened up the possibility of revolutionary participation rather than lumpen-proletarian delinquency. On balance, Lancaster concluded, 'the evangelical sects have accelerated, not impeded, the revolutionary process' (1988: 115).

The FSLN's openness was shown by the fact that, through CEPAD and congressman Sixto, the number of denominations with juridical personality multiplied by five (Miranda 1991: 85). Many of CEPAD's suggestions were incorporated into the constitution.

Since the regime maintained a functioning democracy (and was eventually overthrown democratically), it opened the way for continued Protestant participation. From 1980 to 1984, in the Council of State (which consisted of delegates appointed by leaders of mass organisations and other associations), the Ecumenical Axis was represented by the octogenarian Baptist pastor José María Ruiz. In the 1984 elections, two Baptists were elected to congress on the FSLN ticket: Ruiz and Sixto (ibid.: 84).

Anti-Sandinista Protestants obviously did not enjoy state patronage, but Stoll estimates that by 1983 40 per cent of all pastors were receiving financial aid from an anti-communist source based in Costa Rica (1990: 236). But there is no reason to think the US religious right caused, rather than just made use of, this reticence towards the regime.

On the Atlantic Coast, there were pastors amongst opponents, and Stoll claims a quarter of Moravian churches were closed or destroyed (ibid.: 257). However, the AG, the largest denomination on the Pacific side, doubled its number of church buildings by 1984, despite being the mainstay of CNPEN, a conservative reaction to CEPAD founded in 1981. However, as CNPEN lacked legal incorporation, it was officially a part of CEPAD; according to Stoll, this suited many pastors in rural areas who preferred to keep a foot in both camps.

The AG was the denomination which most identified with an anti-Sandinista position. Whether due to pressure from the Springfield headquarters of the American AG, or to local factors, they were unhappy with CEPAD. In 1989, a CEPAD report is said to have insinuated that it was 'more than a coincidence' that the first pentecostal missionaries had arrived in the country in 1912, the same year as the US marines (Peterson 1995: 312). Even so, the AG hung on in CEPAD for as long as the FSLN was in power, and withdrew after the latter's electoral defeat in 1990, accusing CEPAD of being 'political'. A charitable interpretation is that the AG had been virtually forced to remain in CEPAD since the latter provided a necessary cushion against possible reprisals. An uncharitable interpretation would be that the AG opportunistically withdrew from CEPAD after the change of regime because there were no more concrete advantages to be had. But if the AG thought it might achieve a relationship with the new government by forming a rival Alliance of Evangelical Churches, it was to be disappointed; the post-Sandinista governments, very pro-Catholic, have given far less space to evangelicals than the FSLN.

This was despite the fact that Protestantism was now far more important than in 1979. The 1995 census showed that Protestantism had grown from around 5 per cent to nearly 15 per cent during the Sandinista period. This is inconvenient both for unreconstructed left-wing analysts who insist on seeing evangelicalism as pathological, and for those pentecostal leaders who call for a right-wing vote because the left will persecute the *evangélicos*. The Protestantism which grew was over-whelmingly pentecostal, better able to accompany the vertiginous growth of Managua (Zub 1993: 23). This new pentecostal predominance is reflected in Protestant politics in the 1990s.

The 1990 election in which the FSLN lost power still saw a Baptist elected as the only Protestant. This was Rodolfo Mejía, lawyer and former congressman from before the revolution. Even though a member of Parajón's First Baptist Church, Mejía was in the UNO coalition of Violeta Chamorro.

A study of Protestant attitudes and voting in the 1990 election (Zub 1993) examines whether there is any ground to some analysts' belief that over 80 per cent of Protestants voted for UNO. He examines 248 Managua members of six denominations: AG, Baptists, Church of God (established in 1951 from El Salvador), Misión Cristiana (an atypical pentecostal group, being a 1959 schism from the AG with social projects and membership in the WCC-linked Latin American Council of Churches), Church of Christ (a lay movement founded locally in 1928) and Four-Square (brought from the United States in 1955). Of these, 98.4 per cent affirmed that neither their local church nor denomination had published anything telling them which way to vote; 96.6 per cent denied the existence of 'revelations' in their churches indicating a candidate (ibid.: 64–5). This does not exclude more subtle attempts to influence members' voting, but does suggest a greater neutrality than is often attributed to many churches.

Zub asks whom these evangelicals considered to be responsible for the war between Sandinistas and 'contras'. Asked if 'the FSLN was mainly responsible', 52 per cent replied 'yes' and 31 per cent 'no'. Zub does not say what the general population thought, but the election result suggests it was not so different. AG members answered 57 per cent 'yes' and only 21 per cent 'no', confirming their reputation as bulwarks of anti-Sandinismo. However, when asked whether 'the United States was responsible' (although not 'mainly responsible'), 59 per cent of Protes-tants agreed; even the AG figure was 46 per cent. To the question whether the 'contras' fought 'for democracy' (as the United States asserted), only 37 per cent of evangelicals thought they did, and only 30 per cent of AG members. It would seem that evangelicals were critical of the FSLN and its insistence on the war, but they were not dupes of American and 'contra' propaganda.

When asked about the FSLN's relationship to evangelicals, 8 per cent (AG only 4%) said it had been excellent, 33 per cent (AG 27%) good, 37 per cent (AG 25%) poor, 17 per cent (AG 41%) bad. Even so, sympathy for the FSLN was similar to the general population: 29 per cent compared to 28.3 per cent. The only denomination significantly less disposed was the AG (a mere 4.3%), while Misión Cristiana, Church of Christ and Baptists were all over 35 per cent. There was little sympathy for UNO: 10.5 per cent, with only the Four-Square much higher (34%). Over 35 per cent professed no sympathy for any existing party (69% in the AG).

Of Zub's sample, 51 per cent voted for UNO and 29 per cent for the FSLN. The greatest advantage for UNO was in the Four-Square (69% versus 16%), closely followed by the AG, while the only denomination in which the FSLN won (just) was the Baptist. However, 76 per cent of AG members who voted for UNO denied any sympathy for it, indicating a political chasm which emerging pentecostal politicians would soon try to fill. Of UNO's evangelical voters, 59 per cent did not read newspapers, against 17 per cent of FSLN voters; the higher educational level of left-wing evangelicals is similar to the general population, but a blow for FSLN claims to represent the poorer sectors. Zub discovers that time of conversion influences voting patterns; or perhaps (rather than attributing too much political efficacy to evangelical socialisation) one should say it influences the motives for converting and therefore also the probable voting pattern. Those converting during the first five years of the revolution, years of ideological antagonism and economic restrictions, show a marked tendency to vote for UNO. Pentecostalism was a refuge for the poor anti-Sandinista masses, a functional equivalent of exile in the United States for the rich (ibid.: 105).

There are two limitations to Zub's study. We do not know to what extent the evangelical vote (and differences between denominations) might reflect differences in social composition. Evangelicals might vote in a particular way because they are disproportionately poor, elderly, urban, female or have a dozen other characteristics. To what extent did church teachings, and perceptions regarding the FSLN's relationship to evangelicals, affect the way evangelicals voted? How much religious specificity was there to their behaviour?

The other limitation is that Zub's sample is not weighted socially or denominationally. Numbers interviewed from each denomination do not at all correspond to their weight in the Protestant world (the AG is under-represented). We would have to correct for denominational size to know something about overall evangelical behaviour in the election. If we use as a rough guide the national figures (not just for Managua) given in Zub's introduction, we arrive at the following: evangelicals voted roughly 57 per cent UNO and 32 per cent FSLN, as opposed to overall results of 53 per cent versus 42 per cent for Managua. While confirming greater resistance to the FSLN, this is far from corroborating a sweeping preference for the conservative, American-supported opposition. Much of the difference between Protestants and non-Protestants is accounted for by the sizeable evangelical vote for two small parties which ran independently, the Liberals and the PSC. This apparent search for a 'third alternative' would receive a specifically evangelical colouring in the next election.

Zub portrays evangelical perceptions of politics at the time of the survey, and not at the time of the 1990 election. In the intervening period, the FSLN had lost the moral high ground, as their leaders had distributed state property amongst themselves between losing the election and handing over power. The new government's policies, while ending military service and controlling hyperinflation, contributed to a renewed polarisation. The reduction of the state apparatus, changes in landholding structure and privatisations led to huge unemployment. As Karl says, insufficient regard to social safety nets constrains the already narrow political space, leaving Nicaragua at the brink of renewed conflict (1995: 84). From the evangelical view, post-1990 governments have been too close to the Catholic Church. In the Chamorro government (1990–6), no evangelical had a significant post. Public funds were used to build a new cathedral, and state offices housed the new Catholic university. The giant FSLN acronym on a hill overlooking Managua was replaced by a statue of the Virgin.

Not for nothing did Zub's survey say: 'the most effusive response ... was to the question about an evangelical party' (1993: 101). Of Protestants surveyed, 71 per cent approved the idea. When asked who could solve Nicaragua's economic problems, 31 per cent replied that an evangelical government could, and a further 16 per cent that God could. For many evangelicals, these answers mean the same. Those who wished for an evangelical party were disproportionately female, older, poorer, less educated and inexperienced in party-political life. Zub prognosticates that such a party could be one of the three major forces in the next elections, and would take votes away mostly from the right-wing parties (1993: 77, 106).

In a 1995 survey (Zub 1996a), the same author asked the opinion of 304 pastors: 12 per cent said they would like to be candidates; 42 per cent said they had no sympathy with any existing party, 21 per cent had sympathy with the FSLN, 13 per cent with the PLC (leading member of the UNO government) and only 4.5 per cent with the evangelical PJN (Partido de Justicia Nacional, founded in 1992). However, 30 per cent declared they would vote for an evangelical candidate for president. This leads Zub to foresee the possibility of an evangelical party establishing itself as the third-largest political force in the country. A full 80 per cent of pastors disapproved of the Chamorro government.

By then, several initiatives were under way, although with limited impact. The first evangelical party to obtain registration was the Partido de Justicia Nacional (PJN). Founded in 1992, its main base was in the AG, although lay people of several denominations (and little political experience) were in leadership (Zub 1996b: 38). Having arisen among the laity, it suffered a 'lack of episcopal legitimation', and some evangelicals saw it as not a truly evangelical party because of its lay leadership (Zub 1996a: 113); an interesting comment on the lack of an equivalent of the modern Catholic concept of lay apostolate. It would seem that ecclesiastical leaders are expected to have political leadership as well (whether or not they are actually candidates) – a mentality which has historically been common in the *sects* as well as in the Catholic Church. Lay activism does not imply lay autonomy, and the tasks of an evangelical party must be set by the ecclesiastical hierarchy.

The PJN has links with US organisations around former Republican presidential candidate Pat Robertson which try to link evangelical parties in various countries (Gonzales 1996: 218), infusing them with the agenda of the American religious right. Before long, the PJN was challenged by the Movimiento Evangélico Popular (MEP – no connection with the Brazilian Movimento Evangélico Progressista), organised by pro-Sandinistas. Movimiento Evangélico Popular claims inspiration in figures such as Frank País (Cuban Baptist who joined Castro's forces), Bonhoeffer and Luther King, as well as Central American figures of local renown (Zub 1993: 118). It criticises the UNO government for ignoring evangelicals, and implicitly presents the FSLN as more open to Protestant participation. Already in 1990 the FSLN had presented pastors as candidates in municipal elections (Miranda 1991: 86). In 1996 the pentecostal (Misión Cristiana) leader of the Movimiento Evangélico Popular, pastor Miguel Angel Casco, obtained a decisive victory over some of the historic *comandantes* for a place on the FSLN slate in the upcoming congressional elections (Zub 1996b: 38). In May 1998 Casco, by then a congressman, was elected to the National Directorate of the FSLN with the support of Daniel Ortega. Ortega also supported an evangelical request for an FSLN secretariate for Religious Affairs, and promised to promote evangelical Sandinista candidates for mayoralties and local councils in 2000 (*ALC*, 4 May 1998, 28 May 1998). It is true that, in early 2000, Casco was in open conflict with the Sandinista hierarchy for having revealed details to the press of a controversial pact between the FSLN and the Liberal government, for which he was the FSLN's chief negotiator. Even so, it would seem that the secular tradition of the FSLN leaves it better placed to tap into evangelical strength than the strongly Catholic governing coalition.

However, the most surprising evangelical phenomenon is a party which had not even been created at the time of Zub's 1995 survey but whose characteristics and potential are prefigured in his analysis. The Camino Cristiano Nicaragüense (CCN) is the product of pentecostal leaders with no previous political links. On the contrary, its 1996 presidential candidate, Guillermo Osorno, an AG pastor and former director of an evangelical radio station, had made his name as a media preacher critical of evangelicals in politics (Zub 1997: 11). He credits his conversion to politics to a revelation from God (Zub 1996d: 9). Lack of political experience and academic training did not prevent Osorno from placing third in the presidential race, with 4.1 per cent, albeit far behind the two main candidates. The other evangelical party, PJN, gained a mere 0.3 per cent. Osorno avoided direct confrontation with the Catholic Church (Zub 1996d: 9). Having prophesied he would win, Osorno was obliged to allege fraud to explain his third place. But in truth, it was a remarkable achievement, especially as his party achieved four seats in congress. Zub estimates about ten evangelical deputies: the CCN's four, Casco of the FSLN, and about five from the Atlantic Coast (Zub 1997: 11). By early 2000, the CCN was on the rocks; in the face of much evangelical criticism that Osorno had become a stooge of the government, three deputies broke away to form a new evangelical party (*ALC*, 10 March 2000).

Thus, in the 1990s evangelicals have emerged as an organised political force. The contrast between their numerical growth and their continued marginalisation by law and state has encouraged mobilisation, with some initial success. But denominational divisions, inexperience and lack of qualified people places a limit on how far the phenomenon can go. As Zub concludes, evangelical parties easily succumb to the illusion that 'believers' are incorruptible, that good intentions are all that is needed, and that political power can be safely placed at the service of the church (Zub 1993: 94, 100).

CHAPTER 27

Guatemala

Guatemala is a key case for evangelical politics in the Third World. A lot has been written about it, but much of what we would like to know is still not clear. It has probably the highest percentage of Protestants in Latin America and has produced two charismatic evangelical presidents.

About 60 per cent of the population are Indians, the highest percentage in the Americas. They belong to over twenty ethnic groups and speak as many different languages, which has impeded unified action. The country has a tiny elite of European descent (Spanish, Basque, German). A study of this elite by Casaus (1992) highlights adaptive strategies, now including involvement of oligarchic families in evangelical churches. This began in the 1970s through three elite families (Falla, Castillo and Bianchi), firstly in Verbo church and later in home-grown varieties. Casaus, writing during the government of evangelical Jorge Serrano, stresses how that government had facilitated the return to power of several oligarchic families, including evangelical ones (Alejos, Benfeldt, Zepeda Castillo, Bianchi). 'The oligarchy has not been displaced from power, but has recycled itself, presenting a new image', part of which is the evangelical link. 'The return of these family networks to power takes place, in part, through the appeal of a new social sector, the evangelical pentecostal groups, which give them a new social base for matrimonial and inter-class alliances, with the objective of maintaining hegemony and preserving their power' (ibid.: 297).

We should not read this as meaning that all elite conversions are politically self-interested, much less blatantly cynical. The early ones were probably not (even amongst people who could conceivably have political ambitions), since the risks of an untried strategy would have been high. In later years, the temptation would be greater. The point, however, is not individual motivation but the fact that the political outcome has been to allow part of the elite to reinvent itself and retain its dominance.

It would be interesting to know whether elite evangelicals jettison the racist ideology that Casaus finds amongst two-thirds of the elite: that Indians are inferior, lazy, thieving, lying and drunken, deserving to be worked hard, underpaid and even (for 5% of interviewees) exterminated. Casaus comments that this opinion varies little with sex, age or education, but she does not mention religion, except to comment that Ríos Montt used racist ideology in his counter-insurgency policy.

It is doubtful whether evangelicalism has yet had much substantive impact on the elite. As Villas says, many Anglo-Saxon authors are culturalist, stressing the Catholic and Iberian heritage as impediments to democratisation in Central America; yet this has not prevented Costa Rica being democratic, nor has evangelical growth in Guatemala and El Salvador had a one-directional impact on politics (1996a: 499).

Guatemala has the most unequal land distribution in Latin America. It has also had over thirty years of war (150,000 killed, a million displaced). Guerrillas have been combatted by military control of the countryside and death squads in the cities. Even though democracy returned in 1985, political space is very limited. Topics such as the army's autonomy, poverty and skewed land distribution are off-limits, unless one wishes to invite violence and assassination (Trudeau 1993: 148). This was illustrated in 1998 by the murder of the author of a human-rights report, Monseñor Gerardi, showing that even the Catholic hierarchy enjoys only partial immunity.

Excepting the reformist period from 1944 to 1954, ended by US-supported military intervention, Guatemala has had little room for civil society (Smith 1990: 34). It now belongs to those 'low-intensity democracies' incapable of carrying out meaningful social change (Karl 1995: 72). The growing global gap between rich and poor is most pronounced in Central America. In addition, democracy has never been firmly established in any Latin American country where labour-intensive and domestically owned agriculture is the main export sector (ibid.: 78–9).

Militarisation has accompanied ever-increasing autonomy of the military, first from the United States and now from the oligarchy (Smith 1990: 35). The highlands have become virtual military reservations. Nevertheless, formal democracy has survived, and even showed signs of a developing civil society in the resistance to Serrano's self-coup in 1993. In 1996, a peace accord was finally reached with the guerrillas.

Guatemala was for a time touted as over 30 per cent Protestant. However, much caution must be exercised. There are no government statistics. The evangelical agency Servicio Evangelizador para América

Latina (SEPAL) claimed 31 per cent in 1985, using church membership figures and a multiplier of four. By 1991, SEPAL felt a multiplier of 2.3 would be more realistic, which produced a result of 20 per cent, close to the 19 per cent of a Gallup survey in the same year. When the SEPAL surveys are made methodologically consistent, they show a percentage decline between 1985 and 1991, although continued absolute growth (Grenfell 1995: 47–8). Such stagnation reminds us of South Korea and has occurred at a similar percentage level, although any common factors must be internal since the external (social) factors could scarcely be more contrasting.

The Gallup survey of 1991 showed that Protestants tended to be urban (23.2% in Guatemala City, against 19.3% nationally) and well educated (31% of people with higher education). The latter contrasts with the rest of Latin America. There is also a category of nearly 5 per cent who 'were once evangelicals' (*Consultoria Interdisciplinaria en Desarrollo*, July 1991). Curiously, a 1985 survey found the opposite: against a national average of 20 per cent, the capital city was 16 per cent evangelical whereas the rural Indian Quiché were 25 per cent; and while evangelicals were only 14 per cent in the high income bracket, they were 23 per cent in the low and 21 per cent in the very low (Marco Tulio Cajas, *Perfil y Opinión Política de los Evangélicos Guatemaltecos*, mimeo, 1985). Possibly neither survey was reliable; but there may be a trend for Protestant membership to become more urban and elitist.

Elite charismatic churches have an unusually high profile, but historical Protestantism is weak. The first missionaries arrived from the United States invited and personally escorted by the president, a liberal who had introduced freedom of worship in 1873 and was frustrated that no Protestant missionaries had accepted his invitation to come! His anti-clerical (and even anti-Catholic) policies were enforced rigorously for decades (Garrard-Burnett 1996b: 97). The Presbyterians after 1882, and the holiness missions from the turn of the century, were showered with privileges by liberal governments, but growth was slow. Beginnings of work in indigenous languages after 1919 and the reformist anti-missionary regime of Arbenz (1950–4) laid the basis for the meteoric trajectory of autonomous Protestantism from the 1960s to the 1980s (Garrard-Burnett 1989). In the process, lower-class pentecostal churches and middle- and upper-class charismatic churches became the overwhelming majority, and took the forefront in education and social work.

Protestant penetration of the elite originated in rejection of Vatican II reforms (Smith, D. 1991: 134). The charismatic alternative was blocked by the hierarchy. Some people therefore turned to Protestantism. In addition, the 1976 earthquake had stimulated the arrival of independent charismatic groups from the United States, among them the Church of the Word (Verbo) which soon recruited Ríos Montt. The model was soon copied by members of the elite, such as the former lawyer from a prominent family who founded El Shaddai, the church of Jorge Serrano, as well as Misión de Fe, Fraternidad Cristiana de Guatemala, Jesus es Señor, La Familia de Dios and Lluvias de Gracia. These churches, often called 'neo-pentecostal', usually have strong charismatic leaders, often with contacts with US evangelicals, and emphasise prosperity teaching and spiritual warfare as the prelude to material and spiritual blessings.

Guatemala shows what can happen when Protestantism begins to be practised by significant numbers of the elite. According to Stoll (1994: 108), Protestants are no more than 5 per cent of the elite but are best represented among owners of 'modern' businesses importing technology, and least among the old elite of coffee planters whose requirements for labour control helped to create the death squads. The combination of elite presence, vast popular base and weak state is transforming Protestantism into a new source of political hegemony. Class location makes elite believers receptive to the American religious right and its vision of dominion in which believers take power and remould society from above. 'What brought the evangelical movement into politics was less pastoral activism [the Brazilian case] or North American influence [or solicitation of secular politicians, as in Peru] than the movement's extension upward in the class scale' (ibid.: 107). 'Their performance will test the sweeping claims of evangelists that born-again Christianity can transform economically stunted, repressive societies into models of prosperity and democracy' (Stoll 1991: 189).

In the early 1950s, when missionaries were concerned about Arbenz's socialistic tendencies, Guatemalan Protestants seem to have been favourable to this president who had been brought up as a Protestant (Grenfell 1995: 18–19). But subsequently, politics in Guatemala (oscillating between overt military intervention and covert military tutelage with a democratic façade) became pressed into Cold War moulds. Evangelical churches grew, but no one expected a sudden entry into politics. This changed in 1982, when junior officers who had led a coup invited General Efrain Ríos Montt to take over.

Ríos Montt has been so determinant of the evangelical experience in politics that it is important to understand his trajectory. He is of modest ladino (mixed-race) origin from a largely Indian department, Catholic (a brother is now a bishop) but with an evangelical grandmother who took him to church as a child. He was trained as a regular soldier, but eventually entered the military academy. By the 1960s he was a general. In the early 1970s he became dissatisfied with the way a group of top officers were dominating the political process and carving out huge fortunes (Handy 1986: 395). Later, Ríos was to be accused of having commanded a massacre at that time. To sideline him, he was appointed director of studies at the Inter-American School of Defence Studies in Washington. But the opposition Christian Democrats invited him to be their presidential candidate in 1974. The deepening fissures in the armed forces, as well as their centrality, were expressed by the fact that all three candidates were military men. Ríos almost certainly won, but the ruling clique used fraud to deny him victory. Ríos refused to protest; he departed quietly to be military attaché in Spain, reputedly with a large consolation prize (Grenfell 1995: 53). In 1978, he returned to Guatemala, but the Christian Democrats had not forgiven him and chose another candidate. About this time, a former comrade in arms invited him to a Bible-study group at Verbo church. Ríos became an evangelical.

As Grenfell comments, Ríos' conversion was more an endorsement of his previous strict ethical standards. 'The first evangelical president appears to have undergone remarkably little evangelical secondary socialisation . . . The man responsible for defining the evangelical politician is actually a lot closer to Catholicism than many have realised' (1995: 54). As director of the Polytechnic, before his conversion, he had required every man to carry a New Testament. As presidential candidate in 1974, his style showed all the moralising and haranguing traits for which he later became famous as president (Anfuso and Sczepanski 1984: 49, 62). Had he been allowed to take power in 1974, his presidency might well have been very similar to what it was in the early 1980s; but, since he was still a Catholic, it would not have had any repercussions for Protestantism's public image.

From 1978 to 1982 there was increasing violence and economic collapse. There were also increasing attempts by the army to gain the ideological support of evangelicals in the highland combat zones. However, evangelical churches in the highlands were not uniformly conservative, says Garrard-Burnett (1998: 133). The Presbyterians, with ethnic presbyteries, had the most progressive reputation, but some groups splintered. One Primitive Methodist Church produced an anti-American and quietly pro-guerrilla schism; one Príncipe de Paz church also gained a more leftist faction which suffered at the hands of the military. The EGP guerrillas sought evangelical recruits as being 'more zealous' than Catholics. But the rule was of churches providing a safe haven from political discourse. Some pastors took part in army programmes, but usually out of intimidation rather than ideological predilection.

In 1981 a coalition invited Ríos Montt to run for president. After consultation with Verbo elders, Ríos declined. However, eight days after the 1982 elections, a group of younger officers staged a coup and invited Ríos to lead them. After more consulting with Verbo elders, Ríos accepted, leaving his job as principal of a Verbo day school. It seems that the officers had no knowledge of his new religious convictions (Grenfell 1995: 55).

The junior officers were annoyed by the incompetent counter-insurgency campaign and by corruption. They desired to pursue the war with more vigour, by means of relocation of the rural population in 'model villages'. As Handy (1986) says, Ríos Montt's emergence at their head was at first surprising, since he had kept aloof from politics since 1974. But this was itself a recommendation, and he had personal connections with many of the junior officers from his time as director of the military academy.

For many years, Ríos largely defined Guatemalan perceptions of how an evangelical behaves in politics: honest, committed, ruthless, and obsessed with law and order (Grenfell 1995: 113). In a revealing interview in the American evangelical magazine *Christianity Today*, he says he had no difficulty in readapting to being a church elder after his removal from power. 'For me there is no difference [between head of state and church elder] ... Back then [as president] I was simply ministering to a bigger church.' God had installed him as head of state to make spiritual truths known to the people. To this conception of the nation as a huge church and the head of state as teacher of spiritual truths, we can add the comment by an American evangelical leader, formerly a missionary, after a luncheon engagement together: 'I saw him as a warm and somewhat charismatic individual, but one who was first a military man, secondly an elitist, and thirdly a Christian. I don't believe Verbo gave him enough Christian teaching in a contextualised way'.

Ríos governed for nearly a year and a half. He dissolved congress for corruption and replaced it with a Council of State, presided over by another evangelical, Jorge Serrano Elías. But it is wrong to over-emphasise the evangelical nature of his regime. It was a military government of a particular type. Junior officers had brought him to power, upsetting hierarchy. Military and business had interests in stability and a successful counter-insurgency campaign. If Ríos threatened stability, and if he had too much success against the guerrillas, he would become dispensable. He had not been made president to carry out an 'evangelical' programme, whatever that might mean, and attempts to do so would tend to destabilise his position.

The *raison d'être* of his government was the new counter-insurgency policy known as 'bullets and beans' (*fusiles y frijoles*). Based on 'strategic hamlets', the goal was destruction of autonomous village life. Civil patrols were maintained through enforced conscription (Grenfell 1995: 60). The first stage of this campaign was 'incredibly brutal' (Handy 1986: 403); four hundred villages were destroyed, hundreds of thousands of Indians fled to Mexico and one million were internally displaced (Grenfell 1995: 61). Of course, both before and after Ríos there were military governments which did substantially the same. And no religious concern animated this policy. There was controversy when Ríos offended Catholics by merely shaking the Pope's hand instead of kneeling and kissing his ring; and the Pope's plea for clemency for seven convicted guerrillas was ignored. But at least three of those guerrillas were evangelicals, and one went to his death singing a pentecostal chorus. A pastor in a 'model village' was shot for complaining that civil-patrol duty on Sundays was preventing members from attending church. Several other pastors were arrested, tortured or murdered under Ríos. Protestant identity provided no security for those suspected of subversion, as the thirteen pentecostals burned alive inside their church discovered. Evangelicals who joined the guerrillas were welcomed and often regarded as better fighters, since they viewed the contest as a Manichean conflict between good and evil. However, says Garrard-Burnett, evangelical relief organisations got more freedom than others to work in army-controlled areas; some pastors cooperated willingly with government programmes, while others did so because the army was better able to defend them against the guerrillas than the guerrillas were against the army. Garrard-Burnett concludes that 'conversion in the Ríos Montt years had less to do with the president's own religion or the influence of North American evangelicalism than with his pacification programme' which disrupted peasant life and allowed churches to form freely in the model villages (1998: 154).

Meanwhile, in cities crime decreased dramatically through special courts which administered speedy justice (Grenfell 1995: 63). The counter-insurgency was basically successful. But Ríos wished to go further. His ideal was moral reform, which included not only restraining abuses of authority within the army but forming a new civil-service ethos. While maintaining restrictions on political liberty, he introduced a moral tone into government. The most visible side of this were his Sunday night 'sermons' on television, modelled on Roosevelt's 'fireside chats' but in an 'eccentric haranguing style' (Grenfell 1995: 56). Civil servants were exhorted to personal honesty: 'I don't steal, I don't lie, I don't take advantage.' As Ríos said: 'God loves and disciplines you, he loves and hits you so that you may wake up' (*Crónica*, 28 Apr. 1989: 16).

It seems Ríos Montt also desired a broader conception of a Christian government than just personal honesty. Grenfell asserts he had a political project based on a fundamentalist reading of the Bible (1995: 57), though to what extent he really believed in and tried to implement such ideas is open to doubt. Ríos was, of course, a member of a high-class charismatic church, and such circles have a greater propensity than other Latin American evangelicals to adopt some version of an American political theology called reconstructionism. This theology, which came to the fore in the United States in the 1980s, replaces pre-millennial pessimism about the world with an optimistic post-millennialism. It is the destiny of Christians to govern the nations by a mixture of extreme neoliberal economics and Old Testament theocratic laws. Few politicians adopt the whole package, but several use it selectively to overcome programmatic deficiencies. The optimism and emphasis on analysis and debate are more attractive to higher-class charismatics than to lower-class pentecostals.

On the recommendation of the American director of Gospel Outreach, which had set up Verbo Church, Ríos invited economist R. E. McMaster to make policy suggestions. Following McMaster's March 1983 visit, Ríos told him his analysis was 'in close agreement with mine' (letter of 18 Mar. 1983 from Ríos Montt, in *The Reaper*, 1 Apr. 1983). McMaster's own eccentric account of the trip is in his newsletter.

McMaster stresses that the Guatemalan leadership ('the only on-fire Christian government in today's world') had asked him to teach them 'what Christian economics and government are all about'. He told them there had been only one truly Christian economy since Jeremiah, the USA, and provided 'precise scriptural documentation' on a free market economy and minimal government. 'Point by point we tackled Guatemala's economic problems'; solutions were basically government withdrawal from a series of activities, including labour legislation. McMaster's report is full of impressions of Guatemala and of the momentous significance of his own visit. Guatemala City is clean and paved, with excellent medical and dental care. The country is at peace and in love with its president. Occasional atrocities are quickly punished, and in any case it is self-righteous for Americans to judge Guatemalans by their own standard of human rights (it seems human rights, unlike neoliberal economics, are not universal). 'I toured the country by helicopter... From what I could discern, worker exploitation is declining.' That McMaster was not just a sober free market economist is apparent from comments which pepper the report. 'I stressed ... the probability of the reactivation of earthquakes and volcanic activity in the 1988–1992 time period, when this earth should undergo a period of unequalled ... tribulation.' His visit virtually coincided with that of the Pope. The latter 'addressed the masses; I addressed their leaders. Guatemalans saw these two weeks as the most important since Columbus.'

It is unlikely that Ríos Montt, a general fighting a real war and trying to stay in power, was overly influenced by such a quirky figure. But McMaster's report exemplifies (while exaggerating) a certain type of American influence in Third World evangelical politics. Such currents rarely have the ear of presidents, and even then their influence must not be overestimated. We must not mistake their own triumphalist accounts, devoid of any perception of local political realities, for what right-wing evangelical politics in these countries actually means. The same goes for the Christian-right financial help to the Ríos government. Campus Crusade raised funds for relief in 'model villages'; Jerry Falwell and Pat Robertson launched an aid programme called International Love Lift, whose resources were to be channelled partly through Verbo. Only about $200,000 were actually donated, and impact was minimal (Grenfell 1995: 60). It would be more important to know more about Ríos Montt's local evangelical advisors, Guatemalan and American. There were few Protestants in the government, but McMaster met American Verbo counsellors to the president. Two Verbo elders, Francisco Bianchi, secretary to the president of the Republic, and Alvaro Contreras, secretary to the Private Affairs of the President, were regarded as amongst the most powerful non-military figures. But while they may have established a gatekeeping role in day-to-day affairs, there is no doubting where the real power lay.

Placing the Ríos administration in context nuances both the 'Christian president' myth and that of the bloodthirsty butcher. There is probably truth in a *Christianity Today* article (13 Jan. 1984) by an

American missionary, which claims that Amnesty International wrongly attributed to the Ríos period some incidents which had occurred
earlier. But it is not necessary to say he was exceptionally repressive by
the standards of Guatemalan military governments; it is enough to say
he exemplified those standards. It is in that context that Ríos still enjoys
considerable popularity, as an upright soldier untainted by the corruption of politics (Stoll 1993: 260).

In August 1983 Ríos was overthrown by a coup. The new military
president gave as one reason the need to save the country from religious
fanaticism. Indeed, the Catholic hierarchy was visibly delighted. But the
religious factor was not decisive. Ríos had alienated important civilian
sectors through his dallying with a business tax and rumours of agrarian
reform, and his moralistic preaching had condemned their business and
personal habits. But the key sectors were the military and the United
States. The young officers who had called him to power cooled when he
capitulated to US pressure to punish a young lieutenant responsible for
murdering a USAID employee. The more senior officers, still offended
by the 1982 coup, were exasperated by his stalling on redemocratisation.
And relations with the United States worsened when Ríos refused to
support the 'contra' war in Nicaragua. Two days before Ríos was
overthrown, the coup leader met the US ambassador and the head of
the US command in Panama (Grenfell 1995: 64). It seems that the first
evangelical president in Latin America was ousted by a US-supported
coup, despite conspiracy theories about the supposed role of 'evangelical sects' in promoting American interests in the region.

In 1984 Gospel Outreach published a biography of Ríos Montt
(Anfuso and Sczepanski 1984), an indirect rebuttal to charges commonly
made against him. There was no massacre in the early 1970s (ibid.:
56–7). There was no pay-off to accept defeat in 1974; he wished to avoid
bloodshed (ibid.: 67–8). Far from being racist, he believed racism to be
the root of the country's problems, and said one-third of the delegates to
the Council of State should be Indians. His government did not give
excessive power to members of his church; 'My purpose is not to create
a theocracy ... [but] we need true Christian friends to remind us of our
higher commitments' (ibid.: 156ff.).

The book shows us the type of Protestantism Ríos Montt had been
inducted into. The Verbo elders at the time were mostly Americans,
plus two Guatemalans: advertising executive Alvaro Contreras, and the
manager of the country's largest television station, Francisco Bianchi,
who became his private secretaries when president. There is no feeling

in the book, written soon after his downfall, that his political career might not be over, and it would be enlightening to know how his post-1989 activities are seen by Verbo. With regard to his conversion in 1978, the authors present it as a psychological transformation, enabling him to be less self-righteous, but not as a transformation of mentality. The only difference it seems to have made to his political career was the ability to *wait* for the presidency without resentment. The possibility of a new political world-view is not mooted, and the McMaster visit is not mentioned. It is not clear what Ríos would have done differently as a Catholic in the presidency. When invited to be a candidate for 1982 by a three-party coalition, he met Verbo elders for prayer and fasting. Bianchi is reported as concluding: 'I believe now is not the time. Another door will be opened, a sovereignly opened door … It would be very difficult, even if elected, to bring about meaningful changes' (ibid.: 106–7). The implication is that the coup was a 'sovereignly opened door' and that as military president he would be able to effect changes. Verbo does not seem to have any developed political theology, beyond a rather naive notion of the sovereignty of God. It is ironic that, if Ríos had refused to head the junta in 1982, he might have been elected president in any post-1985 election and had considerably longer in power.

In 1985, partly for international rehabilitation but largely because the rural situation was now secure, the military reinstituted a tutelary democracy. This gave evangelicals their chance in electoral politics, following their rise to visibility with Ríos. The leading figure was to be Jorge Serrano.

Serrano, with degrees in engineering and education, was a business-man who had gone bankrupt in 1981. He had been active in the Catholic charismatic renewal before converting to Protestantism in the late 1970s. In Elim church, founded by a Guatemalan doctor, he soon came to be second in command, with the title of 'prophet'. It is said a family connection with a Verbo elder helped him become president of the non-elected Council of State under Ríos Montt; but the accounts do not explain satisfactorily Serrano's relationship to Ríos. Representative of a different emerging face of Protestantism, Serrano felt well-placed to catalyse the electoral potential. He used non-evangelical funders to organise a group of pastors on a mildly reformist platform. With this base, he was asked to be presidential candidate for a new party, the PDCN, whose base was the cooperative movement. An alliance was later made with the PR, an older party with a reputation for corruption. This was viewed with suspicion by some evangelical leaders. Serrano placed a respectable third for president with 14 per cent. Surveys showed double the preference for him among evangelicals than among the general population (in Marco Tulio Cajas, *La Campaña del '85 – Una Reflexión Necesaria*, mimeo). Even so, it was clear that there was no evangelical electoral bloc. But the example of Ríos had overcome the traditional inferiority complex of evangelicals, and a good number were elected to congress.

Serrano changed church, founded his own party and made contacts abroad. Whether through competition with the leader of Elim, or because his political ambitions were not well received there, he moved to El Shaddai, a new elite church. There he became a lay leader, and at the time of his 1990 presidential campaign was promoting a 'spiritual warfare' project of national exorcism known as 'Jesus is Lord of Guatemala', to free the country from a curse relating to pre-Christian religion. A leaflet by the pastor of El Shaddai explained that 'our entire country was dedicated [in 300 BC] to Satan ... Someone rang me the other day from abroad and gave me a prophecy: the year for Guatemala is 1990. The church will rise up like a giant over this land; the church will prophesy over this nation and will free it from the curse.'

In 1986 Serrano founded Movimiento de Acción Solidaria (MAS), the vehicle for his aspirations. He was later appointed to the Council on National Reconciliation in dialogue with the guerrillas, where he earned a reputation as a conciliator. Meanwhile, evangelical connections in the United States put him in touch with conservative circles such as the International Democratic Union. As 1990 approached, he published *La Participación del Cristiano en la Vida Pública*, a cautious statement of mainstream centre-right evangelicalism, unprogrammatic and non-reconstructionist.

Two months before the election Serrano was running fourth with only 11 per cent (Trudeau 1993: 145). The front-runner with 33 per cent was none other than Ríos Montt, whose running mate was also Protestant, Harris Whitbeck, a businessman, former US marine and leader of the (Methodist) Union Church (*Crónica*, 13 July 1990). The Ríos campaign reputedly received major funding from a former minister of the interior known for human-rights violations. The Catholic Church publicly opposed Ríos, while the US State Department professed neutrality (Trudeau 1993: 145). In the end, Ríos was barred due to a constitutional ban from presidential elections on former participants in coups.

This was Serrano's chance. Whether or not he had only entered the campaign in case his 'mentor' Ríos was disqualified, as he later claimed (ibid.: 149), he is a subordinate figure. The key personage in evangelical politics is still Ríos Montt, and it is this dependence on one man which most distinguishes Guatemala from Brazil. In one survey, most Ríos voters replied that they would transfer to Serrano. Grenfell nuances this: their images were different (Ríos the caudillo, Serrano the sophisticated politician); Ríos instructed his supporters to cast blank ballots; Ríos' support included Catholics; and a survey after the election showed that although 70 per cent knew of Serrano's evangelical affiliation, only half of those regarded it as positive (Grenfell 1995: 79ff.). But it would seem that being an evangelical (rather than just associated with the Ríos government) must be part of the reason why Serrano channelled the Ríos vote more than other candidates. Such was the force of the latter's figure that the image of being an evangelical and of being an honest 'non-political' outsider were still hard to distinguish.

Serrano placed a close second in the first ballot with 24 per cent, and his party became the third largest with eighteen seats. In the run-off, religion became prominent. The rival candidate emphasised Catholic credentials. One senior congressman called on voters to 'defend our religion and our Hispanic American cultures . . . There are international forces wishing to . . . divide us up into small sects . . . With the Protestant sects comes economic and financial domination . . . They want to rip 500 years of Catholicism out of the heart of our people, so that we shall no longer be Guatemalans but have an Anglo-Saxon culture instead.'

This seems to have backfired, since a survey showed that Catholics would vote for Serrano twice as much as for the other candidate. Presumably a similar pattern obtained amongst Protestants, since Serrano emerged victorious with 67 per cent. Many factors may have contributed. His rival was rumoured to be homosexual; Serrano was regarded as against conventional parties and more prone to communicate with the guerrillas.

Serrano's two and a half years in power were marked by the beginnings of civilian control over the military, by the initiation of peace talks and by the recognition of Belize (whose territory Guatemala has traditionally claimed). The last measure, benefiting trade, led to a storm of nationalist protest. On the other hand, his proposed tax reforms benefited large businesses, at the expense of the middle-class and small businesses. And human rights worsened. When indigenous leader Rigoberta Menchú was awarded the Nobel Peace Prize, Serrano was unable or unwilling to prevent a wave of assaults against people associated with her (Grenfell 1995: 180).

Serrano failed to deepen democracy through accountability, and in congress (where he had a minority) he continued vote-buying. Even worse, stories came out about corruption on his own behalf. If people had voted for an honest disciplinarian, they were disappointed. With regard to being disciplinarian, they were bound to be, since he was a civilian leader of a fragile coalition. The evidence of corruption was the final nail in the coffin of the mystique of the evangelical politician. That mystique was seen to belong only to its original owner, Ríos Montt, and not to his religious community (Grenfell 1995: 115).

On 25 May 1993 Serrano carried out what is known, à la Fujimori, as a 'self-coup'. He 'temporarily and partially' suspended the constitution, dissolved congress and the Supreme Court, and announced for within sixty days a Constituent Assembly to rewrite the constitution. The professed reasons were to combat the guerrillas and corruption more efficaciously. In fact, dialogue with the guerrillas had ground to a halt, and Serrano's own reputation had been scarred by revelations about his private life (including a visit to a topless bar in New York) and personal probity (including construction of a multi-million-dollar mansion within a national reserve). Investigations were about to begin. In addition, his autocratic temperament was finding the democratic process frustrating. He had recently lost the support of the Christian Democrats over a proposed neoliberal adjustment.

The 'self-coup' went wrong. Serrano expected popular support and the same international timidity as had characterised reactions to Fujimori (De León 1993: 119). But partly because the situations were perceived to be different, and perhaps because Clinton was now in power instead of Bush, the second condition did not obtain: the United States suspended aid and the Organisation of American States pressed for immediate return to democracy. Internally, a surprisingly broad opposition coalition developed, of business, unions and popular or-ganisations. The media, Constitutional Court, Electoral Court and Human Rights Ombudsman all played key roles. Most crucially, Ser-rano had little military support. Within days, an agreement was reached with the United States and the military to allow his continuance in power through a congressional amnesty. In need of votes for the am-nesty, Serrano tried in vain to bribe the deputies (*Crónica*, 4 June 1993) before fleeing into exile.

For a while, a faction of the military supported the vice-president Gustavo Espina as legitimate successor. Espina was also an evangelical businessman, a recent convert to the charismatic Fraternidad Cristiana. A newsmagazine throws an interesting sidelight on the incident. When Espina was informed of the army's decision to support him, he was in a prayer meeting. Someone commented: 'The prophecy is being fulfilled.

Serrano abandoned the prophecy and now it is Gustavo [Espina] who will be the instrument of the Lord.' The reference was to a prophecy reportedly given when Serrano was still at Elim. An Elim source claims: 'we knew Serrano was anointed to govern Guatemala, but that he would spend two and a half years without really governing... Then would come a period of bloodshed, and after that two years of government in peace and harmony, when the will of God would be done' (*Magazine 21*, 6 June 1993: 7ff.). The story exemplifies various characteristics of much evangelical politics in the Third World: competition between denominations (Elim had no reason to be well disposed to their former member); the use of prophecies as weapons of political legitimation; and the messianic concept of the 'anointed' political leader who fulfils the will of God.

Espina, however, had initially supported the coup, the Constitutional Court declared him ineligible, and the Attorney General threatened to prosecute him for misuse of public funds. Under pressure from the United States and the OAS (Organisation of American States), the military abandoned him, and he also fled into exile.

What was the reaction of the evangelical church? A few churches, the evangelical student organisation and ecumenical groups emitted statements condemning the self-coup. But the Evangelical Alliance did not, and it seems that most of the leadership was in favour. After the crisis had been resolved, the Organización Cívica de Guatemala, an evangelical group initially close to Serrano, placed an advertisement stating its 'satisfaction for the high degree of civic spirit demonstrated... in the last few days'. It then says the Serrano government should be analysed by evangelicals in the following way: (i) that his government was not an evangelical one, but was voted in by the people; (ii) that his fall had no religious element to it, but resulted from the break in constitutional order and antecedent moral problems; and (iii) that his governmental alliances had left the 'most representative evangelical sectors totally marginalised... It is therefore inexact to describe this regime as "evangelical"' (*La Hora*, 10 June 1993). There is no hint of, or even need for, evangelical self-criticism. The same pattern of reaction to disagreeable events involving evangelical politicians has been observed in other countries: the politicians concerned have ceased to be truly evangelical, or have marginalised the real evangelical leadership, and there is thus no blame to be laid on the evangelical community, no feeling that these politicians might be an unacceptable face of the religious community itself projected onto a public screen, and therefore there are no ethical, theological or organisational lessons to be learnt. 'We have been betrayed', is the common line of defence. The same politicians' triumphs are not treated with the same distance, but are regarded as moral triumphs of the church.

Serrano's 'distancing' from evangelical leaders after his election, which did in fact happen and is open to several interpretations (e.g. need for distance from a 'proprietary' relationship to the president desired by some church leaders; pressures of office and the need to limit the access of status-hungry pastors), thus turns out to be providential because it permits a reading of his political and moral failures in terms of estrangement from God and the church. He did not long keep up the initial rhythm of three Bible studies per week. His attendance at El Shaddai became infrequent, and its pastor did not enjoy the influence Verbo elders reputedly had over Ríos Montt. Evangelical deputies in MAS were soon bitter about not getting cabinet positions which went to members of allied parties. Even so, Grenfell says, most evangelicals remember Serrano with shame (1995: 83); but shame for his moral lapses (drunkenness in a topless bar) rather than for his self-coup against the democratic process. A few leaders, however, such as Pr Edmundo Madrid of Lluvias de Gracia, insist that Serrano was innocent. As with cases of corrupt evangelical politicians in Brazil, various readings are possible within the evangelical community; and even those who condemn the person involved may be motivated by the frustration of ethically dubious or unrealistic expectations.

Since then, Ríos Montt has again become the key evangelical figure. In the 1994 congressional elections, his objective was a majority which would allow him to change the constitution and run for president. The evangelical choruses of the 1990 campaign were forgotten, and Ríos talked of a generic Christian identity. Two other parties, MAS and CAN, did appeal directly to the evangelical vote but won no seats. The following year, Ríos was again denied the right to run for president, and his party's candidate came second. In 1999 his party did manage to elect the president, but evangelical dispersion was notable. The second-placed candidate received considerable support from Evangelical Alliance pastors (*ALC*, 16 Aug. 1999). Francisco Bianchi, former advisor to Ríos, ran for president himself but polled very poorly. And significantly, in the first election after the Peace Accord, the leftist coalition which came in third presented as candidate for vice-president the Mayan Presbyterian pastor Vitalino Similox, former general secretary of the Conference of Evangelical Churches.

The literature on Guatemala leaves many unanswered questions.

Little is known about voting habits, especially in congressional elections (the level at which corporate identity is usually influential in other Latin countries). In fact, little is known about Protestant congressmen. In a 1991 interview a MAS deputy told me there had been eleven evangelical deputies elected in 1985, and twenty-two in 1990. Stoll (1991) talks of a quarter of the congress elected in 1990 as evangelical. Grenfell says twenty out of twenty-five MAS deputies were pastors (1995: 95). Even in 1994, a Latin American Theological Fraternity source estimates at least eighteen evangelicals elected to congress. These post-1985 congressmen are the people we need to know more about, to give a better picture of the density of corporate involvement than the concentration on Ríos and Serrano does.

Rather than focusing on the Protestant–Catholic divide, we need to nuance Protestantism internally more. As it grows, internal divisions become more apparent. Wilson's article (1997) is a useful call to look at the popular pentecostals as a corrective to over-absorption with elite neo-pentecostals. The former, dominated by the AG (begun in the late 1920s), the Iglesia de Dios del Evangelio Completo (1916) and Príncipe de Paz (a split from the AG in 1953), number over four hundred thousand, more than double the neo-pentecostals. Almost half of the popular pentecostals are Indians, says Wilson. Ríos Montt and Serrano had little effect on evangelicalism. Wilson asks which is the real pente-costal posture – avoidance of politics or activism? 'In fact, both stances are typical. Pentecostals tend to stay aloof ... until, with little risk of compromise, they can assert their influence... In the interests of ad-vancing their cause they may be tempted to accept help from an otherwise unacceptable source [the state]' (1997: 161).

Wilson's analysis raises the question what 'little risk of compromise' means. Many observers feel that Latin American pentecostals have already considerably compromised their faith by their political activ-ities. The crucial question, of course, is who is making the calculation, what sort of 'influence' they want to assert and what sort of compromise they might consider unacceptable. The answers might differ from one denomination to another, and have a lot to do with internal power structures. We need to know more about these aspects of Guatemalan evangelical politics since, as Wilson says (ibid.: 161), Ríos Montt's politi-cal base is clearly much larger than the Protestant world and Protestant projects are not dependent on him.

Nevertheless, the uniqueness of Guatemala makes it appropriate to raise certain questions. Better-off Protestants are increasingly drawn to visions of dominion theology, which (unlike dispensational pre-millennialism) gives believers a place in the divine plan. The rhetoric of empowerment is most attractive to the elite and middle-class professionals. 'Evangelicals are groping for ways to translate a reformation in personal morality into a reformation in public morality' (Stoll 1994: 108). Spiritual warfare becomes an ideology through which believers take command of society. 'Prayer-warfare against curses and demons could provide a language which actually inspires reform, or it could become a quasi-magical rationale for failing to deal with the structural reasons for national backwardness' (ibid.).

The questions Stoll asks in the early 1990s (Is self-reform afoot in the ruling class? Can charismatic-led top-down reform substantially change political and economic reality?) are given a provisional negative answer in a later work: the social capital generated is wasted in costly experimentation at taking power rather than altering the basic landscape of politics by encouraging the spread of trust (Levine and Stoll 1995). Grenfell shares this pessimism: 'In the US a flourishing evangelical subculture helps to broaden the influence of social capital and simultaneously to reinforce its benefits. Guatemala, by contrast, has neither the resources nor the minimal political space necessary to begin the construction of this necessary second stage' (1995: 107).

However, Grenfell also stresses that Guatemala has yet to elect a president thoroughly socialised by the evangelical tradition (ibid.: 116). Ríos Montt is the central figure of Guatemalan politics as a whole since 1982, even since 1974. It so happens that since 1978 he has also been an evangelical. He is a product of Protestantism's current phase of rapid rise up the social scale; but he may not be typical of the subsequent phase, of a consolidated and substantial minority present at all social levels.

Perhaps Ríos' main significance is for religion in general rather than for Protestantism. As Garrard-Burnett concludes, he 'slashed through a century of state secularism to proclaim a holy crusade', not only against communism but superstition and corruption. Although met with ridicule by sectors of the elite, army and Catholic Church, he enjoyed considerable support in the cities. 'His enduring legacy lies less in his programme than in the fact that he abandoned the ideal of secular government ... [permitting] religion, both Catholic and Protestant, to play an overt role' (1996b: 105ff.).

Conclusion: evangelicals, democracy, nationalism and globalisation in the Third World

This conclusion will attempt, firstly, to delineate the main characteristics of evangelical politics across the three continents; secondly, to look at the implications of Third World evangelical politics for democracy, pluralism, nationalism and globalisation; thirdly, to raise questions regarding the challenge of politics for evangelicalism; and lastly, to ponder the future of evangelical politics in the Third World in the next decades.

EVANGELICAL POLITICS IN THE THIRD WORLD: TOWARDS A CHARACTERISATION

We have examined evangelical politics in twenty-seven countries of Africa, Asia and Latin America. We have used diverse sources: for a few countries, personal fieldwork *in loco;* for many more, interviews and documentary research; and for all cases, extensive bibliographical research. This has resulted, as in most broad-ranging comparative studies, in an unevenness of information from country to country, whether through gaps in research or actual gaps in empirical knowledge. Nevertheless, certain methodological principles which seem appropriate to the object of study have been followed throughout.

One is that too much discussion of evangelical politics in the Third World has been underdetermined by empirical data. One of the *raisons d'être* of this book is that we need to know more about what is actually happening before we jump to conclusions about what it all means. Before anything else, we need to become immersed in the specificities of the religious and political fields, and of the interaction between them, in each national context.

In short, as was said in the African introduction, we need more detailed country-level studies. Underlying this view is the belief that the local religious field (and evangelicalism's place in it) and the local political field (including what Hallencreutz and Westerlund (1996) call 'policies of religion') are vital for understanding evangelical politics; and that a comprehension of the (always internally divided but amazingly variable and changeable) evangelical field itself is also crucial. In other words, that evangelical *organisation, religious location* and *socio-political location* are often more important for understanding its politics than is evangelical *theology*. Theology is important, but as one factor amongst many which may affect evangelical politics in any given context. A study of political behaviour must start out from realism about the actual situation of the churches and the political possibilities and dangers inherent in each context. Size, social and ethnic composition, position relative to other confessions, internal church structures and conflicts, the sociological 'type' (*church, sect, denomination*) of each group, the degree of legitimacy in relation to national myths, the presence or absence (and nature) of international connections – all these constrain political possibilities and affect behaviour. Talk of 'evangelical politics' globally must never lose sight of the fact that local church reality has been very determinant in actual performance.

Talk of 'Protestantism' or 'evangelicalism' or even 'pentecostalism' in general must therefore be accompanied by institutional analysis. The trans-denominational identity of 'evangelical' (or 'born-again') is real, but is nevertheless forged in a field of distinct institutions which vary in antiquity, in global or local insertion, in theological connections, in church government, and so on. It is only by taking churches seriously as dynamically evolving institutions (all of them, including the newest and most difficult to study) that one can throw light on some aspects of their politics.

However, concentration on individual denominations is not enough. The closer Protestants get to power (or the more open the political system), the more important pan-Protestant representation becomes. Hence we need to study attempts to create (or use existing) representative organs, which seek to maximise Protestant strength and (often) to compete politically with other confessions with greater organisational unity. Analysing the success of such ventures (or, alternatively, the extent to which evangelical power-vacuums have been occupied by evangelical politicians) is an important part of our study.

The need for more empirical national-level case-studies is not the only gap we have tried partially to fill. The multiplication of country studies will not by itself take us further than the across-the-board insights without local depth. We also need comparative study of Third World evangelicalism. Previous studies have either been contained within one continent, or have compared a country or group of countries with the developed world. The common denominator of evangelical growth and rise in political activity across Africa, Latin America and parts of Asia has not led to cross-continental comparisons which might reveal the varieties and potentialities of evangelical politics in conditions totally different from those of the northern European and Anglo-Saxon world which has been its traditional location.

Such study, of course, also has the utility of all comparisons – of relativising many explanations and de-parochialising interpretations. Attributing phenomenon A blithely to cause B, which may seem very plausible in Peru, may be scrutinised more closely after discovering that A also exists in Nigeria, where cause B is non-existent. However, that does not necessarily mean the explanation is false. Evangelical religion is multi-faceted, and its politics may not have at all similar roots or fruits in different countries. But at least comparative knowledge helps us avoid extrapolating from specific cases to some supposed 'essence' of evangelicalism.

Our approach implies critical reserve in relation to two theories. One is the 'conspiracy' theory, which supposes American right-wing forces to be behind most political activity by evangelicals in the Third World. The theory builds on certain facts. In some places, evangelicalism has many foreign connections; the question is how important they are. In certain countries (Central America), it is more susceptible than in others (Brazil, Chile). But in personnel and money, Catholicism is more foreign.

Stoll for Spanish America and Fernandes for Brazil have analysed this question. Fernandes (1981) concludes that, despite the tripling of missionaries after the 1964 military coup in Brazil, this has little to do with Protestant growth. Over a third of missionaries work with Indians, a mere 0.2 per cent of the population. And most faith missions are anti-pentecostal, whereas the burgeoning churches are pentecostal. The churches which grow most owe little to missions.

Stoll (1990) says the importance of foreign personnel, money and television programmes in Central America is exaggerated by protagonists and antagonists alike. The religious right was resisted not only by principled opponents but by established conservative missions who feared a backlash.

In this book, the basic premise has been that the American right does indeed try to use evangelical religion (and other religions) in its own interests, but that such activity cannot be assumed a priori to account for a great deal of what Third World actors actually do. The autonomy of Third World evangelicalism, or at least the autonomous appropriation of messages, should be assumed unless proved otherwise, and not vice versa.

The second theory we regard with reserve may be styled the cultural potentiality argument: the 'logic' of voluntaristic evangelicalism will supposedly produce everywhere results similar to those in northern Europe and North America. This theory tends to talk much of the long-term potential, rather than looking at actually existing evangelical politics in its new centres in the Third World. Discussion of potentialities, based on macro-historical comparisons with older Protestantisms, is certainly legitimate, but must be tempered with empirical analysis of what is really happening, and with the awareness that we do not yet have sufficient evidence to guarantee that similarities will produce similar socio-political effects.

Finally, we have proceeded on the assumption that one must often distinguish between actions and pronouncements of church leaders and actual political behaviour of ordinary members, and that more needs to be known about the latter. Although written declarations by erudite churchmen are easier to collect, they can give a mistaken idea of reality.

What we have done in this book, first of all, has been to map out the phenomenon, in so far as it is known. In some cases, we have done little more than say what we do know and suggest what we need to know. The book has thus tried to map out a (largely new) territory, suggesting routes for future study and some methodological principles to orient it. Social scientists, historians and theologians have before them an immense field of study, consisting of the political dimension of Third World evangelicalism.

Besides showing the extent of involvement, we have demonstrated the variety of it. Before we strain after patterns, we should drink in the full range of ways in which evangelicals are politically involved in Africa, Asia and Latin America. This is true not only in the sense that there may be many different projects within one country, but also in the sense that the majority trend in each country varies greatly. The challenge is to detect the factors influencing this variety or, more modestly, to suggest some hypotheses.

The place of evangelicalism in society varies immensely. In Anglophone Africa, Protestants of many persuasions have been amongst the elite since before independence and have a 'natural' place in politics.

Even in some Francophone countries, this applies. Lusophone Africa is somewhat different. Despite Protestant presence in the liberation movements, the Marxist influence complicated its expression in public life until recently. Now, Lusophone African Protestantism may have an important political future, through its combination of elite influence and mass base. In Latin America, on the other hand, Protestantism had to fight its way up politically in a Catholic context. An oppositional identity is thus more pronounced and distinctive than in most of Africa, and is usually not complicated by ethnic divisions. The political operationalising of 'evangelical' identity is thus generally more pronounced in Latin America than in Africa. In some African countries, it is subsumed in a more general 'Christian' identity *vis-à-vis* Muslims. In Korea, on the other hand, despite being a minority religion, it has a secure place in the national myth and does not have a clear-cut religious or anti-religious rival in the political sphere.

In recent years there have been several evangelical presidents of Third World countries: Kérékou, Chiluba, Moi, Obasanjo, Ríos Montt, Serrano, Ramos and Kim Young Sam. In various countries, evangelicals have achieved a significant presence in legislative and/or lower executive levels. In Spanish-speaking Latin America, well over twenty evangelical political parties have been formed (often several in the same country), and have achieved considerable visibility in Colombia, Nicaragua and Venezuela. Evangelicals have trained the leaders of nationalist rebellions (all three groups in Angola), have been hegemonic in ethnic separatist rebellions (Myanmar, India, Sudan), and have enjoyed a complex relationship with guerrilla movements (Mexico). Evangelical churchmen have been central to pro-democracy movements (Kenya). In some places, they are still involved in a basic struggle for political legitimacy (Indonesia, Malaysia). While universalist concerns such as human rights and democracy predominate among some actors, the practice of many is reducible to an ecclesiastical corporatism which seeks to enlist state resources for church aggrandisement (Assemblies of God and Universal Church of the Kingdom of God in Brazil); or to a political imitation of the dominant actor in the religious field, whether Catholicism or Islam (Iglesia Metodista Pentecostal in Chile, much pentecostalism in Nigeria); or to a triumphalism which talks of a divine right of evangelicals to govern (Guatemala, Zambia).

Evangelicalism is being put to a variety of political uses across the globe. That is not surprising; evangelical religion means different things to different people, and holds different positions in the social and religious fields of each country, besides varying from one denomination to another. This is accentuated by 'local subversion', in which local contextual factors in church practice overwhelm the universal heritage of the church; a danger all the greater in churches with local autonomy. Being a decentralised faith, the globalisation of evangelicalism may produce a splintering of political perspectives unable to communicate with each other. Since it has no Rome or Mecca, evangelicalism has difficulty finding a broader view, and its politics tends to be caught up in ethnic, national or local ecclesiastical questions.

This strong localism is its weakness and its strength. It illustrates Casanova's comment on the Janus-face of many religions, as carriers of both inclusive and universalist identities as well as of exclusive, particularist and primordial ones (1994: 4). We have seen examples of particularistic evangelical politics (concern for 'the evangelicals', one denomination or just one local congregation) and of universalistic evangelical politics (having society as a whole as its focus). These stem from different theologies (not only of the public sphere, but of the church itself), but in practice there are many intermediate shades, especially when ethnic questions add to the complexity.

Such variety is perhaps not surprising in view of the classical sociologists' analyses of evangelical religion. Engels thought Protestantism was often at the service of the bourgeoisie, but could at times be revolutionary, albeit (for him) in an unrealistic way. Weber saw it as unintentionally promoting a capitalist rationality in tension with the ethic of universal love. Tocqueville viewed popular Protestantism as having a basic role in democratisation. A domesticating ideology at the service of the status quo, or an unrealistic revolutionary movement, or an (usually unwilling) advanced guard of the iron cage of capitalist rationality, or a buzzing hive of democratic associational life, or ... ? Protestantism in the developed world has done justice to each of these interpretations somewhere or other, at some time or other. Its younger, but strapping, Third World brother is unlikely to be less ambivalent.

Must we therefore conclude that evangelical politics can be absolutely anything at all, or are there inherent limits to the variation? Or even, more cautiously, can we say there are prevailing tendencies (whether we imagine them to be based on sociological qualities of voluntaristic religion, theological qualities of evangelical doctrine, or political qualities of 'right-wing fundamentalism'), deviations from which may exist but will always be somewhat anomalous? Wood (1993) points not only to the 'tremendous latitude in turning imported religion into locally useful sets of beliefs and practices', but also to 'constraints on the possible variations'. There may be aspects of the adoption of Christianity which are 'generalisable social processes'. He thus opts for an intermediate position between orthodox evangelical theology and extreme anthropological relativism. He recognises that some conversions are motivated by expediency and may or may not be followed by deep intellectual commitment; whilst others may be coopted by local traditions. But there may also be unintended consequences of conversion, in which deeper doctrinal knowledge irreversibly alters cultural horizons.

This seems a wise a priori position to adopt with regard to politics. Beyond a certain level, the adoption of evangelicalism may have certain political consequences wherever it occurs; but there is always the possibility of 'manipulation' and 'local subversion', especially in view of its organisational laxity.

What influences the degree and direction of evangelical politics? Wallis and Bruce (1985) distinguish between high-, medium- and low-impact cases. High impact is favoured by proportional representation, low party cohesion, religious access to mass media, strong *sectarianism*, and a threat to (or possibility of gaining) domination. All of these are relevant for some of our cases. But they treat only the developed world (plus apartheid South Africa), and only predominantly Protestant countries. For this reason they do not mention ethnicity, but their stress on institution-building capacity can often mesh with ethnic or regional strongholds.

Works on religion and politics at the global level must be used selectively here. Often, they seem to suppose a stable situation in terms of religious identities, varying only in the degree of political mobilisation of such identities, whereas in fact switching of religion may be rife and may be creating both new conflicts as well as new bases for social cohesion. There is need for greater research into the effect of evangelical expansion on some normative conflicts in the Third World, such as the place of Sarawak within the Malaysian federation, the delicate equilibrium of Nigeria, and the armed struggles in the Sudan, North-East India and Burma. Third World evangelicalism does not fit cyclical theories of religious resurgence, since there it is not a revamped traditionalism. That is one of several reasons why the large literature on global fundamentalism and politics is of limited use for our subject.

Evangelicalism and fundamentalism have a complex relationship. While there is overlap (some evangelicals are fundamentalists), evangelicalism is an older and broader tendency within Protestantism, while the 'fundamentalist' label has been extended in another direction to include phenomena from other religions. Fundamentalism and evangelicalism relate differently to globalisation, the former being more properly a reactive phenomenon of globalisation whereas the latter predates and possibly contributes to it.

The *Fundamentalism Project* illustrates this. The introduction to the volume on the state defines fundamentalism as embracing 'movements of religiously inspired reaction to aspects of global processes of modernisation and secularisation ... the struggle to assert or reassert the norms and beliefs of "traditional religion" in the public order' (Marty and Appleby 1995). But evangelicalism is far from traditional in most of the Third World. Little but Guatemalan neo-pentecostalism is contemplated in the series, and even there the final volume admits how weakly it fits the *Project*'s schema – and this, despite being attributed to 'covert political operations and funding' from the United States (Almond, Sivan and Appleby 1995)! We have seen how unsatisfactory an account that is of Guatemalan evangelical politics.

Cox (1996) talks of supposedly tenuous links between pentecostalism and evangelicalism, and even affirms that evangelicalism does not condone tongues. Other authors, more advisedly, have spoken of the evangelicalisation of pentecostalism and of the pentecostalisation of evangelicalism (Spittler 1994). Pentecostalism is clearly within Bebbington's working definition of evangelicalism which we have adopted, and indeed much of it uses the self-designation 'evangelical' (or *evangélico* in Latin America). As for its relationship with fundamentalism, it is true that some pentecostals come into that category, but the differences are more significant. Pentecostal politics in the Third World cannot be read through the literature on worldwide fundamentalism. Islamic fundamentalism is the predominant influence in recent discussions of global fundamentalism, and its political implications are very different from those of pentecostalism.

Another category of little use to us is Juergensmeyer's (1995) 'religious nationalism', which is in fact one of evangelicalism's main political enemies. 'Religious nationalists' are usually an educated urban religious elite linked with a large, disenfranchised rural constituency. Juergensmeyer claims that what religious activists around the world have in common is a rejection of Westerners and 'secularism'. None of this is very relevant for understanding evangelical politics, which also does not necessarily fit Hallencreutz and Westerlund's concept of 'antisecularism', since its posture towards the secular state varies immensely.

Appeals for tolerance and pluralism, not for a Christian fundamentalism, are the best defence for Third World evangelicals against non-Christian 'religious nationalism'.

Rudolph and Piscatori's work (1997) on religious formations as part of an emergent transnational civil society is more fruitful. They pertinently critique Huntington's (1996) concept of 'clash of civilisations', in which the latter are defined heavily in religious terms while intra-faith conflicts are downplayed. But while rejecting religion as a master variable, they recognise it as a leading definer of culture and an ambiguous factor in a transnational civil society which does not replace but 'thins out' states. Another useful concept is Casanova's (1994) 'deprivatisation of religion', by which religions refuse to accept the ever more marginal position in public life assigned them by secularisation theory, but without necessarily threatening the public/private distinction and democratic pluralism. Certainly, when interpreting evangelical politics, one must avoid the approach that implicitly views religion in politics as a substitute for the failure of 'normal' secular politics, instead of as itself a normal part of politics. (One must also avoid a tendency on the part of some academics, usually expressed implicitly through a choice of negative epithets, to regard the traditional evangelical expansionist impulse, couched in the language of 'winning' a society by converting its members, as inherently politically dangerous.) The limitation of Casanova for our purposes is that his examples are all from the West, and not from non-Western contexts where talk of deprivatisation makes little sense because privatisation never really happened.

What common denominators can be adduced across the three continents? American influence has to be demonstrated rather than presumed, and certainly should not be read off from the claims of American operators. Attempts by institutions such as Pat Robertson's Regent University to organise alliances of evangelical parties in Latin America may sound like confirmation of the 'conspiracy theory', but their efficacy is far from obvious. In most cases, the returns for the American organisers are minimised by the already-established operational agenda of their would-be Latin protégés.

An example is a 1999 course organised by the Leadership Institute in Washington, attended by fifty evangelicals from twelve Latin countries (*ALC*, 18 Oct. 1999). It consisted of training in electoral campaigns, followed by a seminar on 'Christian principles of government'. Analysis must distinguish between the organisers' capacity to attract these people to Washington (probably heavily funded) and their effective influence; it

must also evaluate the attenders (in terms of their real political chances);
and it must ponder the possibility of a hiatus between organisers' and
attenders' main objectives (ideological instruction in 'Christian principles' versus training in electoral techniques).

Another oft-assumed common denominator would be conservatism,
even if not American-controlled. Our cases show plenty of that, but they
nuance the picture by non-conservative examples, as well as the force of
motivations such as ethnicity and ecclesiastical corporatism. Third
World evangelical politics does not often have strong ideological over-
tones, whether conservative or not. It is also not usually dominated by a
single issue, such as abortion in conservative American evangelicalism.
On the whole, Third World countries do not have liberal abortion laws,
and any single-issue politics is more often associated with religious
freedom, democratisation or ethnicity.

Where conservatism is evident, as in much white South African
evangelicalism, it is debatable whether it results from theology. Organisation, rather than doctrine, may have made it even more susceptible to 'local subversion' than other Christian traditions. An example
would be pentecostalism, which seems to have an inbuilt multiracial
thrust; this was manifested against all the odds in the early days in the
United States and South Africa, but later obviated by 'local subversion'.

There is a permanent tension between local and global explanations
of evangelicalism. Accounts entirely in terms of local peculiarities face
the objection that similar phenomena occur elsewhere. And certain
types of global explanation (e.g. in terms of international preachers) rob
local converts of their agency. There is a tension also between different
types of global explanation, which we can call the 'globalised complex
flows' argument and the 'Americanisation' thesis. The latter, in turn,
has 'hard' (orchestrated) and 'soft' (emulationist) versions.

The context of Third World evangelical politics has evident common
denominators. One is the trend to greater social differentiation and
pluralism which is encouraged by globalisation (understood as a cultural
and not merely economic phenomenon). Another is the end of the Cold
War ideological bipolarity, which has created space for an emphasis on
non-economic questions about which evangelicals often have more to
say. Yet another is the advance of global capitalism under neoliberal
auspices. And finally, there is the 'third wave' of democratisation, which
swept Latin America in the 1980s and Africa and parts of Asia in the
1990s, opening up political systems to new actors.

With regard to church–state relations, few Third World contexts have anything similar to the United States tradition of separation. In the US, this tradition is so strong that it constrains all religious actors in politics, whether their doctrine tends in this direction or not (as Tocqueville commented on American Catholicism in the 1830s). Where this tradition is absent, the room for disagreement between religious actors in politics is much greater; and where the existing nation-state itself is questioned, the gap is wider still.

There are also common denominators in the structural position of evangelicalism. In many places, it is growing, fissiparous and voluntarist, and is decidedly non-traditional. Only in some parts of Africa and peripheral Asian regions such as Nagaland (where large-scale conversion is already at least a couple of generations old) has it something of a traditional status. Much less is it a state religion; and only occasionally does it enjoy an unofficial privileged relationship to governments. Usually, Third World evangelicalism does not have strong institutions; it is often composed disproportionately of the poor in poor countries, so its cultural and educational resources are limited. It is divided into many churches, making it impossible to establish a normative 'social doctrine'. It operates a model of competitive pluralism, in competition for members and resources, which does not encourage reflection or costly stances on ethical principle. It often has no international contacts, cutting it off from the history of Christian reflection on politics. It may be an *arriviste* minority inexperienced in the public sphere and still lacking full political legitimacy, but nevertheless confident (even excessively so) about its future. Often its politics cannot be discussed without reference to the religious media.

Another common denominator internal to the evangelical world is the link between politics and unity. Efficacy is often closely tied to unity, whether through the numerical predominance of one church (Baptists among the Naga or Kachin) or through effective representative organisations (Conep in Peru). Often, as real power beckons, pre-existing entities become political footballs (the Brazilian Evangelical Confederation in 1987) and/or new entities are founded as poorly disguised trampolines (the Consejo de Pastores in Chile). Whenever a government starts to contemplate an institutionally divided minority, there will be internal battles for leadership. Or, as in Zambia, government favour will deepen divisions between the favoured and the left-out. The Protestant world is institutionally divided and, in the growing churches of the Third World, institutionally under-endowed. It has no doctrinal basis which obliges unity. It thus allows political interference in internal structuring in a way Catholicism does not. But this political interference (whether from evangelicals or non-evangelicals) rarely achieves its aim, since at the very time that unity becomes concretely rewarding, its achievement becomes harder. In such circumstances, unity would offer the chance of real power, but that serves merely to encourage the emergence of a plethora of would-be unifiers. Persecution (i.e. power-lessness) is the most favourable situation for evangelical unity; any approximation to power makes it less likely.

As for institutional contexts of evangelical mobilisation, what patterns can be observed? Sometimes, the ethnic group is the context for mobil-isation, with the church in a leadership role. At other times, it is the church; even though party affiliation may be required, the denomina-tion (or a segment of it) is the context for important decisions and vote-gathering. Sometimes, mobilisation is through 'evangelical' parties which claim a 'natural right' to receive all evangelical votes. Another mobilisational context is the pan-evangelical 'representative' organism, giving backing to a political project; this happens mostly where there are still evangelical civil rights to conquer, or in elections for constituent assemblies. Finally, there are the specifically political (but non-party) evangelical organisations, whether single-issue or broader, such as the Evangelical Progressive Movement in Brazil (similar in form, though not at all in ideology, to American phenomena such as the Christian Coalition).

What commonalities are there in motivation? In some cases, it can be said that religion is being used for political ends. In most cases, however, people's adoption of a religion has unintended political consequences.

Garvey (1993) asks what causes fundamentalists to become politically active. He detects two groups: those reacting to changes in national identity, and those reacting to government efforts to expand the public sphere. Casanova, speaking of religion more broadly, says that 'what seems to precipitate the religious response are different types of state intervention and administrative colonisation of the lifeworld and the private sphere' (1994: 227). Neither of these statements does justice to most cases of Third World evangelicalism. The idea that a trigger issue is needed is doubtful; when conditions are favourable, issues can be found in abundance by the leaders of mass churches.

Rather than religion being used for political ends, we have more often seen politics being used for religious ends. Casanova points to two preconditions for militancy. Firstly, 'only those religions which either by doctrine or by cultural tradition have a public communal identity will want to assume public roles', that is, especially *churches* in Weber's sense; secondly, however, 'neither doctrine nor historical tradition are per se sufficient ... unless [a religion] is also able to maintain a dynamic and vital profile as a private religion of salvation' (1994: 224). In much of the Third World today, we see Casanova's second factor overwhelming his first: pentecostal groups, without the help of doctrine or tradition, assuming public roles based on their dynamic profile as private religions of salvation. Private success underlies their public role, whether as substitutes-in-waiting for the old publicly dominant religion or, more modestly, as recipients of largesse from the state.

What substantive patterns can we find in evangelical political performance? One is that politicisation often provides a route to political prominence for sectors under-represented due to social deprivation. In some Latin countries, pentecostal electoral success has produced politicians of considerably lower social and educational level than the average (even of those parties which supposedly represent the poor), as well as a larger contingent of non-whites. This achievement (whatever the ambiguity in these politicians' record) is due to the genuinely popular nature of pentecostal churches in which both leaders and led are from humble origins. As in early modern Europe (Mullett 1980: 52–3), *sectarian* Christianity overturns accepted intellectual hierarchies, based on a recognition of the intellectual rights of the common person. When neoliberal policies are making educational inequalities ever starker, a movement which challenges the educational hierarchy in public life has an important role.

Evangelical politics rarely emphasises economic questions. It is not usually dogmatically neoliberal, as the American evangelical right would like; nor is it renowned for opposition to structural adjustment based on a theological critique, such as characterises initiatives linked to the ecumenical movement.

Such a critique is not totally absent. We have seen it in the Evangelical Progressive Movement in Brazil, Concerned Evangelicals in South Africa, Bishop Gitari in Kenya and some statements from Conep in Peru, amongst others. There are in fact Third World networks linking these groups, although analyses usually overlook them. We have even seen similar positions in a leading preacher of the gospel of success, Ghana's Mensa Otabil. But evangelical presidents have effectively promoted neoliberal policies, and there has been a good deal of (usually tacit) support for such measures from evangelical politicians in other countries. Of course, it could be argued that they are only following the trend by which economic policies have been effectively removed from democratic debate.

Although Otabil is unusual amongst prosperity preachers for his position on economic questions, the ideological implications of prosperity doctrine remain unclear. Left-wing proposals for strengthening the domestic market and encouraging small-scale enterprise could be at least as pleasing as neoliberalism to denominations like the Universal Church of the Kingdom of God which counsel members to become self-employed as a necessary complement to giving sacrificially to the church in order to receive many times over from God. In fact, as we saw, since 1995 the UC has abandoned its previous demonisation of the left in Brazil.

On the whole, rather than being ideological, much evangelical politics has shown a calculated caution based on the desire to maximise benefits. We have called this 'corporatism', because its *raison d'être* is to strengthen the churches as corporations, to equip them better for their activities, to reward some of their members individually (in terms of employment, financing or prestige) and to strengthen their position *vis-à-vis* other faiths in the country's 'civil religion'. This basic concern produces a tendency to time-serving and opportunism (since one has to be on the right side of the powers-that-be if concrete results are to ensue), and sometimes even to corruption. It leads to a concern with questions of status (of evangelicalism in general, in competition with other confessions) and prestige (of church leaders); and to a concern with religious freedom in particular rather than with democracy and human rights in general. Although it talks of 'defence of the family', these questions have rather a negative function (avoidance of certain candidates in major elections) than a positive one; it is not the driving force behind the election of corporate candidates.

A pragmatic pro-government stance is supported by the *sectarian* concept of mission. To guarantee optimum conditions for the church, agreements are acceptable. As one candidate in Brazil said: 'Where in the Bible is it written that the servants of the Lord should finance the growth of the kingdom of darkness? Shouldn't it rather be the opposite?' Benefits received are not seen as a betrayal of the evangelical message, but as a sort of tax which 'worldly' power should pay to the truth. This tendency has been responsible for the poor public image of evangelicalism lately in some Third World countries.

While moralisation of political systems has often been a banner of evangelical movements, the practice has frequently been different. While corruption in Brazil has been linked to official candidates of churches, there are also broader factors related to assimilation of the political culture, resistance to more ideological parties which discipline individual practices, and so on. Evangelical presidents Serrano, Chiluba and Kim Young-Sam have all been implicated in scandals.

Another tendency is what we have termed 'triumphalism'. This is the Third World futurist equivalent of nostalgia for 'Christian Europe' or 'Protestant America', but goes beyond. It is predicated on a reading of the Bible rare now in traditionally Protestant countries which have been through wars of religion and the Enlightenment. Old and New Testaments are fused, in a transference of Israel's promised heritage to modern-day evangelicals, granting them a divine right to rule. The utopia of a 'Christian Zambia' or an 'evangelical Guatemala', is alive and well, whatever the remoteness of its implementation due to Protestantism's disunity. This is usually combined with the ritualistic and mystical approach to social blessing characteristic of newer concepts of macro-level spiritual warfare.

Another pattern is the tendency to acquire characteristics of the locally dominant religion in its traditional public role, whether Catholicism or Islam. Evangelicalism thus becomes partially Islamised or Catholicised, all the while involved in a struggle for supremacy. It thus reveals a dependence on the hegemonic model of religion–state relations, rather than representing a substantially different model.

THE IMPLICATIONS OF EVANGELICAL POLITICS

Over all three continents, perhaps the central question is the relationship to democracy. This includes questions such as religious pluralism and religious equality, but goes further. In Africa and parts of Asia, ethnicity and national identity are also crucial.

We shall look first at the specific question of religion and the state. Since the rise of evangelicalism is usually related in the Third World to large-scale conversion, altering the relative strength of religions in the nation-state (or in a given province), it may spark off a complex transition to a new relationship between state and religious field. This is often couched by evangelicals in the language of religious equality. It goes beyond mere freedom to exist as a dissident religion, and beyond freedom of propagation (though these are still burning issues in Muslim contexts and in India). It claims equality of civil status with the dominant religion and equal space in the public sphere and in 'civil religion'. It seeks the same official and unofficial treatment from government and the law as the traditional religion of the country, removing all signs of inferiority.

One can perhaps distinguish a 'genuine' and 'opportunist' use of this transitional context. The 'opportunist' use is the search for a mobilising issue to justify involvement which originates from other motives. 'Brother votes for brother' creates expectations impossible to satisfy, given the variety of demands which evangelical voters have. Only corporate demands could unify such a disparate constituency. If there are obvious civil rights still to conquer as a religious community, there is no problem. If not, there is a tendency to search for more 'rights', for more 'inequalities' or 'humiliations' supposedly suffered by evangelicals.

There are also more 'genuine' claims. In Latin America, we shall see a struggle for religious equality which goes further. It will mainly involve Protestantism, but since pluralism is increasing it will benefit other religions too. When monopoly is broken it tends to lead to pluralism rather than duopoly, even if the latter is what the second-place religion would prefer. There are two main types of religious equality: (a) of freedom of action in the religious sphere; and (b) equality of treatment in the public sphere. This will require adjustments on the part of Latin American states, used to handling a hegemonic and hierarchically organised religious actor, but now obliged to dilute attentions more. It will also require adjustments from divided evangelicalism, on pain of not maximising public potential. A reorganisation of the evangelical field may be necessary to make it capable of having any appreciable public influence. Already the Universal Church in Brazil seeks hegemony in evangelical politics, based on its wealth, media and parliamentarians. But it is doubtful if evangelicalism could ever function as a 'second Catholicism'; rather, it is a different model of the religious field.

What about religious pluralism as it bears on politics? How do evangelicals relate to other faiths in the public square? Beyond cases where persecution or discrimination reigns, we time and again see questions of religious freedom (for others) and acceptance of a non-confessional state as still problematic. This is sometimes because the dominant religion itself does not accept these things. But sometimes evangelical leaders themselves do not accept them, or at least cannot understand and live with the self-restraining implications, especially as their power increases and they face the other side of the dilemma.

Stepan (forthcoming) rightly points out that separation and secularism have no inherent affinity with democracy and that the latter can include a broad range of religion–state relations. What must be maintained are what he calls the 'twin tolerations', in which religious institutions are not allowed to mandate policy to elected governments but have freedom to advance their values in civil society and sponsor organisations in political society.

Casanova's investigation into 'forms of modern public religion which may be viable and desirable' (1994: 7) is relevant here. 'Viable' means not intrinsically incompatible with differentiated modern structures; and 'desirable' signifies strengthening the public sphere of modern civil societies. Casanova concludes that there are indeed legitimate forms of 'public' religion which allow for pluralism of religious belief and freedom of conscience, and raise important questions about the public–private boundary without denying the need for it *per se*. He stresses that *sectarian* Protestantism especially was historically able to embrace modernity and secularisation as a return to the primitive church. (Not so the 'Christian reconstructionists', for whom any pluralism is equivalent to polytheism and is idolatrous.) Casanova thus differs from liberals who interpret any religious mobilisation as anti-modern fundamentalism or as the reaction of traditionalist groups. Religions in the modern world are free to enter the public sphere or not, and they may be carriers not of anti-modern critiques of modernity but of new types of normative critique of the institutionalisation of modernity, all the while presupposing individual freedoms and differentiated structures.

In this context we can ask about the relationship between evangelicals and democracy in the Third World. Rather than asking whether it favours democratisation or authoritarianism, we should ask what sort of evangelicalism might favour what sort of democratisation and in which circumstances.

We can place our discussion in the context of debates about civil society and democratic consolidation. What types of civil society strengthen democracy? Is it possible that social forces which favour democratic *transitions* may be obstacles to democratic *consolidation*, and vice versa?

For many who had lost faith in the state following the collapse of the Eastern bloc, and who did not believe that the market left to its own devices could produce democracy, the revitalisation of civil society seemed the way forward. This was the rediscovery of an ancient tradition, dating back at least to Tocqueville. For some in that tradition,

voluntary associations, below the level of the state but above the individual and the family, promote pluralism and democracy regardless of
whether they are concerned explicitly with public affairs. However, by
the mid 1990s, with the 'third wave' of democratisation receding, civil
society was looked at more critically. A strong civil society, it was now
better realised, does not necessarily mean better chances for democracy.
Civil society can also be uncivil; perhaps institutions do not promote
pluralism and tolerance if they do not actually seek to do so (Fine and
Rai 1997; Uvin 1998). In fact, the same institution can play a mediating
or a polarising role in conflicts, the crucial variable being not its
structure (e.g. whether it is a church) but the values inspiring it (Berger
1998). 'Actually existing' civil society, therefore, does not only contain
elements favourable to democracy; it may contain others which are
politically indifferent, and still others favourable to authoritarianism.
Institutions in civil society can polarise conflicts and contribute to
political instability. In addition, the civil society created by 'religion
from below' may lack connections to formal policy levels and thus fail to
engage the state in consequential fashion (Rudolph 1997b: 252).

Another relevant aspect from recent debates is that democratic transition and consolidation are distinct phases which require distinct virtues. Democracy is largely no longer seen as the product of a high level
of modernisation, but as capable of being crafted anywhere. But more is
known about transition to democracy than about its consolidation. For
some scholars, the key is consensus between elites on a principled
commitment to the rules of the democratic game. For others, it is the
evolution of a democratic culture, which may take generations. This
refers not just to the demanding definitions of democracy which include
socio-economic participatory and egalitarian dimensions, but even to
Diamond's (1997) distinction between electoral democracy and liberal
democracy. The former is a minimal framework (regular, fair and free
elections), while the latter includes a deeper institutional structure of
freedoms, civilian control over the military, accountability of office-
holders and the rule of law through an independent judiciary. While 61
per cent of governments met the former definition in 1996, only 41 per
cent met the latter; in fact, the latter was losing ground outside the
developed world. Consolidation is thus essential if the 'third wave' is to
avoid the reversal which ended previous waves. In this context, some
scholars of African religion affirm that evangelical *sects* may be more
efficacious than 'mainline' churches in democratic *consolidation*, even
though the latter have advantages in democratic *inauguration*. Their

hierarchical (and usually multi-class) structure and international links can help in redemocratisation, but may be a blockage for a long-lasting democratic culture.

Another point is that tooth-and-nail religious competition is not necessarily incompatible with democracy. Rousseau's dictum in *The Social Contract*, that civil and theological intolerance are inseparable, must be questioned. It is not impossible for people to disagree strongly about things they regard as of supreme importance (such as the need to convert others, and even the advisability of exorcising them of demons), and still be good democrats. In fact, they may regard democracy as an aid to genuine conversion, since it avoids the tendency to hypocrisy created by alliances between religion and political power. Soares (1993) suggests this when analysing the 'holy war' of some Brazilian pente-costals against the Afro-Brazilian religions. 'In our holy war there is a dialogue, however abrasive, with the beliefs which are criticised', which is more than can be said for the 'complacent and superior tolerance' of the older churches which 'do not feel their own superiority to be threatened... Warring pentecostalism is carrying out our modernising revolution, based on egalitarian principles.'

Finally, we can ask whether the new mass Protestantism of the Third World might create a fourth Christian wave of democratisation. Witte (1993) speaks of three waves of Christian democratising impulses which accompanied, or even anticipated, Huntington's three waves of demo-cratisation. The first of Witte's waves was Protestant, in the seventeenth and eighteenth centuries. The second was the missionary wave in Africa and Asia, together with a political one, Catholic and Protestant, in Europe and Latin America in the mid twentieth century. The third wave is post-Vatican II Catholic. Our query is if there are signs of a fourth wave associated with the rise of mass Protestantism in Latin America, Africa and parts of Asia. It should be remembered that the second wave was of lay people. Similarly, Third World Protestantism may become more favourable to democracy if its 'lay intellectualism' (Weber) manages to challenge 'priestly' control of its public face.

The first wave was largely an unintended result of the fracturing of the religious field and the experience of wars of religion, rather than the intended result of Protestant leaders' convictions regarding democracy. Even so, 'most of democracy's original exponents were deeply rooted in verities derived from Christian faith and ethics' (De Gruchy 1995: 49).

However, Third World Protestantism is often regarded less optimisti-cally. For some authors, its voluntarism and fissiparousness, and its tendency to create a free social space in which democratic virtues are fostered, mean it will be positive. But other authors, even when not defenders of the conspiracy theory regarding the US Christian right, feel the repressive internal organisation and corporatist interests of many churches make them a danger to democracy.

Theorists who favour the first interpretation often go back to Tocqueville's (1987) study of American democracy in the 1830s. Tocqueville at times praises religion in general, whilst at other times he distinguishes between religions, not all being equally useful to democracy even though all are better than unbelief. The question for us is whether the evangelical Protestantism which grows in the Third World has the characteristics Tocqueville viewed as most beneficial to democracy.

For Tocqueville, democracy generally referred to equality of condition, a democratic social state. This love of equality could, he thought, undermine political liberty, and despotism might result. However, the 'individualism' which drove people asunder and created apathy towards collective action could be combatted by free institutions, the 'immense assemblage of associations' which characterised American society. Crucial amongst these were religious associations. American religion 'taught the art of being free', because it was a 'democratic and republican Christianity'.

Nevertheless, Tocqueville did not regard just any voluntaristic Protestantism as beneficial to democracy. In fact, he saw that Catholicism, as one denomination amongst many, had assimilated the ethos of the American system and was as democratic as Protestantism. This was the triumph of context over confessionalism. On the other hand, he describes characteristics of the free-church Protestantism he regarded as so useful for democracy, implying that one might elsewhere find other types which were not so useful.

One characteristic was clerical self-restraint. Any osmosis between religion and politics is dangerous for religion; and by that he means especially clerical involvement. When a clergyman introduces politics into the sanctuary, he enters the terrain of political contingency, and his religious discourse also becomes affected by contingency. In 1830s America, the clergy in general distanced themselves voluntarily from political power and even showed a professional pride in so doing. They separated themselves from all political parties and fled from any suspicion of personal interest. In a democratic age, the religious leaders who dream of extending their power beyond the religious sphere run the risk of no longer being believed in any sphere.

This self-restraint is doubly difficult, says Tocqueville, because wise democrats feel the need to moralise democracy by means of religion, propagating the taste for the infinite, feelings of awe and the love of non-material pleasures. Democracy favours love of the material, but religions teach men the immortality of the soul, which is the greatest advantage religion brings to democracy. But, he says, it is not easy to say how democratic governments should best guarantee this contribution. State religions are fatal to the church; nor is it good to give religious leaders an indirect political influence over a theoretically lay state. The only way to instil respect for the dogma of immortality is for rulers always to act as though they believed in it; seeing their leaders act thus in great matters, the people will learn to do likewise in smaller ones.

In short, Tocqueville seems to say that the best way to promote Christian influence in politics is through pious and ethical lay politicians (or, if they are lacking, through religiously indifferent politicians who can plausibly fake piety!). Churches should not be politically privileged, whether constitutionally or in practice, nor should church leaders be given unofficial privileges or become elected rulers. And the everyday practice of the churches should purify and restrict an over-ardent and exclusive taste for material well-being. Tocqueville thus provides criteria for evaluating the likely effects on democracy of any specific manifestation of voluntaristic Christianity.

In Latin America, leaving aside the American-orchestrated-expansion theory, two positions have dominated the debate since the 1960s. Willems (1967) said Protestantism helped the transition to a democratic society, whereas D'Epinay (1970) saw it as reproducing authoritarian rural social relations. In the 1990s the debate continued between the heirs of both authors. On the one hand, there are studies which stress Protestantism's democratising potential, talking of a vibrant civil society and drawing analogies with historical effects in other countries. The churches offer a free social space, an experience of solidarity and a new personal identity, as well as responsible participation in a community and, for some, the development of leadership gifts. These authors talk a lot of 'potential' and 'the long run'. Despite what we have shown in this book regarding corporatism, there is an important point: it is no longer a monolithic organisation playing the corporatist game, but a plurality of competing organisations whose actions can politically cancel each other out. It is probably good for democracy that evangelicalism is institutionally divided. Just as modern democracy was helped more by the effects of the Reformation than by the politics of the reformers, Third World democracy may eventually find itself owing more to evangelicalism than to evangelical churchmen and politicians. Dreams of dominance are constantly dashed on the rocks of evangelical division. In addition, despite internal authoritarianism, *sects* can become bulwarks against the culture industry's massification, unwittingly strengthening democracy (as in the Universal Church's opposition to the mighty Globo media empire in Brazil). Churches could therefore, in Tocquevillian and Weberian fashion, become the prototypes of a democracy based on a hive of voluntary associations. Although the value of such arguments is limited when divorced from empirical demonstration of actual trends, they at least make us wary of equally non-empirical projections to the contrary.

This interpretation is defended by David Martin (1990, 1996), who stresses the probable effects of pentecostalism on civil society. Evangelicalism in Latin America 'is a replication (rather than a diffusion) of differentiations long ago achieved in Anglo-American society. [Thus, they] will not seek, as would "fundamentalist" Muslims, to replace one hegemony with another' (1996: 60–1). However, we must ask whether replication or diffusion are the only possibilities. While the many statements of pentecostal intent to replace one hegemony with another are not important if they go against the sociological grain, the question is whether, in a region still marked by a monolithic tradition, the supposed logic of voluntarist religion may not be modified.

On the other side are authors who emphasise the repressive and corporatist nature of pentecostal churches. A leading representative is Bastian (1992, 1997), who questions whether pentecostalism is really Protestant at all. Historical Protestantism began in Latin America within liberal culture, instilling democratic values, whereas pentecostalism evolved from Catholic popular culture which was syncretistic, corporatist and politically passive. There is an elective affinity between pentecostalism and Latin political culture. Bastian mentions evangelical parties, but does not ask why they have so little success and why they are absent in some countries. Nor does he mention differences in political practice between pentecostal churches. He seems to see the corporate vote of the pentecostal electorate as natural, while in fact it is not at all natural, but has to be constructed and reconstructed with difficulty. He does not explain why some pastors go from being intermediaries for secular candidates to being brokers of official denominational candidates.

Gaskill (1997) stresses organisational structures. Protestantism's relationship to democracy depends mainly on the relationship between elites and institutions and on the strategic decisions taken by religious and political leaders. He is correct in part. The trend to official pentecostal candidates in Brazil has to do with the evolution of the religious field and the status of pastors. Gaskill concludes that pentecostalism does not replicate the 'Protestant ethic' in economic life and has contributed to post-authoritarian pluralism. Its interests for the time being coincide, not with a principled defence of democracy, but with any political movement which guarantees resources. This is correct, but leaves aside the fact that the pentecostal churches are Christian, and therefore subject to internal critique based on the Bible and to the influence of the broader evangelical world. It also leaves aside the contrasts between pentecostal churches who share the same 'clientelistic' organisation. Organisational considerations jostle for space with other forces in the evangelical world.

No essentialist or ahistorical concepts (whether static models of voluntaristic religion, ideological models of religion in society, or elitist models which view the 'sects' through the lenses of the religious 'centre') can do justice to the complexity of the evangelical field and the multiple influences on political behaviour. We need to keep long-term potential and current practice in tension, and be aware of new mutations. The political future of Third World Protestantism cannot be deduced from a model of voluntarist religion (since there are many types of civil society), a presumed corporatist essence in pentecostalism, or a typology of ecclesiastical organisation.

Our case-studies suggest that there is often a link between evangelical politics and democratisation. Kim Young-Sam, Chiluba, Serrano and Obasanjo were all elected in fledgling democratic systems. Latin American evangelical parties and the large evangelical presence in the Brazilian Congress are also phenomena of redemocratisation. But what exactly is the link? Do evangelicals merely occupy democratic space, or do they help to consolidate and expand that space? Are they a phenomenon *of* democracy or a phenomenon *for* democracy? The first three aforementioned presidents carried out basically neoliberal policies, with their democratically straitening implications; all three became involved in corruption scandals; and two eventually governed undemocratically. Ríos Montt, of course, made no pretence at democratic governance, although he has since been a successful actor in Guatemala's restricted formal democracy. In India we see evangelicalism as ethnic shaper and quasi-established religion, informing all shades of Naga nationalism, but without developing autonomous reflection on violence or on faith and ethnicity in modern politics. In Kenya, evangelicalism is both bulwark of the Moi regime and one of its most important opponents. Even so, ethnic factors have not been completely overcome. Such cases, which could be multiplied, warn us of the dangers of generalisation.

The few reliable studies of evangelical attitudes (ISER 1996 for Brazil; Fontaine and Bayer 1991 for Chile) suggest that, whatever the behaviour of their ecclesiastical and political elites, the evangelical community as such is not a threat to democracy. The Greater Rio de Janeiro study (ISER 1996) suggests that the intense sociability of Brazilian evangelicalism (85 per cent of weekly attendance at services, with many attending several days a week) makes the churches models of voluntary associationalism. In contrast to the main religious rivals Catholicism and Umbanda, 41 per cent have taken part in elections for their spiritual leaders. Half of them had taken part in administrative meetings of the church during the current year: 'it is difficult to imagine another institution in the country with this level of administrative participation'.

According to the survey, evangelical conversion 'involves a profound break with cultural patterns in relationship between the sexes', an important dimension of democratisation. As for civic participation, low involvement parallels society in general. But in frequency of communication with elected politicians, evangelicals are far above average. Church activity is positively correlated with some forms of social participation, such as unionism and neighbourhood associations. Contradicting certain stereotypes, the most active church members, including those who claim charismatic gifts, show above-average participation in their local communities and professional associations.

Of course, just as Tocqueville talked of a triumph of context over confessionalism in US Catholicism, and fears regarding American fundamentalism are sometimes assuaged by reference to its link to the American heritage of a liberal polity with separation of church and state, it should be remembered that Third World evangelicalism, depending on the country, enjoys few or none of these contextual advantages in relation to its democratic potential. Most countries do not have a similar religion–state tradition such as that which informs the American national myth and constrains all religious actors in US politics, whatever their sociological and theological thrust. On the contrary, favourable internal elements in Third World evangelicalism may be cancelled out by an unfavourable external heritage.

This helps to account for certain characteristics of evangelical politics which are ambiguous or clearly prejudicial to democracy. What we have called corporatism (politics to defend and strengthen the ecclesiastical institution and its leaders) and triumphalism (belief in the divine right of evangelicals to govern) are such examples.

We can illustrate this with the attempt in 1999 by the governor of Rio de Janeiro, Anthony Garotinho, to further his presidential aspirations by making preaching tours all over Brazil. Little known outside his own state, he realised his evangelical identity could give him a nationwide base. This sparked a debate regarding the legitimacy of such actions in a secular democracy. *Pace* the militantly secularist view that would ban all expressions of religiosity from politics, it is no danger to democracy if a ruler is personally religious, or even if he regards his political militancy as inspired by a religious world-view. Moreover, there is in principle nothing undemocratic in appealing for votes to one's own religious sector. What would be undemocratic is to govern in favour of that sector. There are, of course, rights which religious groups can legitimately claim and public offices which individuals from those groups may plausibly aspire to, but any corporate favouritism will be dangerous for democracy. We have seen that evangelical leaders sometimes hope for such state favouritism; we have also seen that, in the context of a pluralistic evangelical field, evangelical heads of state will find it impossible to satisfy such hopes, since favours to some will always leave others resentful. Thus, everything depends on not incurring 'debts' to church leaders in order to be elected, in ways that are irreconcilable with democracy and a non-confessional state. The relationship established during the campaign (both expectations and commitments) will largely determine practice in government. Agreements reached and naive expectations fanned can become a trap, leaving the candidate compromised by proximity to church leaders whose links to undemocratic triumphalism or to insatiable corporatist appetites can easily be exposed.

Corporatism does not support the idea of a correspondence between doctrine and politics according to which evangelicals would be necessarily favourable to a universalist and ethical politics. In addition, it has generally weakened even further the fragile party system, thus undermining what is usually taken to be one of the bases of a stable democracy.

Many countries are experiencing rapid *sectarian* growth in a democratic regime. Corporatist tendencies do carry dangers. *Sectarianism* has difficulty in elaborating a universalist perspective on politics because it has always been excluded or self-excluded from such concerns. Timeserving and vote-selling reflect the *sectarian* concept of mission. To guarantee the best operating conditions, agreements are acceptable. The benefits received (a new roof for the church in exchange for the congregation's votes, or a radio station in exchange for a parliamentarian's crucial vote) are not treason to the gospel, but a tax which 'worldly' power pays to the truth.

On the other hand, corporatist politics provokes internal ideological competition. Even in the official journal of the Brazilian Assemblies of God there are signs of another conception of politics: that of the free citizen who, as an instrument of the Kingdom of God, joins a party without involving the church. Pentecostalism is a branch of Christianity and subject to its universalist ethical impulse.

Before leaving corporatism we should note its effects on the internal organisation of the evangelical field. Each phase has a centralising effect. The selection of candidates follows the lines of ecclesiastical power. The resources obtained follow the same trajectory. The weapons of corporatist politics are size and *sectarian* discipline, excluding individual consciousness-raising of the members (which would open up space for political influence of historical Protestant leaders with greater cultural resources). Corporatism thus weakens internal democracy in the churches involved. Even so, there are limits, since after rejecting the apolitical tradition the leaders cannot close the gates totally to alternative forms of politicisation.

Triumphalism is even more problematic for democracy. It rests on the idea that 'the people of God', identified with the evangelicals, have been chosen not only for eternal salvation or for particular missionary tasks, but also to rule their countries. It is hard for the *sect* to theorise any other political role for itself. It has always seen itself as morally superior; so, in relation to temporal power, it cannot readily accept that it is one player amongst many. It must be indifferent or in charge.

Two sociological problems of this tendency should be noted. Firstly, it does not address the question of how to delimit the group which is supposedly heir to Old Testament theocratic promises, nor the question of how internal political differences should be overcome so as to establish a uniform project. In practice, proposals oscillate between subordination to the leadership of a charismatic politician of evangelical provenance, and more direct control by ecclesiastical leaders. Theocratic projects floated in Latin America and Africa in recent years are more in Wallace's category of 'hierocracy' (rule by clergy) than 'general theocracy' (in which ultimate authority resides in a divine law, usually resulting in rule through a godly laity) (*Encyclopedia of Religion* 1987, 'Theocracy'). The question is: in whose interest is the 'evangelicals in power' banner? Which evangelicals will be in power? The lack of discussion strengthens the power of the main evangelical electoral brokers, namely the leaders of the main denominations and the owners of the main organs of the evangelical media.

Evangelical theocrats see themselves as a sort of vanguard, an enlightened minority every bit as convinced of its right to rule as Marxist vanguards once were. Since, however, this theocratic vanguard has no ready-made policies (unlike Islamists who have only to turn to the sharia), it is not clear what would result. One remedy would be to resort to ready-made radicalised versions of 'Christian politics' on offer from the United States, such as reconstructionism. More likely, however, is that, lacking a programme, theocratic aspirations would become merely hierocratic ambitions and soon turn corrupt and self-serving.

The second sociological problem is the curious return of a concept of territoriality in new versions of macro-level 'spiritual warfare' frequently associated with theocratic currents. The idea of a 'Christian nation' is a return to the territoriality of Christendom, under the aegis of the new charismatic theology of territorial spirits. The sociological problem, however, is the following: how could a territorial concept work within a religious field organised around the principle of voluntarism and a political field characterised by pluralism? It would be necessarily polemical, not tranquil and sure of itself as medieval Christendom was. It would constantly have to prove its territorial right with evidences such as material prosperity. Otherwise, it would need a theodicy to explain why, an exercise in blaming which could degenerate into 'witch-hunts'. The failure of theocratic leaders to prove their efficacy in visible terms would oblige them to seek out mystical saboteurs, as prefigured in Zambian attempts to blame 'Christians who don't pray' for the government's shortcomings. The sacralisation of power in such 'spiritual warfare' concepts (the other side of the coin of its demonisation when in the hands of non-believers), makes criticism impossible. Introducing the dynamic of territoriality into a pluralistic and democratic situation could bring considerable dangers for democracy.

At the same time, there are limits to triumphalism's anti-democratic potential. Whilst power is often attractive, each religion's theological and sociological characteristics can place significant constraints on how the possibility of power is in fact handled. Evangelicalism's emphasis on the cross of Christ (the death of its founder at the hands of the state), its traditional suspicion of 'the world' and insistence on inward transformation of the heart as far more important than outward conformity, all differentiate it from rival theocratic contenders in the Third World such as Islamic fundamentalism. In addition, theocratic tendencies which do arise conflict with evangelicalism's organisational dividedness, the ever-shriller rhetoric of 'unity' reflecting merely an increase in the political prize if that chimera could ever be realised, but not an increasing possibility of its actual realisation.

A final caveat has to do with unintended consequences. As Kalyvas (1998) says, even religious movements entering politics with a theocratic and illiberal project may eventually consolidate democracy. The only European country where a Catholic party won an electoral majority was Belgium, yet Belgian democracy survived. Illiberal groups may evolve towards democracy out of strategic self-interest rather than normative commitment, but the effect is the same.

In burgeoning Third World evangelicalism we see a similar range of postures towards the state (though not necessarily in the same proportions, nor with the same overall effects) as in the history of worldwide Protestantism. One such posture is the rejection of political participation which characterised most Anabaptists of the sixteenth century. The second posture is the ideal of the 'Christian nation', adopted by Calvin in continuity with the Middle Ages. The church is at the centre of society, furnishing its official creed. The pious ruler should promote true religion and morals by political and judicial means. Today, the 'Christian nation' ideal has fragmented into a range of positions, from reconstructionists who defend a theocracy based on Mosaic law, to the liberalism of European territorial churches which asks only for Christian values to retain a certain privilege. In its severe form, the 'Christian nation' implies persecution; in its gentle form, it implies merely discrimination in civil religion, often allied with open support for democracy and human rights. The third posture flourished initially among some early Baptists and the Levellers of the English Civil War, and later spread to other groups, including the Neo-Calvinists who governed Holland for much of the period from the 1890s to the 1940s. This is principled pluralism, of religious freedom in a non-confessional state.

As all three postures have a long history, it is not surprising that Third World evangelicalism also contains all three. This is indeed one of the most significant divisions within worldwide evangelicalism. If we remember that the *sect* is often either a failed *church* or tomorrow's would-be *church*, it is no wonder that even it can oscillate rapidly between an apolitical posture and some form of 'Christian nation' ideal. The 'principled pluralism' position first achieved political importance with the Baptist Roger Williams in Rhode Island and the Levellers in England.

As Wootton stresses with regard to the latter, it is inadequate to see them simply as applying to politics the religious practices of the *sects*, since the latter were intended for exclusive voluntary communities. *Sectarian* theology could only lead to democratic politics if any division of the political world between the godly and the ungodly were overcome. The central theological issue was the relationship between Old and New Testaments. In the view of all 'principled pluralists' since the Levellers, the situation of Old Testament Israel was entirely exceptional; today, the state should limit itself to civil functions according to the principles of natural reason or, as the Kuyperian neo-Calvinists would have it, common grace. Unlike the Civil War Presbyterians, in whose opinion the magistrate was to repress heresy and idolatry as much as to punish murder, the Levellers viewed all modern states as merely civil. The idea of a holy commonwealth was abandoned, and God was no longer expected to hold whole communities responsible for the sins of some in their midst. The question of toleration and a non-confessional state did not, therefore, rest on scepticism or a weakening of religious conviction, but on an understanding of a central theological issue (1991: 440).

This defence of religious toleration and a secular or more properly non-confessional state was based not just on liberal pragmatic arguments (the good of the state), but on theological principle. Evangelicalism reached the Third World largely in this vein, often strengthened by the critique of Catholic or non-Christian 'confusion' of religion and politics. However, the late twentieth century has seen the numerical burgeoning of this evangelicalism and its rise to political influence. In this context, the political restraint shown even by fundamentalist US movements (except for the minority of true reconstructionists) shows signs of being absent in some quarters. It is not, therefore, certain that Third World evangelicalism will be friendly to democracy. Even the argument that its institutional divisions will render it innocuous is uncertain. Not only could a divided evangelical field still be dangerous if it had a broad non-democratic consensus susceptible to manipulation by authoritarian or messianic political leaders, but there is also the possibility of hegemonic groups arising and transforming the intra-evangelical status quo, such as the Universal Church of the Kingdom of God may yet do in Brazil. Will Protestant fragmentation be effectively annulled by the UC's growing dominance? Or will the latter be broken in a few years by adversaries or by internal divisions? The question is important, since in Europe there was an involuntary evolution towards pluralism based on recognition that Christianity was hopelessly divided.

In Brazil, as long as any group has a realistic chance of unifying evangelicalism around a common political project, democracy may well be seen as no more than tactically convenient.

The new religious pluralism will require, throughout Latin America, adjustments in the public sphere in the next decades, to make it more genuinely non-confessional and overcome the remnants of both the 'soft' version of a 'Catholic nation' and the secularist (liberal and Marxist) project which would exclude religion from public life. In this respect, some evangelical complaints are justified. But others go beyond this, towards an 'evangelical nation' project. This is, for the time being, unrealisable. But Latin America, in Martin's (1978) terminology, has been formed not by the 'American' but the 'Latin' pattern. Whatever new hybrid may be emerging, it is not certain that the logic of a monolithic church will disappear completely.

In Guatemala and Nigeria, the concern is not so much a new hegemonic denomination but the rise of a charismaticism which justifies Hollenweger's (1994) concern about the insulation of elite charismatics from dialogue with poor pentecostals. The post-millennial dreams of charismatic elites' accession to power are scant comfort to the disadvantaged of the Third World, an increasing proportion of whom are evangelical. The political implications of prosperity theology (remember Tocqueville on churches benefiting democracy by moderating the taste for material well-being!), spiritual warfare and believers' divine right to rule, could be very different from those of classical Protestant ethics and political doctrine in Europe and North America. Both the regional contexts and the type of evangelicalism growing, raise concerns as to long-term political effects.

Our conclusion on evangelicals and democracy is thus cautious and open-ended. Those who would foreclose the discussion, in positive or negative tone, seem too distant from the complexity of empirical data in diverse situations.

Another important topic is the impact of evangelical politics on questions of nationalism. A recent book on nationalism talks of the primacy of national identities over class, gender and race; 'perhaps only religious attachments have rivalled national loyalties in their scope and fervour' in the modern world (Hutchinson and Smith 1994: 4). This is even truer of the post-Cold War era, in which conflicts between universalistic ideologies have been replaced by more varied causes, including ethnicity, nationalism and religion. Especially potent are amalgams of these. Juergensmeyer (1995) speaks of a rise of 'religious nationalism' around the globe, more powerful than its secular variant. While the Cold War was an internecine quarrel of the West, he says, the conflicts of the future will be intercultural, along cleavages that are primarily religious.

We have seen that religious nationalism is a threat to evangelicals, especially in Asia (Malaysia, India, Indonesia), but also in Islamic Africa (Sudan, Nigeria). (In Latin America, a far softer Catholic variant can still cause problems, but the trend is towards its virtual elimination.) However, there can also be an evangelical version of religious national-ism (Zambia, pentecostals in Nigeria). Thus, while evangelicalism's main problem is with non-evangelical forms of religious nationalism, with effects ranging from mild discrimination to physical elimination, there is also an increasing trend to evangelical nationalism, possibly even more damaging to evangelicalism in the long run.

Resurgent religious nationalism makes the question of evangelical-ism's (or Christianity's) link to national identity crucial in many coun-tries. Such links (or their absence) are not given once and for all, but are in constant flux. This is true even of Muslim countries, where policies towards religious minorities and the actual size of the Christian popula-tion have oscillated over time; how much more so in South and East Asia. The scope for a creative apologetic varies with numerical size of the church, degree of national origin or control of denominations, class, educational and ethnic composition of the church, the existence of creative church thinkers and leaders, the level of democracy and plural-ism in society, and the nature of the major religion. One of the most urgent tasks in many countries, for the churches' own benefit, would seem to be the creative development of a historically and sociologically informed apologetic in defence of evangelicalism's right to exist and positive association with some viable concept of national identity.

What effect can emergent evangelical politics have on non-evangelical religious nationalism? Evangelicalism is thoroughly in-digenised in most of the Third World. To what extent will it still function as a carrier of values, mentalities and practices which develop-ed historically in the West but may not be intrinsically Western (regard-less of whether these are seen as intrinsically evangelical or merely as historically contingent imitations or repetitions of Western evangelical-ism)? The twenty-first century will presumably see an increasing capacity in Africa and Asia to distinguish between the 'Western' ('cul-turally alien and suspect') and a series of other categories regarded as assimilable ('modern', 'global' and even 'Christian'). Will this allow a growing evangelical community to play a role in gradually undermining the ideological legitimacy of religious nationalism? Or will there develop evangelical versions of the same, reinforcing its overall ideological legitimacy while questioning merely the currently dominant project?

Hastings stresses the ambiguity of Christianity in relation to nationalism. He opposes the 'modernist' thesis regarding the genesis of nationalism by rooting it in biblical culture. 'The Bible provided . . . the original model of the nation' (1997: 4, 12). The Bible portrays the world as a world of nations, and Israel as the mirror for national self-imagining. Christianity's adoption of the Old Testament distinguishes it from Islam. There is a Christian thrust to vernacularise, as seen in Bible translation and vernacular liturgy. As a 'religion of translation', Christianity 'has of its nature been a shaper of nations' (ibid.: 187). But Christianity did not start, as did Islam, with any clear political model. When Christians came to power they were able to go in two directions: towards the nation-state or the world empire. Whereas Islam inclined to a world empire based on the *umma* and a single sacred language, Christianity did not go to the other extreme but remained politically ambivalent (ibid.: 201).

In Protestantism, Christianity's tension between vernacularisation and universalism may seem to have been resolved in favour of the former. Yet the link was largely fortuitous (ibid.: 55). Although its greater stress on the Old Testament contributed to nationalism, it was national churches in an Erastian relationship to the state that were most vulnerable in practice. Small non-state churches and very large international ones are less affected. Evangelical Protestantism has frequently combined a universalist spiritual loyalty with a particularist political loyalty. Yet it is from their ranks (Mennonites, Quakers) that the most creative efforts to free Protestantism from nationalist bondage have come (ibid.: 205).

The ambivalence of Christianity to nationalism is mirrored, for Hastings, in the ambivalence of nationalism itself. The nationalism of *jus solis* is inclusivistic, whereas that of *jus sanguinis* is exclusivistic. Nationalism can be an appropriate protest against a universalising uniformity, but it can also deny the divisibility of sovereignty as well as multiple loyalties and identities (ibid.: 33, 182).

Nationalism is often linked to ethnicity, and both to democracy. Recent years have seen a global resurgence of democracy, but also of nationalist and ethnic conflict (Diamond and Plattner 1994: ix). While moderate nationalism can be an ally of democracy, ethnic cleavages present it with a grave danger, their conflicts being less amenable to compromise than material issues. However, accommodative elite practices encouraged by the right political institutions, plus the generation of interests which cross-cut ethnicity, can make ethnically divided democracies possible (ibid.: xx–xxii). Evangelicalism can be a cross-cutting loyalty; however, the mission practice of translating the Bible into every possible dialect, reinforcing and even multiplying ethnic identities and sometimes creating ethnically monolithic denominations, has often complicated this role.

Asian evangelicalism is heavily lodged in ethnic minorities. In these ethnicities which have failed to become nations, evangelicalism may be virtually the established religion. This may be related to the desire to adopt a world religion different from the regionally dominant one. In Latin America, evangelicalism can also be an ethnic revitalisation movement for indigenous peoples.

Is evangelicalism formative in such contexts, or is it rather captive of ethnic agendas? While it may on occasion be adopted for its political usefulness, that is not so in the great majority of instances, and could not explain its continuing hold over generations once the political moment had changed, or in the face of prolonged failure to achieve political goals. However, once adopted, the faith can be put to political use. In any case, a clear separation of 'religious' and 'ethnic' factors is often impossible. Christianity may have helped to create the very ethnic identity (Nagaland). Or ethnic pride and political claims may be the direct result of its adoption: as a Brazilian indigenous evangelical leader once told me, 'when I found Jesus, I felt myself to be more Terena'. At the same time, evangelicalism injects a universalist critique into any ethnic imprisoning of the faith or absolutising of ethnic claims. Of course, many ethnic demands may be justified precisely on the universalist criteria of the gospel, so the coincidence of ethnic interests with evangelical politics does not necessarily mean the captivity of the faith, any more than similar coincidences involving class or national identities might do in the West. However, there is a need for evangelicals to examine questions of group or communitarian rights in democratic contexts, so pressing in the Third World.

Another important question is that of evangelical political parties. These tend to be founded where: (i) it is legally easy to found new parties; (ii) the electoral system favours the existence of many parties; (iii) the political culture is dissatisfied with traditional parties; and (iv) evangelicals find insufficient space in existing parties, or at least cannot get their civil-rights issues heard through them. Where there is no exclusion from the party system, nor evangelical civil rights to conquer, the disadvantages of such parties weigh more: they further divide the evangelical community, and the varied social composition makes it difficult to find a common platform (even on abortion there is no unanimity as to legislative policy, much less with regard to church–state relations, the role of the state, economic policy, etc.). A party must tackle a broad range of questions, something usually beyond the evangelical community's limited educational resources.

Spanish-speaking Latin America has seen over twenty parties in recent years (Bastian's list (1997: 103) contains many errors). These parties rarely include 'evangelical' in their name; the reason is not only the hope of cultivating non-evangelical voters, but the desire to avoid the ire of denominational leaders who would feel slighted by an 'evangelical party' which they had not been consulted about. Founders have generally not been leaders of large denominations, but lower-level pastors or leaders of new groups.

The multiplication of parties should not be confused with strength; they may rather be a sign of weakness and exclusion. Results have been poor, even in terms of evangelical percentages in the electorate. Other modes of mobilisation (e.g. official denominational candidates in existing parties) have been far more successful.

Our study suggests that, *pace* many scholars of globalisation, a globalised world need not lead either to a relativistic homogeneity or to clashing fundamentalisms. Conversion, the main route of evangelical growth in the Third World, is another alternative, with quite different cultural and political implications. Our case-studies are quite clearly not political revivals using religious symbolism, but religious revivals with periodic political incursions but whose dynamism transcends the political realm. The dynamic of conversion places evangelicalism in a very different relationship to global cultural processes from either pan-religious ecumenism (tending to global homogeneity) or fundamentalism (tending to irreducible pockets of anti-pluralism). As generally a non-traditional religion (in local terms) spreading by conversion, its interests are usually the opposite of those of a reactive fundamentalism. For evangelicalism, pluralism and cultural diffuseness would seem to be advantageous, whereas non-Christian fundamentalisms constitute one of its most serious barriers. It may be that evangelicalism flourishes best in a world that is tranquilly religious, rather than one that is either secularised or defensively religious. As Waters says, 'a globalised culture is chaotic rather than orderly... The absolute globalisation of culture would involve the creation of a common but hyperdifferentiated field of value, taste and style opportunities, accessible by each individual without constraint... Islam would not be linked to particular territorially based communities..., but would be universally available' (1995: 125–6). The spread of evangelicalism through conversion fits this picture of hyperdifferentiation, pluralism and de-territorialisation. The continued study of evangelical politics across the globe is important for the understanding of globalising processes.

Evangelicalism can be seen, in fact, as a 'globalisation from below'. If the Reformational concept of 'calling' led in the end to the 'Protestant ethic' which contributed to the 'iron cage' of bureaucratic rationality and the globalisation of rationalised capitalism and the nation-state, the pietistic reconception of calling led to mission and the globalisation of voluntaristic Christianity. Pentecostalism accentuated the contrast. Pentecostalism came indeed to the Third World from America, but from its underside. Born amongst the poor, blacks and women, it was exported at virtually no cost, often by non-Americans, bypassing the usual channels (religious and otherwise) of American wealth and power. It is precisely this counter-establishment Western Christianity that has become the most globalised.

It is worth asking whether Third World evangelicalism can play a role in opposing existing market-driven globalisation. While militant Islam does so in its own way, can evangelicalism adopt a stance which is neither subordinate to neoliberalism nor hostile to the Western (and heavily Christian) heritage of democracy and human rights? Critiques of IMF-recommended policies do exist, but they are occasional and piecemeal rather than systematic and self-aware. Perhaps the increasingly 'social' discourse of prosperity teachers such as the Universal Church in Brazil and Mensah Otabil in Ghana may in the future find common ground with movements of the 'evangelical left'.

THE CHALLENGE OF POLITICS FOR THIRD WORLD EVANGELICALISM

Our study has uncovered considerable activity but very little systematic reflection on that activity. Given the social importance of the phenomenon and its uncertain direction, it would seem to be in everybody's interest that Third World evangelicalism become increasingly self-aware and reflective in its political engagement.

This presupposes comparative empirical knowledge of evangelical politics globally and familiarity with the major Christian traditions of political theology. Greater knowledge can help to avoid irrelevant, impracticable or naive responses, and make it harder for ill-prepared or opportunist leaders to bring disrepute onto their often politically and culturally exposed communities.

Given the variety of political uses to which Christianity and the Bible have been put historically, it is not surprising that variety prevails in today's global evangelicalism. However, it is important, in an increasingly globalised world, that evangelicals in the developed West learn from the social reality and political concerns of fellow-evangelicals elsewhere. Within the Third World, awareness of variety can promote suspicion regarding anyone's claim to have uncovered a definitive 'biblical politics'; but it can also help local politicians see that sometimes they defend positions which would be politically or economically disastrous for their fellow-believers in other parts of the world.

The lack of theorisation about political engagement contrasts with other important Christian currents in the modern world, such as Christian Democracy, Dutch Neo-Calvinism, Liberation Theology or even the New Christian Right. There are obvious constraints on such theorising. Third World countries have limited educational resources, and the evangelical community is often educationally deprived even by local standards. The religious market, with its pressures to be numerically successful and dispute scarce resources, does not encourage deep thinking, ethical teaching or self-denying politics. International church contacts are often non-existent, limiting access to the history of Christian political reflection. And, of course, there are the constraints of the local political systems, with their dominant religion–state models and their often pervasive corruption.

A few lines for reflection can be suggested. In a context which goes from the Asian tigers in crisis to the would-be tigers, to the extreme inequalities of Brazil and South Africa, to the critical cases of Africa, evangelical politics is challenged both by 'local subversion' (the subverting of values of the worldwide church by local interests) and 'global subversion' (subordination to the trends of existing globalisation), with regard to economic systems (from the standpoint of those on the sharp end), geopolitical questions, democracy and gender. The lack of an autonomous vision favours the assimilation of dominant models in which evangelicals merely compete with the locally dominant religion (Islam, Catholicism or whatever) at its own game. Alternatively, a 'biblical model of politics' disseminated by the First World evangelical right is adopted; while others condemn both extremes of the local spectrum as 'ideological' and adopt the locally defined 'centre' as the 'non-ideological' Christian way: a curious reversal of evangelical discourse in most areas of life, in which the average of a non-evangelical society is certainly not affirmed as divinely sanctioned.

In a worldwide context of 'loss of utopia', or of fragmentation into micro-utopias, evangelicalism's non-statist and popular character and radical biblicism could fill a void. While its class location and its shying away from the social sciences have been unfavourable to creative political thinking, this will tend to change. Thus far, it has produced the questionable utopias of an 'evangelical Latin America' or a 'Christian Zambia', but little in the way of sociologically informed theological visions of a different society (rather than just one where evangelicals rule).

Economic policy is vital for a constituency based largely among the poorer sectors of the poorer countries. Also essential is a proper balancing of local and global concerns. The former are represented by questions of ethnicity and nationhood in the light of evangelical faith; the latter by the global challenges of the environment and concepts of human rights. How should evangelicalism relate to the localising forces of ethnic and national identity, while at the same time strengthening commitment to a global community?

Perhaps the key theme is the state. There are many dimensions to this. One is the development of a theology and practice of resistance to tyranny. Another is the question of violence, in situations where evangelicals as such are persecuted or where they are members of oppressed ethnic groups. But these pressing cases are just the tip of the iceberg. More generally, the question of the non-confessional state is problematic. Many evangelical political leaders would still baulk at the words of the Dutch neo-Calvinist Herman Dooyeweerd, when he says the state should 'give proportionally equal ... distribution of its rights and services to all religious communities, including those that are anti-Christian', and must 'do justice to all communities of belief as they concern themselves with education, industry, science and arts' (in Skillen 1974: 433).

How to relate politically to religious pluralism still requires creative thought and action. On the one hand, evangelicals must be bold defenders of pluralism, if only because their disadvantaged brethren in many countries need it urgently. On the other hand, they need to go beyond a secular utilitarian defence of the non-confessional state. As

Sanneh (1996) says, the state as a vehicle for tolerance, human rights, equality and justice must now be conceived in terms hospitable to claims for truth.

The question of power also needs reflection. As a minority tradition-ally marginalised but with a strong sense of destiny, the prospect of converting the ruler or of electing one's own is often seen by Third World evangelicals as the pinnacle of political aspiration and a panacea for national ills. There is little understanding of politics as a *system*, and theologically there is a weak doctrine of sin in which the older Protestant understanding of the need for sinners to control each other in a system of mutual accountability is replaced by the 'messianic' hope in a Chris-tian president or by faith in a 'vanguard' of evangelical leaders with a divine right to rule. If classical Protestant theology has stressed that power relations are inevitable but always dangerous, Third World evangelicalism has tended to stress one side or other of this equation according to its social situation: when impotent, it has stressed the danger of power and the desirability of its total avoidance; when power has beckoned, it has imagined the possibility of an unambiguous exer-cise of power by 'the people of God'. Recent middle-class charismati-cism tends to reduce the solution of political problems to ritualism; complex power relations embedded in political systems are ignored in favour of expressive solutions related to 'territorial spirits'.

Related to this is the question of corruption (cases include presidents Serrano, Chiluba and Kim Young-Sam, as well as numerous congress-men in Brazil and elsewhere). A total picture, of course, includes not only many honest parliamentarians but also some who have had high-profile roles in combatting corruption. Nevertheless, the susceptibility of the evangelical political class has often been above average.

Lastly, there is the question of the specificity of political action *vis-à-vis* Christian morality. One evangelical member of the Brazilian Constitu-ent Assembly of 1988 claimed that 'if everyone were a Christian we should have no need of a Constitution, since we already have one: the Bible. Everything that is praised in the Bible should be prescribed and everything that is condemned there should be proscribed.' This shows the need for reflection on the political role of the Bible and on the distinction between morality and legislation. Newly influential Third World evangelicalism has had little experience in distinguishing political (legislative) tasks from cultural (evangelistic and teaching) tasks.

In all Third World contexts (consolidated or consolidating democ-racies, democratic transitions, dictatorships, separatist movements, wars), there is a need for training, focused especially on the laity. Many churches are reaching social visibility and discovering the need for theoretical and practical expertise in areas which previously seemed irrelevant. Perhaps even more than conventional pastoral training, the churches need people who can interact with their societies in diverse ways.

WHITHER EVANGELICAL POLITICS?

The coming decades are likely to see increasing salience of evangelicals in the politics of Latin America, Africa and Asia. There are imponderables in the extent of this, the evolution of democracy and religious pluralism, especially in Africa and Asia, being the main ones. But there are no convincing reasons to believe it will be a short-lived phenomenon. As Casanova says, decline of religion is not a structural trend worldwide. Religions which accept differentiation and voluntarism are better placed to adopt 'some form of evangelical revivalism as a successful method of religious self-reproduction in a free religious market' (1994: 214). Evangelicalism seems well equipped to flourish globally.

If theories of inevitable secularisation are rejected, what factors could influence the strength of evangelical political involvement? One is numbers. Shrinkage would clearly affect evangelicalism's capacity as a political actor. In fact, the relationship between numerical success and an acceptable political presence may be reciprocal: the latter helps to maintain an attractive public image which facilitates growth, while growth increases political bargaining power. However, the structures which contribute to evangelicalism's grass-roots vitality (such as voluntarism and fission) may hamper the translation of its numerical success into political clout. In any case, the current moment in Latin America and in parts of Africa is a peculiar one which cannot last. Rapid numerical growth will one day stop. And, whether it continues awhile or not, relationship to politics will evolve. Further growth will bring greater political aspirations. Stagnation or decline would lead to more stable membership with a higher percentage of birth-members and fewer converts; this would change the sociological nature of the churches and bring demands for different relations with public life.

Another factor could be disillusionment with the returns of political activity, taking the steam out of evangelical politics. This may be especially the case with triumphalist groups and more local-level corporatism. It would not apply, however, where there are strong corporatist projects (such as the Universal Church), or where there is programmatic participation, especially if based on a fight against anti-evangelical legislation or on ethnic factors. A limitation on political activity could also result from a serious tarnishing of evangelicalism's public image in some countries.

Brazil, as the major Third World democracy with a significant evangelical presence, and the second largest evangelical community in the world, could be a guide to what will happen if conditions are favourable in some Latin American and African countries. But so far, its corporatist pentecostal politics seems to be unique, not only within the continents studied but also historically. Existing sociological literature offers few interpretative clues. The American religious right functions in a very different religious and political context. Despite similar concerns regarding the family and the link with the mass media, the differences (of methods and demands, of background and of prospects) are more decisive. In Brazil, the key figures are denominational heads and not leaders of agencies like the Christian Coalition which mobilise Protestant opinion in the United States. Nor is there in Brazil the nostalgia for a lost past. Brazilian leaders are in a different position in the Protestant field; Protestantism has a different position in the religious world and a different relationship to civil religion and national identity.

The history of Christian *sectarianism* does not give us many parameters either. In Catholic Europe, all Protestant groups remain small. In Protestant Europe, the established churches inhibited the growth of *sects*, or secularisation and unfavourable electoral systems politically marginalised religion. In the United States, Protestant *sects* became *denominations* (and were sociologically transformed) within a generation or two; a process facilitated by the absence of an official church, economic growth, an egalitarian ideology (in which *sects* could acquire respectability), religious tolerance and the entry of new immigrants who pushed the older ones up the social scale (Wilson 1970: 234). Brazilian *sects*, however, grow rapidly but do not win social and cultural respectability; there is still a semi-official church, and no significant immigration or economic expansion. It is in this context that they have launched themselves into politics.

Even in Latin America the Brazilian case is so far unique. In Peru, the sudden entry into politics owed a lot to a secular initiative and affected above all the historical churches. In Guatemala, both Protestant presidents were politicians before their conversion to high-class charismatic churches. In Brazil, on the other hand, the political vanguard are leaders of popular *sects* which have grown so much and so fast that they begin to use the state for their own ends. This may be the first case in history in which Christian *conversionist sects* have achieved such a relationship with the state.

Bibliography

Ackerman, Susan and Lee, Raymond. 1988. *Heaven in Transition: Non-Muslim Religious Innovation and Ethnic Identity in Malaysia*, Honolulu, University of Hawaii Press.

Almond, Gabriel A., Sivan, Emmanuel and Appleby, R. Scott. 1995. 'Examining the Cases', in Marty and Appleby (eds.), pp. 445–82.

Amat y León, Oscar. 1996. 'La Propuesta Misionera y el Desarrollo del Movimiento Carismático Evangélico en el Perú', Master's thesis, CEMAA, Lima.

Anderson, Robert Mapes. 1979. *Vision of the Disinherited: The Making of American Pentecostalism*, New York, Oxford University Press.

Anfuso, Joseph and Sczepanski, David. 1984. *Efrain Ríos Montt: Servant or Dictator?*, Ventura, California, Vision House.

Annis, Sheldon. 1987. *God and Production in a Guatemalan Town*, Austin, University of Texas Press.

Anti-Slavery Society. 1990. *West Papua: Plunder in Paradise*, Report no. 6.

Arana, Pedro. 1987. *Testimonio Político*, Lima, Presencia.

Arroyo, Victor and Paredes, Tito. 1991. 'Perú: Los Evangélicos y el "Fenómeno Fujimori"', in Padilla (ed.), pp. 89–101.

Balcomb, Anthony. 1993. *Third Way Theology*, Pietermaritzburg, Cluster.

Baloi, Obebe. 1995. 'Gestão de Conflitos e Transição Democrática', in Mazula, B. (ed.), *Eleições, Democracia e Desenvolvimento*, Maputo, n/p, pp. 501–27.

Barrett, D. and Johnson T. 1998. 'Annual Statistical Table on Global Mission: 1998', *International Bulletin of Missionary Research*, January, pp. 26–7.

Bastian, Jean-Pierre. 1983. *Protestantismo y Sociedad en México*, Mexico City, Cupsa.

1990. *Historia del Protestantismo en América Latina*, Mexico City, Casa Unida de Publicaciones.

1992. 'Introduction', *Social Compass*, 39 (3), 323–6.

1997. 'Minorités religieuses et confessionnalisation de la politique en Amérique latine', *Archives des Sciences Sociales des Religions*, January–March, 97–114.

Baur, John. 1994. *2000 Years of Christianity in Africa*, Nairobi, Paulinas.

Bebbington, David. 1989. *Evangelicalism in Modern Britain*, London, Unwin Hyman.

Benson, G. P. 1995. 'Ideological Politics versus Biblical Hermeneutics: Kenya's Protestant Churches and the Nyayo State', in Hansen and Twaddle (eds.), pp. 177–99.

Berger, Peter. 1998. 'Conclusion: General Observations on Normative Conflicts and Mediation', in Berger, P. (ed.), *The Limits of Social Cohesion: Conflict and Mediation in Pluralist Societies*, Boulder, Westview Press, pp. 352–79.

Beyer, Peter. 1994. *Religion and Globalization*, London, Sage.

Birmingham, David. 1992. *Frontline Nationalism in Angola and Mozambique*, London, James Currey; Trenton, Africa World Press.

Blancarte, Roberto. 1993. 'Religion and Constitutional Change in Mexico, 1988–1992', *Social Compass*, 40 (4), 555–69.

Bowen, Kurt. 1996. *Evangelism and Apostasy: The Evolution and Impact of Evangelicals in Modern Mexico*, Montreal and Kingston, McGill-Queen's University Press.

Bowen, Roger. 1996. 'Rwanda: Missionary Reflections on a Catastrophe', *Anvil*, 13 (1), 33–44.

Brown, David. 1994. *The State and Ethnic Politics in South East Asia*, London, Routledge.

Bruce, Steve. 1988. *The Rise and Fall of the New Christian Right*, Oxford, Clarendon Press.

Bucana, Juana de. 1995. *La Iglesia Evangélica en Colombia*, Bogotá, Asociación Pro-Cruzada Mundial.

Casanova, José. 1994. *Public Religions in the Modern World*, University of Chicago Press.

Casaus Arzú, Marta. 1992. *Guatemala: Linaje y Racismo*, San José, Flacso.

Chanda, Donald (ed.) n/d. *Democracy in Zambia: Key Speeches of President Chiluba 1991/92*, Lusaka, Africa Press Trust.

Chikulo, Bornwell. 1996. 'Presidential and Parliamentary Elections in the Third Republic: 1991–1994', in Sichone, O. and Chikulo, B. (eds.), *Democracy in Zambia*, Harare, Sapes Books, pp. 25–51.

Claasen, Johan. 1995. 'Independents Made Dependents: African Independent Churches and Government Recognition', *Journal of Theology for Southern Africa*, 91 (June), 15–34.

Cleary, Ed and Stewart-Gambino, Hannah (eds.). 1997. *Power, Politics and Pentecostals in Latin America*, Boulder, Westview Press.

Cohen, Robin. 1997. *Global Diasporas*, London, UCL Press.

'Concerned Evangelicals'. 1986. *Evangelical Witness in South Africa*, Grand Rapids, Eerdmans.

Cox, Harvey. 1988. *The Silencing of Leonardo Boff*, Oak Park, Meyer-Stone.

1996. *Fire From Heaven*, London, Cassell.

Cruz e Silva, Teresa. 1995. 'A. Helgesson – Church, State and People in Mozambique' (review), *Journal of Religion in Africa*, 25 (4), 448.

1998. 'Identity and Political Consciousness in Southern Mozambique, 1930–1974: Two Presbyterian Biographies Contextualised', *Journal of Southern African Studies*, 24 (1), 223–36.

De Gruchy, John. 1984. *Bonhoeffer and South Africa*, Grand Rapids, Eerdmans.
  1995. *Christianity and Democracy*, Cambridge University Press.
De Klerk, Willem Abraham. 1975. *The Puritans in Africa: A Story of Afrikanerdom*, London, Rex Collins.
De León, Francisco Villagrán. 1993. 'Thwarting the Guatemalan Coup', *Journal of Democracy*, 4 (4), 117–24.
Deng, Francis. 1995. *War of Visions: Conflict of Identities in Sudan*, Washington, Brookings Institution.
D'Epinay, Christian Lalive. 1970. *O Refúgio das Massas*, Rio de Janeiro, Paz e Terra.
  1975. *Religion, Dynamique Social et Dépendence: les mouvements protestants en Argentine et au Chili*, Paris, Mouton.
Diamond, Larry. 1997. 'Introduction: In Search of Consolidation', in Diamond, L. (ed.), *Consolidating the Third Wave Democracies*, Baltimore, Johns Hopkins University Press, pp. xv–xlix.
Diamond, Larry and Plattner, Marc. 1994. 'Introduction', in Diamond, L. and Plattner, M. (eds.), *Nationalism, Ethnic Conflict and Democracy*, Baltimore, Johns Hopkins University Press, pp. ix–xxix.
Dickson, Kwesi. 1995. 'The Church and the Quest for Democracy in Ghana', in Gifford (ed.), pp. 261–75.
Dodson, Michael. 1997. 'Pentecostals, Politics and Public Space in Latin America', in Cleary and Stewart-Gambino (eds.), pp. 25–40.
Downs, Frederick. 1991. 'Christian Conversion Movements among the Hill Tribes of North-East India in the Nineteenth and Twentieth Centuries', in Oddie, G. A. (ed.), *Religion in South Asia*, 2nd edn, Delhi, Manohar.
Earle, Duncan. 1992. 'Authority, Social Conflict and the Rise of Protestantism: Religious Conversion in a Mayan Village', *Social Compass*, 39 (3), 377–88.
Encyclopedia of Religion. 1997. Ed. Mircea Eliade, 16 volumes, New York, Macmillan.
Eng, Chan Kok. 1992. 'A Brief Note on Church Growth in Malaysia, 1960–1985', in Hunt, Hing and Roxborough (eds.), pp. 354–78.
Enwerem, Iheanyi. 1992. 'The Politicization of Religion in Modern Nigeria: The Emergence and Politics of the Christian Association of Nigeria (CAN)', PhD thesis, York University, Ontario.
Eyre, Anne. 1995. 'Religion, Politics and Development in Malaysia', in Roberts (ed.), pp. 301–9.
Falla, Jonathan. 1991. *True Love and Bartholomew: Rebels on the Burmese Border*, Cambridge University Press.
Fernandes, Rubem César. 1981. 'As Missões Protestantes em Números', *Cadernos do ISER*, 10, 27–84.
  1992. *Censo Institucional Evangélico CIN 1992: Primeiros Comentários*, Rio de Janeiro, ISER.
Fine, Robert and Rai, Shirin. 1997. 'Understanding Civil Society: A Preface', *Democratization*, 4 (1), 1–6.

Fonseca, Alexandre Brasil. 1997. 'Evangélicos e Mídia no Brasil', Master's thesis, Universidade Federal do Rio de Janeiro.

Fontaine Talavera, Arturo and Bayer, Harald. 1991. 'Retrato del Movimiento Evangélico a la Luz de las Encuestas de Opinión Pública', *Estudios Públicos*, 44, 63–124.

Freston, Paul. 1983. 'The Revolutions in Cuba and Nicaragua: The Lessons for Christian Social Ethics in Latin America', Master's thesis, Regent College, Vancouver.

1993a. 'Protestantes e Política no Brasil: da Constituinte ao Impeachment', PhD thesis, Universidade de Campinas, Brazil.

1993b. 'Brother Votes for Brother: the New Politics of Protestantism in Brazil', in Garrard-Burnett, Virginia and Stoll, David (eds.), *Rethinking Protestantism in Latin America*, Philadelphia, Temple University Press, pp. 66–110.

1994a. 'Breve História do Pentecostalismo Brasileiro', in Antoniazzi, A. et al., *Nem Anjos Nem Demônios: Interpretações Sociológicas do Pentecostalismo*, Petrópolis, Vozes, pp. 67–159.

1994b. 'Popular Protestants in Brazilian Politics: A Novel Turn in Sect–State Relations', *Social Compass*, 41 (4), 537–70.

1995. 'Pentecostalism in Brazil: A Brief History', *Religion*, 25, 119–33.

1996. 'The Protestant Eruption into Modern Brazilian Politics', *Journal of Contemporary Religion*, 11 (2), 147–68.

1998a. 'Evangelicalism and Globalization: General Observations and Some Latin American Dimensions', in Hutchinson and Kalu (eds.), pp. 69–88.

1998b. 'Evangelicals and Politics: A Comparison Between Africa and Latin America', *Journal of Contemporary Religion*, 13 (1), 37–49.

1998c. 'Pentecostalism in Latin America: Characteristics and Controversies', *Social Compass*, 45 (3), 335–58.

Gabriel, Theodore. 1996. *Christian–Muslim Relations: A Case Study of Sarawak, East Malaysia*, Aldershot, Avebury.

Garrard-Burnett, Virginia. 1989. 'Protestantism in Rural Guatemala, 1872–1954', *Latin American Research Review*, 24 (2), 127–42.

1996a. 'Identity, Community and Religious Change among the Maya of Chiapas and Guatemala', mimeo.

1996b. 'Resacralization of the Profane: Government, Religion and Ethnicity in Modern Guatemala', in Westerlund (ed.), pp. 96–116.

1998. *Protestantism in Guatemala: Living in the New Jerusalem*, Austin, University of Texas Press.

Garvey, John. 1993. 'Introduction: Fundamentalism and Politics', in Marty and Appleby 1993b (eds.), pp. 13–27.

Gaskill, Newton. 1997. 'Rethinking Protestantism and Democratic Consolidation in Latin America', *Sociology of Religion*, 58 (1), 69–91.

Gifford, Paul. 1991. *The New Crusaders*, London, Pluto Press.

1993. *Christianity and Politics in Doe's Liberia*, Cambridge University Press.

1994a. 'Ghana's Charismatic Churches', *Journal of Religion in Africa*, 24 (3), 241–65.

1994b. 'Some Recent Developments in African Christianity', *African Affairs*, 93, 373, 513–34.

(ed.). 1995. *The Christian Churches and the Democratisation of Africa*, Leiden, E. J. Brill.

1995. 'Introduction: Democratisation and the Churches', in Gifford (ed.), pp. 1–8.

1996. 'Chiluba's Christian Nation: The Churches in Zambian Politics', paper presented at the African Studies Association of the UK, Bristol (September).

1998. *African Christianity: Its Public Role*, London, Hurst.

Gitari, David. 1996. *In Season and Out of Season: Sermons to a Nation*, Carlisle, Regnum.

Githiga, Gideon. 1997. 'The Church as a Bulwark Against Extremism'. PhD thesis, Open University/Oxford Centre for Mission Studies.

Gold-Biss, Michael. 1993. 'Colombia: Understanding Recent Democratic Transformations in a Violent Polity', *Latin American Research Review*, 28 (1), 215–34.

Gonzáles, Noel. 1996. 'Participación Política de los Evangélicos en Nicaragua', in Gutiérrez (ed.), pp. 207–21.

Grayson, James. 1995. 'Dynamic Complementarity: Korean Confucianism and Christianity', in Roberts (ed.), pp. 76–88.

Grenfell, James. 1995. 'The Participation of Protestants in Politics in Guatemala', Master's thesis, Oxford University.

Gutiérrez, Tomás (ed.). 1996. *Protestantismo y Política en América Latina y el Caribe*, Lima, Cehila.

1996. 'Los Evangélicos, un Nuevo Rostro en la Política Peruana de los '90', in Gutiérrez (ed.), pp. 299–316.

Gyimah-Boadi, E. 1996. 'Civil Society in Africa', *Journal of Democracy*, 7 (2), pp. 118–32.

Hackett, Rosalind. 1995. 'The Gospel of Prosperity in West Africa', in Roberts (ed.), pp. 199–212.

Hale, Frederick. 1993. 'Coming to Terms with Evangelicals and Apartheid', *Journal of Theology for Southern Africa*, 84 (Sept.), 41–56.

Hallencreutz, Carl and Westerlund, David. 1996. 'Introduction: Anti-Secularist Policies of Religion', in Westerlund (ed.), pp. 1–23.

Hamalengwa, Munyonzwe. 1992. *Class Struggles in Zambia 1889–1989 and The Fall of Kenneth Kaunda 1990–1991*, Lanham, University of America Press.

Hammond, Phillip. 1980. 'The Conditions for Civil Religion: A Comparison of the United States and Mexico', in Bellah, R. and Hammond, P. (eds.), *Varieties of Civil Religion*, San Francisco, Harper and Row, pp. 40–85.

Han, Sang-Jin. 1995. 'Economic Development and Democracy', *Korea Journal*, summer, 5–17.

Handy, Jim. 1986. 'Resurgent Democracy and the Guatemalan Military', *Journal of Latin American Studies*, 18 (2), 383–408.

Hansen, Holger Bengt and Twaddle, Michael (eds.). 1995. *Religion and Politics in East Africa*, London, James Currey.

Hardgrave Jr, Robert. 1993. 'India: The Dilemmas of Diversity', *Journal of Democracy*, 4 (4), 54–68.

Hastings, Adrian. 1991. 'Politics and Religion in Southern Africa', in Moyser (ed.), pp. 162–88.

1995. 'The Churches and Democracy: Reviewing a Relationship', in Gifford (ed.), pp. 36–46.

1997. *The Construction of Nationhood: Ethnicity, Religion and Nationalism*, Cambridge University Press.

Hawley, Susan. 1997. 'Protestantism and Indigenous Mobilisation: The Moravian Church among the Miskitu Indians of Nicaragua', *Journal of Latin American Studies*, 29 (1), 111–29.

Haynes, Jeff. 1993. *Religion in Third World Politics*, Buckingham, Open University Press.

1996. *Religion and Politics in Africa*, London, Zed Books.

Hefner, Robert (ed.). 1993. *Conversion to Christianity*, Berkeley, University of California.

1993. 'Of Faith and Commitment: Christian Conversion in Muslim Java', in Hefner (ed.), pp. 99–125.

Helgesson, Alf. 1991. 'Catholics and Protestants in a Clash of Interests in Southern Mozambique', in Hallencreutz, Carl and Palmberg, Mai (eds.), *Religion and Politics in Southern Africa*, Uppsala, Scandinavian Institute of African Studies, pp. 194–206.

1994. *Church, State and People in Mozambique*, University of Uppsala, 1994.

Helmsdorff, Daniela. 1996. 'Participación Política Evangélica en Colombia', *Historia Crítica*, January–June, 79–84.

Henderson, Lawrence. 1990. *A Igreja em Angola*, Lisboa, Editorial Além-Mar.

Hendriks, H. Jurgens. 1995. 'South African Denominational Growth and Decline 1911–1991', *Journal of Theology for Southern Africa*, 91 (June), 35–58.

Hexham, Irving and Poewe, Karla. 1994. 'Charismatic Churches in South Africa: A Critique of Criticisms and Problems of Bias', in Poewe (ed.), pp. 50–69.

Hluna, John V. 1985. *Church and Political Upheaval in Mizoram*, Aizawl, Mizo History Association.

Hollenweger, Walter. 1994. 'The Pentecostal Elites and the Pentecostal Poor: A Missed Dialogue?' in Poewe (ed.), pp. 200–14.

Hong, Young-Gi. 1997. 'The Background of Korean Mega-Churches', mimeo.

1999. 'Nominalism in Korean Protestantism', *Transformation*, October–December, 135–41.

Horam, M. 1988. *Naga Insurgency: The Last Thirty Years*, New Delhi, Cosmo.

Horn, J. Nico. 1994. 'After Apartheid: Reflections on Church Mission in the Changing Social and Political Context of South Africa', *Transformation*, January–March, 25–8.

Hunt, Robert. 1992. 'The Churches and Social Problems', in Hunt, Hing and Roxborough (eds.), pp. 323–53.

Hunt, Robert, Hing, Lee Kam and Roxborough, John (eds.). 1992. *Christianity in West Malaysia: A Denominational History*, Petaling Jaya, Pelanduk.

Hunter, Alan and Chan, Kim-Kwong. 1993. *Protestantism in Contemporary China*, Cambridge University Press.

Huntington, Samuel. 1991. *The Third Wave: Democratization in the late Twentieth Century*, Norman, University of Oklahoma Press.

1996. *The Clash of Civilizations and the Remaking of World Order*, London, Touchstone.

Hutchinson, John and Smith, Anthony (eds.). 1994. *Nationalism*. Oxford University Press.

Hutchinson, Mark and Kalu, Ogbu (eds.). 1998. *A Global Faith*, Sydney, CSAC.

Hutchinson, Sharon. 1996. *Nuer Dilemmas: Coping with Money, War and the State*, Berkeley, University of California Press.

Igwara, Obi. 1995. 'Holy Nigerian Nationalisms and Apocalyptic Visions of the Nation', *Nations and Nationalism*, 1 (3), 327–55.

In, Soo Kim. 1996. *Protestants and the Formation of Modern Korean Nationalism, 1885–1920*, New York, Peter Lang.

ISER. 1996. *Novo Nascimento: Os Evangélicos em Casa, na Igreja e na Política*, Rio de Janeiro, ISER.

Jacobs, Julian. 1990. *The Nagas*, London, Thames and Hudson.

Janelli, Roger L. with Dawnhee Yim. 1993. *Making Capitalism: The Social and Cultural Construction of a South Korean Conglomerate*, Stanford University Press.

Johnstone, Patrick. 1993. *Operation World*, Carlisle, OM.

Jones, Lawrence. 1990. 'Divided Evangelicals in South Africa', in Sahliyeh, E. (ed.), *Religious Resurgence and Politics in the Contemporary World*, Albany, State University of New York Press, pp. 107–19.

Joseph, Richard. 1993. 'The Christian Churches and Democracy in Africa', in Witte (ed.), pp. 231–47.

1997. 'Democratization in Africa after 1989: Comparative and Theoretical Perspectives', *Comparative Politics*, 29 (3), 363–82.

Juergensmeyer, Mark. 1995. 'The New Religious State', *Comparative Politics*, 27 (4), 379–91.

Kalu, Ogbu. 1997. 'The Third Response: Pentecostalism and the Reconstruction of Christian Experience in Africa, 1970–1995', mimeo.

Kalyvas, Stathis. 1998. 'Democracy and Religious Politics: Evidence from Belgium', *Comparative Political Studies*, 31 (3), 292–320.

Kang, Wi Jo. 1997. *Christ and Caesar in Modern Korea*, Albany, State University of New York Press.

Karl, Terry Lynn. 1995. 'The Hybrid Regimes of Central America', *Journal of Democracy*, 6 (3), 72–86.

Kenny, Joseph. 1996. 'Sharia and Christianity in Nigeria: Islam and a "Secular" State', *Journal of Religion in Africa*, 26 (4), 338–64.

Kessler, Juan. 1967. *A Study of the Older Protestant Missions and Churches in Peru and Chile*, Goes, Oosterbaan and Le Cointre.

Keyes, Charles. 1996. 'Being Protestant in Southeast Asian Worlds', *Journal of Southeast Asian Studies*, 27 (2), 280–92.

Kinghorn, Johann. 1990. 'The Theology of Separate Equality: A Critical Outline of the DRC's Position on Apartheid', in Prozesky, Martin (ed.), *Christianity Amidst Apartheid*, Basingstoke, Macmillan, pp. 57–80.

Kinzo, Maria D'Alva Gil. 1988. *O Quadro Partidário e A Constituinte*, Textos IDESP 28, São Paulo, IDESP.

Klaiber, Jeffrey. 1992. *The Catholic Church in Peru, 1821–1985*, Washington, Catholic University of America Press.

Kukah, Matthew Hassan. 1995. 'Christians and Nigeria's Aborted Transition', in Gifford, (ed.), pp. 225–38.

Lagos, Humberto. 1988. *Crisis de la Esperanza*, Santiago, Presor/Lar.

Lancaster, Roger. 1988. *Thanks to God and the Revolution*, New York, Columbia University Press.

Levine, Daniel and Stoll, David. 1995. 'Bridging the Gap between Empowerment and Power in Latin America', mimeo.

Lim, David. 1989. 'Church and State in the Philippines, 1900–1988', *Transformation*, July–September, 27–32.

Limón, Francisco and Clemente, Abel. 1995. 'Iglesias Históricas y Pentecostales: Espíritu de Lucha Social y Participación Política en México: El Caso de Chiapas', in Gutiérrez, Benjamín (ed.), *En la Fuerza del Espíritu: Los Pentecostales en América Latina: Un Desafío a las Iglesias Históricas*, Mexico City, Aipral; Guatemala City, Celep, pp. 175–97.

Linden, Ian. 1977. *Church and Revolution in Rwanda*, Manchester University Press.

   1996. 'Paul Gifford (ed.), *The Christian Churches and the Democratisation of Africa*' (review) *Journal of Religion in Africa*, 26 (2), 224–7.

Longman, Timothy Paul. 1995. 'Christianity and Democratisation in Rwanda: Assessing Church Responses to Political Crisis in the 1990s', in Gifford (ed.), pp. 187–204.

   1998. 'Empowering the Weak and Protecting the Powerful: The Contradictory Nature of Christian Churches in Rwanda, Burundi and the Democratic Republic of the Congo', mimeo.

López, Darío. 1997. 'A Critical Evaluation of the Theological Perspectives of the National Evangelical Council of Peru (CONEP) concerning Human Rights, 1980–1992', PhD thesis, Open University/Oxford Centre for Mission Studies.

Luckham, Robin. 1996. 'Crafting Democratic Control over the Military: A Comparative Analysis of South Korea, Chile and Ghana', *Democratization*, 3 (3), 215–45.

McCullum, Hugh. 1995. *The Angels Have Left Us: The Rwanda Tragedy and the Churches*, Geneva, WCC.

Mallimaci, Fortunato. 1996. 'Protestantismo y Política Partidaria en la Actual Argentina', in Gutiérrez (ed.), pp. 265–89.

Mariano, Ricardo and Pierucci, Antônio Flávio. 1992. 'O Envolvimento dos Pentecostais na Eleição de Collor', *Novos Estudos Cebrap*, 34, 92–106.

Marshall, Paul. 1997. *Their Blood Cries Out*, Dallas, Word Books.

Marshall, Ruth. 1991. 'Power in the Name of Jesus', *Review of African Political Economy*, 52 (Nov.), 21–37.

— 1993. '"Power in the Name of Jesus": Social Transformation and Pentecostalism in Western Nigeria "Revisited"', in Ranger, Terence and Vaughan, Olufemi (eds.), *Legitimacy and the State in Twentieth Century Africa*, Basingstoke, Macmillan, pp. 213–46.

— 1995. '"God is not a Democrat": Pentecostalism and Democratisation in Nigeria', in Gifford (ed.), pp. 239–60.

— 1997. 'Winning Nigeria for Jesus: Pentecostalism, Transnationalism and the Media', paper presented at the XXIV Congress of the Société Internationale de Sociologie des Religions, Toulouse, France, July.

Martin, David. 1978. *A General Theory of Secularization*, Oxford, Blackwell.

— 1990. *Tongues of Fire*, Oxford, Blackwell.

— 1996. *Forbidden Revolutions*, London, SPCK.

Martínez García, Carlos. 1994. 'Linchamiento en Chamula', *La Jornada*, October 2.

— 1995. 'Enfrentamiento o agresión?', *La Jornada*, November 23.

— 1996a. 'Los Evangélicos Expulsados', *Uno Más Uno*, July 11, p. 5.

— 1996b. 'Índios y Evangélicos', *Uno Más Uno*, October 10.

— 1996c. 'Los Problemas para el Ejercicio de la Tolerancia: El Caso de Chiapas', paper presented at the Symposium 'Protestantismo y vida cotidiana en América Latina', Cehila-Protestante, Mexico City, 23–5 October.

Marty, Martin and Appleby, R. Scott (eds.). 1991. *Fundamentalisms Observed*, University of Chicago Press.

— (eds.). 1993a. *Fundamentalisms and Society*, University of Chicago Press.

— (eds.). 1993b. *Fundamentalisms and the State*, University of Chicago Press.

— (eds.). 1994. *Accounting for Fundamentalisms*, University of Chicago Press.

— (eds.). 1995. *Fundamentalisms Comprehended*, University of Chicago Press.

Martz, John. 1992. 'Party Elites and Leadership in Colombia and Venezuela', *Journal of Latin American Studies*, 24 (1), 87–121.

— 1997. *The Politics of Clientelism: Democracy and the State in Colombia*, New Brunswick, Transaction.

Maxwell, David. 1995. 'The Churches and Democratization in Africa: The Case of Zimbabwe', in Gifford (ed.), pp. 108–29.

— 1997a. 'New Perspectives on the History of African Christianity' (review), *Journal of Southern African Studies*, 23 (1), 141–8.

— 1997b. 'Rethinking Christian Independency: The Southern African Pentecostal Movement ca. 1908–1960', mimeo.

— 1998. '"Delivered from the Spirit of Poverty?": Pentecostalism, Prosperity and Modernity in Zimbabwe', *Journal of Religion in Africa*, 28, (3), 350–73.

— Forthcoming. '"Catch the Cockerel before Dawn": Pentecostalism and Politics in Post-Colonial Zimbabwe', *Africa*.

Medhurst, Kenneth. 1984. *The Church and Labour in Colombia*, Manchester University Press.

Metz, Allan. 1994. 'Protestantism in Mexico: Contemporary Contextual Developments', *Journal of Church and State*, 36 (1), 57–78.

Míguez Bonino, José. 1995. *Rostros del Protestantismo Latinoamericano*, Buenos Aires, Nueva Creación; Grand Rapids, Eerdmans.

Mihyo, Paschal. 1995. 'Against Overwhelming Odds: The Zambian Trade Union Movement', in Thomas, Henk (ed.), *Globalization and Third World Trade Unions*, London, Zed Books, pp. 201–13.

Miranda Sáenz, Adolfo. 1991. 'Nicaragua: La Metamorfosis Política de los Evangélicos', in Padilla (ed.), pp. 77–87.

Molebatsi, Caesar and Ngwenya, George. 1994. 'Evangelicals in Politics in South Africa', *Transformation*, October–December, 15–18.

Mondragón, Carlos. 1991. 'México: De la Militancia Revolucionaria al Letargo Social', in Padilla (ed.), pp. 61–76.

Moran, Jonathan. 1996. 'Contradictions Between Economic Liberalization and Democratization: The Case of South Korea', *Democratization*, 3 (4), 459–90.

Moreno, Pablo. 1996. 'Protestantismo y Política en Colombia, 1886–1930', in Gutiérrez (ed.), pp. 73–86.

—— (ed.). 1998. *Evangélicos, Política y Sociedad en Colombia*, Lima, EPOS.

Morier-Genoud, Eric. 1996. 'The Politics of Church and Religion in the First Multiparty Elections of Mozambique', *Internet Journal of African Studies*, 1, 1–10.

Moyser, George (ed.). 1991. *Politics and Religion in the Modern World*, London, Routledge.

Mullet, Michael. 1980. *Radical Religious Movements in Early Modern Europe*, London, George Allen and Unwin.

Munck, Gerardo. 1994. 'Democratic Stability and its Limits: An Analysis of Chile's 1993 Elections', *Journal of Inter-American Studies and World Affairs*, 36 (2), 7–35.

NCCK (National Christian Council of Korea). 1990. *Korean Church: History, Activities*, Seoul, Christian Institute for the Study of Justice and Development.

Ngoenha, Severino Elias. 1999. 'Os Missionários Suíços Face ao Nacionalismo Moçambicano: Entre a Tsonganidade e a Moçambicanidade', *Lusotopie*, 425–36.

Nikkel, Marc. 1991. 'Aspects of Contemporary Religious Change among the Dinka', in *Sudan: Environment and People*, Second International Sudan Studies Conference, University of Durham, April 8–11, pp. 90–100.

Northcott, Michael. 1992. 'Two Hundred Years of Anglican Mission', in Hunt, Hing and Roxborough (eds.), pp. 34–74.

Novaes, Regina. 1982. 'Os Crentes e as Eleições: Uma Experiência no Campo', *Comunicações do ISER*, 2, 3–10.

O'Fahey, R. S. 1995. 'The Past in the Present? The Issue of the Sharia in Sudan', in Hansen and Twaddle (eds.), pp. 32–44.

Ojo, Matthews. 1988. 'The Contextual Significance of the Charismatic Movements in Independent Nigeria', *Africa*, 58 (2), 175–92.

1995. 'The Charismatic Movement in Nigeria Today', *International Bulletin of Missionary Research*, 19 (3), 114–18.

Ossa, Manuel. 1990. *Espiritualidad Popular y Acción Política: El Pastor Victor Mora y la Misión Wesleyana Nacional*, Santiago, Rehue.

Padilla, René (ed.). 1991. *De la Marginación al Compromiso: Los Evangélicos y la Política en América Latina*, Buenos Aires, FTL.

Palma, Irma (ed.). 1988. *En Tierra Extraña: Itinerario del Pueblo Pentecostal Chileno*, Santiago, Amerinda.

Panter-Brick, Keith. 1994. 'Prospects for Democracy in Zambia', *Government and Opposition*, 29 (2), 231–47.

Peel, John. 1996. 'The Politicisation of Religion in Nigeria: Three Studies', *Africa*, 66 (4), 607–11.

Peterson, Douglas. 1995. 'A Pentecostal Theology of Social Concern in Central America', PhD thesis, Open University/Oxford Centre for Mission Studies.

Pierucci, Antônio Flávio de Oliveira. 1989. 'Representantes de Deus em Brasília: A Bancada Evangélica na Constituinte', *Ciências Sociais Hoje*, 104–32.

Pirouet, M. Louise. 1995. 'The Churches and Human Rights in Kenya and Uganda since Independence', in Hansen and Twaddle (eds.), pp. 247–59.

Poewe, Karla (ed.). 1994. *Charismatic Christianity as a Global Culture*, Columbia, University of South Carolina Press.

Pollitt, Penelope. 1981. 'Religion and Politics in a Coal-Mining Community in Southern Chile', PhD thesis, University of Cambridge.

Prandi, Reginaldo and Pierucci, Antônio Flávio. 1994. 'Religiões e Voto no Brasil', paper presented at the congress of the National Association for Research in the Social Sciences, Caxambu, Brazil (November).

Prunier, Gérard. 1995. *The Rwanda Crisis*, London, Hurst.

Ranger, Terence. 1986. 'Religious Movements and Politics in Sub-Saharan Africa', *African Studies Review*, 29 (2), 1–69.

1995a. *Are We Not Also Men?* London, James Currey.

1995b. 'Conference Summary and Conclusion', in Gifford (ed.), pp. 14–35.

Rao, O. M. 1994. *Focus on North East Indian Christianity*, Delhi, SPCK.

Rapaport, Joanne. 1984. 'Las Misiones Protestantes y la Resistencia Indígena en el Sur de Colombia', *América Indígena*, 44 (1), 111–26.

Ribeiro, Darcy. 1983. *Os Brasileiros: 1. Teoria do Brasil*, Petrópolis, Vozes.

Roberts, Richard (ed.). 1995. *Religion and the Transformations of Capitalism*, London, Routledge.

Robertson, Roland. 1992. *Globalization*, London, Sage.

Romero, Eduardo. 1994. 'Observing Protestant Participation in Peruvian Politics', *Latinoamericanist*, spring, 6–10.

Rose, Susan. 1996. 'The Politics of Philippine Fundamentalism', in Westerlund (ed.), pp. 323–55.

Ross, Kenneth. 1995a. 'Christian Social Witness in Malawi 1992–93', *Journal of Theology for Southern Africa*, 90, March, pp. 17–30.

1995b. 'Christian Faith and National Identity: The Malawi Experience', *Journal of Theology for Southern Africa*, 93 (December), 51–62.

Roxborough, John. 1992. 'The Story of Ecumenism', in Hunt, Hing and Roxborough (eds.), pp. 277–322.

Rudolph, Susanne. 1997a. 'Introduction: Religion, States and Transnational Civil Society', in Rudolph and Piscatori (eds.), pp. 1–24.

1997b. 'Dehomogenizing Religious Formations', in Rudolph and Piscatori (eds.), pp. 243–61.

Rudolph, Susanne and Piscatori, James (eds.). 1997. *Transnational Religion and Fading States*, Boulder, Westview Press.

1997. 'Preface', in Rudolph and Piscatori (eds.), pp. vii–viii.

Sabar-Friedman, Galia. 1997. 'Church and State in Kenya, 1986–1992: The Churches' Involvement in the "Game of Change"', *African Affairs*, 96, 382, 25–52.

Sanneh, Lamin. 1996. *Piety and Power*, Maryknoll, Orbis.

Saracco, Norberto. 1989. 'Argentine Pentecostalism: Its History and Theology', PhD thesis, University of Birmingham.

(ed.). 1992. *Directorio y Censo Evangélico*, Buenos Aires, n/p.

Schoffeleers, Matthew. 1988. 'The Zion Christian Church and the Apartheid Regime', mimeo.

1990. 'Ritual Healing and Political Acquiescence: The Case of the Zionist Churches in Southern Africa', paper presented at the Conference on Power and Prayer, Amsterdam (December).

Schubert, Benedict. 1999. 'Os Protestantes na Guerra Angolana depois da Independência', *Lusotopie*, 405–13.

Scott, Luis. 1991. *La Sal de la Tierra: Una Historia Socio-Política de los Evangélicos en la Ciudad de México 1964–1991*, Mexico City, Kyrios.

Sepúlveda, Juan. 1996. 'Reinterpreting Chilean Pentecostalism', *Social Compass*, 43 (3), 299–318.

Shenk, David. 1997. *Justice, Reconciliation and Peace in Africa*, Nairobi, Uzima.

Sichone, Owen. 1996. 'Democracy and Crisis in Zambia', in Sichone, Owen and Chikulo, Bornwell (eds.), *Democracy in Zambia*, Harare, Sapes Books, pp. 109–28.

Sierpe, Diego. 1993. 'Ni Bendito, ni Maldito: Los Evangélicos entre la Democracia y el Fascismo', in Hallencreutz, C. et al., *Iglesia y Sociedad en Chile*, Universidad de Uppsala, pp. 73–108.

Sigmund, Paul. 1999. 'Introduction', in Sigmund, P. (ed.), *Religious Freedom and Evangelization in Latin America*, Maryknoll, Orbis, pp. 1–8.

Sinclair, Christopher. 1993. 'Evangelical Belief in Contemporary England', *Archives de Sciences Sociales des Religions*, 82 (April–June), 169–81.

Skillen, James. 1974. 'The Development of Calvinistic Political Theory in the Netherlands', PhD thesis, Duke University.

Smith, Brian. 1982. *The Church and Politics in Chile*, Princeton University Press.

Smith, Carol. 1990. 'The Militarization of Civil Society in Guatemala: Economic Reorganization as a Continuation of War', *Latin American Perspectives*, 17 (4), pp. 8–41.

Smith, Dennis. 1991. 'Coming of Age: A Reflection on Pentecostals, Politics and Popular Religion in Guatemala', *Pneuma*, 13 (2), 131–9.

Smith, Martin. 1991. *Burma: Insurgency and the Politics of Ethnicity*, London, Zed Books.

1994. *Ethnic Groups in Burma*, London, Anti-Slavery International.

Soares, Luiz Eduardo. 1993. 'A Guerra dos Pentecostais contra os Afro-Brasileiros: Dimensões Democráticas do Conflito Religioso no Brasil', *Comunicações do ISER*, 44, 43–50.

Spittler, Russell. 1994. 'Are Pentecostals and Charismatics Fundamentalists? A Review of American Uses of These Categories', in Poewe (ed.), pp. 103–16.

Spyer, Patricia. 1994. 'Serial Conversion/Conversion to Seriality: Religion, State and Numbers in Aru, Eastern Indonesia', in van der Weer (ed.), pp. 171–98.

Stepan, Alfred. Forthcoming. *Arguing Comparative Politics*. Oxford University Press.

Stoll, David. 1990. *Is Latin America Turning Protestant?* Berkeley, University of California Press.

1991. 'Guatemala Elects Born-Again President', *Christian Century*, 108 (6), 189–90.

1993. *Between Two Armies: In the Ixil Towns of Guatemala*, New York, Columbia University Press.

1994. '"Jesus is Lord of Guatemala": Evangelical Reform in a Death-Squad State', in Marty and Appleby (eds.), pp. 99–123.

Swain, Tony and Trompf, Gary. 1995. *The Religions of Oceania*, London, Routledge.

Sylvestre, Josué. 1986. *Irmão Vota em Irmão*, Brasília, Pergaminho.

Tate, C. Neal. 1990. 'The Revival of Church and State in the Philippines', in Sahliyeh, Emile (ed.), *Religious Resurgence and Politics in the Contemporary World*, Albany, State University of New York Press, pp. 141–59.

Tegenfeldt, Herman. 1974. *A Century of Growth: The Kachin Baptist Church of Burma*, South Pasadena, William Carey Library.

Tennekes, Hans. 1985. *El Movimiento Pentecostal en la Sociedad Chilena*, Iquique, CIREN.

'Theological Reflection on Public Policy: Representing Christianity in the South African Parliament'. 1997. *Journal of Theology for Southern Africa*, 98 (July), 81–8.

Thomas, M. M. 1992. *Nagas Towards AD 2000*, Madras, Centre for Research on New International Economic Order.

Thompson, Mark. 1996. 'Off the Endangered List: Philippine Democratization in Comparative Perspective', *Comparative Politics*, 28 (2), 179–205.

Throup, David. 1995. '"Render unto Caesar the Things that are Caesar's":

The Politics of Church–State Conflict in Kenya, 1978–1990', in Hansen and Twaddle (eds.), pp. 143–76.

Timberman, David. 1992. 'The Philippines at the Polls', *Journal of Democracy*, 3 (4), 110–24.

Tocqueville, Alexis De, 1987. *A Democracia na América*, 3rd edn, Belo Horizonte, Itatiaia; São Paulo, Edusp.

Trudeau, Robert. 1993. *Guatemalan Politics: The Popular Struggle for Democracy*, Boulder, Lynne Rienner.

Tu, Weiming. 1999. 'The Quest for Meaning: Religion in the People's Republic of China', in Berger, Peter (ed.), *The Desecularization of the World*, Washington, Ethics and Public Policy Center, pp. 85–101.

Uvin, Peter. 1998. *Aiding Violence: The Development Enterprise in Rwanda*, West Hartford, Kumarian Press.

Van der Weer, Peter (ed.). 1994. *Conversion to Modernities: The Globalization of Christianity*, London, Routledge.

Vencer, Jun. 1999. 'Church and State: A Biblical Framework', *Berita Necf*, July–August, 4–11.

Villas, Carlos. 1996a. 'Prospects for Democratisation in a Post-Revolutionary Setting: Central America', *Journal of Latin American Studies*, 28 (2), 461–503.

Villa-Vicencio, Charles. 1995. 'Abortion: An Appeal for Reason', *Journal of Theology for Southern Africa*, 92 (Sept.), 72–5.

Vines, Alex. 1991. *Renamo: From Terrorism to Democracy in Mozambique?* Centre for Southern African Studies, University of York.

Vines, Alex and Wilson, Ken. 1995. 'Churches and the Peace Process in Mozambique', in Gifford (ed.), pp. 130–47.

Waliggo, John Mary. 1995. 'The Role of Christian Churches in the Democratisation Process in Uganda 1980–1993', in Gifford (ed.), pp. 205–24.

Walker, David. 1994. '"Evangelicals and Apartheid" Revisited: A Response to Frederick Hale', *Journal of Theology for Southern Africa*, 89 (Dec.), 42–50.

Wallis, Roy and Bruce, Steve. 1985. 'Sketch for a Theory of Conservative Protestant Politics', *Social Compass*, 32 (2–3), 145–61.

Walls, Andrew. 1996. *The Missionary Movement in Christian History*, Edinburgh, T. and T. Clark.

Walshe, Peter. 1995. 'Christianity and Democratisation in South Africa: The Prophetic Voice within Phlegmatic Churches', in Gifford (ed.), pp. 74–94.

Ward, Kevin. 1995. 'The Church of Uganda Amidst Conflict', in Hansen and Twaddle (eds.), pp. 72–105.

Waters, Malcolm. 1995. *Globalization*, London, Routledge.

Webster, John. 1992. *The Dalit Christians: A History*, Delhi, ISPCK.

Westerlund, David (ed.). 1996. *Questioning the Secular State*, London, Hurst.

White, Gordon. 1995. 'Civil Society, Democratization and Development (II): Two Country Cases', *Democratization*, 2 (2), 56–84.

Willems, Emílio. 1967. *Followers of the New Faith: Culture Change and the Rise of Protestantism in Brazil and Chile*, Nashville, Vanderbilt University Press.

Willis, Avery. 1977. *Why Two Million Came to Christ*, South Pasadena, William Carey Library.

Wilson, Bryan. 1959. 'The Pentecostalist Minister: Role Conflicts and Status Contradictions', *American Journal of Sociology*, 64 (5), 494–504.

1970. *Religious Sects: A Sociological Study*, London, World University Library.

Wilson, Everett. 1997. 'Guatemalan Pentecostals: Something of Their Own', in Cleary and Stewart-Gambino (eds.), pp. 139–62.

Witte Jr, John (ed.) 1993. *Christianity and Democracy in Global Context*, Boulder, Westview Press.

Wood, Peter. 1993. 'Afterword: Boundaries and Horizons', in Hefner (ed.), pp. 305–21.

Wootton, David. 1991. 'Leveller Democracy and the Puritan Revolution', in Burns, J. H. (ed.), *The Cambridge History of Political Thought 1450–1700*, Cambridge University Press, pp. 412–42.

Zaluar, Alba. 1985. *A Máquina e a Revolta*, São Paulo, Brasiliense.

Zavala, Rubén. 1989. *Historia de las Asambleas de Dios del Perú*, Lima, Ediciones Dios es Amor.

Zub, Roberto. 1993. *Protestantismo y Elecciones en Nicaragua*, Managua, Ediciones Nicarao.

1996a. *Oficio y Modelos Pastorales*, Managua, CIEETS/Visión Mundial/IN-DEF.

1996b. 'Percepciones acerca del Poder en las Iglesias Evangélicas Nicaragüenses', *Xilotl*, 9 (17), 21–43.

1996c. 'Clamor por un Partido Evangélico', *Confidencial*, 9 (Sept.), 9–10.

1996d. 'Evangélicos: La Sorpresa Electoral', *Confidencial*, 15 (13–19 Oct.), 9.

1996e. 'Análisis', *Confidencial*, 20 (17–23 Nov.), 12–13.

1997. 'La Religión en el Marketing Político', *Signos de Vida*, March, 10–13.

Index